Advance Praise for
Raymond E. Brown and the Catholic Biblical Renewal

"Donald Senior reveals the unpretentious brilliance of Raymond E. Brown (1928–98) in the context of turbulent times in Catholicism. He portrays a complex man of prodigious learning for whom scholarship and church life were mutually enriching. Senior shows us a priest with a rich network of friends and a deep life of faith who nonetheless was burdened by harassment from right-wing critics. His book traces the path by which Vatican officials came to embrace new modes of biblical scholarship; he describes the significance of this scholarship for the church and for enhanced relations with Protestants and Jews. As one privileged to have known Raymond E. Brown, I highly recommend this book for the witness it bears to one of the most important teachers of the twentieth century—and whose legacy continues to inspire."

> —Mary C. Boys, SNJM, vice-president of academic affairs
> and dean, Union Theological Seminary

"Fr. Raymond E. Brown was without doubt a central figure in the development of twentieth-century Catholic biblical scholarship. Combining rigorous historical criticism of Scripture with devotion to the church's teachings, he produced highly respected works of meticulous scholarship sensitive to their theological implications. Donald Senior's intellectual biography carefully reviews Brown's scholarly accomplishments while tracing the history of his influential academic career and recording the controversies within Catholic circles engendered by his embrace of critical methods. Anyone interested in the development of Catholic biblical scholarship since Vatican II will welcome this biography of, as Senior says, 'the most well-known and most appreciated Catholic teacher of the Bible of his generation.'"

> —Harold W. Attridge, Sterling Professor of Divinity,
> Yale Divinity School

"Fr. Raymond E. Brown was during his lifetime the leading biblical scholar/ exegete in the United States. His books were reviewed by the *New York Times Sunday Book Review*. He helped save what could be saved of the Roman Catholic diocesan priesthood. His thesis on how the Gospel of John, the three letters of John, and the extra chapter in John (chapter 21) all fit together is probably the boldest and most brilliant and satisfying thesis by any American scholar in the field of New Testament studies since the founding of the republic. This biography tells the whole story."

> —Benedict Thomas Viviano, OP, Fribourg University,
> Switzerland, and Aquinas Institute, St. Louis, MO

"Raymond E. Brown was an extraordinary human being whose influence in biblical studies and the church has been profound. In this biography, Donald Senior provides invaluable insights into Brown's major writings and delightful perspectives on Brown as a person, based on interviews with those who knew him well. Brown was both priest and scholar, deeply Catholic and ecumenically engaged. I highly recommend this volume for all who want to better understand his remarkable life and legacy."

—Craig R. Koester, vice president for academic affairs,
Luther Seminary, St. Paul, MN

"Fr. Raymond E. Brown was a brilliant, influential, respected, ecumenical, and sometimes controversial biblical scholar. Fr. Donald Senior has given us a wonderful gift in this insightful intellectual biography and analysis of Brown's work. Senior helpfully situates Brown's scholarly and popular activity within Brown's own spirituality, the changing times of twentieth-century Catholicism, and the wider academic and religious spheres in which he moved. Readers of this volume will come to know, or know better, the premier American Catholic biblical scholar of the last century—and his ongoing significance."

—Michael J. Gorman, Raymond E. Brown Chair in
Biblical Studies and Theology
St. Mary's Seminary and University, Baltimore, MD

"Catholics and Protestants alike owe Donald Senior, CP, enormous thanks for this careful, balanced, and insightful treatment of the life of Raymond E. Brown, SS. This biography identifies the religious commitments, intellectual qualities, and personal characteristics that were the essence of who Fr. Brown was. He had a natural intellectual rigor that few people share. His life was primarily one of work and service. He lived simply, but he did not have a hermit's existence. Brown was regularly engaged with friends, other people, and a variety of interests, not simply with his academic pursuits and achievements. As readers will learn, along with Brown's great erudition, he was a multifaceted person who enjoyed opera, travel, and many different kinds of people.

In all aspects of his life, Brown was true to his Christian faith and loyal to his commitments, particularly to the church. Donald Senior brings these dimensions of Brown's life to the fore, and readers are able to meet the Raymond E. Brown known to those who were fortunate to have known him well."

—Marion L. Soards, professor of New Testament studies,
Louisville Presbyterian Theological Seminary

RAYMOND E. BROWN AND THE CATHOLIC BIBLICAL RENEWAL

RAYMOND E. BROWN AND THE CATHOLIC BIBLICAL RENEWAL

DONALD SENIOR, CP
FOREWORD BY RONALD D. WITHERUP, PSS

Paulist Press
New York / Mahwah, NJ

Photo Credits: Archives of the U.S. Province of the Society of Saint Sulpice

The Scripture quotations contained herein are from the New Revised Standard Version: Catholic Edition, Copyright © 1989 and 1993, by the Division of Christian Education of the National Council of the Churches of Christ in the United States of America. Used by permission. All rights reserved.

Jacket image courtesy of Associated Sulpicians of the U.S. Archives, Associated Archives of St. Mary's Seminary & University.
Jacket design by Joe Gallagher
Book design by Lynn Else

Library of Congress Cataloging-in-Publication Data is available upon request.

ISBN 978-0-8091-0644-8 (hardcover)
ISBN 978-1-58768-703-7 (e-book)

Published by Paulist Press
997 Macarthur Boulevard
Mahwah, NJ 07430

www.paulistpress.com

Printed and bound in the
United States of America

CONTENTS

FOREWORD

Twenty years, from one point of view, does not seem like a very long time to offer an objective historical perspective. When, only a few years after his death, I raised the possibility with several historians about writing a biography of Raymond E. Brown—by most estimations the most important American Catholic biblical scholar of the twentieth century—they demurred. Some thought it too recent; others, after learning of the dearth of correspondence in Brown's files, felt there was too little information to write a biography in the traditional sense of the term. After all, most historians rely on letters, journals, and personal memoirs to reconstruct the "life and times" of a great person. There was precious little of that kind of material in Brown's personnel files, now housed at the Associated Archives of the Sulpicians at St. Mary's Seminary and University in Baltimore. Yet Brown's enormous written legacy, seen in his extensive scholarly and popular writings over a forty-year period, does provide an objective framework from which to summarize and analyze the life of this towering biblical exegete. These resources have, in fact, provided much of the foundation for this biography.

Although it has taken two decades to arrive at this point, I believe the reader of this book will find that the right person has been chosen as the author. When Paulist Press and I approached Passionist Father Donald Senior, CP, about the possibility of writing this biography, he immediately embraced the project. Even knowing that it might be a challenge to come up with the kind of information that normally undergirds a full biography, Fr. Senior generously agreed to this task, both out of respect for the legacy of Fr. Brown and out of interest in truly trying to explain his importance in the context of modern biblical scholarship as it moves further into the twenty-first century. While we Sulpicians are, I believe, justifiably proud of Brown's achievements as a confrere, at the same time, we also desired to have someone from outside our community, yet familiar with biblical studies, to analyze the impact of Brown's life and scholarship.

I can say without hesitation that Fr. Senior is eminently qualified to undertake this project. A noted biblical scholar with impeccable credentials and an impressive publishing record, he also knew Brown personally and engaged him over the years in professional conversations. Although not trained as a historian per se, Fr. Senior is himself steeped in the history of biblical interpretation and the most prominent figures in it, as well as with the practice of the historical-critical method(s) of biblical interpretation, which was the hallmark of Brown's scholarship. Senior's own historical perspective, then, is well developed and highly esteemed. Another advantage is that, like Brown, Senior also served on the Pontifical Biblical Commission, giving him an international and ecclesial perspective that is hard to surpass.

Given this context, I would like to offer a few personal observations about this volume, designed from the beginning as an intellectual biography of Raymond Brown. The first is that, despite the lack of substantial correspondence, Senior has done a remarkable job plumbing the depths of the fairly limited number of letters, interviews, and personal documents left in Brown's estate. Senior has ferreted out some of Brown's own comments about his life experience—he was notoriously reticent to share much of his personal family history, for example—and has gleaned from recent interviews of those who knew Brown personally many observations that help to provide a more intimate and human portrait of the man, which heretofore has been elusive. In consequence, this biography fills in some lacunae from previous accounts of Brown's life and provides a fuller context to understand him and his importance. A few anecdotes that Senior recounts also brought a smile to my face, as I remembered some of Brown's idiosyncrasies that were so well known to his friends and colleagues.

Second, as was pointed out by others just after his untimely death in 1998—and now enhanced in this book—Senior fleshes out Brown's commitment to biblical scholarship as a true *churchman*. For Brown, biblical scholarship was never simply about exercising his tremendous intellectual gifts or about exegeting the Bible for its own sake. Everything Brown did as a scholar was done in the service of the church. Despite his fascination with the technical aspects of exegesis, Brown's Christian faith was his uppermost motivation. His commitments as a Roman Catholic, as a priest, and as a Sulpician were always central to his identity. His broad experience in ecumenical and interfaith conversations never constrained his personal faith but indeed strengthened it. He believed firmly that proper, scientific study of the Bible could both challenge and support every church's identity, including his own Roman Catholic Church. This is an aspect of Brown's life, however, that ended up causing him much anxiety. In my judgment, Brown's ultraright Catholic critics who branded him a heretic in the 1970s and '80s never appreciated or understood his true, conservative commitment to his Catholic faith. Senior carefully explains this aspect of Brown's career in chapter 8 of this book, which offers the most comprehensive, objective analysis of attacks on Brown to date.

A third point relates, from another angle, to the controversies that sometimes swirled around Brown's scholarship as it related to sensitive themes in the church's contemporary life. What struck me once more in reading Senior's analysis of Brown's life and scholarly career is how often Brown's scholarship led him to take well-reasoned, carefully explained, and moderate positions, which ultimately led him to middle-of-the-road stances that some interpreted as avoiding controversial conclusions. Brown was not interested in grandstanding to impress or shock his readers. His unwavering commitment to scholarship, in fact, forced him not to push his deductions beyond what the evidence would allow. Thus, in the context of a divided Catholic Church that emerged after the Second Vatican Council (1962–65), he criticized both "left" and "right" for exaggerated positions that Brown thought the evidence from honest biblical interpretation could not bear.[1] Taking such moderate positions, however, paradoxically embroiled him in further controversies. It earned him criticism from *both* sides of the spectrum. Even if, as is so often the case, the "truth" stands somewhere in the middle, this position is often uncomfortable and invites all-around criticism. This is all the truer when divisions become more and more pronounced, which has been the case in the Catholic Church in the wake of the Second Vatican Council down to our own day.

Finally, I offer a personal observation about the long-term value of Senior's biography of Brown. If it is true that twenty years is not a long time to digest the impact and fruit of an important figure like Brown, nevertheless Senior's study clearly shows that Brown's scholarship still casts a long shadow on biblical studies today, and not simply in the field of Johannine studies for which he is so famous. This book shows that some of the same methodological issues Brown addressed some forty years ago continue to impact biblical scholarship today. Granted that, methodologically, biblical studies have moved far beyond what Brown's interests were, some of the same basic issues he addressed remain at the heart of contemporary biblical controversies, especially the value and limits of the historical-critical method.[2] As the struggle to identify the most helpful approaches to biblical studies in a postmodern context remains, so too does the figure of Raymond E. Brown also remain as a touchstone for many neuralgic issues that resist easy, or perhaps superficial, resolution.

The reader of this biography, then, will not only be rewarded by a historical analysis of the life and scholarship of Fr. Brown, but will also gain a more comprehensive perspective on why his legacy endures. I congratulate Fr. Senior and Paulist Press for having the courage to undertake this study. For those of us who knew Brown personally, it is gratifying finally to see such a comprehensive and well-rounded discussion of his remarkable career. To a newer generation of scholars, priests, seminarians, students of the Bible, and interested laypeople, who may have only run across the name of Brown in one or another scholarly footnote, this book provides a reliable guide to help you understand why he is rightly considered one of the giants of Catholic biblical scholarship in the twentieth century.

Ronald D. Witherup, PSS
Sulpician Generalate, Paris

INTRODUCTION

THE SECOND VATICAN COUNCIL AND THE CATHOLIC BIBLICAL RENEWAL

Raymond E. Brown, SS, was the foremost American Catholic biblical scholar of the twentieth century, with tremendous influence within and beyond the Catholic community.[1] One might even reasonably claim he was among the most respected biblical scholars in the world, across the entire spectrum of Christianity. His life spanned an exceptional period of dynamic change in the Catholic Church, particularly regarding the role of the Bible in Catholic life and thought.

Brown was born in 1928, was ordained a Catholic priest in 1953, received his doctorate from Johns Hopkins University in 1958, and pursued a distinguished career in teaching, lecturing, and writing over the next forty years until his death in 1998. That lifetime witnessed a remarkable period of change in both the wider world and within the Catholic Church. Brown was a high school student during World War II, was called back from studies at the Gregorian University in Rome by his bishop in 1950 at the outbreak of the Korean War, and witnessed first-hand the social turmoil that descended on the United States in the late 1960s in the wake of the Vietnam War, affecting even the seminary in which he first taught. We should also note the onset of technology, particularly the use of the computer that marked the end of the twentieth century and the beginning of the twenty-first. Brown himself was a late user, only discovering the potential of a laptop computer for his writing in the final few years of his life. Once discovered, though, he used it to the full. One friend claimed that Brown never took extended vacations until he realized that he could bring his work with him by means of his beloved laptop.

At the same time, powerful currents were sweeping through the Catholic Church that would have a personal impact on Brown's own life. In 1943, while he was a junior in high school, Pope Pius XII published an encyclical, *Divino Afflante Spiritu*, that reversed years of suspicion and restraint imposed on biblical scholarship within the church and would encourage a whole generation of Catholic scholars to pursue advanced degrees in biblical studies, including Brown himself. On October 11, 1962, Pope John XXIII convened the first session of the Second Vatican Council, a watershed event that would reaffirm the central role of the Scriptures within the church's life and further ratify the surge in Catholic biblical scholarship. Brown himself, at the request of his bishop, would spend a short time at that opening session of the Council, and its Decree on Divine Revelation (*Dei Verbum*) published at the end of the Council in 1965 would be a bulwark for his own leading (and often controversial) role as a premier Catholic biblical scholar.

The renewal of the liturgy and the strong affirmation of the role of the Scriptures that were hallmarks of the Council's reforms would spur an explosion in the U.S. Catholic community of workshops, courses, and publications that made access to the Scriptures an exciting feature of the post–Vatican II era. Brown himself would be a major contributor to this renewal through his prolific publications, both on the scholarly and popular level, and through the thousands of workshops, courses, and lectures that he would give throughout his career, both in the United States and across the English-speaking world. Another dramatic impact of the Council was to transform centuries of rancor and suspicion among various Christian denominations into a period of remarkable ecumenical interaction and harmony. Brown himself stood at the center of that movement, being the first Catholic representative on the International Faith and Order Commission, a leading promoter of collaborative biblical scholarship with Protestant colleagues, and a pathfinder in his role as a Catholic priest teaching at one of the most prestigious Protestant seminaries in the United States.

To review the life of Raymond Brown is, then, also to be plunged into a review of one of the most remarkable periods in the history of the Catholic Church. Although personal bibliographical information, particularly about the early years of Brown's life, is somewhat sparse, it is important to try as much as possible to retrace his personal life, his formation as a Sulpician priest, his professional preparation as a biblical scholar, and the contours of his teaching and publishing career along with his deep commitment to share the fruits of biblical scholarship with a wide audience through his popular articles and presentations. Brown's exceptional personal gifts and his formative experiences explain a lot about his future professional life and the impact it had on the Catholic Church in the United States. At the same time, tracking the evolution of his publications and his reflections on his methodology illumines the struggle within Roman Catholicism to absorb historical-critical methods of studying the Bible, while attempting to maintain Catholic tradition and doctrine. Brown stood at the very epicenter of that struggle—a struggle whose reverberations are still part of the atmosphere of Catholicism today.

ANTICIPATING THE STORY: THE CATHOLIC CHURCH AND BIBLICAL SCHOLARSHIP

To appreciate the context of Raymond Brown's life and career, it is important to briefly sketch the evolution of biblical scholarship in the Catholic Church over the past one hundred years. Brown himself suggested one could divide that period into three major segments: 1900 to 1940, 1940 to 1970, and 1970 to 2000.[2]

1900 to 1940

The first period, 1900 to 1940, dealt with the lingering legacy of the Protestant Reformation and the Enlightenment. One of the central principles of the Reformation was an ardent appeal to Scripture as the essential authenticating norm of church life. *Sola Scriptura* (Scripture alone) was the lens for detecting the excesses perceived in the Medieval church: its aberrant forms of piety, its overemphasis on church structures and authority, and its political compromises with the secular realm. The same univocal focus on Scripture posed a challenge to the Catholic appeal to tradition and the development of doctrine that underwrote the teachings and structure of the church. At the same time, the turn to human reason and confidence in the empirical view of reality that grew out of the Enlightenment were perceived by many church authorities as a threat to the role of the supernatural and the transcendent within that reality. Rationalism would ultimately sweep through the intellectual realm of Europe and challenge the moral authority of the church.

At the Council of Trent (1545–63), the Catholic Church would mount the "counter-reformation," in effect tacitly agreeing with the reformers about the need to renew the life of the church and its clergy while clarifying, with more precision and a greater historical sense, the teachings of the church.[3] Through the Council of Trent, the church would also push back on the Protestant appeal to Scripture alone, reaffirming the role of tradition and the Spirit's ongoing guidance of the church's magisterium. The Bible always had a prominent place within the life of the church, with biblical characters and stories incorporated into its liturgy and devotions, etched in the statuary and stained-glass windows of its places of worship, portrayed in its popular festivals and pageants, and in varying degrees, the subject of its catechesis and preaching. Because a majority of Christians were mainly illiterate until the modern era, reading or studying the Bible would be rare among ordinary Catholics. However, through its monastic institutions and at the heart of its theology in the Medieval universities, reading, studying, commenting on, and, in fact, preserving the Scriptures, the church had an enduring commitment to the Bible as essential to its life.

Yet, in the wake of the Reformation and in reaction to the perceived assaults of rationalism, the Catholic Church over time adopted a defensive posture regarding the role of the Scriptures in Catholic life. Individual devotion to reading and studying the Bible, even as the invention of the printing press made this more of a possibility, was discouraged out of fear of "private interpretation" of Scripture. For Catholic laity to read the Bible without the guidance of the church's teaching authority could lead one astray, as the proliferation of various Protestant denominations appeared to confirm. Similarly, the development of empirical thinking and historical methodology in various fields of inquiry turned to critical analysis of the Bible as well as other types of literature. Rationalist assumptions questioned the role of the miraculous in biblical narratives such as the account of the exodus of Israel from the grip of Pharaoh or in Jesus's multiplication of the loaves or walking on the water. Scholars such as H. R. Reimarus (whose work on the life of Jesus was published posthumously in 1798) and David Friedrich Strauss (who, in 1835, attempted to find "reasonable" explanations for what was presented as evidence of the transcendent by allegedly naïve believers) questioned the historical reliability of the Gospels and offered a more rational portrayal of the Jesus of history, one different from the theological portrayal in the Gospels themselves. For many church authorities, it was not simply the conclusions of such research that were to be rejected, the historical methodology itself was seen as subversive of the sacred and historically reliable character of the Bible.

Armed with this perspective at the end of the nineteenth and the beginning of the twentieth centuries, the leadership of the Roman Catholic Church ushered in a period of profound suspicion regarding this type of biblical scholarship and moved to protect the faithful from what was considered its corrosive influence. To that end, Catholic scholars who seemed to adopt historical-critical methods were put under suspicion by church authorities. A prime example is that of Pére Marie-Joseph Lagrange, OP (1855–1938), the French Dominican who in 1890 founded what would become the prestigious École Biblique in Jerusalem, a Catholic graduate school dedicated to biblical scholarship.[4] Lagrange prized studying the Bible in the land and context in which it was first composed. The original small band of faculty and students that formed the school immersed themselves in study of the Scriptures and in firsthand archaeological exploration. Lagrange himself would spend time (especially during the winter months) in the warmth of the Cairo museum, studying ancient Semitic literature and culture and noting its influence on the Bible itself. He would eventually compose a commentary on Genesis that incorporated some of this research. However, this commentary and other writings on the Bible produced by Lagrange and his colleagues would raise alarm with church authorities, and he was for a time forbidden to publish his research. In fact, his commentary on Genesis was never published. His own role at the École Biblique and, in fact, its existence as a Catholic biblical center, would be continually under threat. Later, Lagrange turned his attention to commentaries on the New Testament and even studies of patristic writings to avoid the suspicions directed at his Old Testament studies.

Ultimately, Lagrange's deep personal piety and unwavering loyalty to the church would blunt the suspicions of church authorities. A contemporary of Lagrange was the French Catholic priest Alfred Loisy (1857–1940), who took a different tack. Loisy's writings, particularly his two-volume commentary on the Synoptic Gospels, were considered too radical and were condemned by church authorities. His bold resistance led ultimately to his excommunication in 1908, a step that would cast a long shadow over Catholic biblical scholarship. Lagrange, on the other hand, would seek to be in accord with church authority and was never formally censored or excommunicated. While he personally suffered from these attacks, he tenaciously demonstrated that historical research of the Scriptures was not incompatible with Catholic faith or with reverence for the Bible as the Word of God—a stance that would be echoed later in the perspectives of many pioneering Catholic scholars, including Raymond Brown himself. This loyal stance of Lagrange would ultimately be the best defense against his critics.

The concern of Catholic Church authority about a scientific approach to the Bible reached its high tide during the pontificate of Pius X (1903–14), who mounted a serious reaction against what was designated as the heresy of "modernism." Modernism referred to the perceived pernicious influence of rationalism and reductionism on church dogma. Included in this was the mounting suspicion against modern methods of biblical exegesis. Leo XIII, Pius X's predecessor, had published a moderate view of the impact of biblical studies on Catholic faith in his 1893 encyclical *Providentissimus Deus.* Leo acknowledged the importance of biblical studies for Catholic theology and encouraged the use of the original biblical languages and respect for the historical context in which the Scriptures were composed. He also acknowledged that the "truth" of the Scriptures did not necessarily extend to scientific matters. His encyclical would be an important precedent for the liberating encyclical of Pius XII in 1943. Pius X took a far more suspicious view, however, and believed that proponents of such modern methods of biblical study within the church needed to be resisted: "They want them to be treated with oil, soap and caresses. But they should be beaten with fists. In a duel, you don't count or measure the blows, you strike as you can."[5]

Particularly important were the decrees of the Pontifical Biblical Commission during this period. This commission had been established by Pope Leo XIII in 1902. Staffed by three cardinals and twelve consultors, its main purpose was to protect and defend the integrity of the Catholic faith in biblical matters. In a series of decrees published under Pius X between 1905 and 1915, the Commission stoutly defended a traditional view of the Bible over against the views of modern biblical exploration. For example, it asserted that Moses was the true author of the Pentateuch (although acknowledging that he may have drawn on other sources and was aided by some coauthors) and affirmed the literal historical character of the early chapters of Genesis, including the account of Creation and the narratives of the first annals of humanity. Other decrees asserted that Matthew was the first Gospel to be written and was to be dated before the destruction of Jerusalem and perhaps even before the writings of Paul. It also affirmed that the apostle John was the sole author of the Gospel of John and that the discourses of Jesus contained in the Fourth Gospel were the actual words of Jesus and not the composition of the evangelist.

Later in the twentieth century, the binding force of such strong conservative views found in these decrees would be tacitly set aside. Under Pope Paul VI, the function of the Pontifical Biblical Commission would no longer be primarily to monitor biblical scholarship but was now composed of an international set of biblical scholars whose purpose was to advise the Vatican and the pope on biblical matters of importance for the life and teaching of the church. As we will note later, Raymond Brown himself would serve two sets of terms on the Commission.[6] However, for Catholic biblical scholarship in the early part of the twentieth century, the decrees of the Commission had a profound chilling effect. This was particularly true in the United States, where the repressive atmosphere of the church regarding biblical studies had a negative impact on the work of biblical professors at Catholic University and elsewhere.[7]

1940 to 1970

The atmosphere of suspicion against modern biblical scholarship that characterized the reaction of Catholic Church authorities during the first half of the twentieth century would dramatically change in the period that led from the pontificate of Pope Pius XII through the Second Vatican Council (1962–65) and its aftermath. The turning point came with the encyclical *Divino Afflante Spiritu*, promulgated by Pius XII in 1943. As Raymond Brown himself and others would declare, this document was in effect the Magna Carta of modern Catholic biblical scholarship. The formal occasion for the encyclical was the fiftieth anniversary of Leo XIII's *Providentissimus Deus*, but Pius XII's statement went far beyond that of its predecessor. As Leo had done, Pius XII stressed the importance of respect for the sacredness of the Bible and the need to pursue biblical scholarship in harmony with the church's teachings. However, he also called for a return to the original biblical languages as the basis of biblical study rather than dependence on the

Latin or Vulgate version that had been a staple of Catholic biblical translations for centuries. In a reversal of previous trends, he also endorsed the use of historical-critical methods in study of the Scriptures, noting that they helped exegetes discover the original meaning and context of the Scriptures. Also important at the time was Pius's defense of Catholic biblical scholars, urging that their work be evaluated by others "not only with equity and justice, but with charity." Their severe critics "should abhor that intemperate zeal which imagines that whatever is new should for that very reason be opposed or suspected."[8] This admonition was a direct response to numerous attacks on Catholic biblical scholars mounted by anonymous pamphlets sent to Italian bishops at that time. The Pontifical Biblical Commission itself had responded to these attacks in a letter sent to the Italian hierarchy in 1941.[9] The anonymous pamphlet had accused church authorities of supporting the kind of critical exegesis that would undermine the truth of the Bible and Christian piety. The letter of the Commission refuted these claims step-by-step and appealed to the encyclical of Leo XIII, which had encouraged openness toward historical-critical analysis.

What, then, had taken place between the repressive atmosphere under Pius X and the liberating decree of Pius XII? For one thing, in the spirit of scholars such as Lagrange, other Catholic scholars in Germany, at the Pontifical Biblical Institute in Rome, and within the École Biblique in Jerusalem and elsewhere, were working quietly on less controversial topics such as studies of the biblical languages, archaeology, and biblical geography. A particularly important influence was that of Augustin Bea, SJ (1881–1968), who had been a professor and rector at the Pontifical Biblical Institute, a consultor on the Pontifical Biblical Commission, and whose integrity and erudition were respected by both Pius XII and his predecessor Pius XI. Bea played a substantial role in the formulation of *Divino Afflante Spiritu*. Later, at Vatican II, he would also be a leading champion of ecumenism. As would be proven time after time, the religious character and church loyalty of such scholars, coupled with the integrity of their scholarship, would have a decisive influence on the church's acceptance of modern biblical scholarship.

Pius XII's encyclical was a decisive turning point for Catholic biblical scholarship. One of its immediate impacts was to inspire a whole generation of bright priests and religious, mainly but not exclusively men at this point, to pursue advanced degrees in biblical studies. From this surge would come a generation of outstanding American Catholic biblical scholars who would themselves train—and inspire—a further wave of Catholic exegetes. Raymond Brown himself was someone whose path to biblical scholarship opened at this time. Other outstanding Catholic scholars would be his colleagues, names such as Joseph Fitzmyer, SJ; Roland Murphy, OCarm (the three of whom would become the coeditors of the groundbreaking *Jerome Biblical Commentary*); Barnabas Ahern, CP; George MacRae, SJ; Eugene Maly; Patrick Skehan; Carroll Stuhlmueller, CP; Mother Kathryn Sullivan, RSCJ; and Bruce Vawter, CM—to name only a few. This "greatest generation" of scholars and teachers would themselves prepare a host of Catholic biblical scholars who would serve in various capacities in the post–Vatican II church.

At the same time, however, suspicion of biblical scholars still lingered in the minds of some church leaders and led to the continuing censure of some prominent Catholic scholars. Even in the early years of the pontificate of Pope John XXIII, some professors at the Pontifical Biblical Institute in Rome were forced by lower-level Roman authorities to leave their teaching positions, such as Stanislaus Lyonnet, SJ, and Maximilian Zerwick, SJ. The same negative atmosphere was present in the United States during this period. Edward F. Siegman, a member of the Society of the Precious Blood and a beloved figure among his peers, was forced out of his post at the Catholic University of America in 1961 at the instigation of Msgr. Joseph Fenton, a professor of theology at the Catholic University. Siegmann was editor of the *Catholic Biblical Quarterly* and is credited for lifting that journal to the professional quality and respect it earns today. Fenton was a formidable critic of modern biblical scholarship and saw himself as a guardian of orthodoxy. He was backed at that time by Archbishop Egidio Vagnozzi, the Apostolic Delegate (1958–67), who, as we will see later, also attempted to suppress the writings of Raymond Brown himself.[10]

But the tide would turn with the convocation of the Second Vatican Council by Pope John XXIII and its fundamental agenda of reform. By chance, Raymond Brown was visiting Rome from his fellowship year in Jerusalem and was able to secure a ticket for the ceremony where John XXIII was "crowned" (as Brown would put it) as pope on November 4, 1958. In January 1959, the new pope, whom many thought would be a brief caretaker after the long pontificate of Pius XII, stunned the ecclesiastical world by announcing his intention to convene an ecumenical council. The first session of the Council would begin on October 11, 1962. (Brown would not be present for the opening but did attend part of the first session in November 1962 as a consultor invited by his bishop, Joseph Hurley of St. Augustine, Florida.)

One of the first schemas to be presented to the Council, in October 1962, dealt with divine revelation. Because it was judged to be very inadequate by a large number of bishops, it could not achieve the requisite two-thirds vote needed for it to be approved. It was also disappointing to biblical scholars around the world. In fact, in August of that year, even before the formal submission of the schema, a meeting of the U.S. Catholic Biblical Association had gained access to a copy and lamented its tone and content. The proposed document seemed to ignore Pius XII's *Divino Afflante Spiritu* of 1943 and hark back to the restrictive tones of the Pius X era. For example, on the question of the truth of the Bible, the schema asserted that "it is completely forbidden to admit that the sacred author could have erred, since divine inspiration of its very nature precludes and rejects all error in everything, both religious and profane." It also rejected out of hand modern historical-critical methods in studying the Gospels. Providentially, Pope John XXIII had the schema withdrawn and astutely appointed both the champion of the conservatives, Cardinal Alfredo Ottaviani, and the hero of the progressives, Cardinal Bea, to cochair a committee that would prepare a revision. Their work would continue all during the remaining sessions of the Council and would be submitted for approval in the very last session in the fall of 1965. It was a very different document from the original schema that was withdrawn from consideration in the opening session; the content and tone had benefited by the overall progress of the Council in the intervening years and passed with only a handful of dissenting votes.[11]

In 1964, a year before the approval of *Dei Verbum* ("The Word of God," the title given to the Council's final version of The Dogmatic Constitution on Divine Revelation), the Pontifical Biblical Commission issued a statement on "the Historical Truth of the Gospels" that would have a profound impact on the formulation of *Dei Verbum* itself and signaled the growing acceptance of modern biblical scholarship within the Catholic Church. The rationale of the relatively brief statement was to defend "the abiding truth and authority of the Gospels in their full light."[12] Recapitulating the affirmations of Pius XII's encyclical, the text urged scholars to study the Scriptures in their original language and to be aware of the context and literary form of the biblical texts. Especially important was the statement's description of the "three stages" that led to the formulation of the Gospels, beginning with the taproot of the gospel traditions in the life of Jesus, then circulating and being influenced by their use in the life of the apostolic church, and finally being composed by the work of the evangelists in the context of their respective communities. The statement concluded,

> Unless the exegete pays attention to all these things which pertain to the origin and composition of the Gospels and makes proper use of all the laudable achievements of recent research, he will not fulfil his task of probing into what the sacred writers intended and what they really said. From the results of the new investigations it is apparent that the doctrine and the life of Jesus were not simply reported for the sole purpose of being remembered, but were "preached" so as to offer the Church a basis of faith and of morals. The interpreter (then), by tirelessly scrutinizing the testimony of the Evangelists, will be able to illustrate more profoundly the perennial theological value of the Gospels and bring out clearly how necessary and important the Church's interpretation is.[13]

This view of the evolution of the Gospels and its implications for the kind of historical reliability characteristic of the gospel materials would be repeated by *Dei Verbum* and become a staple of subsequent official church pronouncements and of Catholic biblical scholarship itself. As we will note, this perspective was also a foundational principle of Brown's own methodology.[14]

Ultimately the Council's Dogmatic Constitution on Divine Revelation, *Dei Verbum*, was more encompassing than the brief statement of the Pontifical Biblical Commission. A fundamental contribution was to present the notion of revelation itself not as a communication of formal doctrinal propositions but as a divine self-revelation transmitted through the creation of the world and the human person, present in history, particularly in the history of God's chosen people, Israel, and culminating in the person of Jesus Christ, the Word of God made flesh. The entirety of the Scriptures, both the Old and the New Testament, are the privileged and inspired transmission of this divine revelation. This transmission of the Word of God was entrusted to the apostles by the risen Christ and continues in the apostolic church founded in his name until the end of time.

This overall portrayal of divine revelation enabled Vatican II to address in a fresh way several key issues of great importance for the interpretation of Scripture within the church. Rather than portraying Scripture and Tradition as two separate conduits of revelation, the Council saw both Scripture and Tradition as "bound together, and communicating one with the other" (no. 9). "Sacred Tradition and sacred Scripture make up a single sacred deposit of the Word of God, which is entrusted to the Church" (no. 10). This formulation ratified the teaching authority of the church but also made it accountable to Scripture. The church is viewed as both the servant of the Word and its authentic interpreter.[15]

Dei Verbum also affirmed a more nuanced understanding of the so-called inerrancy of the Bible. Instead of the untenable claim of the original schema that the inspired Scriptures could not contain error in any realm of truth, "religious or profane," the Council's statement recognizes that the truth of the Bible does not necessarily extend to all types of knowledge but "that the books of Scripture, firmly, faithfully and without error, teach *that truth which God, for the sake of our salvation*, wished to see confided to the sacred Scripture" (no. 11; italics added). This notion of the inerrancy of the Scripture makes room for what had already been acknowledged in the encyclicals of both Leo XIII and Pius XII, namely, that the Bible should not be expected to be without error in matters such as science or history. Equally important for the modern church's understanding of the nature of the Bible was the Council's affirmation that the Scriptures, while divinely inspired, were, nevertheless, composed by human authors, with all the conditions required for the composition of any literature within its own linguistic, cultural, and historical contexts. "Hence the exegete must look for that meaning which the sacred writer, in a determined situation and given the circumstances of his time and culture, intended to express and did in fact express, through the medium of a contemporary literary form. Rightly to understand what the sacred author wanted to affirm in his work, due attention must be paid both to the customary and characteristic patterns of perception, speech and narrative which prevailed at the age of the sacred writer, and to the conventions which the people of his time followed in their dealings with one another" (no. 12).

Dei Verbum goes on to reflect on both the Old and the New Testaments from this vantagepoint, seeing both as the inspired Word of God but transmitted in a thoroughly human context. In referring to the emergence of the Gospels, the Council absorbs the threefold stages of composition already affirmed by the 1964 statement of the Pontifical Biblical Commission's "Instruction on the Historical Truth of the Gospels," and explicitly cites this document.[16]

These affirmations of *Dei Verbum* about the nature of revelation, the meaning of the truth of the Bible, and the manner of the human composition of the Scriptures were, in fact, a decisive confirmation of the acceptance of the historical-critical methodology of biblical exegesis by the official church.

The concluding pastoral directives of *Dei Verbum* were equally important for the Catholic biblical renewal that would take place in the postconciliar period. The recommendations in its final chapter are comprehensive in scope. The Eucharist is central to the life of the church because it enables the faithful "to partake of the bread of life and to offer it to the faithful from the one table of the Word of God and the Body of Christ." Therefore, liturgical preaching "should be nourished and ruled by sacred Scripture." In a statement that stands in dramatic contrast to more traditional Catholic concerns about "private interpretation" of Scripture on the part of laity, the Council affirmed that "access to sacred Scripture ought to be open wide to the Christian faithful." To this end, translations need to be made "especially from the original texts of the sacred books" and, remarkably, it recommends that "these translations [be] made in a joint effort with the separated brethren" so that "they may be used by all Christians." The statement goes on to encourage deeper study of the meaning of the Scriptures, including acquaintance with patristic reflections on Scripture. It also urges "sons [*sic*] of the Church who are engaged in biblical studies constantly to renew their efforts" and declares that study of Scripture "should be the very soul of sacred theology." The ministry of the Word—"pastoral preaching, catechetics and all forms of Christian Instruction, among which the liturgical homily should hold pride of place—is healthily nourished and thrives in holiness through the Word of Scripture."

> Therefore, all clerics, particularly priests of Christ and others who, as deacons or catechists, are officially engaged in the ministry of the Word, should immerse themselves in the Scriptures by constant sacred reading and diligent study.

Additionally, given the encouragement of the laity to have access to the Scriptures, the Council urges bishops to see to the publication of the Bible with "translations of the sacred texts which are equipped with necessary and really adequate explanations." The statement even encourages that "editions of Scripture, provided with suitable notes, should be prepared for the use of even non-Christians, and adapted to their circumstances."

Dei Verbum concludes with an earnest hope: "Just as from constant attendance at the Eucharistic mystery the life of the Church draws increase, so a new impulse of spiritual life may be expected from increased veneration of the Word of God, which stands forever."

Even though the final text of *Dei Verbum*—like most of the Council's declarations—bears evidence of compromise and leaves many questions unresolved, it was and remains one of the most remarkable and far-reaching contributions of the Second Vatican Council to the life of the Catholic Church. For those Catholic biblical scholars who had been burdened with suspicion on the part of some church authorities, it was an act of liberation. For those who would now take up the ministry of biblical scholarship within the church, it was an inspiration and an enduring support. For Raymond Brown, who began his work of biblical teaching and scholarship just as the Council was concluding, the pastoral exhortations of *Dei Verbum* would define his priestly vocation and the entirety of his professional career.

1970 to 2000

It will take generations for the church to absorb fully the sweeping results of Vatican II into its life. Nevertheless, the immediate impact of the Council in the period 1970 to 2000, particularly on the Catholic biblical renewal, was dramatic. This period spanned the professional life of Raymond Brown, and the events that swirled through the Catholic Church, particularly in the United States, will be taken up in much more detail in what follows in this book.

There were some immediate and visible implementations of *Dei Verbum*'s recommendations. Closely following the completion of the Council, the Vatican published a directive for a three-year Lectionary that dramatically expanded the exposure of Catholics to the Bible within the context of both the Sunday and daily Eucharistic liturgies. Substantial portions of the three Synoptic Gospels were assigned to the Sunday readings on a rotating three-year basis, with large segments of John's Gospel read yearly. Accompanying the gospel readings was a wide range of readings from the Old Testament and Psalms, along with continuing selections from the writings of Paul and other New Testament texts. Paralleling the Sunday cycle of readings were ongoing daily readings from the Old Testament, the Gospels, the Pauline writings, and other New Testament texts. For the first time in Catholic liturgical history, those who participated in the Eucharist were exposed to major segments of the biblical writings.[17]

Accompanying this important liturgical innovation was a series of directives from the Vatican emphasizing that the sermon, or more properly the homily, was an integral part of the Eucharist and was to focus on an amplification of the biblical message and its relationship to the Eucharist. The United States Conference of Bishops would follow up this by emphasizing the need for a biblical focus in preaching, in their directives for priestly formation, and in subsequent formal statements on preaching.[18] Similarly, revisions of seminary curricula incorporated much more study of the Scriptures within its requirements.

The Council's recommendation that theologians and bishops give more attention to the Bible as the foundation of Catholic teaching also had some immediate impact. For example, the works of influential Catholic theologians, such as Walter Kasper's *Jesus the Christ* (1974) and Edward Schillebeeckx's *Jesus: An Experiment in Christology* (1979), included a rich biblical basis for their work.[19] New studies of Catholic ecclesiology such as Avery Dulles's widely read 1974 work *Models of the Church* also turned to the Scriptures as a primary source.[20] In formulating some of their most influential pastoral statements, the U.S. bishops would begin with a biblical foundation, such as those in U.S. bishops' statements on the morality of nuclear warfare (1983) and on economic justice (1986).[21]

There is no question that the impact of the Council also encouraged a whole generation of priests and religious to pursue graduate work in Scripture. In the immediate wake of the Council, most of those who took up graduate work in Scripture were priests, both diocesan and religious—as envisaged in the language of *Dei Verbum* itself.[22] Later, however, women religious and laity, both women and men, would begin to swell the ranks of Catholic biblical scholarship. At first, such students were formed primarily in Catholic European universities such as the Pontifical Biblical Institute and the Gregorian University in Rome,[23] the University of Louvain in Belgium, and Catholic faculties in German Universities such as Munich, Münster, Heidelberg, Regensburg, or

Tübingen (where both Hans Küng and Joseph Ratzinger would make their marks) or at the Institut Catholique in Paris and the University of Freiburg in Switzerland. A smaller yet significant number of students would venture to pursue graduate studies at the École Biblique in Jerusalem. Later, as we will see in the case of Raymond Brown himself, increasing numbers of Catholic students would seek degrees at American universities, such as the divinity schools of Harvard, Yale, Princeton, and the University of Chicago, or in the Semitic departments of a university such as Johns Hopkins, the alma mater of Brown. Opportunities to pursue a doctorate in Scripture at Catholic universities in the United States was—and is—still limited. Catholic University was one long-standing option through its Semitics department; later St. Louis University and the University of Notre Dame would build up their Bible departments at the graduate level.

In the immediate wake of the Council there was also an explosion of Catholic interest in the Bible on a popular level. Bible study groups sprang up in parishes across the country. Numerous dioceses sponsored workshops on the Bible for their clergy as well as for catechists and the general public. In several places, annual Bible study weeks sponsored by dioceses or Catholic colleges and universities were established, notably in Chicago; Denver; San Francisco; Dallas, Pennsylvania; Georgetown; Burlington, Vermont; and Buffalo—to name only some longer enduring examples. Similarly, Catholic publishers and commercial publishers with an eye to the Catholic market began to produce a wide range of commentary series, monographs, textbooks, and various devotional works on the Bible at a rate never before seen. For example, as we will discuss later, Raymond Brown produced numerous popular publications through Paulist Press. The Benedictine Liturgical Press of Collegeville, Minnesota, would contribute to this avalanche of biblical publications, including the founding of a popular journal, *The Bible Today*, which was first published in 1962 while the Council was still in session and continues to this day. At the time of the Council, Liturgical Press would also inaugurate the Collegeville "Reading Guides" series, which sold hundreds of thousands of booklet-sized commentaries on each book of the Bible. As we will see, Raymond Brown's commentary on the Gospel of John in this popular series would go on to sell over a million copies. At the same time, Prentice-Hall, a commercial press, would publish in 1968—with Brown as a coeditor—one of the most notable and influential fruits of nascent Catholic biblical scholarship, *The Jerome Biblical Commentary.*

The impetus to ecumenical collaboration prompted by the Council also had an impact on the Catholic biblical renewal in this period. Biblical studies by Catholic authors were being published in Protestant biblical series, such as the *Anchor Bible Commentaries*, in which a number of Catholic scholars were early contributors, including Raymond Brown, Joseph Fitzmyer, and Mitchell Dahood. Catholic schools of theology routinely used biblical studies by Protestant authors in their courses and vice versa. Catholic biblical scholars joined what had been essentially Protestant professional societies such as the Society of Biblical Literature and the European *Studiorum Novi Testamenti Societas*, with several rising to become the presidents of these associations, such as Brown himself, Joseph Fitzmyer, SJ, and George MacRae, SJ, who would serve as executive secretary of the Society of Biblical Literature for several years. Increasing numbers of Protestant scholars would also become regular members of the Catholic Biblical Association, drawn to its meetings by their more intimate atmosphere and openness to engagement with theological and pastoral issues. (In 1984, the CBA would elect for the first time a noted Protestant scholar, Paul Achtemeier, as its president.) Catholic scholars began to serve on the editorial boards of biblical journals that previously were exclusively a Protestant domain, such as the *Journal of Biblical Literature*. True to the recommendation of *Dei Verbum*, such a classic Protestant translation of the Bible as the Revised Standard Version would be published in a "Catholic edition" that would incorporate for the sake of Catholic readers the so-called apocryphal or "deutero-canonical" writings not considered part of the canon by Protestants. Ecumenical collaboration and mutual respect in the realm of biblical scholarship is still vigorous, and, in fact, largely taken for granted—a lasting impact of the Council.

Yet this postconciliar period, 1970 to 2000 (and beyond), was not all sweetness and light. While the enthusiasm generated by the Council remained strong, there were other factors at work, both within the church and in the wider society, that brought a more sober tone. The election of Pope Paul VI, who succeeded the beloved John XXIII, was considered a continuing vindication of the Council's work. Six days after his election, the pope announced that the work of the Council (which had been suspended with the death of Pope John XXIII) would continue. The new pope's journey to the Holy Land less than a year after his election was a symbolic endorsement of the Council's spirit of renewal, including its turn to the Scriptures for spiritual inspiration. But, for many, the publication of the encyclical *Humanae Vitae* in 1968 and its reaffirmation of the church's prohibition of contraception took some of the luster off the postconciliar enthusiasm. The election of John Paul II in 1978 would follow (after the shockingly brief reign of John Paul I). As bishop of Krakow, Cardinal Karol Wojtyla had been an active participant in the Council and a supporter of its work. But the turmoil and polarities that were becoming apparent in the post–Vatican II years and what was perceived as a slackening of doctrinal teaching and church discipline, prompted Pope John Paul II to take a more rigorous stance, quelling perceived "dissent" and imposing stricter conformity in matters of liturgical practice and church discipline. Concerns about moral values and faltering discipline were no doubt accentuated in the United States by the growing unease with the Vietnam War and the widespread social unrest that characterized political and social life in the late 1960s and '70s.

These tensions were certainly evident in the Catholic community of the United States. While most Catholics seemed to welcome such Council reforms as the use of the vernacular in the liturgy, a greater sense of openness and inclusion, the encouragement of lay participation in the life of the church, ecumenical outreach, and greater access to the Bible, others sensed a danger that the church was going astray and being too accommodating to modernity. In the biblical realm, concerns about the historicity of the Gospels and the conformity of biblical scholarship to the church's doctrine and teaching authority returned to the forefront for some theologians and bishops. In some instances, these concerns were stoked by irresponsible statements on the part of self-proclaimed progressives, who, for example, in preaching and popular teaching, would dismiss out of hand the historical nature of the Gospels or call into question the connection between key church doctrines and the Scriptures. Such sensational claims could prove shocking and even scandalous to Catholics in the pew unprepared to judge their validity or context. This was also a time of dramatic changes in Catholic religious life that led to a substantial number of resignations on the part of many religious men and women. Questions about the validity of mandatory celibacy, fueled in part by slackening social norms regarding sexual behavior in the wider society, also led to numerous departures from the diocesan priesthood in the United States and Europe.

THE RATIONALE AND PLAN OF THIS BOOK

Raymond Brown was a leading Catholic biblical scholar who perhaps more than any other individual spearheaded the dynamic Catholic biblical renewal in the span of time we have been considering. He was also a faithful priest and churchman who believed it was his vocation to help spread devotion to the Scriptures as the Word of God across the church, particularly in the United States. His driving energy to accomplish this and the public success he enjoyed in doing so would also make him a very visible target for those who saw in many of the changes in the post–Vatican II church a threat to Catholic orthodoxy and the undoing of the church's mission. It is this remarkable moment in the life of the modern church that is the focus of the study to follow—a period whose dynamics continue to reverberate and a period embodied in the life and career of Raymond E. Brown.

In inviting me to write this biography, the publishers described their view of the work as an "intellectual biography." I take that to mean that the intended purpose is to describe and assess the impact of Raymond Brown's scholarship rather than focusing exclusively on the details of his life. In many ways, that concept of the work is fortunate for me since there are many aspects of Brown's personal experience, such as his early family life, his decision to become a priest, or some of his personal reactions to contemporary events and personages, that are not directly available or reported only second hand. No members of his immediate family have survived. He was not a heavily introspective man. He kept no diary and most of his correspondence found in the Associated Archives at St. Mary's Seminary and University in Baltimore, where his personal effects have been preserved, deals with practical matters such as his financial obligations to his Sulpician community or arrangements for his lectures and publications. Brown poured his life and thought into his work of teaching, lecturing, research, and writing. As we will discuss, he had exceptional work habits but was not in any way a grim workaholic. He enjoyed friendships and savored the ordinary pleasures of a normal human life. But his own views about the church and its theology and about some of the controversial issues previously mentioned are addressed not in personal journals or letters but in his prolific writings, especially in the many popular publications that flowed from his pen. Yet, as with any human being, the backdrop of Brown's life—his family, his education, his love for his native New York, his many deep friendships, his abiding loyalty to his Sulpician community and to the priesthood, his teaching experiences, and the controversies and personal attacks against him—all of these not only shaped his personality but also the character of his biblical scholarship and its impact on the life of the post–Vatican II church.

Preparatory Years

Accordingly, in the opening chapters we will begin, as much as the somewhat sparse sources allow, by sketching Brown's family origin, his formation as a priest and Sulpician, and his graduate educational experiences. The latter—particularly his pursuit of a doctorate in Semitic studies at Johns Hopkins University under the tutelage of William Foxwell Albright—would profoundly influence the trajectory of Brown's subsequent career and the quality of his scholarship.

The settings for Brown's teaching career are also important to track, beginning with his first teaching assignments at St. Charles Seminary College in Catonsville, Maryland, then for several years in the early '60s at St. Mary's Seminary and University in Baltimore. In a remarkably short time, Brown's reputation as a brilliant scholar and inspiring teacher was widespread. His decision to move from St. Mary's to accept a position in New York was monumental and in many ways difficult for Brown, both on a personal level as a loyal Sulpician as well as for his scholarly career. He first received a joint appointment with the Jesuit Woodstock theologate and Union Theological Seminary (1971–74), then, with the close of the New York Woodstock theologate, his tenured appointment at Union, that in turn led to his appointment as a Distinguished Professor (1971–90). His time as a faculty member at Union would be a period of exceptional productivity for Brown and extended his reputation as a leading Catholic biblical scholar worldwide.

Another significant transition would come in 1990 with his decision to retire from teaching at Union and to take up residence at St. Patrick's Seminary in Menlo Park, California. As we will discuss, Brown, who at that time was only sixty-two years old, was not "retiring" in the full sense of the term, but had decided to leave behind full-time teaching and directing doctoral students to focus exclusively on research and writing. St. Patrick's was a Sulpician seminary serving the Archdiocese of San Francisco, and Brown would find there a compatible environment for what he intended to do. Here, too, Brown's productivity was remarkable, with several of his major works finding completion during this last period of his life. In 1998, this "retirement" period of hard work would be cut short by Brown's untimely death.

His Publications

Much of this study of Raymond Brown will concentrate on his prolific publications. The intent is not to offer "book reviews" of these publications but to note Brown's characteristic methodology, his views on the significant and often sensitive and controversial topics he was willing to tackle, and to note the lasting impact of his scholarship. As a deliberate strategy, Brown composed popular-level studies of the same issues he addressed in his more technical major works. The driving intent of this approach was to forcefully bring the Scriptures into the church, both on a scholarly and popular level. As we will note, the topics Brown covered in his written works were also the subject of the literally thousands of lectures, workshops, and audio tapes he produced over the length of his teaching career. In many cases, these lectures "road tested" Brown's approach to various issues and later would work their way into his written publications.

A Public Scholar, a Churchman, an Ecumenist

Raymond Brown was also what might be called a "public" scholar. As we will note, his work was not confined to the classroom, the lecture hall, or the written word. He was active on a national and even international level in numerous organizations and church commissions, such as a member of the Pontifical Biblical Commission, a contributor to the Catholic–Lutheran and Catholic–Methodist ecumenical dialogues, a member of the international Faith and Order commission, serving as president of the most prestigious professional associations, and so on. He would be a leading figure in the ecumenical commitment of the Catholic Church as well as a pioneer in encouraging close collaboration with Jewish scholars.

The Target of Opposition

Brown's prominence as a scholar and a churchman also made him a target of those who found his work troubling or dangerous. This was no doubt the most painful dimension of Brown's experience as a Catholic priest and as a biblical scholar. His championing of the historical-critical method in biblical interpretation was attacked by his foes as heretical and destructive of the church's teachings. The drumbeat of opposition to him never ended, even with his death. In his letters and in comments to friends and colleagues, as well as in some of his publications, Brown lamented such opposition and, occasionally, struck back. But he was also shrewd in taking steps to insulate himself from some of these attacks—cultivating the support of bishops and other church officials, fashioning behind-the-scenes responses for others to disseminate. One of the greatest frustrations for some of his opponents was that, despite their unrelenting public accusations, Brown maintained the support of many key bishops and was implicitly endorsed by the highest level of church authority in Rome. As we have seen with other pioneers in scriptural studies, church loyalty and personal integrity mattered.

Assessment

Our study of Raymond Brown will conclude with an attempt to assess his lasting impact on the Catholic Church, particularly in the United States. His sudden and unexpected death in 1998 at the age of seventy was a jolting shock to his colleagues and many admirers. Yet his vast body of published works remains and his championing of the historical-critical approach to biblical study is still endorsed as essential by the Catholic Church, even as the limitations of that method and the need to include other approaches to biblical interpretation have become more apparent. The Second Vatican Council itself continues to be interpreted and assessed, even as it has made an indelible mark on the life of the Catholic Church. So, too, the work of Raymond Brown and the vital role of the Scriptures in the life and thought of the church he stood for will continue to be a dimension of the contemporary church.

PURPOSE AND ACKNOWLEDGMENTS

In acknowledging my debt to the many people who made this work possible, I would like first to say a word about my own personal relationship with Raymond Brown. I completed my doctoral work in Scripture at the University of Louvain in 1972 and immediately began teaching at Catholic Theological Union (CTU) in Chicago, a major school of theology sponsored by several religious communities. I cannot clearly remember the first time I personally met Raymond Brown, but I had certainly read and studied many of his publications during my seminary and graduate education. I do remember encountering him at a Catholic Biblical Association meeting in Milwaukee shortly after I began teaching at CTU. He was always affable, unassuming, and gracious. I think he saw himself as an informal mentor to many of us who were beginning our work as biblical faculty. Over the years, I would receive from him a number of offprints of his articles and even copies of his books, with the salutation "Best Wishes, Ray." When he was in the midst of his major work, *The Death of the Messiah*, he flattered me with a telephone call or two to discuss the approach he was taking. As he did for so many younger scholars, I discovered that Raymond Brown was the one who had recommended me to be a part of some publishing project or speaking engagement. After he moved to California, I gave some lectures in the Vatican II Institute, a program of renewal for priests that was housed at St. Patrick's Seminary in Menlo Park. Ray made it clear to me that I should come and visit with him in his office at the seminary whenever I was there, which I gladly did. As fate would have it, I was president of the Catholic Biblical Association at the time of the 1998 annual meeting in Scranton, Pennsylvania, when word of his sudden death reached us during the opening liturgy of the meeting. It fell to me to make the announcement to the assembled members—each of whom knew and admired Ray Brown as I did. I will never forget the reaction of shock and sorrow that swept through the university chapel at that moment.[24]

So, for me, the opportunity to pay homage to Raymond Brown in this work is a great and unexpected privilege. My intended audience is, first, that whole generation of priests, religious, and laity who love the Bible and recall the name of Raymond Brown and the important contribution he made. This would also include many Protestant and Jewish friends and admirers of Brown. Hopefully, seeing the man and his work up close will deepen their appreciation for him. I also write for a younger generation of Catholics—and other Christians—who may have heard of Raymond Brown in only a vague way, if at all. His contribution should not be forgotten, and those who will lead and animate the church of the future should count him as a model of both enduring loyalty to the church and of courageous intellectual leadership—both of which should go hand in hand. Finally, the life and work of Raymond

Brown are in many ways a commentary on one of the most remarkable periods in the history of the modern Catholic Church. For all who care about the church and its future, I hope this glimpse of the church's life at a unique time will be informative.

It would be an exaggeration for me to claim Raymond Brown as a close friend, but I surely considered him as one of my personal heroes and one whose commitment to biblical scholarship at the service of the church remains an inspiration. I thank Paulist Press and the Sulpician community for the honor of inviting me to write this account of his life. Those two great Catholic institutions were embodied for me in a special way in the Very Rev. Ronald Witherup, PSS, currently Superior General of the Society of St. Sulpice, and Rev. Mark-David Janus, CSP, President of Paulist Press. It so happens that the Sulpicians and the Paulists have a long history of collaboration. The Sulpicians who founded St. Mary's Seminary and University in the eighteenth century had, a century later, welcomed the seminarians of the newly established Paulist community, begun by Isaac Hecker in New York in 1858. Aware of that connection and admiring the commitment of the Paulist Press to quality Catholic publishing, Raymond Brown made it a point to submit many of his more popular publications to the Paulists. Fr. Ronald Witherup has had a long and deep connection with Raymond Brown; Brown had guided him into graduate biblical studies, was a colleague when Witherup himself began his teaching career, was Dean of St. Patrick's Seminary in Menlo Park when Brown had resided there, and would be Brown's provincial religious superior at the time of his death in 1998. To Fr. Witherup fell the sad task of taking care of Brown's personal effects. I am grateful to him for inviting me to write this biography of his cherished friend and fellow religious and for his wonderful guidance and encouragement throughout the process of composing this work.

My thanks to the Very Rev. John Kemper, PSS, current Provincial Superior of the Sulpicians, for his unflagging support of the project and for his warm hospitality during my visits to St. Mary's and its archives. Thanks, too, to Msgr. David Fulton, Director of the Center for Continuing Formation at St. Mary's, for his genial hospitality during those visits.

Special thanks also are due to Christopher Bellitto, who served as editorial liaison on behalf of Paulist Press throughout the project. His warm and friendly manner and his professional and timely assistance step-by-step as the manuscript took shape, have been invaluable to me.

Early in the process, I had the benefit of conferring at length with

Sr. Mary C. Boys, SNJM, Dean of Academic Affairs and Skinner and McAlpin Professor of Practical Theology at Union Theological Seminary in New York. Mary, a graduate of Union herself and a doctoral student and good friend of Raymond Brown, was a prime source of information about his days at Union. She also generously provided me with a host of materials from Brown's tenure at Union. I am also grateful to Beth Bidlack, Associate Dean at Union and former director of its Burke Library. She was tireless in tracking down information about Brown's doctoral students during his time at Union.

Two other great friends of Brown were in the Union orbit when he was there and were completely generous in sharing information about him. Dr. Phyllis Trible served as the Baldwin Professor of Sacred Literature at Union from 1980 to 1998, during Brown's own tenure there. She was most gracious in sharing with me her fount of memories of her deep friendship and close collaboration with Brown as his faculty colleague. Rabbi Burton L. Visotzky was appointed to the faculty of Jewish Theological Seminary of America in 1977, Union Seminary's close neighbor, following his ordination to the Rabbinate, and continues to serve there as the Appleman Professor of Midrash and Interreligious Studies. He warmly welcomed me and offered valuable insight into his fellow "rabbi," as he called Brown, and briefed me on their collaboration and friendship.

I was fortunate to be able to interview at length many of Brown's fellow religious, faculty colleagues, doctoral students, and academic collaborators, including John Kselman, PSS, a former student of Brown and later a biblical colleague, who was Brown's prime editor for most of his major works; Robert Leavitt, PSS, who was also a student of Brown and later the president-rector of St. Mary's Seminary and University, was instrumental in establishing the Raymond E. Brown Johannine Collection at St. Mary's, a research center that honors Brown's legacy; and Fr. Michael Barré, PSS, a retired faculty member of St. Mary's and a fellow religious and friend of Brown. Numerous former students, scholarly colleagues, and those who had been touched by his writings and lectures sent me notes of encouragement and words of appreciation for Brown—for all of them I am most grateful. Their admiration for Raymond Brown after all these years reinforced my own appreciation for this outstanding priest and scholar. I also had the opportunity for numerous personal interviews with friends and collaborators of Brown, including Fr. John Meier, currently Professor of New Testament at the

University of Notre Dame and a close associate of Brown, especially from their New York days; John Donahue, SJ, a friend and collaborator with Brown, as well as one who was mentored by him; Sr. Sandra Schneiders, IHM, who was inspired by Brown at the beginning of her scholarly career and later was a trusted colleague of his; and Benedict Viviano, OP, whose trove of knowledge about Catholic biblical scholars, including Raymond Brown, was most helpful. I was also fortunate to learn much from former doctoral students of Brown—all of whom spoke of him with delight and reverence. These included Professor Craig Koester, Academic Dean and Professor of New Testament at Luther Seminary; Professor Claudia Setzer, Professor of Biblical Studies at Manhattan College; and Professor Marion Soards, Brown's assistant when at Union and now Professor of New Testament at Louisville Presbyterian Seminary.

Special thanks, too, to John and Rosemary Croghan of Winnetka, Illinois, who were dear friends of Raymond Brown, who in turn thoroughly enjoyed their friendship and the warm hospitality of their home on many occasions. Their memories of Brown and the correspondence they collected from him were most valuable. Thanks, too, to their son Dr. John Croghan for his help in understanding the circumstances of Brown's final days.

Especially helpful was the transcript of the Oral History Interview of Raymond Brown conducted by Fr. John Endres, SJ, on December 3, 1996. Sponsored by the Catholic Biblical Association, this project was a unique and immensely valuable instance in which Brown reflected in a personal way on his own vocation as a biblical scholar. A copy exists in the St. Mary's Archives; which brings me to what proved to be absolutely essential to the whole project, namely, full access to the Associated Archives at St. Mary's Seminary and University.

As noted on its website, this unique resource is "located on the campus of the nation's first Roman Catholic seminary, this program brings together the archives of the Archdiocese of Baltimore (est. 1789), St. Mary's Seminary and University (est. 1791), and the Associated Sulpicians of the United States (U.S. province, est. 1903), making it one of the most significant repositories for records relating to the early history of the Catholic Church in the United States." All of Raymond Brown's personal effects and the entirety of his archives are located there. Unless otherwise indicated, all quotations from Brown's correspondence and other documentation are from the archives and used with permission of the Sulpician community. What makes the Associated Archives at St. Mary's invaluable is not only its unique collection of documents but the superb professionalism and generosity of its director and staff. I want to thank in a special way Tricia T. Pyne, PhD, Director of the Archives, and her staff, particularly Ms. Alison Foley, MLS, who serves as reference archivist. At every turn and for every request, their professional help was fully available to me and this project.

Closer to home, I want to thank Ms. Lissa Romell, the Administrative Assistant of my local Passionist community in Chicago, who patiently transcribed hours of interviews and helped in countless ways with the preparation of the manuscript. All of it done with aplomb and never a complaint. I should also thank the fellow Passionists of my community in Hyde Park, Chicago, for my commandeering so much of Lissa's time and their having to listen so often to my anecdotes about Raymond Brown! Other Chicago friends, too, were patient with me during the writing of this biography and gave feedback on the material as it went along.

Finally, a word of dedication. I have had the privilege of spending the entirety of my professional life (so far) at CTU, serving on its faculty and, for twenty-three years, as its president. Raymond Brown and his peers in the Catholic biblical guild were the pathfinders and pioneers who paved the way for me and my distinguished biblical colleagues at CTU. I am truly grateful for the years of research, writing, and teaching at this wonderful institution that has been my lot since I finished graduate school many moons ago. As a very small token of that appreciation, I dedicate this work to the students, staff, faculty, and administration of Catholic Theological Union.

Donald Senior, CP
The Feast of the Epiphany
January 6, 2018

CHAPTER 1

PREPARATION

FAMILY, VOCATION, EDUCATION

For a man who wrote nearly fifty books and over three hundred articles and reviews, Raymond Brown wrote relatively little about his own family life and the early years of his education and seminary experience.[1] This was not because he wished to keep these formative years a secret or was hesitant in any way about them. From start to finish, Brown was someone who focused on his work at hand and did not spend a lot of time discussing or documenting his inner thoughts and feelings.[2] As all who knew him could testify, he was gregarious and outgoing but was more reticent about discussing his own family history and his own internal personal reflections. Yet what is known about his early years up to and including his seminary formation and his rich graduate educational experiences would profoundly shape his character and prepare for the exceptional professional career that lay ahead of him.

THE NEW YORKER AND HIS FAMILY

Raymond Edward Brown was born in the Bronx, New York, on May 22, 1928, the first of two children of Reuben Haynor Brown and Loretta Agnes Sullivan, and baptized June 3, 1928, at St. Thomas Aquinas Church, at 1900 Crotona Parkway. At that time, the family lived at 136 Daily Avenue in the heart of the Bronx. That Bronx origin never left him, even though he lived elsewhere from his senior year in high school in Florida in 1944 until his move from Baltimore back to New York in 1971. Anyone who met Fr. Raymond Brown in his later life, distinguished looking and famed scholar and author that he was, would be startled by a Bronx accent reminiscent of James Cagney. Brown attended primary school and the first three years of high school at All Hallows School, taught by the Irish Christian Brothers. Later in 1994, when receiving from the school the honor of being inducted into its "Hall of Fame," he would credit the brothers with teaching him how to do public speaking and to write a complete sentence. He also credited the school with giving him a "solid, firm teaching in Catholic faith [that] helped him discern his vocation," one of the rare instances on record when Brown talked about the inception of his call to priesthood.[3]

Brown was close to both his parents and in later life he would lament that his heavy schedule of teaching and lecturing prevented him from being able to visit with them as often as he would have liked. Colleagues and friends familiar with his office in Baltimore, New York, or in Menlo Park noted that a photo of his father and mother was always on his desk. He told friends that his mother was a kind and gentle person. One of Brown's closest friends in later life was Kateri Sullivan, an Immaculate Heart of Mary Sister in Los Angeles, California; he confided to another friend that Sullivan's warm and gracious demeanor reminded him of his mother.[4]

Brown's father was involved in real estate and finance and was apparently a somewhat strict figure. When observing some behaviors of students that annoyed Brown at St. Mary's in Baltimore or at Union Theological Seminary, he would mutter, "My father would never put up with that!" Brown's father was apparently gifted mechanically and took pride in a number of renovation projects on public buildings[5] and homes in the New York and New Jersey area. In a 1994 letter to Sue Albert, a family friend from Wyckoff, New Jersey, Brown thanked her for sending photos of a house renovated by his father and one that the young Brown family would eventually reside in for a time. "Nothing you could have done would have won my heart as much as to send me photos…of the house on Upper Saddle River Road [located in Montvale, New Jersey, about thirty miles northwest of New York City]. Because my father redid houses frequently, we lived in many lovely houses in NY, NJ, and Florida; but none captivated my heart the way that house did." Brown's letter goes on to describe in detail the various renovations his father had put into the house and lamented the fact that subsequent owners had not kept up the property. He also noted, "The buildings were not in great shape; he never showed it to my mother or me until he had redone everything." "My father," he wrote, "could fix anything."

Brown may have inherited his father's discipline and eye for detail but not his mechanical skill. Brown's personal correspondence is full of meticulous details about his finances, his travel plans, and the process of publishing his books. But Brown was awkward and unsure when faced with a simple practical task. His assistant at Union, now Professor Marion Soards at Louisville Presbyterian Seminary, recalls finding Brown one day struggling to install a small holder for his toothbrush on the wall of his bathroom. When Brown left for a moment to take a telephone call, Soards quickly completed the simple task of fastening it to the wall. When Brown returned, he was totally amazed that Soards had accomplished what to him seemed a formidable project.

The family moved to Florida in 1944. The precise reason for the move is not known, but later, at the time of his father's death, Brown would note that locating in Florida had been more of his mother's desire than that of his father. Perhaps the multiple moves and the cold winters of New York were factors. Later, Brown himself, when teaching at Union, would regularly flee New York in the winter to go to the Caribbean, often in the company of a good friend and a priest of the nearby Trenton Diocese, Msgr. Joseph Shenrock, himself deeply involved in ecumenical work. Brown would usually arrange to give some talks on one of the Islands to offer some rationale for the trip and spend his free time enjoying swimming at the beach and pursuing his writing. Brown attended St. Paul's High School in St. Petersburg for his senior year.[6] The family would eventually settle in Miami Shores, a suburb of Miami itself. At that time, its population was less than five thousand, but it would later double in size and become a predominantly Hispanic population. When the Brown family moved there, the Miami area was still part of the Diocese of St. Augustine, which virtually covered the whole state. For the rest of his life, mainly for taxation purposes, Brown would list his official address as that of St. Rose of Lima Parish in Miami Shores, his family's local church.

Brown's mother, Loretta, would pass away from cancer in 1963 while he was teaching at St. Mary's in Baltimore. His father also suffered from cancer and died in 1973 after Brown had joined the faculty at Union Theological in New York. The loss of his wife devastated Brown's father, and the ten years of his widowhood would be extremely difficult for him and for his two sons who tried to encourage him. Brown made an extra effort to spend time with his father. At one point in writing to the then rector of St. Mary's, Fr. Van Antwerp, Brown mentions that he and his brother were both tending to their father who was keeping vigil for his wife's impending death: "Mother is failing rapidly.…My dad becomes increasingly difficult to handle. He is frustrated as her death so patently approaches, and becomes more irritable and emotionally upset. My brother is here again (this is his 25th year as a Brother) and he had a few weeks' vacation coming.…He and I spend our time trying to keep one another sane."[7] After her death, Brown's father found being a widower a torment; he became deeply depressed and lost weight. Brown, in consultation with his brother, was determined to have his father close out the house in Miami Shores, with all of its memories of his mother, and bring his father to New York: "If only we could sell this house down here! I must admit I am worn out trying to think of topics of conversation to get his mind off my mother. 1963 will go down as the year of great exhaustion."[8] His father had loved living in New York, and his son Raymond would be able to see to his good care there. However, his father's condition worsened and the planned move never took place. The fact that both his parents died of cancer and at a relatively younger age (his mother was sixty-six; his father, seventy-four) made Brown himself wary that he, too, might have to face cancer. That was not to be the case, but his death at seventy turned out to be the average between the age of both his parents at their passing.

There is little mention in Brown's personal correspondence of his relationship to his younger brother, Robert. Robert had become a Christian Brother in the early 1960s but later left the community and married, moved to Scranton, Pennsylvania, and had one son. Robert Brown would pass away only a couple of years after his brother Raymond's own death. There is no hint of any great tension between the two brothers, but the scarcity of reference to his brother and the testimony of his colleagues suggest that they did not have a close relationship. At one point, Brown confided to a friend that he had been invited to visit his brother and his family for a Thanksgiving celebration and went, but without much enthusiasm. As his nephew was growing up, Brown made some efforts through correspondence to interest him in his hobby of stamp collecting and even his own biblical work but never got very far.

After his father's death in May 1973, Brown had responded to his provincial who had expressed his sympathy for his loss: "I shall miss him deeply as I close out the family side of my life." Brown's life would be blessed with abundant close friendships, but the family support that had been the anchor of his early life was now behind him. In the second volume of his Anchor Bible commentary on the Gospel of John, he dedicated the entire work to his father: "This completed commentary is dedicated to my father in his seventieth year. A small gesture of gratitude for a lifetime of generosity."[9]

THE SULPICIANS AND SEMINARY TRAINING

After his high school graduation from St. Paul's High School in Petersburg, Brown entered St. Charles College in Catonsville, Maryland, in the fall of 1945 to begin his seminary education. St. Charles, a venerable college founded in 1848 on land originally deeded to the Diocese of Baltimore by Charles Carroll, one of the signers of the Declaration of Independence, had moved to Catonsville from its first location in Ellicott City, Maryland, after a devastating fire in 1911. It was staffed by the Sulpicians and served as a college seminary for diocesan candidates.[10] The Diocese of St. Augustine sent their seminarians to St. Charles for their initial seminary preparation. This continued a long connection with the Sulpicians, since the first bishop of the newly formed Diocese of St. Augustine in 1870 had been a Sulpician, Jean-Pierre Augustin Verot. The details of Brown's decision to enter the seminary are unknown. His comment about the influence of the Christian Brothers at All Hallows on his vocation suggests he had been thinking about this step all during his high school years.

It was here at St. Charles that he would have his first contact with the Sulpician community that would be at the center of the rest of his life. The Society of St. Sulpice was founded in France by Jean-Jacques Olier (1608–57). Olier, a contemporary of such luminaries as St. Francis De Sales (for whom Olier had served as an altar boy at his Mass and was impressed with his sermons) and St. Vincent de Paul, was part of a resurgence of Catholic life in France inspired by the reforms of the Council of Trent. A singular legacy of Olier was his creative mission to reform the preparation of diocesan priests. Ultimately, he and his colleagues had founded a seminary connected with the parish of St. Sulpice in Paris in 1641. The intent was that the core group of priests surrounding Olier would collectively run the seminary, with themselves embodying the ideals of the priesthood and being an influence on the seminarians they were preparing. His vision of seminary education included both intellectual rigor and the cultivation of a deep interior spiritual life. The seminarians took most of their courses at the Sorbonne (which Olier also wanted to reform) and some at the parish. Particularly important was the role priest-formators were to play as spiritual guides and confessors for the seminarians. Olier himself was not especially interested in forming a large religious order, but the effectiveness of his methods and his reputation for genuine holiness soon brought many requests for assistance to his doorstep from other bishops in France and beyond. Olier died after a series of strokes in 1657, and it was left to his successors to gradually build his initial modest initiative into a large and formal community of diocesan priests.

After a series of negotiations and proposals, the still young Sulpician community was invited in 1791 by the progressive bishop John Carroll of Baltimore to establish a college and seminary in Baltimore, a diocese at that time whose boundaries incorporated virtually the entire United States, numbering some thirty thousand Catholics. St. Sulpice Seminary (its name later changed to St. Mary's Seminary) would be the first Catholic seminary in the newly established United States. It remains the flagship seminary of the Sulpician community in the United States.[11]

To a remarkable degree, the Society of St. Sulpice retains the ideals and purpose forged by Olier. The Society is not a religious order in the usual sense of the term. Rather, it remains a group of diocesan priests who are released by their respective bishops to become part of the Sulpician society; they do not take religious vows but are bound together by their collective mission. Their primary work remains that of seminary education for diocesan priests, with members of the Society serving as faculty and as spiritual advisors and confessors responsible for the formation of seminarians. As we will see, that mix—the pursuit of theological scholarship and respect for the priesthood—would form the foundation of Brown's lifelong mission.

It is unlikely that Brown had gone to St. Charles College with the idea of joining the Sulpicians. His formal application to join the Society would come only in 1951, but undoubtedly his first experience of the Sulpicians on the faculty at St. Charles began the process. From the outset, Brown's superior intellectual gifts were recognized, and in 1946 he was enrolled in The Catholic University of America in Washington, DC, for the remainder of his philosophy training.[12] Brown was awarded a Basselin scholarship, a scholarship for "the very best and brightest" seminarians endowed by the lumber magnate Theodore Basselin at the Theological College of Catholic University. Brown graduated from Catholic University in 1949.

At the completion of his philosophy program, Brown, in recognition of his intellectual gifts, was sent by his bishop to Rome in 1949 to begin his theological studies at the Gregorian University, the famed Pontifical University staffed by the Jesuits. During what would turn out to be a brief sojourn, Brown lived at the Pontifical Belgian College, an institution founded in 1844 to serve as a residence for Belgian seminarians studying in Rome. Although there seems to be no record of why he took up residence there, it is likely that it was the opportunity to learn French and German in the international atmosphere of this residence. It is interesting that another foreign student and young priest, Karol Wojtyla, later to become Pope John Paul II, for the same purpose of learning languages, had also stayed at this college from 1946 to 1948 while completing his doctoral dissertation at the Angelicum University. They missed being there together by only a few months. Brown had completed only one year of theological studies at the Gregorian when his bishop, Joseph Hurley, called him back to the United States. It was 1950 and the Korean War had broken out. Based on his own earlier experience of trying to get seminarians out of Europe at the beginning of World War II, Hurley feared that the conflict could mushroom into a world war and Brown would be stranded in Rome.

THE LURE OF THE BIBLE

This turn of events brought Brown back to Baltimore where he would complete his theological studies in preparation for priesthood at St. Mary's Seminary, but this shift also led to one of the most significant developments in his life—his discovery of biblical studies as his first love and the start of a lifelong vocation of teaching Scripture. To mesh his first year of courses in Rome with the curriculum at St. Mary's, Brown met with the Dean, Fr. Edward A. Cerny, SS, to work things out.[13] Brown himself describes the encounter and its aftermath:

> I approached the Dean, telling him what I had had in Rome;
> but those were very regimental days. He just said, "You take

7

all Second Theology courses whether you've had them or not in Rome." And I said, "Well, that's fine, I don't mind retaking the systematic and moral courses, but I didn't have all your biblical courses." (In St. Mary's a great deal of Bible was taught in first year.) He replied, "That's not our fault." I pressed him about what I had to do about this in order to get a degree, but he told me to go to the professors and see what they would say. So I went to the professor of Bible; and he said that he didn't have time to give me a private course, but if I wanted to study the whole Old Testament on my own and take an examination, he'd hear the examination. Well, he didn't tell me how much to study, so I started reading the Old Testament and studying. I was fortunate enough to be able to read French and Italian and some German, so that actually I was reading better books than were available in English. And when I took the exam, he was highly complimentary. He virtually told me, "I didn't mean you had to know that much."[14]

The amazed biblical professor went on to ask Brown about his experience.[15] "He asked me whether I was interested in Bible. I said it was the most interesting thing I had ever done in my life; it was fascinating." There was a short leap from here to Brown's commitment to a life of teaching the Scriptures. "I'd always wanted to teach. In fact, I told my own Bishop that when I joined the Diocese of St. Augustine. The professor said, 'We do need teachers of Bible.' So I applied to the Bishop of St. Augustine, asking if he would release me to the Sulpicians with the understanding that I would teach Bible. It just happened that the first Bishop of St. Augustine, back in the last century, had been a Sulpician, and nobody had ever gone to the Sulpicians since. Consequently he sort of felt an obligation to release me. And that's how I got into Biblical Studies."[16]

Brown would go on to complete his theological studies at St. Mary's in preparation for his ordination. He received the usual sequence of degrees awarded at a pontifical graduate program such as St. Mary's had: a "Baccalaureate in Sacred Theology" (STB) in 1951 and a "Licentiate in Sacred Theology" (STL) in 1953.[17] In 1952, during his fourth year of theological studies, in preparation for his licentiate degree, Brown wrote a paper on the history of the concept of *sensus plenior*, a particularly Catholic concept that asserted that the biblical text of the Old

Testament included a "fuller sense or meaning" beyond the intent or consciousness of the biblical author, a meaning that pointed to the fullness of revelation in Christ.[18] This would lead to the first of a long string of Brown's publications. Again, Brown's own words best describe what happened:

> The professor thought that it [Brown's STL thesis] was quite good. I had been reading the *Catholic Biblical Quarterly* [the professional journal of the Catholic Biblical Association of America], and I asked him whether I could send an article on it to that periodical. There really hadn't been a history written in English on the *sensus plenior* theory. So I took a chance and sent it over. Ed Siegman, a Precious Blood priest, who was a wonderful man, really one of the heroes of American Biblical studies, sent for me. I went over and saw him at Catholic University. He judged it a good article and said, "I'm going to publish it, because we're anxious to encourage young biblical scholars." And so he published it in 1953 in the *Catholic Biblical Quarterly*. That is, more or less, what got me involved on a professional level.[19]

ORDINATION TO PRIESTHOOD

One other step would complete Brown's formal association with the Sulpicians and forever mark his life. He was ordained a priest by Bishop Hurley in Miami, Florida, on May 23, 1953. Although there is no record of his personal feelings or reflections about this momentous day itself, being a priest (and a Sulpician) would define Brown's own personal identity for the rest of his life. He was in many ways a classic and traditional Catholic priest. He was devoted to celebrating the Eucharist every day no matter where he was. That was relatively easy to do in his assignments to Sulpician seminaries in Baltimore and eventually at Menlo Park, California. But that fidelity was also apparent in New York, where he would regularly celebrate Mass at Corpus Christi parish across the street from Union Seminary. On vacation, during visits to such places as national parks or in the Caribbean, he would also habitually celebrate Mass, even in very informal settings. As his colleagues and provincial superior noted, Brown was not scrupulous or obsessed about this. If circumstances did not permit him to celebrate Mass on a given occasion, he accepted that serenely, but daily Eucharist was an integral part of his life.

He was never embarrassed about his role as a priest and made it a habit to wear his Roman collar wherever he would go and whenever he taught or lectured. He was not rigid about this either and in informal settings would wear casual clothing. In fact, the universal testimony of those who knew him was that he was a terrible dresser, forever wearing the same flannel shirts, threadbare sweaters, tattered pants, and battered shoes or sandals.[20] He kidded more than one of his faculty colleagues that wearing his Roman collar was not simply a religious statement but a way for him to avoid having to acquire a better wardrobe! In fact, as will be noted later, Brown's limited wardrobe was matched by a stark simplicity in every aspect of his material life: an uncluttered apartment with little furniture, scant personal possessions beyond things needed for his work, living, dining, and traveling modestly. No doubt this was due in part to Brown's singular concentration on his intellectual pursuits, but it also sprang from a deeply spiritual instinct that unobtrusively marked his entire life.

A YEAR OF SOLITUDE

After his ordination, Brown received his first teaching assignment at St. Charles College in Catonsville in the fall of 1953, at the time a college-level seminary staffed by the Sulpicians. This would be a typically active period for him. While teaching, he completed his doctoral dissertation on the meaning of *Sensus Plenior* and received his Doctorate in Sacred Theology (STD) *summa cum laude* from St. Mary's (1955). As we will note later, during the period 1955–58, he also pursued a master's degree in Semitic Languages at Johns Hopkins University, and later enrolled in their doctoral program—a step that would have an enormous influence on his entire professional career.[21]

It was also at this time that Brown would take the definitive formal steps to join the Sulpicians, even though his relationship with them was already firm. As noted earlier, in March of 1951, while still a seminarian, he had received Bishop Hurley's permission to join the community. Acceptance involved a formal vote by the Sulpician faculty of St. Mary's.

In a follow-up letter, the seminary rector James Laubacher reported to Fr. Lloyd P. McDonald, the provincial, that the vote for Raymond Brown was favorable. Out of fourteen votes cast, ten were favorable, two abstained because they were not familiar enough with the candidate, and one voted "no" because he was "not sure he [Brown] would be a good community man." The letter also noted that at the faculty meeting, "some commented that his external appearance gave the impression of an air of superiority, but others felt that was not real."[22]

Later, after completing his first two years of teaching at St. Charles and with the conclusion of his first year of master's study at Johns Hopkins, Brown would take another important step required for full affiliation with the Society of St. Sulpice. From 1955 to 1956, Brown, along with other candidates, would enter a "year of solitude" at a house on the grounds of St. Mary's.[23] This year of solitude was intended to be a year of intense formation in the history and spirituality of the Sulpicians. Similar to a novitiate for a religious order, extended time was given to daily prayer, spiritual direction, and study of Sulpician history, spirituality, pedagogy, and traditions. A year apart from study and teaching was not exactly Brown's cup of tea, although he readily entered this phase of his preparation as a Sulpician. He confessed that he spent a lot of time honing his skills in the biblical languages.[24]

Two of the Sulpician priests who oversaw the year of solitude wrote candid evaluations of his character and aptitude for Sulpician life, even though their hesitations about him did not translate into a rejection of his candidacy for the Sulpicians:

> Father Brown has a mind of some depth and range. He has made excellent use of his intellectual gifts and there is every reason believing he will become a learned and successful teacher. His academic interest in Sacred Scripture has interfered with his getting any great good out of his year of Solitude. His active mind seems to find the periods of prayer trying and his restlessness expresses itself in some rather disedifying postures in Chapel. There is ample justification for thinking that Father Brown expects to exercise his greatest influence as a teacher and not as a Director for he knows wherein he excels. Besides, he is so wrapped up in his own thoughts, plans, and projects that he will find it rather difficult indeed to listen long enough to learn the problems and troubles of others.

Through a process of unsuspected rationalization I believe that he tends if not theoretically at least practically to put moral goodness and intelligence on an *ex aequo* basis. He possesses considerable natural goodness himself and there seems to be an underlying solid priestliness of character that inspires confidence and trust. His judgment is fairly good and healthy interest and participation in athletics has kept a good balance in his life.[25]

A similar evaluation was that of Fr. John S. McDonough, SS, who would later serve as provincial superior.

Father Brown presents a serious, though pleasant and almost boyishly innocent personality. His mind is very active and wide of range. He is an extrovert, every [*sic*] and constantly expressing his view and thoughts, and given to outshouting others of a group in conversation. But he is not mean, nor intentionally overbearing. He just isn't interested in the views and thoughts of others, but forever occupied with his own thoughts, forming his own ideas, and intent on expressing them. Throughout this year, Solitude has been quite a minor interest to him. He has enjoyed, even more than the others, the daily vacation from Solitude throughout breakfast time. There he has his mail, rather extensive, to read; and there is consulted and discussed matters with the Scripture Professors, more frequently than not having books, notebooks, and manuscript [*sic*] to present or receive. His real interest and principal daily occupation seems to have been Scriptural Studies. He has been regular in attending common exercises and to me suggests the piety of a good boy. At the thanksgiving after Mass however, when he has finally gotten there, he has more often than not sprawled out with feet on the kneeler and head on arms atop the back of the forward pew, or occasionally leafing through some book. It is difficult for me to see him listening to a student's personal problems, or to imagine him having sympathetic understanding of his difficulties.[26]

Although these characterizations are expressed through the somewhat gimlet eyes of the evaluators, those who knew Raymond Brown in later life can easily recognize at this early date the later urbane and accomplished professor and scholar: very bright, gregarious, intensely fixed on his scholarly pursuits, absorbed in his love of the Scriptures, strongly self-confident in his own views, and, through it all, a fundamental goodness. While, as we will note later and as these evaluators perceived, he could be impatient with listening to the complaints or problems of some students, in fact, as his teaching experience progressed, he would also prove to be a most sympathetic and endearing friend to his colleagues and graduate students alike.

OPENING TO A NEW WORLD: DOCTORAL STUDIES AT JOHNS HOPKINS UNIVERSITY

Along with his ordination as a Sulpician priest and his discovery of a fascination with biblical studies, Raymond Brown's entry into the ecumenical world of graduate studies at Johns Hopkins University would be a fundamental transformative experience, having a lifelong impact. The towering figure in the Near Eastern Studies department at Johns Hopkins at that time was Professor William Foxwell Albright, himself a most distinguished alumnus of Johns Hopkins. Albright was recognized as the "father" of the realm of modern biblical archaeology, and his work had enormous influence. Bucking the trend set by German literary critics of that era who were skeptical about the historical reliability of the Bible, Albright maintained that the basic biblical account of ancient Israel's history was fundamentally accurate and compatible with the findings of archaeology. He also inspired and trained the first generation of Israeli archaeologists and had a significant role in the deciphering and interpretation of the Dead Sea Scrolls. Albright had served as the director of the American School of Oriental Research (ASOR) in Jerusalem from 1922 to 1929 and again from 1933 to 1936. (In 1970, a year before Albright's death, the Jerusalem school would be renamed the W. F. Albright Institute of Archaeological Research in recognition of its most renowned former director.)

The list of Albright's students who became noted scholars themselves is remarkable: John Bright, Frank Moore Cross, David Noel Freedman—to name but a trio of luminaries. Equally remarkable for the time, Albright also mentored a number of distinguished Catholic scholars, including several Jesuits such as Joseph Fitzmyer, Roger O'Callaghan, Mitchell Dahood, William Moran, John Huesman, and Thomas Leahy. Moran and Dahood would go on to become members of the faculty of the Pontifical Biblical Institute in Rome. Of course, Brown himself would join this honor roll, but first he had to negotiate admittance into Johns Hopkins with his Sulpician superiors. Johns Hopkins was only a short distance from St. Mary's and Brown easily got permission to pursue a master's degree in Semitic Studies there while teaching at St. Charles and before his year of solitude in 1955. Brown at first assumed that receiving the master's degree would be the end of his stint at Johns Hopkins. Whether he would be able to pursue a doctorate in Scripture was not certain. At that time, as Brown himself noted, "relatively few teachers of Bible got doctorates partly because of the myth, and it was largely a myth, that the doctorate in Sacred Scripture in Rome was the hardest-to-get degree in the world. It wasn't so, but compared to some other Roman degrees, it was respectable."[27]

In a long letter to his then provincial, Fr. McDonald, dated March 10, 1955, Brown laid out in detail, at his superior's request, some possible avenues for his graduate preparation for teaching Scripture. By May of that year (1955), he noted, he would have already earned several degrees: his M.A. in philosophy (from Catholic University), the STD in theology (from St. Mary's), and his master's in Semitic languages from Johns Hopkins. What to do next? He could go to the Pontifical Biblical Institute in Rome for two years to acquire a licentiate in Scripture, but he believed that "the training presented is inadequate" since the program is designed for those "who have no biblical background at all." Furthermore, he noted, "The Institute is especially weak on languages."

Another option (one obviously Brown preferred) was to pursue another year at Johns Hopkins, followed by a year abroad either at the Biblicum in Rome, which he was not enthusiastic about, or, preferably, a year at the École Biblique, the famed Dominican graduate biblical school in Jerusalem. The latter, he noted, was a strong option because of its superior courses, its in-depth approach to the biblical languages, and the location in Jerusalem. After a year of courses at the École Biblique, he noted, he would be equipped to receive the SSL before the Biblical Commission in Rome.[28] However, he conceded that the unstable political situation in Jerusalem introduced an uncertain note for planning.

If the second option were adopted, then after two years of further study (e.g., one year at Johns Hopkins and one year abroad at the École), he would have an SSL and a master's in Semitics from Johns Hopkins and be well prepared to acquire a PhD in Semitics from Hopkins. He also added, "I might also mention that there is a possibility that the year at Hopkins might be on a scholarship," no doubt to nudge his provincial in the right direction. He concludes his letter with the kind of deference that would mark his correspondence with his Sulpician superiors all his life. "I have written this explanation to clarify the situation as you requested; I stress that they are only suggestions or possibilities, and any decision you make will be accepted without question."

In fact, it was Albright himself who had pressed Brown to pursue a doctorate at Johns Hopkins. As Brown noted, "I went for a year [to complete the master's program] and Albright asked me, 'What would you do with a master's degree?' (I already had a masters in Philosophy and a license in Theology.). He said, 'You can't teach with a master's degree. I'll put you down for studying for a doctorate.'"[29] Brown used the time during his year of solitude to bone up on his biblical languages and, at the end of the year, sought permission from his provincial Fr. McDonald to continue to the doctorate. "Well, all right, go on and get a doctorate at Hopkins" was the reply.[30] The fact that several Jesuits were already enrolled in the program and that another Sulpician colleague had earlier enjoyed taking some courses there paved the way for Brown. It was also known that Albright, a son of missionaries and a devout Methodist, was sympathetic to Catholics; his wife was a practicing Catholic and one of his sons would go on to become a Christian Brother. The ecumenical atmosphere that would mushroom after the Second Vatican Council had not yet taken hold, and for a Catholic priest to do advanced studies at a secular university was still a novelty. As we will see, the professional and ecumenical spirit he discovered at Johns Hopkins, and the stint in Jerusalem at ASOR that was part of his program, would open entirely new horizons for Brown and remain a lifelong influence.

Brown excelled during his two years of doctoral studies at Hopkins. While there, his mentor, Albright, conducted a seminar on the Dead Sea Scrolls, the cache of invaluable texts that had been discovered only a decade earlier and were a growing source of fascination as scholars were engaged in the work of deciphering and eventually publishing this trove of ancient manuscripts, most of them biblical texts.[31] Albright was impressed with the paper that Brown prepared for the seminar and urged him to publish it, which he did, appearing in the *Catholic Biblical Quarterly* as "The Messianism of Qumran,"[32] the second of his scholarly publications on the

Scrolls, joining the article that Siegman had accepted for publication while Brown was completing his doctorate at St. Mary's.[33] His doctoral dissertation would be on the subject of the Semitic notion of *mystērion* or "mystery," a topic also prompted by Albright's scholarly interest in the fact that this term (in Hebrew, *raz* and *sod*) was found in some of the sectarian writings at Qumran. Brown explored the possible connection between this concept in the Qumran writings and its echoes in the Pauline literature. His dissertation was titled "The Semitic Background of the Pauline *Mysterion*." From this doctoral research Brown would later mine a number of articles and a monograph.[34]

Jerusalem

Albright's interest in the Dead Sea Scrolls and his mentoring of Brown in this direction laid the groundwork for another significant turn in Brown's academic formation. Joseph Fitzmyer had completed his doctoral work the year before Brown and, at Albright's prompting, had gone to ASOR in Jerusalem for a year to work on composing a concordance of the yet unpublished Dead Sea Scrolls. After he had completed his doctoral work, Albright suggested to Brown that he also ought to go to Jerusalem and pick up the task that Fitzmyer had begun. Albright also counseled Brown to apply for a fellowship at ASOR. Surely the recommendation of the American School's most distinguished former director helped the young scholar Brown to successfully acquire the fellowship! Brown left for Jerusalem and this chapter in his life in the fall of 1958. He took up residence at the ASOR headquarters in East Jerusalem near the École Biblique. His time in Jerusalem would overlap with Fitzmyer's stay for about a month. The incredibly prolific Fitzmyer had by that time produced over 19,500 individual handwritten cards, covering a great deal of the nonbiblical texts found in the Scrolls! This is the same work that Brown would now take up. With obvious excitement he describes their work in a 1948 letter to Fr. McDonald, no doubt also thereby assuring his religious superior that he was doing important things and not wasting time:

> Briefly, here is what I am doing. The largest body of the material found at Qumran belongs to the Fourth Cave: many thousands of fragments of various sizes. The work of identifying these fragments and joining them, and identifying them as

parts of the original hundreds of manuscripts plaed [sic] in this cave has been going of [sic] for four years. The mss. are roughly two-fifths biblical and three-fifths non-biblical. There are four scholars working the non-biblical material and two on the biblical material. Some time ago it was realized that a concordance of the vocabulary of the non-biblical material would be an absolute necessity. Many of the comginations [sic] of words and expressions are entirely new, and the only way these scholars are ever going to be able to fill in lacunae is to have a concordance of all these expressions which are common at Qumran. For this purpose, Fr. Fitzmyer, S.J., now at Woodstock, was sent over (the Rockefeller Foundation supplies the funds) last year to begin the concordance. After a year's work he had some 19,500 cards in the concordance files. (The documents are in Hebrew and Aramaic.) He covered most of the Aramaic material. Yours truly has stepped into his shoes and is continuing the same work. As soon as the scholars have worked over a ms., they hand it over to me and I begin to put its words into the concordance. This means discussing the forms and syntax with them to come to an agreement how we file the worlds [sic]. I get the advantage of seeing all this material and its contents years before it is published, and learning a great deal about Qumran language and thought. (The New Testament parallels in wording get more interesting every day; the scholars have the advantage of a close recheck on their work and the occasional catching of a *lapsus.*)[35]

Eventually the combined work of these two young scholars would form the basis of a concordance published by Clarendon Press of Oxford University.[36] Brown's association with Fitzmyer both at Johns Hopkins and in Jerusalem would forge a close friendship that would last the rest of these two great scholars' lives.[37] They shared a passion for biblical scholarship, a fierce defense of the historical-critical method, a staggering capacity for scholarly publications, and a common interest in stamp collecting! Both would amass over their adult lives extensive stamp collections and would often compare notes on their progress.

Brown's stay in Jerusalem and his work in the famous "scrollery" of the Rockefeller Museum in Jerusalem, the studio where the Dead

Sea Scrolls were kept, also brought him into contact with other prominent scholars who were involved with editing the Scrolls, with whom he would later collaborate over the years of his professional career. For example, Roland DeVaux, the Dominican scholar and faculty member at the École Biblique who was the first chief excavator at Qumran; the brilliant John Strugnell, one of the original members of the committee working on the Scrolls and who would later become professor of Christian Origins at Harvard and, in 1984, editor in chief of the Scrolls, succeeding the famed Dominican scholar and École Biblique professor Pierre Benoit; John Allegro, the British archaeologist and scholar whose later sensational theories about the Scrolls would prove controversial;[38] Jósef Milik, the Polish scholar and Catholic priest who was also involved early on with DeVaux and the excavation team at Qumran and would later be a key publisher of some of the Scrolls; Jean Starcky, the French scholar and priest who also took a prominent role in the later publication of the Scrolls; and not least, Msgr. Patrick Skehan, who would go on to be the long-term chair of the Semitics department at the Catholic University of America and was a highly influential member of the Catholic Biblical Association. He was also a friend of Albright and more than once Albright tapped Skehan to replace him as a visiting professor at Johns Hopkins when Albright would take leave for more extended stays in the Middle East. Brown paid a special tribute to Skehan in his oral history interview:

> Pat Skehan was a wonderful person, especially when I worked with him in Jerusalem. Pat was really brilliant. His mind was the closest I've ever seen to genius, next to Albright. But also a very shy person. I finally got to be very good friends with Pat, and the only way I could really tap his mind was to tell him, "Quit being polite, assuming I know things. Treat me as an absolute idiot." I got him to write for the JBC.[39] But I warned him, "You're always saying to people, I don't have to tell you this. You do have to tell this." But once you persuaded him that you really didn't know, he could be extremely helpful as a teacher. He could read Palestinian Arabic newspapers. He enjoyed that, for he liked to see how they used modern words. I always thought one of his major feats was reading Hebrew upside-down because he used to have the student

read the Hebrew Bible while he stood in front of the student and read it upside-down.[40]

Brown also used his time at ASOR to take advantage of being in Jerusalem. He took some classes at the École Biblique with such Dominican luminaries as Pierre Benoit, noted especially for his knowledge of the history and archaeology of Jerusalem, and Marie-Émile Boismard, who would later be one of the creators of *The Jerusalem Bible.*[41] Brown was very impressed with the depth and quality of these courses and would continue to contrast them with the academic quality of courses in Rome. He wrote from Jerusalem in 1958, "I have no desire to go and study in Rome; I think I have had all that I can take; I dropped in at a few of the courses while I was in Rome and the Biblical Institute is pretty horrible.... I am dropping in on some courses over at the École Biblique—really superb; in twenty-five years of going to school I have not seen any better courses. Currently I am following Fr. Benoit's course on the Synoptic Gospels, Fr. Boismard on St. John, and Fr. DeVaux on the early sections of the Pentateuch. When I compare it with what I have seen and heard of the Biblical Institute in Rome, there is no comparison."[42] He also appreciated the gracious welcome he received from the Dominicans at the École Biblique, including DeVaux, Benoit, and Boismard. He took the opportunity to travel throughout the surrounding region, not only in Israel itself but to Damascus and to Dura-Europas in Syria as well as to Petra and Amman in Jordan, joining groups either from ASOR or the École who were visiting various archaeological sites.

The team working on the Scrolls wanted Brown to continue in Jerusalem for another year, but his provincial wanted him to come back and start teaching at St. Mary's; so he had to bid farewell to Jerusalem and to an experience that had been so enjoyable and formative. There is little doubt that Brown's stint in Jerusalem and his expertise in the Dead Sea Scrolls made a profound impression on him personally and professionally, particularly regarding the Jewish context of the New Testament. As we will see later, it also helped reinforce for him the importance of combatting Christian anti-Semitism and of forging strong collaborative relationships with Jewish scholars.[43]

Brown's time at Johns Hopkins, especially the mentoring he received from Albright and the ecumenical contacts with his fellow students there, plus his sojourn in Jerusalem—also made possible because of Albright's guidance and sponsorship—was now at an end. But the experience had opened a whole new world for Brown, who previously had been educated solely within a Catholic framework and the relatively confined world of seminary life. Brown would be grateful for Albright's mentoring for the rest of his life. When asked many years later what he had learned from Albright, Brown had replied, "What it meant to be a Christian gentleman." In fact, Brown had learned much more from Albright, but no doubt Albright's sympathy with Brown's religious motivation had made the young Sulpician priest's entrance into a new world of universal critical scholarship a much more peaceful transition.

Rome Again

While Brown was in Jerusalem, he took time off in the fall of 1958 to go to Rome to take the baccalaureate examination in Scripture before the Pontifical Biblical Commission. Since St. Mary's Seminary offered a "pontifical" degree, its faculty members were also required to hold a "pontifical" degree, and this meant Brown himself had to acquire one. Since Brown had not attended the Pontifical Biblical Institute, he had to be tested by the Pontifical Biblical Commission itself. He wisely decided not to go for broke and attempt to also acquire the more advanced licentiate degree at the same time but simply to be tested for the baccalaureate. In 1963, when Brown himself was already an accomplished scholar and teacher, he would return to Rome and receive the licentiate, at last capping his long list of graduate degrees.

Brown's arrival in Rome happened to coincide with a historic moment. Pope Pius XII, the towering pontiff who had reigned since 1939 all during World War II and whose encyclical *Divino Afflante Spiritu* had opened the path for the Catholic biblical renewal, died after serving nineteen years on the throne of Peter.[44] Brown arrived in Rome shortly after the pope's death. As he was preparing for his examination before the Commission, Brown had hoped to stay at the Sulpician headquarters in Rome. However, there was no room and he was put up in a *pensione* near the Vatican. As a consolation prize, his superiors offered him a ticket to the coronation of Cardinal Giuseppe Roncalli as the new Pope John XXIII on November 4, 1958.[45] The new pope was seventy-six years old when he was elected, and many of the cardinal electors thought of his reign as a brief and quiet interlude after the long papacy of his predecessor, Pius XII. The next January, barely three months after his installation, Pope John (now St. Pope John XXIII) startled the Vatican curia assembled January 29, 1959, for their annual Mass in the Basilica of St. Paul Outside-the-Walls by announcing his intention to convene an ecumenical council.[46] The Second Vatican Council convened by Pope John would begin the fall of 1962, and as we will see, Brown was there with his bishop for a brief stay during the first session. From the Council in the fall of 1965 would emerge a document that would be a bulwark for Brown's own work as a Catholic biblical scholar, namely, the Council's Dogmatic Constitution on Divine Revelation, *Dei Verbum*. As noted previously, that document would consolidate the gains of Catholic biblical scholarship begun under Pius XII and would open a new chapter for the Catholic biblical renewal.[47]

Brown successfully completed his examination before the Commission. In a letter to his provincial, he confessed that it had been prudent not to attempt gaining the license degree at the same time. Counting his seminary years at Catholic University in philosophy, his one year of theology at the Gregorian, and then three years at St. Mary's, plus his two years of doctoral work at Johns Hopkins, he had been immersed in graduate studies for twelve years. It was time to put his exceptional intellectual gifts and his rich education in theology and Scripture in the service of his ministry of teaching. And so, he was grateful to return to Baltimore and to begin his career as a faculty member at St. Mary's, teaching Scripture as he longed to do.

This period of seminary and academic formation had a decisive impact on Raymond Brown. He had advanced to the priesthood that he had been working toward since his graduation from high school, and he had discovered his Sulpician vocation that would enable him to take up the ministry of teaching and scholarship to which he had long aspired. His discovery of his fascination with Scripture was triggered by the seemingly accidental requirement to learn the Old Testament on his own because of the gap in his theological studies in transferring from the Gregorian to St. Mary's, a happy accident, indeed. Having completed his seminary education, he was ready to enter into the new world of graduate studies at Johns Hopkins University under the tutelage of one of the foremost biblical scholars of the twentieth century, William Foxwell Albright. Brown's own personal study of the biblical languages, his graduate work in Semitics at Johns Hopkins, and his firsthand work on the Dead Sea Scrolls in Jerusalem would lay the groundwork for the quality of his own biblical scholarship. Likewise, these encounters with Albright and his cadre of brilliant students, plus the connections with other prominent scholars Brown would make in Jerusalem, prepared the way for a life of close ecumenical collaboration with a broad array of colleagues, as well as prepared Brown for the leadership role he would play in professional societies such as the Catholic Biblical Association, the Society of Biblical Literature, and the European-based Society of New Testament Studies. Joined to this was the fact that even in this formative period, Brown had begun his work of publication, especially with his early articles in the *Catholic Biblical Quarterly* on *Sensus Plenior* and on the Qumran writings. Equally important was exposure to certain influences that would contribute to the characteristics of his own biblical scholarship. In William Foxwell Albright, he experienced a mentor whose scholarship was instinctively generous in estimating the historical value of the Scriptures, a view that Brown would share. Albright was by no means naïve on this point, but he was inclined to find a more credible historical grounding in the biblical traditions than the Bultmanian school and some later archaeologists would. Albright was also the one whose expertise in the Dead Sea Scrolls and whose seminar and teaching on this topic led Brown into an appreciation of the world of Judaism contemporary with the New Testament period and the profound influence of Judaism on Jesus and on the writings of the New Testament.

As he took up his teaching role at St. Mary's in the fall of 1959, Brown's preparation for his new role as a scholar and teacher of the Bible had been rich and deep. It was now time for Brown to repay the debt he owed to his mentors and his community by taking up his Sulpician mission.

CHAPTER 2

PRIEST, TEACHER, AND SCHOLAR

In the fall of 1959, armed with an array of advanced degrees, deeply committed to his Sulpician and priestly vocation, enriched by exposure to world-class scholars, and having experienced the international settings of Jerusalem and Rome, Raymond Brown would at long last launch his teaching of graduate biblical studies at St. Mary's Seminary and University in Baltimore, Maryland. The odyssey of biblical scholarship and teaching that began here would, over the next thirty-nine years, take him to appointments in New York (1971–90) and to Menlo Park, California (1991–98). He was now thirty-one years old and ready to work. The range of experiences that would define his career—graduate teaching, prolific publishing, public lecturing, ecumenical involvement, and his growing significance as a leading Catholic scholar in the biblical field—would all take root during his tenure at St. Mary's.

ST. MARY'S BALTIMORE (1959–71)

As noted previously, the Sulpicians had founded St. Mary's Seminary in 1791 at the invitation of Bishop John Carroll of Baltimore, at a time when the United States itself was in its infancy. Brown was an alumnus of this distinguished seminary and now was returning as a member of its faculty. He was thrilled to begin his teaching career and threw himself into it. The seminary was thriving and drew seminarians from several dioceses whose bishops prized the quality of formation and education provided by the Sulpicians. Students from his years teaching at St. Mary's remember him as someone both revered and, to an extent, feared. Although Brown had taught briefly at the college level at St. Charles, this would be his first experience at the graduate level. As is often the case with beginning faculty, Brown took a rather severe approach, particularly in the discipline he demanded of his students. He instructed them that once they entered the threshold of his classroom, all talking and other commotion was to cease. He also advised students that if they had not prepared for class, they should alert him at the outset and he would not call on them. But if they did not prepare and failed to confess this to him, and if he called on them and discovered that they were unprepared, then they could expect a reprimand. Such was the case, in fact, for one student who was dressed down by Brown in one of his classes and who later would go on to be a Harvard Professor (and a close friend of Brown).[1]

Classroom lectures were Brown's forte then and for the rest of his career. He seldom used notes but presented the subject matter with exceptional clarity, completing the lecture right on time and with a conclusion that itself seemed to be perfectly timed. His superb teaching quickly was recognized by students and faculty alike, and led to the young scholar acquiring almost immediate legendary status. Having been taught by Fr. Brown became a badge of honor for many St. Mary's alums. His preferred mode of teaching was certainly the lecture format; throughout his teaching career, he would be less adept at conducting seminars or leading discussions.

At the same time, the early evaluations of Brown during his formation that questioned how he might fare with the other dimensions of the Sulpician mission proved somewhat true. In addition to teaching, Sulpicians were ordinarily expected to serve as spiritual directors and confessors for the seminarians in their care. Although he dutifully carried out this part of his responsibilities, he was not comfortable in doing so. Even in the case of having to mentor students academically, Brown showed a certain reluctance in having to spend too much time in casual interaction with them, preferring to concentrate on his scholarship and teaching. Students who entered his office in these early days with a question discovered that the only chair in the room was the one Brown was sitting in—and if they had a question or concern it had to be transmitted standing and, preferably, succinctly. He was even less inclined to spend time as a spiritual director or guide for the students. It was never a case that he was indifferent or unfriendly to them, but simply that this was not his forte or the center of his interest. In fact, as we will see, as his time at St. Mary's advanced into the somewhat turbulent years of the mid-to-late 1960s, Brown would become increasingly uncomfortable with what he considered immature or inappropriate behavior on the part of the seminarians—making the formational dimension of his role as a Sulpician faculty member even more challenging.

Along with his commitment to teaching, it was during his tenure at St. Mary's that his work of publishing began to accelerate. As noted earlier, he had already published articles in the *Catholic Biblical Quarterly* while completing his STD at St. Mary's.[2] One writing assignment that would have major implications for his future was composing in 1960 a brief commentary on the Gospel and Epistles of John for the newly established *New Testament Reading Guides* published by Liturgical Press.[3] As was customary for Sulpicians, Brown had first cleared this assignment with his provincial, writing to say how excited he was about this new project.[4] Brown's booklet commentary on John's Gospel and Letters would go on to sell more than a million copies over the years. Equally important, this early writing assignment steered Brown deeper into Johannine studies and would lead to his two major contributions in the Anchor Bible series on the Johannine literature.[5] As we will note later, his connection with his mentor, Albright, opened the door for him not only to be a contributor to the Anchor Bible project but to have a decisive influence on the shape this series would ultimately take.[6]

Joining his work on the Johannine literature, another major writing project from his time in Baltimore was the publication of the first edition of *The Jerome Biblical Commentary* (1965). The idea for this major Catholic project originated with Brown, but he worked in close collaboration with two outstanding Catholic colleagues, Joseph Fitzmyer, SJ, and Roland Murphy, OCarm.[7] The goal was to produce a one-volume resource that would provide commentaries on each book of the Bible plus several topical articles on subjects related to biblical history and interpretation. The contributors to the volume were all Catholic scholars and represented the growing maturity of Catholic biblical scholarship now coming into its own in the wake of the Second Vatican Council. *The Jerome Biblical Commentary* would be an instant success and would go through a complete revision in 1990. Even though Brown was still in his thirties, his work on *The Jerome Biblical Commentary* established the young scholar as already an outstanding and influential leader among Roman Catholic biblical scholars, a role he would retain all his professional life.

Joining his teaching and publishing work, Brown's amazing energy was also turning to an increasing number of public lectures and workshops throughout the country. In this he was catching the wave of popular interest in the Bible that was surging through Catholic parishes and educational institutions, stimulated by the Second Vatican Council itself. He had already caught the eye of some prestigious graduate schools, invited in 1963 to give the Lagrange lecture at the Aquinas Institute of Theology (at that time located in Dubuque, Iowa), serving as "co-president" and giving a paper at the 1966 Journées Bibliques at the University of Louvain, also in 1966 giving the Thomas More Lecture at Yale University, the Kearnes Seminary Lecture at the Divinity School of Duke University in 1967, and the Charles McDonald Lecture at the University of Sydney, Australia, in 1969. Along with these important academic recognitions, Brown was giving an increasing number of lectures and workshops for Catholic parishes and dioceses throughout the country—something he would continue to do right up to the time of his death in 1998. As we will see, only in the last few years of his life did he determine to cut back on the number of lectures and workshops, not because of flagging energy but to spend more time writing.[8]

An unusual interlude in his teaching work at this time took place when his bishop, Joseph P. Hurley, invited Brown to accompany him to the opening session of the Vatican Council in November 1962. He was not the bishop's official *peritus*, that is, his designated theological advisor or "expert" that each bishop at the Council was allowed to bring with him. Because his bishop may not have considered Brown experienced enough for this official role, he was more of an informal consultant. While Brown appreciated the chance to see history in the making, his stint in Rome would be short-lived. He grew weary of being Hurley's "dinner companion" as he put it and was anxious to get back to teaching. In addition, he was concerned about his father who was in distress about his wife's failing health. Fortunately, in giving clearance for Brown to go to Rome, his provincial had written to the bishop thanking him for the trust the bishop had placed in Brown in inviting him to accompany him to the coming Council, but, at the same time, laying the ground work for limiting Brown's stay in Rome: "It is an honor and a privilege not only for him but for the Society. We regret the necessity of having to limit in some way the time that Father Brown can afford to take from his Seminary duties. (Father Cerny, 'our senior Scripture man,' has had recurrent heart attacks and is not teaching. This means that Father Brown will have extra work in a house of almost 400 seminarians.) We trust, however, that he can be with you in Rome when you would most need him."[9] Fortified with this good excuse, Brown was able to return to Baltimore after about a month and resume his teaching and his burgeoning lecture and publication career.

Another commitment that began during these early years and would continue throughout his professional life was his involvement in ecumenical work.[10] This, too, was spurred by the spirit of the Second Vatican Council that had invited Protestant and Orthodox participation in the Council and, more personally for Brown, by his graduate work in the ecumenical environment of Johns Hopkins. When visiting Rome in November of 1962 with his bishop, Brown had the good fortune of meeting Msgr. Johannes Willebrands, the Dutch ecumenist who would later become a cardinal, and had been appointed by Pope John XXIII as the secretary of the newly established Secretariat for Promoting Christian Unity. Through Willebrands, Brown would be invited to give a paper at the 1963 plenary meeting of the World Council of Churches Faith and Order Commission to be held in Montreal. Inspired by the ecumenical atmosphere of the Vatican Council then in session, the organizers were looking for a Roman Catholic response to a paper given by the famed German exegete Ernst Käsemann. So began Brown's ecumenical career at the highest level. He himself believed that probably a Protestant colleague from his Johns Hopkins days had recommended him for this initial ecumenical venture.[11] In 1968, he would be appointed as the first Roman Catholic member of the Faith and Order Commission and, at the same time, be appointed by Pope Paul VI as a Consultor of the Vatican Secretariat for Christian Unity. In the United States, he would also become a member of a national commission for bilateral discussions between the Lutheran and Roman Catholic churches (1965–74), as well as participating in the international Methodist/Roman Catholic Dialogue.

LOOKING TO NEW HORIZONS

Brown was committed to his work at St. Mary's both because of his love of teaching and because of his loyalty to his Sulpician community. In serving as a faculty member at St. Mary's he was doing precisely what the mission of the Sulpicians had been founded to do and what he perceived his own vocation to be. Yet as the years moved on, Brown began to be restless in his stay there and started to think about moving to a new realm.

Several factors contributed to his unease. One, no doubt, was the changing environment of the seminary itself. Outside the doors of St. Mary's, the world was churning. In 1963, President John F. Kennedy was assassinated and the Vietnam War was heating up. Mounting casualties and the conduct of the war would eventually lead to the end of Lyndon Johnson's presidency, propelled by unrest and protests throughout the country culminating in the chaos of the Democratic convention in Chicago in 1968 and the narrow victory of Richard Nixon as president. In that same incredible year of 1968, Martin Luther King was assassinated on April 4, Robert Kennedy assassinated June 6, and Neil Armstrong landed on the moon July 20. Along with this political turmoil something of a social revolution was reverberating not only through the United States but in much of the Western world. It was the time of the Beatles and the sexual revolution. In Paris, the philosopher-president of the Sorbonne, Paul Ricoeur, had to resign in the wake of student riots, and students at the medieval University of Louvain went on strike for several weeks, even precipitating a fall of the Belgian government. In the church itself, particularly in Europe and North America, the ranks of priests and religious that had surged to new highs in the aftermath of World War II, suddenly were hit with waves of resignations, often coupled with questions about priestly celibacy.

That spirit of wrenching social upheaval and a questioning of traditional values and mores inevitably made an impact on the young men who were entering the seminary in the mid to late sixties. The expectation that Sulpician faculty would also be involved in formation work and spiritual direction, a role Brown was never enthusiastic about, became increasingly challenging for him. He mentions being shocked with some of the students' views on moral issues such as masturbation and celibacy, and their casualness about not reciting the daily breviary or attending Mass. He especially could not abide that some students were skipping class. He also detected a breakdown in the seminary's discipline, once complaining about the noise of students playing soccer in the corridor outside his own room. Never a sound sleeper, Brown also complained about the creaking noise coming from the doors on the toilet stalls in the public restroom on the floor below his bedroom. In an attempt to remove this nuisance, the seminary went so far as to replace the doors with curtains! Later, he was able to move to another room in a quieter part of the seminary. It helped, for a while.

What Brown perceived as a slackening of commitment to academic preparation in favor of more extensive pastoral experience was also very troubling to him.[12] He was by no means indifferent to the essential pastoral purpose of the priesthood and the proper role of pastoral training in the seminary curriculum. All during his time at St. Mary's, Brown himself faithfully celebrated Mass and preached every Sunday that he was available at Our Lady of the Assumption Parish in Govans, Maryland (a suburb of Baltimore). But he firmly believed that solid academic preparation should be primary in the seminary curriculum and was the only sure foundation for sound pastoral practice. More than once in his letters, he expressed some frustration with the seminary leadership when he felt this academic emphasis was eroding. His faculty peers also detected Brown's frustration. In a faculty evaluation from the 1967–68 school year, it was noted about "Father Brown," "Academically, of course, he is doing an outstanding job. In his relationships with the students it is evident that they accept his scholarship, but he relates poorly to them because of his conservative tendencies. He too finds it difficult to accept the present program of seminary work."

The period of the late sixties was also a time of some upheaval in many religious communities. The Vatican Council had invited religious communities to renew themselves, particularly by being attentive to the original charism and particular mission of their founding. This often meant a revision of the religious communities' rules and constitutions, a revision that required many hours of discussion and debate among the members. The Sulpician community was no exception. Brown himself seemed to be less enthusiastic about some of the changes introduced in their revised rule of life that gave greater emphasis to the pastoral dimension of the seminary curriculum, and he subsequently wrote to a fellow Sulpician that the changes were "a disaster."[13]

No doubt, too, a painful experience that occurred during his time in Baltimore also took the luster off his initial enthusiasm. Beginning in 1962, Brown would find himself embroiled in a controversy with the Apostolic Delegate Egidio Vagnozzi that would also involve the archbishop of Baltimore, Lawrence Shehan. Shehan, a Baltimore native, was appointed archbishop of Baltimore in 1961 and would later be named a cardinal by Pope Paul VI. He was an amiable and pastoral bishop, and seen as a strong supporter of the pastoral reforms of the Council in which he himself was deeply involved. As we will note later, Brown had deep respect for Shehan and considered him "a father," affection that Shehan also felt toward Brown himself. Yet through a series of mis-understandings the two found themselves publicly at odds over some of Brown's writings concerning the Petrine office presented in the New Testament.[14] The dispute would linger for several years without full res-olution and remained a difficult and painful experience for both men.

Beyond his restlessness with conditions at St. Mary's and in the Archdiocese of Baltimore, Brown felt the tug of a possible new phase in his vocation as a scholar and teacher, and wondered if he should not consider a new context for his work. Already in 1965, he had written to his provincial, Fr. McDonald, explaining that he had turned down an invitation from Lancaster Theological Seminary, a United Church of Christ institution, to teach a course in their master's program for the second semester in 1966. It would involve a long drive and Brown was already overcommitted for that period. He added,

> However, I might share with you my hope that when a more important Protestant seminary asks a similar question, I would very much like to accept. I believe that the time is ripe for Catholics to teach NT at the most important divinity schools in this country, like Union, Yale, and Harvard. This is one of the greatest services we can render to the Church, and if I am ever fortunate enough to be asked, I deeply hope that the Society may be in a position to think of letting me go.[15]

In early 1967, Brown received just such an invitation from John C. Bennett, then president of Union Theological Seminary in New York, to consider teaching as a visiting professor during the spring semester of 1968. Brown wrote a long letter to his provincial, Fr. Lloyd McDonald, asking permission of the provincial and the provincial council members to accept the offer.[16] The rationale he offered was twofold—the ecu-menical implications of the invitation and the opportunity for Brown himself to spread his academic wings. He noted that Union was "the most prestigious Protestant non-university divinity school in the USA." And, "they have had a long-standing practice of inviting famous bib-lical scholars as visiting professors; Oscar Cullmann[17]was the visiting professor this past year. I could almost swear that such an invitation has never been directed to a Catholic in New Testament before. (There probably have been very few Catholics at Union, and invitations would be first extended in non-sensitive fields.) Therefore this is a gesture that is of importance for the Church, and the appointment of a Catholic would attract a great deal of attention. That it would also do the Sulpicians and St. Mary's some good is also a factor." Brown went on to confess that his own ecumenical experience had led him to a desire to teach in a Protestant seminary, "in order to see what the mentality and life is really like."

In addition, he believed that teaching at Union would also add to his experience as a scholar and teacher.

> As for the teaching, this also would be helpful, for it would give me an opportunity to do a type of teaching that I can never do in one of our seminaries. I have been told that the two courses will each have about 25 class hours per semester, and even in the general course I can choose to devote all that time to one book of the NT or to a few chapters. This is quite different from our survey courses where no more than a few classes are devoted to a book. I am curious to see whether I could meet the demands of more detailed teaching.

While anxious to accept this opportunity, Brown wanted to make sure his superiors did not see this as a "permanent shift" or as somehow slackening his commitment to the Sulpicians. "I assure you that I will do nothing without the permission of my superiors. I am reasonably sure that at the moment a place like Union is very far away from hiring permanently a Catholic, and I am not at all sure that I would like to live permanently in a non-Catholic atmosphere." Brown gave his superior assurances that he would return to St. Mary's frequently during his semester at Union and went into detail about how adjustments could be made at St. Mary's to fill in for his absence and how his expected salary at Union ($6,000), minus the cost of his meals, would be donated to St. Mary's to defray any costs of hiring a replacement.[18]

His final argument was that this kind of ecumenical opportunity, despite the demands on "the manpower shortage in our seminaries," was worth taking; "I think it is important for Sulpician prestige and outlook to make the sacrifice. We have sacrificed men for a South American mission; an ecumenical tie-in with major non-Catholic seminaries is just such a mission, in my estimation."

Brown was given permission to take up the visiting professorship at Union, and the experience would eventually lead, three years later, to his leaving St. Mary's and beginning an entirely new chapter of his life in a return to his origins in New York. During the semester that Brown spent at Union, President Bennett also invited as visiting faculty such Catholic luminaries as the theologian Hans Küng of the University of Tübingen and innovative moral theologian Bernard Häring of the Lateran University in Rome—both heroes of the Second Vatican Council. Bennett had become president of Union in 1963 and was slated to retire in 1970. He was especially ecumenically minded and considered his invitation to these Catholic scholars as one of the great achievements of his tenure as president.[19] Of the three, only Brown would later join the Union faculty full time.

A PERMANENT STEP

Even though Brown did not anticipate that Union would be ready yet for a full-time Catholic faculty member, the call came shortly after his sabbatical year when President Bennet, himself nearing retirement, sent a letter of invitation. In the time between Brown's experience as a visiting professor in 1968 and the invitation from Union to take up a permanent position in New York, the Jesuits had moved their Woodstock theologate from Maryland to New York City and had established educational collaboration with Union Theological Seminary and the nearby Jewish Theological Seminary.[20] The offer to Brown was extended in 1970 to a joint appointment, shared with Woodstock and Union. His reasons for finally making the decision to permanently leave St. Mary's, his Sulpician base, and move to New York were spelled out in a definitive letter dated January 31, 1970, to Fr. Paul Purta, a classmate of Brown's who was now also his provincial.

Brown noted that he had been receiving for some time offers from other institutions of higher learning, but the joint Woodstock-Union invitation to accept the "Omori-Woodstock Professorship of Biblical Studies" was the most attractive to him.[21] To his previous rationale offered in his discussions with Fr. McDonald about ecumenism and teaching experience in a prestigious academic setting such as Union, he added a new perspective:

> I feel that the work which I am entering is Sulpician work, for in the future many Catholic seminarians will be trained in seminaries such as Union. Our own seminaries are in the process of becoming less and less residential, and soon the idea of closed formation will be gone. An increasing number of students will think of seminaries as divinity schools, and some will wish to go to ecumenical or non-Catholic ones. This has already begun at Union, for there are students there who intend to ask a bishop for ordination at the terminus of their course. (I am not indicating that I think this is a good way to prepare a man for the priesthood but I am just facing facts.) The Sulpicians should have a few men teaching in non-Catholic or ecumenical seminaries if they wish to be involved in all aspects of the Catholic seminary apostolate today.

As Brown would often do, he suggested to his provincial how the event of his move might be made public. "I might add that if my leaving St. Mary's were announced precisely in this light, then no harmful reflection will be cast on St. Mary's, something that I wish to avoid." He also thought that through his presence at Union he might be able to influence "a bright but unattached Catholic student at Union who wants to be a priest and is academically oriented to the Sulpicians."

Brown's prediction of such a development in Catholic seminary education would not come true. If anything, concerns about seminary discipline and the perceived turbulence of the times prompted Catholic Church authorities, particularly during the pontificate of John Paul II, to intensify the residential and formational components of seminary training and to be suspicious of outside influences.[22] What is striking about Brown's rationale in this letter is his concern to view the step he was about to take in leaving St. Mary's as in continuity with his Sulpician commitment. Much of this same letter to Fr. Purta is taken up with Brown's proposals concerning the financial aspects of his move. He wanted to emphasize both his strong desire to remain within the Sulpician fold but, at the same time, to assure his provincial that he would not be a financial burden on the community and, in fact, would continue to pay more than his share. He absolved the community of any need to pay into his retirement. He would take care of that himself but also held out the hope that he could "spend retirement in Sulpician company." He also added a review of his financial history with the Sulpicians, noting that his father had paid his tuition when he was in the seminary and that Brown himself had not accepted any salary from the community during his teaching years at St. Mary's. In fact, he had made generous contributions to the community from his lectures and publications and had the Sulpicians as the beneficiary of the life-insurance policy that would be provided by Union Seminary.

Brown's generosity to his Sulpician community would continue all the rest of his life, including the major part of his estate. Discussion of the details of his financial contributions, his various tax obligations, and his retirement benefits would command much of his correspondence with subsequent provincials and treasurers of the community.

He closed his letter to his provincial on a poignant note: "All of you who know [me] know how difficult it has been for me to come to the decision to leave St. Mary's, and I suspect when in 1971 I finally pull away for the last time, [I] shall leave a major part of my heart behind. But I think it will be good for me to get away and get some perspective. We never know: it may well be that in five or ten years I shall judge that [I] made a mistake and that I should return to give more of my active years to Sulpician seminaries." As we will note, Brown would eventually return to a Sulpician seminary—St. Patrick's in Menlo Park—for the last phase of his life, but not as a repeat of his faculty role at St. Mary's.

UNION THEOLOGICAL SEMINARY NEW YORK (1971-90)

The New York phase of Brown's career would be one of the most energetic and productive periods of his life. He was now forty-three and had already made his mark as a leading Catholic biblical scholar, not only in the United States, but through his contacts in Jerusalem and Rome and his increasing involvement in ecumenical work, such as the Faith and Order Commission, he was also building an international reputation. Given the spirit of the times and the more free-wheeling environment at Union, Brown would hardly escape some of the mounting concerns he had had at St. Mary's about the quality of seminary training and student behavior—if anything, the situation at Union would be far more challenging to Brown's religious sensibilities. But being in a context where he did not have direct responsibility for student behavior or for the ultimate direction of the school, Brown was not as personally affected by some of the chaos that swirled through Union (and many other American higher education institutions) in those days.[23] He was ultimately able to carve out a convenient teaching schedule that left ample time for his other scholarly interests, and his status as a distinguished professor and something of an "outsider" as a Catholic priest in a Protestant seminary enabled him to keep a tranquil distance from the politics and controversies of the school. At the same time, Brown would find among some of his colleagues at Union deep lifelong friendships and stimulating educational alliances. The result was that his nearly twenty years at Union would be the most productive and academically satisfying of his entire life.

He would also thrive in the dynamic urban environment of New York City, his birthplace, taking advantage of its vast cultural and educational opportunities. For example, Brown had developed a great love of the opera, so much so that some jokingly suggested that access to the Metropolitan Opera was the real reason for his move to New York. Throughout his stay there he had season tickets and would be seen taking the subway from Union to the opera house in Lincoln Center, with the Italian libretto on his lap and armed with a pair of full-sized binoculars.[24] He kept among his personal effects a notebook, cataloguing each performance he had witnessed and noting the artists involved. He also made it a point to avoid sitting through performances of an opera he had already seen; when a repeat opera came along, he would give his tickets to students or colleagues at Union.

Having his own residence in McGiffert Hall on the campus of Union also facilitated another lifelong and perhaps surprising devotion of Brown, namely, to television and old movies! His fellow Sulpicians and other friends throughout his life were struck by how Brown liked to have the television on while he worked, something like "white noise," and that he loved the reruns of old movies. A favorite genre for him was detective stories; a special delight for him was the long-running series *Mannix* (1967–75). Brown delighted in figuring out the plot long before the story had reached its end. That investigative curiosity was part of Brown's make-up and no doubt fueled some of his delight in determining the historical background of the biblical texts he explored in such detail. In fact, in the preface to his book on the Johannine community, Brown refers to his biblical investigation as "detective work."[25]

As noted earlier, the original idea was that Brown would share a joint appointment between Woodstock and Union. An important stipulation was that if, for some reason, Woodstock ceased to exist or returned to its original setting in Maryland, then Brown would continue as a tenured professor at Union. No doubt the somewhat experimental nature of Woodstock's move to New York had raised this possibility, providentially, since Woodstock would close only three years into Brown's time in New York. A partner with Union in funding Brown's position was Auburn Theological Seminary. Due to declining enrollments, Auburn had closed its doors in upstate New York in 1939 and merged with Union, its fellow Presbyterian Seminary. While retaining its board of trustees and its endowment, Auburn ceased to grant degrees and instead developed some specialized educational programs—a tradition that continues today. Auburn joined with Union in supporting Brown's professorship, named the Auburn Chair of Biblical Studies, which Brown formally acquired in 1971. Later, in 1981, he would advance to the rank of "distinguished professor." Brown even seems to have been somewhat relieved that from now on he would belong entirely to Union rather than splitting time and energy with Woodstock. It was to experience the freedom of teaching in the new context of a Protestant seminary, liberated from some of the concerns and constraints of a Catholic institution, that had been his hope in the first place.

In Brown's negotiations with Union, he was willing to trade off higher salary considerations in favor of acquiring more sabbatical time. His arrangement was that he could take a half-sabbatical every two years—paving the way both for the extensive research time as well as the many opportunities for lecturing and teaching in other settings that would be the hallmark of this period of his life.[26] When he became "distinguished professor," Brown was also not obliged to be involved in committee work. Occasionally, he would agree to some ad hoc committee assignments, such as search committees, but otherwise he savored this freedom. As it would evolve, Brown was deeply involved and present to the life of Union Seminary, particularly through his teaching, interaction with students, and relationships with his faculty colleagues. However, he hovered at the edge of the everyday direction of the school that most faculty would have to spend time on, often sitting in the back benches of faculty meetings (though he was at times very vocal on certain issues).[27]

As he had foreseen, teaching at Union enabled Brown to do far more than the type of survey courses that dominated the seminary biblical curriculum at St. Mary's. He developed semester courses on some of the topics that would become the focus of his major publications, such as the Johannine literature and the Passion Narratives. His course on the Gospel of John soon became his trademark and a magnet for students at Union. Several of his former students recall the classroom at times being standing room only, with Brown giving his usual brilliant and inspiring lectures without notes (except for any occasional small card on which he had scribbled a few words). His student assistant at the time, Marion Soards, noted that Brown had in his office the galley sheets of his commentary on John's Gospel and had annotated it extensively. In preparation for class, he would read over the galleys and that would be sufficient for him to give his fluid lecture. Unfailingly, he brought the lecture to a close right at the proper time, with a perfect conclusion. The more rigid class discipline he had imposed on his students in his early teaching days at St. Mary's had given way to a more confident and more relaxed style enjoyed by the graduate students who took his courses at Union.

Brown was far less successful in seminar settings, taking a much more hands-off approach that led at times to some uncertainty among his students. Sr. Mary Boys, whose doctoral dissertation Brown directed and who years later would become the Academic Dean of Union, remembers being part of a seminar on Ephesians and Colossians. Brown would begin the seminar session by giving an hour-long lecture on the topic and then invite the assigned students to offer his or her paper, leaving the students to wonder what more could be said on the topic beyond what Brown had already mentioned! The seminar sessions also brought out another curious personal habit of Brown. Once he had finished his own introduction to the session, he would invariably fall asleep. If a question was posed to him or some debate arose, Brown seemed to arouse and join right in, but otherwise he would be constantly nodding off. Students in his seminar used to joke among themselves about how soon he would fall asleep after the beginning of the seminar discussion. This was a habit noted by so many people who were close to Brown over the years. Some had even wondered if he had some physical condition that inclined him this way, but most thought it was related to his notorious sleep habits. Brown was an insomniac and would work far into the night and rise early in the morning; he may have been simply sleep deprived.

THE GIFT OF FRIENDSHIP

Another life-giving aspect of his time at Union was the strong friendships he developed while there. Brown stepped into a Bible department that included George Landes (1928–2016), whom Brown had first met while they were both in graduate studies at Johns Hopkins. Landes would teach Old Testament and related topics at Union for thirty-nine years before retiring in 1995. George Landes was an ordained Presbyterian minister and, from all accounts, a gentle and genial presence on the faculty. Another biblical colleague that would work even more closely with Brown, was New Testament scholar J. Louis Martyn (1925–2015). Martyn had begun teaching at Union in 1959 and, in 1967, was appointed as the Edward Robinson Professor of Biblical Theology. Martyn, who had begun his adult work life as a plumber before turning to biblical studies, was a down-to-earth and engaging colleague. Brown developed a deep friendship with him and enjoyed the company of both Martyn and his wife Dorothy all during his time at Union.[28] Both Martyn and Brown were particularly interested in the Johannine literature and, like Brown, Martyn developed a working hypothesis about the evolution of the Johannine community, beginning with its deep roots in Palestinian Judaism and ultimately moving into the realm of the wider Hellenistic world of the first century.[29] Emphasizing the Jewish roots of the Johannine literature was a more recent turn in Johannine scholarship, and both scholars would become leading exponents of this view. The two of them would conduct joint seminars on the topic, dazzling their students with their combined erudition.

No colleague was closer to Brown at Union than the distinguished Old Testament scholar Phyllis Trible. Trible recalls first meeting Brown when she had begun her teaching career at Wake Forest University. Brown was a speaker at an ecumenical gathering. While there he had learned that the recently published (1968) *The Jerome Biblical Commentary* had received an award, news, she noted, that he had received with typical modesty. Later, Brown was part of the search committee that recommended Trible to the Union faculty when she moved from

Andover Newton to be appointed Baldwin Professor of Sacred Literature in 1980. At a dinner with some of the Union faculty the evening of her interviews, Trible ended up sitting next to Brown. When he noticed that she had ordered calves liver as her entrée, he leaned over and said with a smile, "You just lost my vote. My mother used to make me eat that stuff and I can't stand it." Trible felt from this first encounter they just "clicked" and over the years developed a wonderful friendship, filled with mutual affection and respect. In many ways, the two were unlikely friends. Trible was becoming famous for pioneering feminist perspectives for biblical interpretation[30] and was an elegant daughter of the South, raised as a devout Southern Baptist and an alumna of Meredith College in Raleigh, North Carolina, and of Union itself. Brown was a Roman Catholic priest with strong Bronx and New York roots and characteristics. Yet they would maintain strong bonds until the end of Brown's life, sharing a love of the opera, travel, and a certain aversion to the inevitable political intrigues of faculty life.

Brown's friendship with Phyllis Trible points to an important dimension of Brown's life that seems to have flowered at Union but was consistent all his life, namely, his capacity for friendships, especially with women. Virtually all those who knew Brown up close testify to his ability to develop lasting friends. He would ply friends with postcards during his travels, be in contact with regular telephone calls, and would remember significant moments in their lives. This was obviously true of some of his Sulpician brothers, but his network of friends extended far beyond that circle. Upon Brown's death, a cascade of personal notes flowed into the Sulpician community, most of them expressing deep affection for Brown and genuine grief at his loss. At Union itself, Brown was close to his administrative assistant, Eileen Tobin. She was a bright and talented woman who had never had the opportunity for higher education. She was devoted to Brown and he, in turn, treated her with warm respect.[31]

Another very close friend was Kateri Sullivan (1936–2015). She was an Immaculate Heart of Mary Sister located in Los Angeles. Brown had apparently met her early on when giving a workshop in the area in 1968. Her gentle and friendly manner had reminded him of his own mother, as he later confided to Trible. She also was part of a large and robust Irish family and over time, particularly when Brown was located on the West Coast, the Dodds clan (Dodds, the family name of her sister's husband) seems to have adopted him as one of their own family members. He would stay with them when he was in the area and thoroughly enjoyed their company. When Brown was still at Union and was about to go on one of his sabbaticals in Rome in 1988, he had entrusted to Kateri the task of taking care of his various financial obligations, writing to her with amazingly detailed instructions. She in turn would chide Brown on the sad state of his wardrobe. In a 1998 letter written to Fr. Ronald Witherup, the Sulpician provincial, shortly after Brown's death—which she mourned greatly—she confessed, "For years I gave him no peace about his pants. Several times I told him, 'This is the last time this jacket lining or pants pocked can be mended.' He told me I'd be sorry for my critical attitude because he was leaving his personal effects to me, and then I'd have to treat his pants with reverence and respect."[32] In the same letter she suggested that along with the books and awards that were to grace a memorial space at the Seminary library in Baltimore, there should also be a case that displayed his tattered jacket, his weather-beaten beret, and his trademark Roman collar.[33]

Brown was a classic priest and there is no evidence anywhere that he was ever less than faithful to his vows, yet his friendships with women were evident to all who knew him. While he cherished their company, he was also scrupulous never to travel alone with a woman, always arranging to have at least one other person along. Brown loved to travel and to visit new places, including national parks and museums. During these times, he was not inclined to talk shop but to engage in conversation about a wide range of topics, drawing on what seemed to be an endless supply of detailed information. Just before his death, he had been planning a trip to Sicily with his two dear friends, Phyllis Trible and Kateri Sullivan, a journey that sadly never took place. Earlier, the same trio had enjoyed a visit to Rome, with Brown having arranged for his two women friends to stay at Rome's Lay Centre.[34]

Brown's appreciation of women was apparent not only in his many lasting friendships with women but also in his professional work. He was particularly solicitous to the women graduate students at Union and supportive of their future careers and was always willing to give workshops and lectures to women religious. He also supported a few of his women students financially, helping them with tuition and debt payments. He also highlighted in his writings the role of women in the New Testament.[35] This may have been due, in part, to his distress about the way women were sometimes treated in the church. One notorious example involved his dear friend Kateri Sullivan, who was a member of the Immaculate Heart of Mary Sisters, a community that had been suppressed in 1967 by Cardinal James McIntyre of Los Angeles. The sisters had abandoned their traditional religious garb and other customs in response to the reforms of Vatican II. In reaction, McIntyre no longer permitted the sisters to teach in the archdiocese. When the Vatican was asked to adjudicate the dispute, the sisters were given the draconian choice of either returning to their former discipline under the authority of the archbishop or seeking dispensation from their vows. This was a wrenching experience for the women of the community, forcing upon even the elderly sisters the choice of either submitting to the cardinal's will or having to resign from the community they had belonged to for their entire adult lives. Of the 380 members of the community, 315 chose to seek dispensation and formed their own independent organization, among whom was Kateri Sullivan.

Another important friend and colleague during Brown's time at Union was Msgr. Myles Bourke, the longtime pastor of Corpus Christi parish, located across the street from Union. Bourke (1917–2004) was a highly respected New Testament scholar himself, who had taught for many years at St. Joseph's Seminary in Dunwoodie, the seminary of the Archdiocese of New York, and was a remarkable leader of the Catholic biblical movement, often playing a leading role in the deliberations of the Catholic Biblical Association, where he served as president and, for many years, as Chairman of its Board of Trustees. He was a dignified and elegant man, always immaculately dressed in his high Roman collar. He was a progressive mentor to many of the New York Catholic clergy and the quality of the liturgical and intellectual life of Corpus Christi parish under his leadership was considered a model. He and Brown developed a strong friendship. Brown would habitually say morning Mass at Corpus Christi and frequently dined at the rectory. Bourke had been appointed to the Board of Trustees of Union in 1971 and, in this role, kept Brown informed about some of the events and issues in which Union was embroiled at the time.

In the growing ecumenical spirit of the times, increasing numbers of Catholic students began to come to Union for their graduate work. No doubt some of this increase was due to Brown's own presence on the faculty. He made it a point to be something of an informal chaplain to the Catholic students, hosting gatherings and meals at his apartment in Union's McGiffert Hall, having informal Masses with them, and giving some of them his unused opera tickets. Mary Boys recalls the thrill of taking classes with Brown. At one point, she had gone to him to speak about an idea she had for her doctoral dissertation, dealing with the role of the Bible in religious education. To her surprise and delight, Brown offered to be her doctoral director, a conversation, she noted, that would change her life. With her, as with a number of his doctoral students, Brown's care for them would sustain far beyond the completion of their time at Union. Several noted that Brown made it a point to recommend them for academic positions—a valuable and effective recommendation given the wide network of Brown's contacts and the respect he enjoyed.

Even though Brown extended hospitality to his students, particularly the Catholics to whom he felt a special obligation, his own domestic skills were severely lacking. When he wasn't dining at the Corpus Christi rectory, he would open cans of spaghetti and lace it with hot sauce, from a supply he stashed in the Union cafeteria kitchen. Recognizing his own inadequacies, he had hired a woman to come in occasionally to clean his apartment. She had to remind him that she would need tools such as mops and buckets to do the work. Consequently, Brown called Mary Boys to purchase a mop for him since he wasn't sure how to do this himself. (She recalls traveling on the subway to school carrying the mop she had purchased for him!)

Brown enjoyed dining out, although his longtime publisher at Paulist Press, Fr. Kevin Lynch, noted that Brown was not comfortable in very expensive restaurants. He also enjoyed an evening cocktail (usually a Manhattan, sometimes two) before dinner. Lynch recalls the delight on Brown's face when at receptions Paulist Press held at some religious conventions, one of the staff would have a Manhattan at the ready when Brown, one of their star authors, appeared.

At the same time, Brown lived a simple and frugal life, with dedication to his scholarly work commanding his time and attention. When eating on his own, as noted earlier, he would quickly grab something out of a can. Sometimes when working with others on a rare committee assignment, he would suggest they save time by working through lunch—a suggestion that was mostly unwelcome by his colleagues. Visitors to his apartment at McGiffert Hall remember how sparsely furnished it was, with an abundance of books and little else except the essentials of a desk, a bed, and a few sticks of furniture. As noted, his threadbare wardrobe was legendary. Once when Brown and Trible were going to a meeting in New York City, he inadvertently left his raincoat in the trunk of the cab. When it pulled away, he realized that he had forgotten his coat and wanted to contact the cab company to retrieve it. Remembering how tattered it was, Trible persuaded him to buy a new one at Macy's instead. When this was later reported to Kateri Sullivan, she thanked Phyllis for liberating Brown from his embarrassing coat.

Across the street from Union Seminary is the famed Jewish Theological Seminary of America, an institution with whom Union had maintained a long and respectful collaboration. In 1964, the ecumenically minded President Bennett worked out a formal relationship between the two schools that allowed an exchange of credits. When Brown was on the Union faculty, he had struck up a friendship with a brilliant rabbinic student, Burton Visotzky, who had taken Brown's course on the Gospel of John. As noted previously, Brown's interest in Judaism and its essential place in the development of early Christianity and the New Testament had been quickened by his ASOR sojourn in Jerusalem and through his association with Albright at Johns Hopkins. Brown believed that it was crucial for Christian biblical students to be better informed about Judaism and Jewish literature. Visotzky became an important dialogue partner with Brown (and Visotzky considered Brown his "personal rabbi"). At one point Brown arranged for Visotzky to conduct a seminar on rabbinic literature for Union students. Visotzky recalls his nervousness as the time of the seminar drew near, nervousness compounded when he realized that Brown was present not only to introduce Visotzky to the students but that he intended to participate in the seminar himself. His nervousness was eased, however, when he noted that Brown nodded off to sleep only a few minutes into the opening lecture.[36]

THE FINAL MOVE: ST. PATRICK'S IN MENLO PARK

The nearly twenty years Brown would spend at Union were amazingly productive and personally satisfying. His publications during this period were numerous, including major works such as *The Birth of the Messiah* (1977), *The Community of the Beloved Disciple* (1979), the Anchor Bible Commentary on *The Epistles of John* (1982), *Antioch and Rome* (1983, done in collaboration with John Meier), and one of his own personal favorites, *The Churches the Apostles Left Behind* (1984).

Along with a host of other more popular works during this time, most published with Paulist Press, he also produced two notable ecumenical works in collaboration with Protestant scholars, a collaboration no doubt stimulated by the ecumenical environment of Union Seminary, namely, *Peter in the New Testament* (1973) and *Mary in the New Testament* (1978). He also maintained a punishing schedule of lectures, workshops, and brief teaching stints throughout the country and some abroad as well. To flee the January cold in New York, he often gave workshops in various parts of the Caribbean, usually accompanied by his friend Msgr. Joseph Shenrock, a priest of the Diocese of Trenton.

Academic honors and other recognitions began to mount as well. While at Union, he received honorary doctorates from the University of Edinburgh (1972), the University of Uppsala (1974), DePaul University in Chicago (1975), Louvain University in Belgium (1976), St. Anselm's College in Manchester, New Hampshire (1977), Boston College (1977), Fordham University (1977), Glasgow University (1978), Dominican School of Theology in Berkeley (1979), Loyola College in Baltimore (1980), Immaculate Conception Seminary in Darlington, New Jersey (1980), Wagner College, Staten Island (1981), Hofstra University, Hempstead, New York (1985), Providence College in Rhode Island (1987), Episcopal Theological Seminary in Virginia (1987), LeMoyne College, Syracuse (1988), The Catholic University of America (1989), Rockhurst College, Kansas City (1989), St. Francis Xavier University, Nova Scotia (1990), St. John's University, Jamaica, New York (1990), and Weston School of Theology, Cambridge, Massachusetts (1990). Once when awaiting the start of an academic procession, a faculty colleague at Union noticed that Brown had pinned several of his most cherished academic medals on the lapels of his academic robe. The faculty member joked that so many honors must be a compensation for a celibate life—to which Brown responded with a twinkle in his eye, "There are no compensations for a celibate life."

Now his sixtieth birthday was on the horizon, and he began to think about the next steps his life should take. He thought he had at least a decade ahead of him before he would have to consider retirement, and he would like to spend it in research and writing. Already in 1984, he had written to his provincial, Fr. Edward Frazer, and raised the idea of moving to St. Patrick's, the Sulpician seminary in Menlo Park, California, which served the Archdiocese of San Francisco and several other western dioceses. He was not thinking of returning to seminary teaching but considering how he might, in fact, move into "semi-retirement," focusing on research and writing while being relieved of his teaching duties and the responsibility of directing doctoral students.

Also prompting him to consider a move was that many of the same problems that had motivated him to move from St. Mary's in 1971 were also nagging him at Union. Reflecting the spirit of the times, student activism had intensified at Union, so much so that Brown groused that the students seemed to be taking over the direction of the school. When someone asked him about the dress code at Union, he quipped, "Most of them wear clothes"! His concern about academic excellence—another problem he had detected at St. Mary's—was also on his mind about the direction Union would go. Already in 1974, he had expressed his concern in a letter to the then President of St. Mary's, William J. Lee, noting that he had discussed with Paul Purta, his provincial, "that there were certain non-academic movements being discussed for Union's future that were making all the tenured faculty uneasy about the destiny of this institution. The great tradition of scholarship that had brought me here in the first place was in peril."[37] That crisis, in fact, passed, in Brown's view, with the forced resignation in 1975 of then president J. Brooke Mosley who had succeeded president Bennett.[38]

As his time at Union progressed and his academic reputation grew, Brown also continued to be wooed by other institutions, as had already been happening toward the end of his tenure at St. Mary's. A particularly attractive offer came in 1984 from the Chandler School of Theology at Emory University, offering him appointment to the newly created position as the Woodruff Professor of Theology that included minimal teaching duties and ample resources for research (Brown noted that they had "a lot of funds from Coca Cola"). Brown had even visited the campus and was impressed with the opportunities there.

Ultimately, however, Brown's decision to move on was not based on any negative experience at Union or the lure of academic positions elsewhere. Overall, he had been content there and had thrived in the academic setting of the school and the wider context of New York. He felt that it was time to retire altogether from the formal academic world as a member of the faculty and, instead, to find a congenial circumstance where he could intensify his writing and research at the service of the church, unencumbered with any other obligations or constraints. The place that beckoned to him was St. Patrick's Seminary in Menlo Park. He would be in a Sulpician setting, paving the way for a smoother entry into his retirement years "in the company of Sulpicians" as he had earlier hoped,[39] when that time would eventually come. He would have access to the library and academic resources of the seminary but not have to do teaching or be part of the seminary faculty. He could also enjoy the warmth of the California sun, and the seminary was equipped with an outdoor swimming pool; swimming was one of his favorite activities. An added plus was that the then archbishop of San Francisco was John Quinn (1929–2017), who was a personal friend and constant episcopal support for Brown, and had first broached the possibility of Brown moving to California.

Brown spelled out his sentiments in leaving Union in a letter he sent to the president, Donald Shriver, in April 1989, indicating his desire to retire as of June 30, 1990:

> I am in good health, and I would like to take advantage of that blessing to use the good years of early retirement to complete some writing projects I have long had in mind. Even though Union has been very generous in freeing time to write, the work that I hope to accomplish is too detailed and complicated to be done while I am guiding a large number of doctoral candidates.[40] If I retire in 1990, I am promised a room plus space for my library at the seminary of the Archdiocese of San Francisco...so that I could stay there and write....The seminary is run by priests of my own group, many of whom I taught; accordingly for the next decade, if I have good health that long, I would be among friends. Very kindly the St. Patrick's Seminary is not requiring that I teach or become a faculty member, and that is important to me. I shall be proud that my last formal position was Auburn Distinguished Professor of Biblical Studies at Union.

He went on to express his gracious appreciation for Union and the time he had spent there:

> I do not find this letter easy to write. I shall be leaving behind excellent colleagues in the Biblical Field, some of them now close friends for a long time....Above all I shall be leaving a place that has been home to me for twenty years and where I have done the most productive work of my life. Some of

those years have been publicly turbulent, and yet amidst all the pressures never have seminary administrators treated me with anything other than complete courtesy…no promise made to me at Union was ever broken, and more kindness was shown to me than I expected or deserved.

Besides what I shall leave behind, the thought of retirement and of the changes it brings is a bit frightening. Even when begun at 62, it forces me to face aging. I have to hope that freedom from the obligations of everyday seminary work will be true freedom, not stagnation. But when all is weighed, I think retirement is the right thing to do.[41]

Brown had first run a draft of this resignation letter by his provincial, Gerald L. Brown, a couple of weeks earlier, making sure he had the permission of his superior to take this step.[42] In another communication with Gerald Brown, he also discussed some of the financial arrangements; a concern for taxation purposes was that the province would not designate California as his permanent residence and thereby inadvertently make Brown liable for additional taxes. Brown had always maintained Florida as his permanent residence for taxation purposes and wanted to ensure it would stay that way. However, he added, "You and I both know that the real issue is not monetary, but I hope that what I can do in my latter years will be helpful for the church."[43]

Another important encouragement for Brown's move to California was his close friendship with Archbishop John Quinn of San Francisco. The archbishop would make it a point to meet with Brown whenever he had visited at St. Patrick's and encouraged him to think of moving to California when Brown started to think of retiring. Quinn was a constant supporter of Brown's work and was eager to have an eminent scholar like Brown take up residence at St. Patrick's, his archdiocesan seminary. But a possible fly in the ointment was that Archbishop Quinn's enthusiasm at having Brown in his archdiocese and at the seminary had led him to hope that Brown could serve as a spiritual director for the seminarians—a prospect that frightened Brown and was not at all in his plans. Brown had written in July of 1988 to Quinn about his planned move to St. Patrick's, following up on a conversation that he had already had with the archbishop on the matter. His reason for writing was to ask Quinn's formal permission to take up residence in the archdiocese and at the seminary, but more important for Brown was to spell out to the archbishop what the exact purpose of his move was. As Brown confided to his provincial, he had tried to head off Quinn's suggestion: "I told him [Quinn] that I felt I could be doing more for the Church writing commentaries than in spiritual direction....And he recognized that. But the remark scared me as to his priorities. It is still my firm belief that the great weakness of American priests is not a lack of spirituality but a lack of depth. They really have nothing substantial to communicate to the people."[44] Now as the move to Menlo Park was about to happen, Brown wanted to communicate clearly his plans to the archbishop:

> In terms of what I would do at St. Patrick's, I would not plan to be a faculty member or to teach on any regular basis. I have assured Father Coleman [Fr. Gerald Coleman, PSS, then President of St. Patrick's] that I would be happy to give lectures from time to time, for the students, for the public, for the priests. And occasionally I would be happy to go into Scripture classes and give lectures. But my main task would be research. I have several books that I wish to write, and the press of duties at Union have prevented me from doing this. At the moment my health is good; and if God spares me, I would look forward to staying at St. Patrick's as long as I am healthy enough not to have to go to a retirement home. Obviously, when it does become necessary to go to a retirement home, I would turn to the Sulpicians and our home in Baltimore. But my fondest hope is that it would be a decade or more at St. Patrick's before *real* retirement becomes necessary.[45]

Brown would move to California in July of 1990. He had asked president Donald Schriver to extend his stay at McGiffert hall by one month ("free of charge") since his lease would expire on June 30, the end of his tenure at Union. He packed up his things for the move, including his precious stamp collection. As fate would have it, Brown wrapped his collection in plastic bags and in transit many of his stamps were damaged by extensive mildew triggered by moisture trapped in the wrapping. This had been an important and cherished hobby for Brown, one that he shared with his friend and colleague Joseph Fitzmyer. In his will, Brown had anticipated that his collection, which he was entrusting to the Sulpicians as part of his estate, would be very valuable. He hoped that a younger Sulpician might keep up the collection but, if not, it should be appraised and sold. Unfortunately, because of the damage to the collection in the move to California, the value of the stamps plummeted, and the eventual appraisal estimated the worth at around $13,000—an amount far below what Brown seemed to have expected. Providentially, he would never know of this outcome. He bade farewell to his many friends and colleagues at Union and in the city. In the few days before he moved, he invited his dear friend Phyllis Trible to accompany him on a last round of museum visits, and with that he had completed the New York phase of his life.

In fact, Brown's sojourn at Menlo Park would fulfill his hopes. A minor problem was securing a desirable room at the seminary. At first, he had his eye on a suite that the previous rector of the seminary had used but gave up on that when the new rector stated he himself planned to use that space. Ultimately, Brown found a compatible location for his bedroom, an office, and his personal library, which was considerable. (Brown estimated that it consisted of 8,000 volumes at the time of his move.) He had mentioned to Archbishop Quinn that he intended to pay for his own expenses at the seminary and that he wanted to place no financial burden either on the Sulpicians or the archdiocese. Earlier Quinn had offered Brown free use of a house that was maintained by the archdiocese for the bishop on the seminary grounds, but Brown declined. When the time did come for him to retire, he said he would like to donate a portion of his library to the seminary, as a "gesture of gratitude for the hospitality that would enable me to use these final years of my life productively in writing."[46]

His routine at St. Patrick's would be peaceful and conducive to the research and writing he was committed to do.[47] He usually celebrated daily Mass for the Mexican sisters who maintained the dining facilities for the seminary, and he enjoyed the Mexican food, laced with hot sauce, that they prepared for him. He also used the swimming pool on a regular basis (using the same pair of tattered swim trunks that were almost completely worn through![48]). As he had promised, he would give an occasional lecture at the seminary and gave some "mini-courses" at the Vatican II Institute, a Sulpician program for the continuing education for priests, conducted on the seminary campus. From time to time, he would give lectures at nearby parishes. He usually declined any stipend for this work but did let it be known that he was willing to accept a good bottle of wine in compensation! As a result, he had on hand a collection of good wines that he shared with his Sulpician confreres. He still traveled to give workshops and lectures at programs around the country and abroad, but he was also considering cutting back his extensive lecture schedule in favor of devoting more time to writing.[49] As we will note later, he also did some international work, including accepting reappointment to the Pontifical Biblical Commission by the Prefect of the Congregation for the Doctrine of the Faith, Cardinal Joseph Ratzinger, an official affirmation that meant a great deal to Brown.

In fact, Brown would never completely withdraw from his routine of lectures and workshops. At the time of his death, he had committed to several such opportunities.[50] But compared to his pace while at St. Mary's and Union, he was dedicating much more of his time to writing. Right up to the last days of his life, he would be engaged in the work of biblical scholarship that he had sensed was his calling from the very beginning.

THE PUBLIC SCHOLAR

The accumulation of Raymond Brown's teaching, thesis direction, lecturing, and publications on both a popular and a scholarly level over nearly forty years of his professional life was prodigious. Also significant was the vast network of relationships he had established with scholars and religious leaders around the world. This had begun with his entrance into the world of ecumenical scholarship during his formative years at Johns Hopkins and his stint in Jerusalem during his fellowship year there. It had continued through his exposure to the Vatican world through his gaining pontifical degrees before the Pontifical Biblical Commission, through his serendipitous exposure to the opening session of the Second Vatican Council by invitation of his bishop, and later by his membership on the Pontifical Biblical Commission and his sabbatical teaching experiences at the Roman Pontifical Biblical Institute and the North American College. His ecumenical work, including his holding of a chair at a highly respected Protestant seminary, which we will track later, also forged trusting relationships with a host of American and European Protestant biblical scholars.[51] All this thrust Brown into a very public role as perhaps the best known Catholic biblical scholar of his time. It would also, as we will consider, make him a target of opportunity for those ultraconservative Catholics who chaffed that one whose work they considered heretical and destructive had achieved such prominence and acclaim.[52]

Some aspects of Brown's public role deserve a closer look. We have already noted the list of honorary doctorates Brown had received during his tenure at Union Theological Seminary. That list of honors would continue until the end of his life, including recognition from a prestigious private university such as Northwestern University in Chicago, which honored Brown in 1995.[53] Early in his career at Union he had received honorary doctorates from the University of Edinburgh (1972) and the University of Glasgow (1978)—both highly significant and unusual ecumenical recognitions of Brown's work, particularly his commentary on the Gospel of John and his contribution on the Faith and Order Commission.[54] A special place in Brown's heart was earned by the University of Uppsala, which conferred the honorary doctorate on him in 1974. The history of this prestigious Swedish university mirrored the story of the Reformation itself. It was founded in 1477 by an initiative of the Catholic primate of Sweden, Archbishop Jakob Ulvsson, and ratified by Pope Sixtus IV. At the time of the reformation in the mid-sixteenth century, the University lost its Catholic sponsorship under the reign of the Lutheran King Gustav I Vasa. In 1971, three years before Brown received his honorary doctorate, the University was reconstituted as a state university and no longer officially connected with the Lutheran Church. Brown was the first Catholic scholar to be honored by the University at its well-known, elaborate conferral ceremony where the recipient is given a special hat and robe, plus a laurel crown—to be worn the day of the ceremony—and a gold ring. Brown wore this ring on the middle finger of his left hand for the rest of his life, obviously a sign of the pride and satisfaction he took in this singular recognition.

Equally impressive were the awards that Brown received, including several awards from various press associations for his publications and medals and recognitions from a number of organizations and institutions, including honorary memberships in the American Academy of Arts and Sciences, the British Academy, as well as the Phi Beta Kappa Society, considered the most prestigious American award for excellence in the arts and sciences.[55]

Brown took an active role in the professional organizations that served biblical scholarship. In fact, he would become the president of all three major associations—the Catholic Biblical Association of America

(CBA), the Society of Biblical Literature (SBL) and the European based *Studiorum Novi Testamenti Societas* (SNTS, the Society for the Study of the New Testament)—the first scholar to achieve this. He was active early in the Catholic Biblical Association of America, joining as a "student member" in 1951. The Association at that time was almost all clerics. "Mother Kathryn Sullivan was the one nun, I remember." "Later," Brown noted, "the CBA became a very interesting group of scholars, and some of the best articles in the *CBQ* in those days came out of papers at the Conventions."[56] Brown would be elected president of the CBA from 1971 to 1972. As was customary, his presidential address on "The Relationship of the 'Secret Gospel of Mark' to the Fourth Gospel" was ultimately published in the association's official journal, *The Catholic Biblical Quarterly*, a journal written by and for biblical scholars.[57] Throughout his life, but particularly in his earlier years, Brown was a regular contributor to the *CBQ*, publishing 19 articles and 29 reviews in its pages. In later years, his attendance at the CBA annual meetings became less frequent; Brown preferred to attend the SNTS meetings in Europe that took place in late summer, roughly parallel to the CBA meetings.

In 1977, Brown was elected as president of the SBL, succeeding his longtime friend and editorial colleague, David Noel Freedman. The SBL is a large, nonsectarian, but mainly Protestant, organization that includes biblical scholars from various denominations across North America and, increasingly in recent years, from other parts of the world. Brown was the second Catholic to serve as president of the organization; the brilliant and outspoken John L. McKenzie, who had served as president in 1966 was the first.[58] Brown's presidential address given at the end of his one-year term at the SBL meeting in San Francisco was titled "'Other Sheep Not of This Fold': The Johannine Perspective on Christian Diversity in the Late First Century." His probing of the evolution of the Johannine community in this address would be an important preparation for his full-blown treatment of the issue in *The Community of the Beloved Disciple*.[59]

Brown was elected president of the SNTS in 1986 at the organization's meeting in Atlanta, Georgia, one of the few times it had met in the United States.[60] Brown was the first Catholic scholar from North America to be so honored, but not the first Catholic elected president of this prestigious association. Highly respected Catholic European scholars such as Pierre Benoit, OP (1962), Rudolf Schnackenburg (1966), Beda Rigaux, OFM (1974), Xavier Léon-Dufour, SJ (1980), and Jacques

Dupont, OSB (1984) had preceded him. Those familiar with the sterling reputation of the scholars on this list can recognize what a singular honor this was for Brown.

For his presidential address to the SNTS, Brown chose to challenge the growing trend of some scholars who were ascribing more historical and religious value to noncanonical works than to the canonical Gospels themselves. In this instance he critiqued the views of John Dominic Crossan about the priority of "The Gospel of Peter" to that of the Synoptics.[61]

As is normally the case with such organizations, the office of "president" is mainly honorary in nature, with an Executive Director administering the organization. Those elected president are scholars who have the respect of their peers in the association. For a Catholic scholar to be recognized in this way by all three of the major biblical associations speaks for itself.

THE PONTIFICAL BIBLICAL COMMISSION

In 1972, Brown received an invitation to become a member of the Pontifical Biblical Commission. In many ways, this appointment was the highest possible approbation of Brown's work as a Catholic scholar, short of being named a bishop. As noted earlier, the membership and function of the Biblical Commission had been significantly changed during Pope Paul VI's reorganization of the Vatican curia after the Second Vatican Council.[62] Originally an independent body, the Commission was now lodged under the umbrella of the Congregation for the Doctrine of the Faith (popularly known as the "Holy Office"—perhaps the most powerful Vatican secretariat within the curia). Its membership was composed of twenty biblical scholars from around the world; Brown would be the lone American on the Commission. Its function was no longer to ride herd on Catholic biblical scholars, but to promote sound biblical scholarship—including, as in the past, offering examinations for those seeking an STL or SSD from the Commission—and to serve as something of a "think tank" on behalf of the Secretariat and the pope on matters of biblical interpretation.

Brown received notice of his appointment May 27, 1972, in a letter from the then secretary of state, Cardinal Jean-Marie Villot, forwarded

by the Apostolic Delegate to the United States, Archbishop Luigi Rai-
mondi, and sent to the Jesuit theologate, Woodstock College (even
though Brown resided at Union Theological Seminary). The process
by which a scholar is appointed to the Commission is undefined but
includes nomination by one's national hierarchy and approval by the
Prefect of the Congregation for the Doctrine of the Faith, who at the
time of Brown's appointment was the Croatian cardinal, Franjo Šeper.
Clearly Brown must have passed muster with these various prelates. He
was joined on the Commission by several well-known European Catholic scholars, including such luminaries as Albert Deschamps (who was
"Rector Magnificus" of the University of Louvain and would serve as
"Secretary" of the commission), Pierre Benoit, OP, and Jean-Dominique
Barthelemy, OP, both of the École Biblique in Jerusalem, Henri Cazelles
(a fellow Sulpician), Ignace de la Potterie, SJ, Joachim Gnilka, Jean Gre-
lot, Lucien Legrand, MEP, Stanislaus Lyonnet, SJ (a faculty member at
the Pontifical Biblical Institute), Ceslaus Spicq, OP, David Stanley, SJ (a
Canadian scholar), and Carlo Maria Martini, SJ, who at that time was
the rector of the Biblical Institute and would later be appointed by Paul
VI in 1978 as rector of the Gregorian University. He would go on to be
appointed as archbishop of Milan by Pope John Paul II and later named
a cardinal, one who was constantly discussed as equipped for the papal
office itself.

This appointment must have been viewed by Brown as a blessing,
placing his name among the most respected Catholic scholars in the
world and inoculating him as it did from some of the opposition that
was mounting against him at this time on the part of ultraconservative Catholics.[63] As things turned out, it was a mixed blessing. On the
agenda of the Commission was some routine work on upgrading the
regulations for taking examinations for the Pontifical degrees in Scripture before the Commission (as Brown himself had done some years
before) and discussions about defining what is a characteristic Catholic
approach to biblical interpretation.[64] But, in 1975, the Commission was
asked by the Congregation of the Doctrine of the Faith to prepare a
statement on the relevance of the Bible for the question of ordination
of women to the priesthood—in service of a broader document on the
question that was being planned by the Congregation itself. The Biblical Commission completed its statement in the spring of 1976, with the
end result being a judicious and cautious approach to what everyone
understood was a highly sensitive topic.[65] Although the Commission's

statement included a more extensive exposition, the bottom line was expressed in three basic conclusions, accompanied by a vote tally of the members of the Commission: (1) the New Testament does not settle in a clear way and once and for all whether women can be ordained priests (seventeen votes for; none against); (2) the scriptural grounds alone are not enough to exclude the possibility of ordaining women (twelve votes for; five against); (3) Christ's plan would not be transgressed by permitting the ordination of women (twelve votes for; five against).[66]

It is clear that in this matter the Biblical Commission and the Congregation for the Doctrine of the Faith were on a collision course. Several months after the formulation of the Commission's statement, the Congregation itself would issue a Declaration that would conclude: "...the Sacred Congregation for the Doctrine of the Faith judges it necessary to recall that the Church, in fidelity to the example of the Lord, does not consider herself authorized to admit women to priestly ordination."[67] The embarrassment this caused was compounded by the fact that the members of the Commission were among the most highly respected Catholic biblical scholars in the world and hardly considered rebels by nature. When it became clear that the work of the Biblical Commission would be suppressed, one of its members, David Stanley, SJ, a Canadian scholar and, at that time, a professor at the Gregorian University, resigned from the Commission in protest at the Congregation's "complete disregard" for the biblical evidence—he would later lose his position at the Gregorian as a consequence. Worse yet, the Commission's full report was leaked to the press, revealing for all to see the strong dissent of the scholars on the Commission from the stance of the Congregation for the Doctrine of the Faith.

We do not know Brown's own personal position or what precise role he played in the formulation of the Commission's statement. The Commission's usual working procedures preclude this type of information. Their statements are formed over time, with the input of individuals and subcommittees woven together into a final consensus text, upon which the Commission as a whole then votes. The Biblical Commission is not authorized to publish its own reports—they are at the service of the Prefect of the Congregation and the pope himself, who ultimately authorize for publication any statement of the Commission—which in fact usually happens. But, at the same time, we know that Brown, in view of the unanimous vote of the Commission, supported the view that the biblical evidence did not preclude ordination of women. And, from his earlier article on the subject, one suspects that he voted with the majority on the other two statements of the Commission.[68]

In any case, further disaster happened when Brown himself was accused of being the one who leaked the Commission's statement to the press. He was mortified by this accusation, which he believed called into question his integrity and his loyalty to the church. He vigorously denied the accusation. A journalist named John Muthig, who worked for the Catholic press service and later for the American Catholic magazine *St. Anthony's Messenger*, had acquired a copy of the statement (for a price) and called Brown to find out about the circumstances of the Commission's document. Muthig reported that in a conversation about the leak of the document with Fr. Richard Malone, a staff member of the National Conference of Catholic Bishops who also assisted at the Congregation for the Doctrine of the Faith, Brown's name had come up.[69] Muthig himself had told Malone he would not reveal his source but could certify that "Raymond Brown was *not* his source" (emphasis original). Brown wrote immediately to Malone to clarify matters. Malone replied that he was leery of Muthig (whom he described as a "newsman on the rise who wants to be a Woodward [i.e., Kenneth Woodward, at that time the religion editor for *Newsweek*] at the expense of the Catholic Church") and raised Brown's name only as an appeal to Muthig that reputations could be damaged if anyone were falsely accused of the leak. Malone asked Brown's forgiveness for even using his name in this manner. Vatican officials, Malone noted, usually assume that the source of a leak is associated with someone who is from the country where the leaked document is published—in this case the United States, thus fingering Brown as the prime suspect. He assured Brown that, upon hearing from Muthig that Brown was innocent, he had immediately contacted Jerome Hamer, OP, secretary of the Congregation for the Doctrine of the Faith, to assure him that Brown was not the source of the leak. Malone also informed Brown that he had learned that the source of the leak turned out to be a staff member within the Vatican itself.[70]

Nevertheless, the damage was done, and Brown believed he remained under a cloud of suspicion. One of the consequences was that the terms of most of the members of the Biblical Commission were not renewed. It is customary that members of the Commission are appointed for two consecutive five-year terms. For most of the members of the ill-fated Commission that had taken up the question of women's ordination, there would be no second term, including Raymond Brown. Later, Msgr. Albert Deschamps, the secretary of the Commission (who survived the purge), wrote a personal letter to Brown apologizing for the situation and expressing his own embarrassment that a scholar of Brown's stature and integrity would be subject to this.[71]

Brown's association with the Pontifical Biblical Commission would have a happier ending. In February 1996, Brown would be delighted to learn that he was reappointed to the Biblical Commission by no less than Pope John Paul II, an invitation received through the good graces of none other than Cardinal Joseph Ratzinger, the long-term prefect of the Congregation for the Doctrine of the Faith.[72] Brown contacted his friend Joe Reynolds in the provincial office and urged him to make this appointment more widely known, seeing it as a removal of the shadow cast by his prior experience on the Commission and a further vindication of his good standing with Vatican authorities.[73]

The work facing the Commission this time around was the prospect, urged by John Paul II himself, of making a substantial statement on the Christian Scriptures and the Jews. The pope noted that the Church had issued several statements about its relationship with Judaism in questions of liturgy and catechetics, but not in the area of Scripture itself. This would finally appear in 2002 as one of the Commission's most important post–Vatican II texts, *The Jewish People and Their Sacred Scriptures in the Christian Bible*.[74] In this instance, we have clear evidence that Brown, even though he was on the Commission only a short time—he attended his first session in the spring of 1997—would have a significant impact on the scope and content of the Commission's statement. Upon receiving a proposed sketch of the Commission's planned statement shortly after his appointment, he had written to Albert Vanhoye, SJ, the distinguished Belgian scholar who was secretary of the Commission and, at that time, a faculty member at the Pontifical Biblical Institute.[75] Brown recommended that the scope of the Commission's study be extended to include both the Old and the New Testaments, and that it hit head on some of the New Testament texts that had served as a source of consternation for the Jewish community and a prompt for Christian anti-Semitism. Brown was opposed to solving the problem by means of removing or altering such texts, as had been attempted in a recent American Bible Society version of the Bible. Instead, Brown suggested, "It would be helpful if we commented on the meaning of hostile references to the 'Jews' and how they should be understood today in

a way that is not offensive ecumenically."[76] Vanhoye replied, expressing his gratitude for Brown's suggestions and affirming that he would
adopt them for the working schema of the Commission. He added, "I
am moreover very happy to count on your competence and your experience."[77]

The final document published by the Commission would appear
in 2002, three years after Brown's death, but it is clear from his own
working notes that he had composed significant portions of what would
be the final text, particularly on providing the historical and social context for some of the more problematic New Testament texts referring to
the Jews.[78] By a stroke of providence, Brown's contribution to this key
Vatican text came at a time when his own views about Judaism and the
New Testament were at their greatest maturity.[79]

Brown's dedication to his work on so many levels was unwavering
and because of it, he would leave an indelible mark on biblical scholarship and on the church that he always desired to serve. It is to a closer
look at other dimensions of this remarkable academic and ecclesiastical
career that we can now turn.

CHAPTER 3

INTERPRETER OF THE WORD

Raymond Brown's lifelong contribution as a priest and scholar was to proclaim with extraordinary energy and effectiveness the Word of God to the church. Although a consummate scholar, there was no doubt that ultimately his motivation and driving purpose was pastoral, namely, to bring the riches of the Catholic biblical renewal to the life of the church. If one could summarize the impact of his lifelong ministry, it would be that he was a dedicated interpreter of the Word of God.

He carried out this ministry in several ways. For thirty-seven years of his adult life, Brown was a teacher, beginning with his short stint at St. Charles Minor Seminary in 1953, through his time on the faculty of St. Mary's Seminary and University (1959–71), and concluding with his "retirement" in 1990 from Union Theological Seminary, where he had spent twenty years. During those teaching years, he educated a whole generation of Catholic seminarians, now veteran priests, and numerous graduate students at Union, many of whom went on to become pastors and professors in a variety of Christian denominations. Many of the doctoral candidates he guided at Union advanced to become distinguished scholars and intellectual leaders in their own right.[1] Through the lectures and workshops that he gave throughout his career, including his last years at St. Patrick's Seminary in Menlo Park, California— over a thousand by his own estimate—he touched innumerable priests, religious, and laity who were dazzled by the depth and clarity of his biblical teaching. Many of those lectures were amplified and reached even more audiences through the numerous taped recordings made of his presentations.[2] It would not be an exaggeration to say that Raymond Brown became the most well-known and most appreciated Catholic teacher of the Bible of his generation.

Despite this amazing oral legacy, Brown's most enduring impact is likely to be his written works, particularly his major works that have left an indelible mark on biblical scholarship. His range of publications was amazingly wide—including small booklets on the liturgical readings meant to be of assistance for homily preparation, devotional works on aspects of the liturgical seasons and their biblical readings, popular books written for an educated but nonprofessional audience often on controversial issues involving biblical questions such as the virginal conception of Jesus, the origin of the priesthood and the episcopate, the New Testament portrayals of the figures of Mary and Peter, and, finally, several major works on an academic and technical level including commentaries and topical matters.[3]

Those familiar with his working habits noted that his more popular works were not derivative from his major technical works, but, rather, he would be at work on his writing for a wider nontechnical audience at the same time he was doing exhaustive research on his major technical publications. In the case of his popular works, his lectures to a wide variety of audiences were the seedbeds for his writings. In almost every instance, Brown noted that the chapters in such works as *Biblical Reflections on Crises Facing the Church* (1975) or *The Critical Meaning of the Bible* (1981) and many others were adapted from lectures he gave in different parts of the country. In his 1990 work *Responses to 101 Questions on the Bible*, Brown states that his choice of topics and his responses were drawn from years of interactions with the audiences of his lectures.[4]

Before considering in subsequent chapters the range of topics that Brown engaged in his writings and some of the positions he espoused, we turn first to his approach to biblical interpretation.[5]

ENDORSING THE HISTORICAL-CRITICAL METHOD

Standing back from Brown's library of publications (as well as the content of his lectures) one is struck by two driving forces that shaped his work. First of all, he became an indefatigable practitioner and proponent of the so-called historical-critical method as a legitimate and even essential component of biblical exegesis and interpretation.[6]

Although later in his career he would somewhat grudgingly acknowledge the value of other methods beyond the historical-critical, he was never at home with them.[7] Brown would certainly have agreed with the description of the historical-critical method provided by his colleague Joseph Fitzmyer, SJ, in an important defense of the method published in 1989 in *Theological Studies*:

> The method is called "historical-critical" because it borrows its techniques of interpreting the Bible from historical and literary criticism. It recognizes that the Bible, though containing the Word of God, is an ancient record, composed indeed by a multiplicity of authors over a long period of time in antiquity. Being such an ancient composition, it has to be studied and analyzed like other ancients [*sic*] records. Since much of it presents a narrative account of events that affected the lives of ancient Jews and early Christians, the various accounts have to be analyzed against their proper human and historical background, in their contemporary contexts, and in their original languages. In effect, this method applies to the Bible all the critical techniques of classical philology, and in doing so it refuses apriori to exclude any critical analysis in its quest for the meaning of the text.[8]

Fitzmyer's inclusion of a recognition that the Bible contains "the Word of God" reveals the same theological conviction about Scripture shared by Brown—a conviction that would not necessarily be accepted by some practitioners of the historical-critical method. Brown himself acknowledged that some proponents of historical criticism would work from a very different set of assumptions that would be antithetical to Catholic faith—a critique that led church officials to oppose the historical-critical method in the first place, as we noted earlier.[9] Brown forthrightly opposed such assumptions: "For many people Historical Criticism has had almost an aura of pure science in studying the sources from which a biblical book was composed: their historical value; the circumstances of composition; the author; and the objective contents. Yet, since historical investigation was often combined with an antipathy toward theology, the results have appeared barren to readers looking for spiritual meaning applicable to their lives. Indeed, this critical approach does not seem to explain the NT as vitally important religious literature."[10] But, as Brown went on to say, "When one strips off some of the abuses…Historical Criticism is concerned with the commonsense observation that readers of any book of Scripture will want to know what the author of that book tried to convey."[11]

The endorsement of the historical-critical method of biblical exegesis by Brown and other contemporary Catholic biblical scholars was no doubt due in part to the timing of Raymond Brown's entrance into the world of Catholic biblical scholarship. As we have noted earlier, when Brown began his professional career as a biblical scholar and teacher in the late 1950s, the Catholic Church on an official level had just emerged from a period where historical inquiry into the background and content of the Scriptures was under severe suspicion. The liberating impact of Pius XII's *Divino Afflante Spiritu* and its subsequent strong ratification by the Second Vatican Council lifted the cloud of suspicion from Catholic biblical scholarship.[12] At the same time, the generous use of Scripture in the decrees of the Second Vatican Council and the rapid implementation of the pastoral directives about the Bible found in *Dei Verbum*, the Council's Dogmatic Constitution on Divine Revelation, led to a surge of popular interest in the Bible and its meaning for Catholic life. Brown would be at the forefront of this dynamic biblical renewal in Catholicism, particularly in the United States. He and other Catholic scholars at this time proved to be enthusiastic practitioners and advocates of the historical-critical approach to Scripture, believing that it ultimately led to new insights into the meaning of the Scriptures for Catholic life.[13]

Another key motivation for Brown's biblical scholarship was his conviction that a thorough historical exposition of the biblical materials, pursued with rigor and integrity, was fully compatible with authentic Catholic doctrinal and pastoral tradition. On this point, Brown and other Catholic scholars who held similar convictions, such as Brown's friend and colleague Joseph Fitzmyer, SJ, would be met with some degree of skepticism and opposition, both from those who thought that making room for such doctrinal concerns led to a compromise of historical methodology, but especially from those within the Catholic community who were convinced that the use of historical-critical methods in biblical interpretation inevitably led to a conflict with or betrayal of Catholic teaching. As a leading voice in the American Catholic community, particularly in the wake of the Council, Brown would become a prime target of such critics within the church.[14]

This dual focus on scholarly integrity and fidelity to Catholic tradition reflected, in fact, the deepest commitments of Brown's life as a Catholic priest and as a Sulpician—his devotion to rigorous scholarship and his tenacious loyalty to the Catholic Church. His explanations of his own method of biblical interpretation, whose formulation he tinkered with throughout his professional career, also reflect this dual and interrelated loyalty.

THE LITERAL MEANING PLUS: "WHAT THE BIBLE MEANT AND WHAT THE BIBLE MEANS"

As one commentator noted, "As regards hermeneutical theory, Brown travels light."[15] His interests were directed more to the practice of biblical interpretation rather than to extensive theorizing about a particular method or reflecting on the philosophical underpinnings of a particular approach. This is not to say he hesitated to address questions of method or was incapable of doing so. He discussed the proper method for biblical analysis and interpretation at several key points in his writings. Early on, in his book *The Critical Meaning of the Bible*, Brown examines at length the historical-critical approach to the Bible and its implications for the church.[16] He returned to the question in his articles on the *Sensus Plenior* and on hermeneutics in the first and second editions of *The Jerome Biblical Commentary*.[17] Perhaps his most mature exposition of method is found in his *An Introduction to the New Testament*, a work completed less than two years before his death.[18]

Brown's own articulation of his method, while undergoing some development over time, consistently attempted to hold on to both fundamental dimensions of Scripture reflected in Fitzmyer's definition quoted ealier, namely, a rigorous application of the historical-critical method to discern the "literal" sense of the text and exploring the meaning of Scripture within the traditions and teaching of the Catholic Church—a distinction that Brown variously referred to as the "literal" and the "more than literal" meanings" or "what the Bible meant" as distinct from what it "means," or the "literal" and "wider meanings" of Scripture, or a somewhat less precise term, the "plus-value" meaning of the text.

At its most basic level, this bifurcated perspective involves respecting first of all the "literal" level of the text, which Brown defined, as he would in his introduction to *The Death of the Messiah*:[19] "The literal sense means what the biblical authors intended and conveyed to their audiences by what they wrote."[20] He was also aware that to speak of "what the biblical authors intended" is shorthand for the complex background and layers of meaning a text acquired in the course of its formulation.[21] This is especially true when we are dealing with an ancient text such as the Bible where the experiences, suppositions, language, and literary style of the authors are surely vastly different than our own modern perspectives and experiences. Because the biblical authors wrote in different times and places, they do not necessarily share a common background among themselves. In the case of the Gospels, for example, a saying of Jesus found in one of the Gospels might have its origin in Jesus's own words but was also shaped by the apostolic preaching and teaching of the early community, and may have experienced further transformation as it is incorporated by the evangelist into the written narrative of the Gospel.[22] Once again, he defended the historical-critical method as essential in the attempt to retrieve this literal sense, even though the historical-critical method was not the only valid approach. "When one strips off some of the abuses (e.g., overenthusiasm for detecting sources, arbitrary judgments about historical circumstances) Historical Criticism is concerned with the commonsense observation that readers of any book of Scripture will want to know what the author of that book tried to convey."[23]

Especially in his later writings, such as his *An Introduction to the New Testament*, but already to an extent in his earlier discussions of method, Brown realized that in the search to construct the "literal meaning," that is, the attempt to discern "the intention of the author" from an analysis of the author's written text was challenging.[24] As he put it, "A more delicate issue is the relationship between what the written words convey and what the writers intended. There is a span of possibilities: According to the skill of the writer, a writing may convey what the author wished, or something less, or the opposite, or something other than the author wished or foresaw. In interpreting any work, however, one must start by supposing a *general* correspondence between what the author intended and what the author conveyed. Only by exception, then, do commentators on the Bible have to alert readers to instances where what the words seem to convey may not be what the author intended."[25]

Increasingly, he recognized an aspect of textuality that has been emphasized in modern hermeneutics, namely, the realization that written texts take on a "life of their own." A written text can convey a range of meanings that may go beyond or even in a different direction from the original conscious intent of its author. As Brown noted, "Once a work is written, it enters into dialogue with its readers, including future readers. In modern contextual approaches to hermeneutics…the literary work is not simply the written text as once completed; it comes into being when writing and reader interact. The text is not simply an object on which the interpreter works analytically to extract a permanently univocal meaning; it is a structure that is engaged by readers in the process of achieving meaning and is therefore open to more than one valid meaning. Once written, a text is no longer under the author's control and can never be interpreted twice from the same situation. Although the hermeneutical phraseology is recent, there has been an ongoing meaningful engagement with the text through the centuries."[26]

This same complexity is true in determining the identity and circumstances of the original audiences to whom the various biblical texts were addressed. Brown appeals to the example of Mark 7:3, where the evangelist explains in some detail the Jewish custom of ritual purification before meals, thereby inferring that the author was either Jewish or very familiar with Jewish customs, whereas his intended audience was not.[27] Thus, the probings of historical-criticism into the literary forms, the social and cultural context of the era in which a biblical text was formed, and the probable identity and circumstances of the recipients of a text, as well as other factors, all figure in the attempt to describe the "literal sense."

It should also be noted—since this would become one of the controversial points about the results of using this method—that in many cases probing the "literal" sense also involves judgements about the history behind the text. In other words, it becomes a matter not simply of what the author intended to convey through the written text, but also how one judges the historicity of the events referred to in the author's text. For example, Matthew and Luke both affirm the virginal conception of Jesus, but was there in fact a virginal conception or is this solely some kind of theological assertion in narrative form? As we will see, this is the kind of historical question that Brown would tackle in his pursuit of the "literal" sense of Scripture.[28]

THE WIDER SENSE

The attempt to discover the "more than literal" or "wider" sense of Scripture also involves a complex process. Brown's search to find an organic connection between the literal and more-than-literal meaning of Scripture was first apparent in his exposition of the notion of *Sensus Plenior* ("the fuller sense"), which was the subject of his doctoral dissertation at St. Mary's and the first of his published books, *The Sensus Plenior of Sacred Scripture.*[29] This approach, which was mainly endorsed by Catholic exegetes, attempted to account for a christological reading of Old Testament texts by asserting that infused in the biblical text by God was a level of meaning not intended by or apparent to the original authors. Identifying Christ with the suffering servant passages from Isaiah 53 or understanding Isaiah 7:14 as a prefigurement of the virginal conception of Jesus would be classic examples of this type of interpretation. Such "theological interpretation" of the Old Testament as prefiguring Christ in a variety of ways was typical of patristic interpretation of the Bible.[30] Brown noted that the terminology of a "fuller sense" originated in 1925 by Catholic scholar A. Fernandez and was held in sway in Catholic circles for several decades thereafter. Brown defined "*sensus plenior*" in his article on hermeneutics in the 1990 edition of *The New Jerome Biblical Commentary*, an article that was mainly written by Brown but also with the collaboration of Sandra Schneiders, a colleague who, as already noted, helped Brown become more aware of modern trends in textual interpretation:[31] "The SPlen [*sic*] is the deeper meaning, intended by God but not clearly intended by the human author, that is seen to exist in the words of Scripture when they are studied in the light of further revelation or of development in the understanding of revelation."[32]

As Brown observed, the hypothesis of a "fuller sense" of Scripture was based on the scholastic notion of "instrumental causality" as applied to revelation and the biblical text. God, as the ultimate author or "first cause" of Scripture, used the human author as an "instrument" to compose the text of the Scriptures. As an "instrument," the human author or authors were fully engaged in the composition of the text but were constrained by the limits of their own human capacity, that is, their literary style; the cultural, social, and religious context of their times; their limited scientific knowledge, and so on. Yet God, as the divine "author" or originator of Scripture, could infuse into the text a level of meaning of which the human author might be unaware, but of which later interpreters, conscious of the full span of revelation and salvation history, could detect. One of the intents of this notion of *Sensus Plenior* was to respect the human reality of the biblical author as a true "instrument" in the composition of the Bible and thus honoring the importance of the literal sense of the Scriptures and protecting biblical interpretation from what were perceived as some of the excesses of patristic interpretation that departed far from the literal sense.

However, as Brown himself conceded early on, this approach to biblical interpretation was too tied into scholastic philosophy and its notion of instrumental causality to be useful to modern scholarship.[33] It also seemed to assume that there is a single author for every biblical book, which cannot be the case. Consequently, he himself would no longer appeal to the idea of a *sensus plenior* to explain the wider meaning of the Scriptures beyond the intention of the author.

In elaborating the search for the more-than-literal meaning of the Scriptures, Brown was convinced that there must be a continuing connection between the literal meaning and the more-than-literal meaning. In other words, the literal meaning of the text, discovered primarily through historical-critical methodology, serves as a "control" on the range of more-than-literal meanings. Yet Brown recognized that an appreciation of the "more-than-literal" or "wider" meaning of the biblical text was essential for a Catholic perspective on interpretation of Scripture.

In discussing that "wider meaning" of Scripture in *An Introduction to the New Testament*, Brown cited three factors that lead to this more-than-literal sense. First is the fundamental faith conviction that the ultimate source of biblical revelation was God, expressed in the traditional formula that God was the ultimate "author" of Scripture. As Brown explained, this was "'authorship' not in the sense that God dictated the Bible to human copyists; but that the composition of biblical books by human writers was part of God's providence, so that the OT and the NT might articulate revelation and provide enduring guidance for God's people."[34] Thus, both the conviction that the Scriptures originated with God and were divinely inspired already adds a profound layer of meaning to the biblical text.

Brown also recognized that another wider meaning of the Scriptures is accrued when a particular biblical book is viewed within the context of the canon of Scripture.[35] At this basic level, for example, the inspired books of the Hebrew Scriptures sacred to Judaism are incorporated into the Christian Scriptures along with the New Testament books as the "Old Testament" and are now read in the light of Christian revelation and faith. Similarly, the canonical setting of individual books gives them a new layer of meaning. For example, the so-called Deutero-Pauline writings (such as the Pastoral Letters) are joined in the canon with the "authentic" Pauline letters and are thus seen as part of the evolving theological legacy of Paul.

Finally, other levels of meaning of a biblical text can emerge in the process of the church itself or an individual reader or groups of readers encountering the biblical text and reading and interpreting it from the perspective of their own setting and experience. Thus, the Catholic attempt to relate later Christian dogma and practice to their biblical foundations represents the search for a more-than-literal sense of Scripture, for example, relating the papacy to the ministry of Peter and the dogma of the virginal conception of Jesus to its biblical source or in the establishment of the ordained priesthood and episcopate—to cite examples that would become the subject of Brown's own work of biblical interpretation.[36] Individuals, too, approach the Scriptures seeking more than a literal meaning in the text. As he put it, "People have continued finding in the NT meaning for their own lives as they face new issues; they have asked what the NT books *mean* and not simply what they meant."[37]

AN INCARNATIONAL APPROACH

The implications of Brown's method of interpretation and its theological foundation were addressed in detail by Kevin Duffy, a Marist priest. Duffy completed a doctoral dissertation on Brown's methodology in 1990 at Heythrop College, the Catholic faculty at the University of London, and later published a distillation of his work in an article for *The Heythrop Journal*, "The Ecclesial Hermeneutic of Raymond E. Brown."[38] The latter used Brown's interpretation of the virginal conception of Jesus as an illustration of Brown's method in action. As a courtesy, Duffy sent a copy of his dissertation to Brown at its completion in July of 1990 and asked him if he would have any comments. Brown replied in some detail a few months later, apologizing for the delay, which was due to his move from New York to Menlo Park, California. Brown generally approved of Duffy's work, complimenting him on its accuracy and the courtesy shown to Brown's contributions, but he did offer two points of concern. One was that Duffy may have misunderstood Brown's viewpoint on whether the virginal conception of Jesus was a part of the church's "infallible magisterium." Brown insisted he himself had always thought it *was* part of the ordinary magisterium of Catholic dogma, but, at one point, he was unsure if he was correct about this. Later feedback from theologians assured him that his original conviction was correct.[39] Second, Brown did not agree with Duffy's judgment that there was a lack of social concern in his exegesis, such as minimal reference to liberation theology. Brown responded, "I do resist interpretations that have Jesus or Paul dealing with social problems they never dealt with; I do not resist the application of their principles and attitudes to [contemporary] problems they did not deal with."

Brown ended the letter with one final observation, asking Duffy in the future to use his middle initial in referring to him: "There are four Raymond Browns who have written in Scripture and theology in this century, and several of their writings are constantly being attributed to me even in scientific bibliographies because people do not pay attention to the middle E." Duffy responded to Brown's letter, writing from the Marist House of Studies in Leuven, Belgium, where he was now the local superior. He thanked Brown for his response and for the permission to cite his 1990 letter in his future work. (As noted, Duffy did include reference to Brown's letter in his *Heythrop Journal* article—and was careful to use the middle *E* in Brown's name.)

"THE PHILOSOPHY OF THE METHOD" AND THE "PHILOSOPHY OF THE PRACTITIONER OF THE METHOD"

Duffy's careful and detailed analysis of Brown's methodology helps clarify some of its nuances. He highlights a distinction that Brown made between "the philosophy of the method" and the "philosophy of the practitioner of the method"—a distinction somewhat overshadowed by Brown's more extensive discussion of the fundamental difference between the "literal" and the "more-than-literal" aspects of interpretation.[40] The "philosophy of the method" refers to the tools and procedures utilized to analyze the literal meaning of the text, such as tracing the sources of a document, observing the nuances of the language and literary structure of the text, its social and historical context, the historical and social context of its intended audience, and so on. From this perspective, rigorous and "objective" application of the "philosophy of the method" and its components would be required of all practitioners, no matter what their religious or philosophical views.

However, as Brown noted, there is also the "philosophy of the practitioner of the method," which introduces an important and inescapable reality into the process of determining the literal meaning of a biblical text. The "philosophy of the practitioner" would include the assumptions of the exegete about such things as divine revelation, the possibility of miracles, the authority of church teaching, and so on. Duffy illustrates this in reviewing Brown's discussion of the virginal conception. Brown would assert that applying the "philosophy of the method" to the question of whether the virginal conception of Jesus was a historical fact would result in the conclusion that it is an "open" question. This could be a conclusion shared by all those who would explore the text from a historical-critical perspective. However, viewing the evidence from the viewpoint of a believing Catholic exegete such as Brown would represent, "the philosophy of the practitioner of the method" would lead him to conclude that the evidence favors historicity. Thus, Brown is bringing to bear on his analysis of the gospel's assertion of the virginal conception of Jesus both his use of the historical-critical method and his confidence in the teaching authority of the church, that is, "his philosophy" as a practitioner of the method. The result, Duffy points out, is a "blurring" or a "bridging" between the literal sense and the more-than-literal sense.

This is precisely where Brown's loyalty and commitment to the truth of the church's teaching authority came into play. As he pointed out, the early church did not learn its fundamental faith commitments from reading the New Testament; rather, the Scriptures were considered an expression of the faith of the community and emerged from that faith. The Scriptures were, in a real sense, the "book of the church." In the instance under discussion, the church did not come to its belief in the virginal conception of Jesus by reading the infancy narratives of Matthew and Luke. Rather, Matthew and Luke were expressing a faith conviction they already had as part of the faith community of the early church. Brown was convinced that ultimately there would be no inherent contradiction between faith and reason; that is, ultimately the results of a rational process such as the historical-critical method would in the end not prove contradictory to the Spirit-guided teaching of the church. In other words, the coherence of faith and reason would not permit the clash in a strict sense between a denial of the fact of the virginal conception proven by application of the historical-critical method and the affirmation of the fact of the virginal conception asserted by the magisterium of the church.

Brown conceded, however, that "tension" can exist between the church's teaching and the biblical data that is appealed to in support of it. As Brown noted, "Tension is not an improper relationship between what the Scripture meant to its authors and what it has come to mean in the Church." He went on to add, "Yet personally I would not accept the opposite extreme which allows the literal meaning and the church interpretation to be contradictory in the strict sense."[41] While one would hope in the ability of church theologians and leaders to see "a congruous development from the literal sense of Scripture to the church interpretation of Scripture (or church doctrine based on Scripture)," Brown conceded that is not always the case, such as in the development of Marian doctrine and piety, particularly squaring such development with the stark views of Mary in the Gospel of Mark. Church teaching draws some of its components from some trends in Scripture but not others. However, Brown believed that such "tension" need not be viewed as a negative but could be a source of helping clarify church teaching and "modifying exaggerations"—paving the way to further development of the church's teaching and strengthening its fidelity to the gospel.[42]

THE "RATZINGER" CONFERENCE

One of the most important of Brown's writings for his views on the strengths and limitations of the historical-critical method is the "addenda" he wrote for the final version of his address to the January 1988 Erasmus Conference held in New York on biblical interpretation, sponsored by the Rockford Institute and its Center on Religion and Society under the leadership of Dr. Richard John Neuhaus. Brown's paper at the conference dealt with the contribution of the historical-critical method to ecumenism.[43] At the same conference, the guest of honor, Cardinal Joseph Ratzinger, had sharply criticized certain aspects of the historical-critical method and its use in biblical interpretation.[44] In the light of Ratzinger's critique, Brown was prompted to compare his own views with that of the cardinal, doing so in a very respectful but forthright manner.

A fundamental point made by Brown was that Ratzinger's view of the historical-critical method was influenced by his European context, where employers of the method often used it to discredit any transcendent or inherently sacred aspect of the biblical text. However, Brown's vantage point on the method was influenced by a very different experience, where biblical scholars employed the method in the service of the community of faith.

Brown went on to note both "convergences" and some "differences" between his presentation and that of Cardinal Ratzinger. Convergences included opposition to the kind of "radical criticism" that denied any divine intervention and viewed the Bible simply as a historical artifact. Both also agreed that equally misguided was a "fundamentalist" approach that purported in Ratzinger's words "to take the Bible again in its literal purity, just as it stands and just as the average reader understands it to be."[45] Such a "simplistic literalism" was inadequate. Brown noted that at the Emmaus conference itself, some in the audience asked Ratzinger if the church should not go back to an earlier period before the application of historical criticism to the Scriptures, a view that the cardinal rejected. Likewise, Ratzinger and Brown agreed that the historical-critical method had made a positive contribution to our understanding of the Scriptures. Here, no doubt, Brown was more optimistic about the results than Ratzinger. Ratzinger's point, Brown noted, was not a rejection of the historical-critical method itself but a critique of some of the philosophy of its practitioners and a call for "an honest recognition of its limits."[46] At the same time, Ratzinger affirmed—and Brown agreed—that it was not acceptable simply to impose later church traditions onto the meaning of the biblical text.[47]

On the level of "differences," Brown returned to the fact that his own view was more "optimistic" than that of the cardinal. At the conference, Ratzinger had praised "moderate" users of the historical-critical method and had explicitly referred to Brown himself as an example. In a quotation that would become an important support for Brown and a point of consternation to his critics, Ratzinger replied to a questioner who seemed to be critical of Brown, "I wish we had many scholars like Father Brown."[48] Brown identified the reason why some employers of the method were "moderates"; "The 'lines of development' approach in my paper shows that the so-called moderate positions are accepted because of the thesis that the Bible is the book of the church and that liturgy, church history, and the *sensus fidelium* are major hermeneutical tools."[49] Here, of course, was an approach that was exemplified time and again in Brown's own writings. Brown's optimism was not simply theoretical; he described the positive impact that such a moderate use of the historical-critical method of biblical interpretation had. He referred to the reaction that he personally had received from his use of the method in his work on the infancy narratives in *The Birth of the Messiah.* "Through lectures in every state, and the majority of the dioceses of this country, and through my writing, I have encountered warm enthusiasm for the religious, spiritual, and ecclesiastical wealth of the Scriptures as I interpret them with a strong component of historical criticism. From a book like *The Birth of the Messiah,* I have had now close to a thousand testimonials by clergy of all churches who have found great enrichment for their sermons and teaching." He had a similar experience in feedback concerning his commentaries on the Johannine literature: "My love for the Gospel of John has caught others and made it a factor in their lives. This is what makes me optimistic about the contributions of modern day exegesis."[50]

At the same time, Brown realized that there were causes for concern, a realization, he noted, that brought him closer to the more cautious perspective of Cardinal Ratzinger. The challenge for American biblical scholarship was not so much the influence of Bultmann and Dibelius cited by Ratzinger. Of greater concern on the American scene was the trend on the part of some academics on the university level "to disintegrate the canon," by those who gave equal importance to extracanonical texts, both "for the reconstruction of earliest Christianity but also for what the church of today should be (usually in the direction of less structure and less hierarchical authority)."[51] Similarly, some would claim that such extracanonical texts represented the earliest form of Christianity only to be suppressed by "the more institutional writers of the canonical works."[52]

There were other causes for concern. One was the state of religious education at the college as well as the primary and secondary levels. Many students at Catholic colleges were provided with inadequate theological education or, in the case of biblical studies, with overspecialization at the expense of a broader acquaintance with the Scriptures. Many college professors themselves had good technical training but were poorly equipped theologically. At the primary and secondary levels, many Catholic school teachers had very inadequate religious education themselves. A lament could also be made about the quality of preaching. While some advances had taken place, many priests seemed unable to deal directly or effectively with the Scriptures in their homilies.

Finally, Brown turned to the question of the philosophical groundings of the historical-critical method, a concern expressed by Cardinal Ratzinger. Here his distinction discussed earlier between the "philosophy of the method" and the "philosophy of the practitioner of the method" was germane. The fact that moderate biblical scholars, who considered themselves part of the community of faith, could effectively use the historical-critical method in a constructive way indicated that the problem was not with the intrinsic philosophical foundation of the method itself but with the assumptions—or philosophy—that some scholars who discounted the reality of the transcendent brought to their work.[53] Rather than fixating on one or other philosophical approach to exegetical method, Brown, in his typical pragmatic way, was interested "in a context in which various methods and background can be brought into play in a complementary way to give us as holistic a view of the Scriptures as possible."[54]

AN ECCLESIAL HERMENEUTIC

In concluding his analysis of Brown's methodology, Duffy believes that it ultimately rests on the fundamental doctrine of the incarnation. Church tradition, expressed in *Dei Verbum*, drew a parallel between the mystery of the "Word made flesh," whereby the divine fully assumes human reality in the person of Jesus Christ, and with the fusion of the divine and the human dimensions of Scripture that is, at once, both divinely inspired and expressed in authentically human language. As *Dei Verbum* stated, "Indeed the words of God, expressed in the words of men, are in every way like human language, just as the Word of the eternal Father, when he took on himself the flesh of human weakness, became like men."[55] The incarnation provides the doctrinal basis for both recognizing the sacredness of Scripture as the inspired Word of

God, while at the same time accepting the fully human nature of the biblical text and thus paving the way for using every legitimate means of analyzing a biblical text in the same manner one would analyze any ancient text. Brown reflected on this in *The Critical Meaning of the Bible*: "The fact that the 'word' of the Bible is human and time-conditioned makes it no less 'of God.' In the Bible God communicates Himself to the extraordinary extent that one can say that there is something 'of God' in the words. All other works, patristic, Thomistic, and ecclesiastic, are words about God; only the Bible is the word of God."[56]

Brown also affirmed that some of the fundamental "tensions" inherent in the life of faith, including dealing with Scripture as the Word of God, stem from faith in the incarnation: "I have a sense according to which Christianity, stemming from the incarnation, has to preserve attitudes that are in tension—the incarnation involving the fully divine and the fully human in Jesus, is a primary tension. The church and the sacraments, instituted by Christ and yet going beyond any blueprint or expressed detailed plan uttered by Jesus, involve a tension. So also does a ministry, identifiable with the community from whence the ministry springs and yet set apart for service in the presence of God and representing Christ the priest."[57]

As a consequence, Brown was convinced that use of the historical-critical method in interpreting the Scriptures was not simply an arbitrary choice of method but a necessity resulting from the doctrine of the incarnation, which affirmed the authentically human dimension of the Scriptures as the Word of God. As Duffy concludes, "New methods and approaches explore dimensions of the human reality of biblical texts inaccessible to classical historical criticism. But they will be fruitful in a Roman Catholic context to the extent that they too are based on the same implicitly chalcendonian grasp of the economy of salvation that makes historical criticism an ineliminable ingredient in biblical interpretation. This grasp is at the heart of an ecclesial hermeneutics."[58]

Armed with this "ecclesial" method of interpretation, Brown would go on to fearlessly address some of the most challenging issues facing the church in the modern era.

CHAPTER 4

ENGAGING CRITICAL ISSUES IN THE CHURCH

As noted in the previous chapter, the terms *ecclesial* and *incarnational* seem most apt to describe Raymond Brown's method of biblical interpretation. A constant concern of his biblical exploration was to underscore the ultimate coherence between the message of the Bible and the teaching and practice of the church. In this sense, Brown's approach was truly "ecclesial," reflecting the fundamental criterion for authentic Catholic biblical scholarship later emphasized by Pope Benedict XVI, who, in his response to the General Synod of 2008 on the role of the Scriptures in the life and mission of the church, would challenge Catholic scholars to ply their work in the service of the community of faith.[1] Brown's exegetical method was also "incarnational" in the sense that he tenaciously believed that the biblical texts were grounded in history and could not be properly understood without taking into account the original historical, social, and cultural contexts of the Scriptures. Christian faith itself was grounded in the historical reality of Jesus Christ, the Word made flesh. For that reason, Brown insisted on the primacy of the historical-critical method of biblical inquiry.[2] As his own career of teaching and writing developed, he recognized that the historical-critical method was not the only legitimate approach to biblical interpretation, but for him it remained an anchor for all other approaches.

This combination of rigorous historical-critical inquiry and concern for the vitality of the church and its teaching is evident in virtually every lecture and publication Brown composed over the length of his remarkable career. He was convinced that sound biblical scholarship in the service of the community of faith would not only provide a foundation for the church's life and teaching but would also challenge the church in its ongoing responsibility of constant reform and renewal. He recognized that biblical scholarship and theology were not the only voices to be heard—ultimately, decisions about the life and direction of the church were the responsibility of legitimate church authority, namely, the bishops and the pope. But he did not hesitate to bring the results of his biblical scholarship into the ongoing discussion of the church's life at both the academic and popular levels.

Most of Brown's popular publications appeared during the period from the late 1960s, in the immediate aftermath of the Second Vatican Council, and on through the postconciliar period presided over by Pope Paul VI and Pope John Paul II during the 1980s and '90s. As we will see, virtually every lecture Brown gave on a popular level was triggered by the sometime turbulent debates that ran through Roman Catholicism during this period, particularly within the United States. Resignations from the priesthood and religious life began to mushroom, accompanied by debates about the nature of priesthood and the requirements of priestly celibacy. Religious communities, prompted by the reforms of the Council, were researching their founding charisms and raising substantial questions about their mission and their way of life, including the wearing of the religious habit. The quest for more collegiality in the church's governance raised questions about episcopal authority and even about the nature of the papal office. The resurgence of the Catholic biblical movement that was also a product of the Council had an impact on Catholic theology, raising questions about scholastic methods and traditions and subsequently causing alarm in some more traditional Catholics who feared an erosion of Catholic doctrine. At the same time, enthusiasm for ecumenical dialogue—again prompted by the spirit of the Council—not only fostered life-giving relationships among Catholics and Protestants but also contributed to debates about the Catholic Church's ecclesiology and sacramental practices.

Much of this debate and its accompanying reassessment of the church's theology and practice was exhilarating for those who experienced it, but it also brought some degree of chaos and acrimony. Some Catholics of a more traditional bent feared that the church was unraveling and losing its soul. Others on the liberal side of the equation chafed under what they considered the church's hesitancy and the slow pace of true reform. Much of Brown's work took place during the papacy of John Paul II, who was the first non-Italian pope in centuries and whose tenure would be second in length only to Pope Pius IX. John Paul II was elected to the Petrine office in 1978 after the shocking death of John Paul I (who was pope for only thirty-three days, one of the shortest reigns in papal history) and would be a dominating figure in the church until his death in 2005. The tensions in the postconciliar church would intensify during Pope John Paul II's time in office and would be the focus of much of his pastoral concerns. There is no doubt that this remarkable pope saw an important part of his mandate as that of restoring church discipline and reaffirming doctrinal stability. For example, discussions of collegiality were tempered and such questions as ordination of women ruled out entirely. Some significant theologians were sanctioned and even silenced. At the same time, this pope also drew attention to the church's social teaching and, through a multitude of papal visits, emphasized the universality and diversity of the church's global life.

The issues and atmosphere of this period in the church's life during the final decades of the twentieth century made a strong impact on Brown's pastoral and popular writings and dictated the topics that absorbed him. While his focus was always on the biblical aspects of these issues, it is not difficult to detect in his writings his own personal views about these various controversies and debates. In his popular publications, even more so than in his major academic works, one also learns a lot about Raymond Brown the human being and priest.[3] Clearly, as we will see in the following sampling of his writings, the "philosophy of the practitioner of the method" had a major influence on Brown's work.[4]

REACHING FOR A POPULAR AUDIENCE

From the outset of his scholarly work, Brown did not shy away from popularization. Bringing the message of the Scriptures to the wider church was a fundamental drive of his ministry, both as a scholar and a Catholic priest. His commitment to popular writing coincided with Brown's active pastoral practice as a priest throughout his academic career, as noted earlier.[5] When he was on the faculty of St. Mary's in Baltimore, he celebrated Mass and preached each Sunday on a regular basis at a local parish; during his stay at Union Theological Seminary in

New York, he was a regular celebrant of Mass at Corpus Christi parish across the street; in his final years at Menlo Park, he took turns celebrating the daily Mass for the sisters who ran the seminary food service. He occasionally gave retreats to priests and sisters. Many of his graduate students, particularly at Union Theological Seminary, turned to him as a priest for spiritual guidance, including Protestant students. Brown never shied from his identity as a Catholic priest.

One of his first publications to catch popular attention was his 1960 contribution to the newly established series *New Testament Reading Guides*, published by Liturgical Press of St. John's Benedictine Abbey in Collegeville, Minnesota.[6] Brown had written to his provincial expressing his excitement about the project, which he described as a publication for a lay audience but drawing on serious biblical scholarship. Brown's commentary—which prefigured his major two-volume commentary on the Gospel of John and a further volume on the Johannine Letters in the Anchor Bible series—flew off the shelf and would go on, in Brown's own estimate, to sell more than a million copies over the lifetime of this successful series.

Another major publishing project geared to bringing the Bible to a wider Catholic audience was *The Jerome Biblical Commentary*.[7] Brown saw the need for such a one-volume commentary on the whole Bible from his own dissatisfaction in using an earlier work, *A Catholic Commentary on Sacred Scripture*, edited by Bernard Orchard and published in 1953.[8] Brown believed that because there had been so many developments in biblical scholarship in recent decades and particularly since many new Catholic scholars were now in the field that the time was right for a major new effort.[9] He had talked over the idea with Roland Murphy, the acclaimed Carmelite Old Testament scholar, of having it published by the Catholic Biblical Association itself. In a letter sharing his plans with his provincial Fr. McDonald and seeking his permission he wrote,

> Fr. Roland Murphy and I have been drawing up plans for a Commentary on the whole Bible to be approved and published by the Catholic Biblical Association. We would be the editorial board, in the sense of listing the articles, determining the contents and format, and lining up the contributors. We would exercise the right of rejection. But we plan to get another man to do the actual editorial work of getting the

articles to jibe with one another. I would expect to contribute some articles to this commentary if it ever gets beyond the drawing board. We hope to submit our plans to the 1961 CB [*sic*] meeting for approval. Neither of us plans to put too much actual time; someone else can do the work and get the glory. We want to be sure it starts (we need it desperately) and that i[t] has quality. I hope these writings meet with your approval; please inform me if they don't.[10]

The reaction of the Catholic Biblical Association to the proposed project at its summer 1961 meeting was positive, but it would be published through Prentice-Hall. In a follow-up letter in September 1961, Brown described the current plan for the project: "As I mentioned in the Feb 12 note, Fr. Murphy, OCarm, and I were thinking of editing a Commentary on Sacred Scripture (a large two volume affair—some 8000 typed pages of MS—designed to become the seminary text book in the USA). We have decided to bring in Fr. J. Fitzmyer, SJ, as a third editor. I will take the General Introduction, Fr. Murphy will take the OT, and Fr. Fitzmyer will take the NT....I will make some short personal contributions to the Commentary, but my main work with [*sic*] be as editor."[11]

No less than Cardinal Augustin Bea, SJ, the great hero of the Second Vatican Council who encouraged Pius XII's encyclical *Divino Afflante Spiritu* and its liberating effect on Catholic biblical studies, wrote a laudatory foreword to the volume. Fitzmyer confessed that he himself had tried to organize a Catholic commentary series but "was having little success in rounding up potential authors," so he was eager to join Brown and Murphy in their proposed venture. But there was still a struggle to get the work completed: "After a number of stormy years spent in prodding procrastinating contributors, we managed to publish the JBC in December of 1968."[12] Here, too, this publishing project would prove to be immensely popular, with over three hundred thousand copies sold in the United States and Canada.

A second revised edition, two-thirds of which included new authors and articles, appeared as *The New Jerome Biblical Commentary* in 1990 with the same trio as editors.[13] This time another luminary of the church with solid biblical credentials, Cardinal Carlo Maria Martini, archbishop of Milan, would write the foreword. Before his ordination as bishop, the Jesuit Martini had been rector of the Pontifical Biblical Institute and was a published author in his own right. He described this new edition as "born of the patient and devoted dedication of the best of English-speaking Catholic exegetes."[14] It should be noted that Brown himself was involved in the writing of seven of the nineteen topical articles included in the volume and did yeoman work in personally recruiting authors for the various commentaries and articles. This edition, too, would become a widespread resource for Catholic biblical study for college and university work and graced the personal libraries of pastors and teachers throughout the country. The volume almost did not make it into print. Brown was disturbed that the projected purchase price of the revised edition was out of range for students' budgets and threatened to withdraw from the project. He reluctantly agreed to go ahead when the publisher explained the costs of publishing such a massive, multiauthored volume.

Another major biblical project, prompted also by the biblical renewal surrounding the Second Vatican Council, was a new translation of the Bible sponsored by the American Catholic bishops to be titled the New American Bible (NAB), first published in 1970. The history of how the first and subsequent editions of this translation evolved is complicated, caught up in part with intrachurch disputes about the style of translation especially for liturgical use, the content of the annotations that accompanied the translation, and the question of inclusive language.[15] The NAB was preceded by the Confraternity of Christian Doctrine edition begun in the early 1940s, based on the Vulgate, the prevailing Latin translation traced back to Jerome. However, with the publication of Pius XII's *Divino Afflante Spiritu* and its exhortation for biblical scholars to make new translations based on the original biblical languages, the earlier work of the Confraternity translation was put aside in favor of new efforts based on the Hebrew and Greek texts, taking place during the 1950s and '60s. This translation was finally published in 1970 as the New American Bible. Prompted by Vatican II's Decree on Divine Revelation, *Dei Verbum*, and its call for annotated editions of the Bible, the NAB also included official annotations and footnotes that were considered an integral part of the translation itself.

Brown did considerable work on the translation of John's Gospel for this project. However, the nearly completed text was entrusted to a final literary editor who made a substantial number of changes that became highly controversial. Many felt the final version was too colloquial and, in fact, had introduced errors into the text.[16] For his part, Brown was dismayed by what had happened to his translation of John and finally withdrew his name from the list of translators. The dissatis-faction experienced by Brown and others would be vindicated when an entirely new translation of the New Testament replaced the first edition in 1986. Brown himself would not be involved in any further biblical translation work, preferring to pour his energy and biblical prowess into engagement with other pastoral issues.

CRISES FACING THE CHURCH

Brown selected the topics of his more popular biblical publications mostly because they were issues in play in the post–Vatican II church. Some of his lectures and articles were dry runs for the major academic works he was undertaking, such as topics related to the infancy narra-tives in the time running up to his publication of *The Birth of the Mes-siah* (1977), and on the passion narratives preparing for his two-volume study, *The Death of the Messiah* (1994).[17] But most of his lectures and more popular publications were prompted by issues then under debate in the church of his day.[18]

Priest and Bishop

One of Brown's most influential works—and a source of consid-erable controversy on the part of some of his critics—was his study of the biblical foundations for the Catholic hierarchical order of priest and bishop, a study that also spilled over into his views on the papal office itself. This topic was taken up primarily in his 1970 publication *Priest and Bishop: Biblical Reflections*, a work he dedicated to his friend and mentor, Msgr. Patrick Skehan, professor in the Catholic University's Semitics department.[19] From the outset, Brown stated that the moti-vation for writing his book was the ongoing debate about the nature of Catholic priesthood and questions about episcopal authority. "With the whole Christian world looking on, we Catholics have entered a sometimes acrimonious debate with ourselves as to what should be expected of those who are in the special ministry of the Church, i.e., the priesthood—What manner of life should our priests live and what work should they do? Also under review is the role of the bishop, said traditionally to possess the fullness of the priesthood. We are asking whether the authority structure on all levels should be more collegial or

democratic and what such a change would mean in light of the traditional theology of the episcopate."[20] He also noted the "immediate" origins of his study. The chapter on priesthood was prompted by a request
from a diocese to offer a paper on the biblical origins of the priesthood
as a contribution to a debate about what were the proper functions of
Catholic priests. The chapter on bishops was triggered by Brown's experience of discovering a growing gap between some bishops and their
priests, with the bishops believing that their office as "successors of the
apostles" required them to be "responsible for all the major decisions of
the Church." His study of the episcopate was also inspired by his ecumenical involvement and his awareness of the obstacle posed by Catholic claims to "apostolic succession." Brown was convinced "both for the
internal health of the Roman Catholic Church and for its relationship
to other Christian bodies it was imperative that Catholics know some
of the limitations of the claim that the episcopate stands in apostolic
succession."[21]

Brown began his work with the disclaimer that he was not providing an exhaustive biblical study of these issues but would focus on
certain aspects of the question. He anticipated that even with this limited scope, his conclusions might be controversial—and in this he was
surely correct. He saw himself as occupying the middle ground between
"conservative readers" who would be dismayed at what they perceived
as questioning traditional ideas about the origin of the priesthood and
episcopate, and "liberals" who might be angered that Brown found biblical support for some traditional ideals of the priesthood and episcopate. Standing in the middle ground on most church issues was always
Brown's preference.

Our goal here is not to repeat all of Brown's carefully laid out case
but to note his way of approach and some of his major conclusions. His
study of the origins of the priesthood and the role of bishop follows a
pattern that would be typical of so much of his work on pastoral topics.
After a statement of the issue in question and a survey of traditional
church teaching and practice, he would then examine the pertinent biblical data, using the historical-critical method, and then, based on the
conclusions of his biblical inquiry, turn rapidly to the implications for
current church issues, typically ending up supporting official Catholic
teaching but casting it in a way compatible with its biblical roots. It
should be noted that, although Brown would not describe himself as a

theologian, many of his writings would go into considerable depth in articulating the nuances of the church's theological positions.

He began his study of the biblical origins of priesthood by noting that the term *priest* is not used in reference to any church minister in the New Testament, but reserved for the singular role of Jesus as "priest" in the Letter to the Hebrews, or applied to the priestly role of the entire people of God in the First Letter of Peter, which refers to Christians as a "holy priesthood, to offer spiritual sacrifices acceptable to God through Jesus Christ" (1 Pet 2:5). Brown observed that this text refers primarily to the holiness of God's people and not to the exercise of cult. He also objected to the term "priesthood of the laity" since 1 Peter is speaking of the entirety of the Christian community. To contrast the so-called priesthood of the laity with the cultic priesthood of the Old Testament and apply it to the Christian community is, in Brown's view, an error found in the interpretation of both Martin Luther and Hans Küng. The term *priest*, which will only be used of a specific Christian ministry in the second century, finds its origin in the Old Testament priesthood. Brown surveyed the functions of the priesthood within the temple economy of Israel and found there some traits that will come into play in later Christian notions of priesthood, such as the expectation of holiness on the part of the priest, a certain "separation" from the people at large because of their sacred work, the need for financial support, the roles of proclaiming God's Word, teaching, and offering sacrifice. From the point of view of the earliest Jewish Christian community, the Old Testament priesthood remained valid, as the Jerusalem Christians themselves frequented the temple and were involved in its cultic activity.

The application of the term *priest* to a specific Christian ministry would take place only after the New Testament period and only when developing Christian theology highlighted sacrificial aspects of the Eucharist itself, a realization, Brown believed, that was not yet apparent during the earliest decades of the church. Only later when the Christian community would begin to experience itself as a separate community from Judaism and when the Eucharist was seen as an "unbloody" sacrifice replacing the sacrifices of the no longer existing Jerusalem temple, would the term *priest* be applied to those who presided at the Eucharist.

There were, however, other ministerial roles that would later be combined within the role of the Christian priesthood. Brown listed the role of "disciple" as one called to give the entirety of his life and energy to following Christ, and that of "apostle" as one sent forth as Paul was to proclaim the gospel to the world in homage to the risen Christ. Other aspects of the apostolic role exemplified by Paul would also contribute to the notion of priestly ministry, namely, that of prayer, suffering, fraternal correction, and taking up collections on behalf of the community.

Also critical for the fully developed role of "priest" in the postapostolic church was the New Testament category of the "presbyter-bishop," which developed as the early communities themselves became more established. It seems that at the earliest stages of the community, there was no real distinction between the role of *presbyter* or "elder" and that of the *episkopos* or "bishop." Only later would the leadership evolve into the central authority of a single bishop over a local community, with the collaboration of other "elders" or presbyters. In contrast to the itinerant and charismatic style of an "apostle" in the Pauline mode, the presbyter-bishop was residential and concerned about the ongoing well-being of a local community—and thus more "institutional" in character.

Missing from this list of New Testament categories, Brown noted, is the role of "presider" at Eucharist. The New Testament is silent about who presided at the Eucharist. There is no compelling reason to believe that only "apostles" or "presbyter-bishops" performed this role. This brings Brown to one of his most radical conclusions, "radical" at least from the viewpoint of the more traditional description of the origin of the priesthood. "Thus there is simply no compelling evidence for the classic thesis that the members of the Twelve always presided when they were present, and that there was a chain of ordination passing the power of presiding at the Eucharist from the Twelve to missionary apostles to presbyter-bishops."[22] Although Brown did not discuss the origin of other priestly functions such as the authority to forgive sins or anoint the sick, he noted that the same question about such an apostolic "chain of ordination" would apply. "The more plausible substitute for the chain theory is the thesis that sacramental 'powers' were part of the mission of the Church and that there were diverse ways in which the Church (or the communities) designated individuals to exercise those powers—the essential element always being church or community consent (which was tantamount to ordination, whether or not that consent was signified by a special ceremony such as the laying on of hands.)."[23] Later, Brown observed, such consent by the church would be more formalized and those empowered to preside at Eucharist would be reserved to bishops and priests, as these roles themselves were more clearly designated and formally defined. Evidence for this development, he observed, can be found in the second and later century writings of Clement, Ignatius of Antioch, and Tertullian, with traces also found in the Didache.

Consequences for Priesthood and Episcopate

While from the viewpoint of biblical and historical scholarship Brown's portrayal of the origin of the priesthood and episcopate would not be surprising, such a portrayal was a radical change from the traditional Catholic narrative about the origin of these key hierarchical structures. Both traditional Vatican texts and more popular Catholic devotion would trace the "ordination" of the apostles as priests by Jesus himself at the Last Supper and would see the apostles in turn ordaining bishops to preside over local churches and through them and the laying on of hands, ordaining priests to be the celebrants of the Eucharist. No wonder, as we will consider later, some church officials such as Cardinal Lawrence J. Shehan, Brown's own bishop in Baltimore, and others would be alarmed at what they considered an undermining of Christ's institution of the essential structures of the church.[24]

Although Brown would, in a sense, "let the chips fall" in describing as clearly as he could the probable historical origins of these church offices, his goal was not to undermine Catholic Church order but to bring relief to some of its problems. First, he found in the New Testament roles that ultimately contributed to the profile of the Catholic priest, biblical support for many of the key qualities and functions traditionally attributed to the priest. Even the echoes of the Old Testament role of the priest provided some important antecedents such as the notion of holiness, and the role of teaching and proclaiming God's will. New Testament antecedents such as that of discipleship affirmed the need for lifelong devotion to Christ, for taking on a style of life that reflected Jesus's own rejection of possessions for the sake of the gospel, and argued in favor of the permanency of priestly commitment as opposed to the "part time" ministry being proposed by some. Celibacy, too, could find its roots in the radical nature of Jesus's own devotion to his mission, and even though mandatory celibacy would be imposed later in the church's history, Brown maintained it had strong biblical roots. Likewise, the mandate to teach and preach the gospel and to lead the community of the faithful—all had roots in the various New Testament roles that would later be merged into the role of the priest. The aspect of apostolic suffering for the sake of the mission exemplified by

Paul was also an important reality for the contemporary priesthood to keep in mind and not give in to discouragement or easy complaint.

At the same time, Brown believed that part of the tension and debate about the role of the priest in the contemporary church stemmed from the combination of multiple roles and ideals that have been woven into the job description of the modern priesthood. Roles that were at one time carried out by multiple individuals in the early Christian community have been totally absorbed by the ideal of the contemporary priesthood. Perhaps it was time that some of the roles heaped on the priest should be unbundled and assigned to other ministerial roles within the church.

In a similar vein, Brown also defended the Catholic conviction that the bishops were the "successors" to the apostles; obviously there was not succession in the sense that the "chain" theory of ordination claimed, but from another perspective there *was* a connection with the New Testament role of the "apostle." The answer might be found in the differing definitions of *apostle* found in the theology of Luke-Acts on the one hand and that of Paul on the other. Luke gave attention to the role of the "Twelve apostles" as the bridge between the ministry of Jesus and the founding of the community. For the most part, the Lucan apostles were not missionaries nor were they presiders over local churches. They were, however, responsible for key decisions taken early on that would have an impact on the whole church, such as the establishment of leadership for the Hellenistic Jewish Christians and the momentous decision to accept Gentiles into the community. For Paul, on the other hand, being designated as an "apostle" meant encountering the risen Christ, accepting the role of missionary to the Gentiles, and experiencing in his own life the death and resurrection of Jesus. Paul, in turn, recognized in such figures as Peter and James, the overall authority of the "Twelve," even if sometimes grudgingly. While not being a resident pastor of a local church, however, Paul was dedicated to founding and nurturing local communities, while the Twelve portrayed by Luke seemed to view their role in relation to the entirety of the Christian community.

The formal role of the presbyter-bishop that would emerge in the second century and beyond combined various aspects of both the "Twelve" portrayed by Luke and the missionary "apostle" exemplified by Paul. Similar to the Twelve, the bishop would be more "residential" than the charismatic and itinerant role of the Pauline apostle. However, the "bishops" would draw on both models in their essential role of "pastoral care"; Paul would appoint leaders in local communities who would continue the pastoral care the apostle had initiated in founding these communities.[25] So Brown concludes, "Although quite different in many ways from the Pauline missionary apostles, the presbyter-bishops did eventually succeed to these apostles in the exercise of pastoral care over the churches the apostles had founded." Likewise, "the affirmation that the episcopate was divinely established or established by Christ himself can be defended in the nuanced sense that the episcopate gradually emerged in a church that stemmed from Christ and this emergence was (in the eyes of faith) guided by the Holy Spirit."[26]

This eventual combination in the later role of the presbyter-bishop of both the Lucan notion of the "Twelve Apostles" and the Pauline notion of the missionary apostle became a strength as well as a liability. Here, Brown would make his leap to the contemporary scene. Some bishops, burdened by the belief that they are the direct successors of the apostles, could be tempted to believe they were required to make all pastoral decisions, even in the case of issues that were not their expertise. The inclusion of the ideal of the Pauline missionary apostle in the mix suggests that in addition to pastoral care for a local church, the bishop must also have the innovative and charismatic power to pronounce on other more extensive issues, beyond their local competence. Thus, as in the case of the priesthood, tracing the biblical origins of these roles reveals some of the inordinate expectations that might be laid on bishops and priests. Some relief, Brown suggests, might be found if bishops, for example, who were willing to count more on the expertise and advice of theologians and other resource persons—not to diminish their episcopal authority but to find collegial support for their responsibilities.[27]

The Papacy

Brown also turned his attention to the biblical underpinnings of the papacy, both in his 1975 work, *Biblical Reflections on Crises Facing the Church*, and in his 1990 book, *Responses to 101 Questions on the Bible*. In both instances, the prompt for his study was his concern about the obstacles that Catholic claims for papal authority posed for ecumenism.[28] The chapter in *Biblical Reflections on Crises Facing the Church* is titled "An Ecumenical Understanding of Peter and a Theology of the Papacy," already a hint of how Brown would proceed: a historical-critical study of the role of Peter in the New Testament would then be related to ecclesial and theological claims about the papacy. Brown would draw substantially on the 1973 study *Peter in the New Testament* that was a byproduct of his participation for several years in the official dialogue between Lutherans and Roman Catholics.[29] A succinct presentation of his view is found in the series of questions Brown poses in *Responses to 101 Questions on the Bible*, specifically questions 97 to 100. The first asks about the New Testament evidence for Peter's role in the church: "Would the early Christians have recognized him [Peter] as the head of the church?"[30] Brown responds by emphasizing the important distinction between the historical role of Peter during his lifetime and the symbolic dimensions of the role attributed to Peter in the later New Testament writings, what he would designate as the "Petrine trajectory." The "historical" Peter apparently was something of a leader among the early disciples of Jesus, the first called among the disciples and often speaking on their behalf. However, in the postresurrection portrayals of Peter, his role expands. In Luke's Gospel and the Acts of the Apostles, he is the most important member of the Twelve; in such texts as Matthew 16:16; Luke 22:31–34; and John 21:17–19, Peter is ascribed significant pastoral leadership in relation to the community of disciples, with "enormous symbolic value for the foundation and overall pastoral care of the church."[31] But, Brown notes that Peter is not the sole leader in the early church—there are other figures such as James, the brother of the Lord who is a significant leader of the Jerusalem community, along with Paul who towers as the missionary to the Gentiles. Nor is there any indication that Peter was designated as the leader of any local church.

A related question is whether Peter can be described as "the first of the bishops of Rome" (question no. 99). In response, Brown notes that by the end of the second century, Irenaeus lists Peter as the first bishop of Rome. Yet during the lifetime of Peter, the authority structure of the community in Rome would not yet be that developed, and it is unlikely that Peter would have been considered "bishop of Rome" by his contemporaries. But Peter did visit Rome and was martyred there, so Brown states, "I would suggest that in the 60s, when Peter came to Rome, this first among the Twelve was the most prominent figure in the Roman Church. In the language of the end of the second century, that would have caused him to be listed as the bishop of the Church of Rome, even if Peter's contemporaries in the 60s might not have used that term for him."[32]

Taking things a step further, Brown asks, "Would Christians of New Testament times have looked on Peter as the Pope?" (question no.

100). Once again, he cautions that we must be careful not to attribute later terminology and its implications to circumstances in the first century. Certain historical developments would lead to the full evolution of the papal ministry: (1) the role of Rome as the imperial capital, (2) the tradition that the apostles Peter and Paul were martyred there, and (3) the role of the presbyters of Rome during the second century in "resisting heretical ideas and insisting on the purity of the Christian faith."[33] "All these factors colored the description of the bishop of Rome as the pope, since they contributed to an understanding of the Holy See as having responsibility toward and for the scattered churches of the empire and for preserving orthodox faith."[34] Thus, Brown concludes, "Perhaps the proper way of phrasing an answerable question pertinent to the 60s is not, 'Would the Christians of that period have looked on Peter as the pope?' but 'Would Christians of that period have looked on Peter as having roles that would contribute in an essential way to the development of the role of the papacy in the subsequent church?' I think the answer is yes."[35]

In considering the ecumenical implications of this view of the papacy, Brown notes that, from the vantage point of faith, the Spirit guided the early church to develop and adapt its authority structures in a certain trajectory as it met new historical circumstances and demands. Does that suggest that further adaptation could be undertaken? As he notes, "The very notion of a Petrine trajectory in the NT where the image of Peter was adapted to meet the needs of a Church after his death supposes the possibility for the continued adaptability of this image to meet the needs of the present Church or the Church of the future."[36]

Women's Ordination

In at least one published essay, Brown also tackled the issue of women's ordination, found in a chapter in *Biblical Reflections on Crises Facing the Church*, derived from a lecture given in 1975.[37] At the outset, he cites an experience he had at Union Theological Seminary where he spotted a Jesuit seminarian from Woodstock (at that time in a collaborative arrangement with Union) in secular garb passing a Protestant woman seminarian wearing a Roman collar—leading Brown to wonder if he were seeing a vision of the future! Ordination of women, he surmised, would become another issue effecting ecumenical relations between Roman Catholicism and other ecclesial bodies. It should be noted that Brown's essay on this topic preceded by almost twenty years Pope John Paul II's controversial 1994 apostolic letter *Ordinatio Sacerdotalis*, which declared that "the Church has no authority whatsoever to confer priestly ordination on women and that this judgment is to be definitively held by all the Church's faithful."[38] This declaration effectively put on hold any public discussion of this topic in Catholic circles.[39]

Brown's approach to this issue deviates a bit from his usual pattern of relating contemporary church debates to the biblical evidence. In fact, he notes that he is not going to concentrate on some of the controversial New Testament texts dealing with women, such as 1 Corinthians 14:33–34, where Paul apparently states, "Women should be silent in the churches," or even reaching back to the question of whether the Creation account in Genesis 2 provides evidence for the subordination of women to men. He does note, however, that such texts "cannot be repeated as normative today in a different sociology [*sic*] without first investigating whether the change of social condition does not require a different expression of God's will for His people."[40] Before considering the biblical connections to this issue, he first notes several "nontheological factors" that pose serious difficulties if Catholic women were ordained priests, such as economics (whether there would be job availability, although he concedes that in the case of the Roman Catholic Church the clergy shortage offsets this), social factors such as traditional views about the role of women in some cultures, sexual factors such as what would be the impact of celibate men and women working in close proximity or studying together in seminaries (Brown wryly notes that the presence of women in seminaries would undoubtedly lift the intellectual tone), organizational difficulties, such as having women as bishops, and ecumenical difficulties such as the impact on Roman Catholicism's relationship with the Orthodox churches. Brown allows some humor to break through on this topic. For example, he asks his audience to consider how the ordination of women would play out in the Italian church, in a country where the "Italian women's liberation movement…has scarcely dawned" or, he confesses, he himself "would be staggered at the thought of a woman monsignor. Madame, you may have come a long way, but after all!"[41]

When Brown turns from his list of nontheological factors to the most important theological factor—whether the New Testament supports the ordination of women—he emphatically states that he himself is not in a position to give a firm answer. As a biblical scholar and theologian, he was willing to contribute to this question but was not authorized to give a final answer. He also confessed that as a celibate male and coming from a family without a female sibling, he felt particularly unqualified to discuss the proper role of women in the church. Instead he proposed situating the question within the context of New Testament ecclesiologies. Specifically, he wanted to explore "how the acceptance or refusal of NT criticism shapes one's ecclesiology, and how one's ecclesiology or view of the Church is often decisive as to whether one thinks that women can or should be ordained."[42] To that end, he proposed three basic ecclesiological models:

1. A "blueprint ecclesiology" that "supposes that God has given us a blueprint of the Church in which all the basic structures and ways of sanctification were mapped out" ahead of time. While minor adjustments might be made, the basic hierarchical structure of the church built on the apostles and prophets such as stated in Ephesians 2:20 cannot be altered. In this view, "blueprint ecclesiology does not allow for the ordination of women, for they were not sketched by God into the hierarchical section of the building." This view would also affirm that Jesus "thought about the Church and clearly founded it during his ministry or immediately after the resurrection." In such a "blueprint ecclesiology...it is clear that if Jesus wanted women priests, he would not have ordained only men." Brown labeled this reasoning as a prime example of Catholic "fundamentalism,"[43] but, in fact, it is an argument that appears in official Catholic statements on the matter such as *Ordinatio Sacerdotalis* itself, which cites as one of the reasons militating against the ordination of women "the example recorded in the Sacred Scriptures of Christ choosing his Apostles only from among men." Brown argued that the basis for this type of blueprint ecclesiology was "shaken" by the Pontifical Biblical Commission's 1964 statement on the historical truth of the Gospels and by Vatican II's Dogmatic Constitution on Divine Revelation, *Dei Verbum*, both of which affirm that the Gospels represent a "developing first-century tradition, a tradition

that begins with Jesus but goes beyond him," as the life of the church unfolded under the guidance of the Spirit.

2. Another type of ecclesiology Brown labels as "Erector-set" ecclesiology.[44] In this view of the church and its development, "Christians are free to go ahead and build the Church as utility directs. God (or Jesus) gave a commission to build a community but no blueprint. He gave some of the components, like pieces in an erector set, but no book of instructions, other than that the Church should be so built as to serve well the people of God who live in it."[45] This view of the church would pave the way for later innovations, such as the ordination of women. "If Jesus did not specify everything, and if many ecclesiastical developments were the product of the Holy Spirit's leading the Christian community, why cannot the Holy Spirit lead in another direction at a later period?"[46] Brown points to the example of the Christian priesthood itself, which, as noted earlier, appears as a development beyond the New Testament period. While Brown admits the growing popularity of this view of the church among some Catholics, he has some serious reservations about it. "In place of a historically dubious blueprint ecclesiology, they [the adherents of this view] tend to construct a sociological model of the Church that may be equally insensitive to the complexities of history."[47]

3. Brown confesses he has no convenient label for what he views as the preferable middle way ecclesiology that proposes neither a fixed blueprint nor an "an invitation to build anything you want." In this middle way, so characteristic of Brown's moderate approach noted earlier, the "will of Christ" and the guidance of the Spirit are determinative for the nature and structures of the church as it develops through the centuries, even when discerning the will of Christ is not always clear. "History and sociology almost certainly played a role in the development of Church structure, especially the pattern of the single bishop and the college of presbyters which had emerged by the end of the first century; but our earliest testimonies to this structure see it as symbolically

preserving the model of Jesus surrounded by his disciples. And so the will of Christ has meaning in this ecclesiology, even if the working out of that will is conceived in a subtler way than it is proposed in blueprint ecclesiology."[48]

Applying this middle-ground ecclesiology to the issue of women's ordination is not an easy task, Brown concedes. The "age-long custom of ordaining only men" cannot be easily dismissed, but, at the same time, others "may judge that the breaking down of human barriers by the grace of Christ, the barriers of origin, race, and social rank, will only be complete when the barrier of sex is broken within the Church. They may see equality of women in ministry as the final working out of Galatians 3:28: "There is neither Jew nor Greek; there is neither slave nor free; there is neither male nor female; for you are all one in Christ Jesus."[49] Likewise, some would note that the traditional identification of the priest as "another Christ" in a very special way, necessitates that the priest be male. However, Brown notes that "others will choose to attach the symbolism not to maleness but to humanity."[50] God's grace comes to us not through maleness as such but through a "human being like us in everything except sin." "If the theology of the priest as another Christ is meant to draw attention to the continued mediatorship of *humanity* in God's giving of grace, one might argue that a priesthood involving both males and females is a better symbol of humanity and overcomes the biological limitation of the incarnation."[51]

Brown concludes his discussion of this topic by noting that there can be "honest and intelligent disagreement among theologians" on this issue. However, he also observes that no matter how the Roman Catholic Church decides this issue, "a better context of that decision will be created by giving women public roles in relation to the celebration of the eucharist"—he refers here to altar girls, women lectors, incorporating women into "dialogue sermons," and having women as ministers of communion. He also urged the "encouragement of women theologians, the constitution of theology schools for Catholic women, and the introduction of women professors into Catholic seminaries."[52]

Brown remained uncertain on how the ordination question in the Catholic Church would be resolved. But, he observes that neither the pope nor bishop nor theologian "could have predicted what the Catholic attitude toward ecumenism would be in 1965. Am I wrong in 1975 in suspecting that the Holy Spirit who moved the Roman Catholic Church through an amazing decade of change with regard to ecumenism might very well move the Church through another amazing decade of change as regards the role of women?"[53] The future of this issue would turn out to be much more complex and controversial than Brown could discern at this stage. Without doubt Catholic women, at least in the United States, became more visible in some liturgical and ministerial roles, although opportunities for preaching remained limited, and the advance of women in biblical and theological graduate work would be substantial. But the question of the ordination of women, especially in the wake of John Paul II's *Ordinatio Sacerdotalis*, would remain muted and controversial.

Concluding Reflections on Church Order

Raymond Brown's treatment of the various issues stemming from post–Vatican II debates about church order are a parade example of his biblical methodology, with both its "ecclesial" and "incarnational" qualities in full view. His instinct was to approach the biblical data from the vantage point, or presenting cause, of pastoral concerns in the church of his own day, such as debates about the role of the priest, the authority of the bishop, the claims of the papacy, and the possibility of ordaining women to the priesthood. In tackling these issues, Brown would first apply historical-critical methodology to effectively "de-construct" some aspects of the traditional assumptions about these issues in Catholic tradition. A prime example would be his critique, based on the New Testament materials, of the "chain" type of apostolic succession that affirmed that Christ ordained the apostles as priests and bishops at the Last Supper, that the apostles then ordained successors in various local churches, and that, in turn, these early individual "bishops" of local churches would ordain priests to assist them in their pastoral work. A similar "deconstruction" would be applied to the notion that Peter, as the "first bishop of Rome," was recognized as pope by the early church.

In each case, however, Brown would reconstruct continuity with church tradition by affirming that Christ did in fact constitute the community of faith and that, under the guidance of the Spirit sent by the risen Christ, essential structures would emerge and ultimately be the biblical basis for the hierarchical structure of the church, even as these structures would only develop over time. In this, he once again appealed to the church's affirmation in *Dei Verbum* that the Gospels themselves developed over time—rooted in the life and mission of the historical Jesus but developing under the guidance of the Spirit well beyond that stage. He noted more than once the importance of Pope John XXIII's opening statement at the beginning of the Second Vatican Council: "For the deposit of faith, the truths contained in our venerable doctrine, are one thing; the fashion in which they are expressed, but with the same meaning and the same judgement, is another thing. This way of speaking will require a great deal of work and, it may be, much patience: types of presentation must be introduced which are more in accord with a teaching authority which is primarily pastoral in character."[54]

Not all of Brown's concern was with historical issues. He moved readily from his reflections on the biblical materials and their implications for the development of the church's teaching and structures to reflections on the implications for the spiritual life and pastoral practice of the church and its leaders. Thus, the various roles that would be merged in priesthood, such as disciple and apostle, led to Brown's affirmation of the need for the priest's personal devotion to Christ, for enduring fidelity in one's vocation, to a justification for priestly celibacy, to the need for collegiality and the sharing of responsibility for decision-making, to increased roles for women, and so on. As we will note later in chapter 7, much of his approach to the biblical background for the church's structure and pastoral life was connected to his ecumenical commitment. How Roman Catholic claims for priesthood, for apostolic succession, for the role of the papacy, and the question of women's ordination would impact relations with Protestant and Orthodox churches was a consistent concern throughout his popular writings.[55]

What also emerges in Brown's discussion of these issues is the fact that he was in many ways an "old fashioned" priest himself, though the term "old fashioned" is not meant as a negative characterization. Courageous and bold as he was in his discussion of the historical roots of Catholic Church order, one can easily detect Brown's own moderate perspectives. He was fully committed to a vision of the priesthood that was celibate, permanent, loyal, and one that prized sacramental life and strong theological formation. In various asides, he also revealed his impatience with extreme views on both sides of the spectrum. For example, he branded those who used the argument that women could not be ordained since Jesus did not "ordain" his own mother as "Catholic fundamentalists," while those who characterized the role of the priest solely as being as a "man for others" were "pseudo-Bonhoefferian." He was not sympathetic to fellow priests who seemed to lament the hardships of their role, citing as he did the apostolic sufferings of Paul the Apostle. His views on women's ordination and their role in the church was strikingly liberal for his day and reflected Brown's strong relationship with women friends and his support of his women graduate students; at the same time, some of his tone in dealing with the issue of women's ordination shows that he was a man—and a cleric—of his time, with no expectation that this issue would be resolved any time soon nor considering it an urgent pastoral priority. Those who knew Raymond Brown personally attest that this was the vision of priesthood that Brown embodied.

DOCTRINAL ISSUES AND THE CHALLENGE TO CRITICAL BIBLICAL SCHOLARSHIP

While most of the issues that Brown tackled in his more popular writings stemmed from pastoral debates within postconciliar Catholicism, some of his most important writings concerned the impact of the biblical renewal on Catholic dogma. This was particularly true with his discussion of the virginal conception of Jesus and the question of bodily resurrection, topics directly engaged in his 1973 work *The Virginal Conception & Bodily Resurrection of Jesus.*[56] As Brown himself noted, these issues were not on the same plane: for some, the question of the virginal conception of Jesus was more esoteric and farther down on the level of the essential truths of Christian teaching. The resurrection of Jesus, on the other hand, was affirmed on virtually every page of the New Testament. Yet both issues were highly sensitive for traditional Catholic faith and were being questioned by some modern theologians and biblical scholars. Put more specifically was the virginal conception of Jesus based on the historical fact that Mary conceived Jesus without human sexual intervention? In affirming the resurrection of Jesus, did this mean *bodily* resurrection, with the tomb actually being empty? The answers to these questions were important because they also touched on the most fundamental question of all: Who was Jesus Christ? How does the church's Christology relate to these two questions?

Brown forthrightly noted that the application of historical methods of biblical inquiry to traditional dogmatic teachings was viewed negatively by many ultratraditional Catholics. "With the conviction that they are protecting the faith, fundamentalist editorial and column writers hurl charges of heresy and Modernism at attempts, no matter how careful, to apply contemporary biblical or historical criticism to Catholic doctrines."[57] An underlying concern for Brown was the impact of what he termed "right-wing vigilanteeism" on the "continuing progress of Catholic biblical studies in this century, especially since…a main thrust of these studies will be to help in the clarification of Catholic doctrine for our times."[58] In his extensive introduction to his engagement with the doctrines of the virginal conception and bodily resurrection, Brown had reviewed the evolution of biblical scholarship in modern Catholicism, noting that the current postconciliar period was an opportunity for the teaching and practice of the church to digest and be nourished by the flourishing of biblical scholarship.[59] He feared that the sweeping condemnations of biblical scholarship coming from some far-right quarters would blunt this progress and, in fact, would undermine the legitimate authority of the church's hierarchy by posing as more orthodox and more vigorous in defense of church teaching than the bishops themselves.

At the same time, Brown emphasized that he was sympathetic to the legitimate concerns of Catholics who were not ideologues in these matters but wondered how some of the questions being raised about these traditional teachings of the church were to be properly understood. To address such legitimate concerns in an informed and respectful manner (and without what he termed "shock techniques") was, in fact, a fundamental purpose of Brown's scholarly and pastoral mission, and it finds a strong expression in this book. He states such a purpose in its opening pages:

> But much of the truly conservative sensitivity is not fundamentalist: it recognizes the limitations of past (and of all) formulations of truth; but it insists that despite the limitation there was a grasp of truth in these formulations. This valid conservatism fears that a change in the formulation or in the understanding of the formulation may result in a loss of the insight into truth. In writing this book I have sought to speak to both the complexities and the sensitivities. While I try to show how critical biblical scholarship would nuance our approach to the Gospel accounts, I seek to do this with enough explanation so that the reader who is open to conviction may see that

a *truly* conservative attitude (as opposed to a fundamentalist attitude) need not be affronted by modern approaches to the Bible and to theology.[60]

It would be hard to express Brown's overall purpose and style more accurately than this.

The Problem of the Virginal Conception

In treating the question of the historicity of the virginal conception, Brown drew on several previous presentations. In his typically courageous fashion, he chose this topic for his inaugural lecture in the James Memorial Chapel of Union Theological Seminary when he was installed as Auburn Professor of Biblical Studies in November 1971. In a letter to his provincial, he confessed that he was sleepless and nervous the night before ("the worst strain of my life"), realizing the sensitivity of this issue, particularly doing so as he began his tenure as the lone Catholic faculty member in a Protestant seminary.[61]

At the outset, he noted that most modern mainline Protestant theologians would answer "no" to the question of the historicity of the virginal conception of Jesus, preferring to see it as a *theologoumenon,* that is, as a metaphorical or symbolic expression in narrative form of the unique and marvelous character of Jesus as viewed by Christian faith. At the same time, official Catholic teaching and most Catholic and Orthodox theologians would uphold as the ordinary magisterium of the church the historical basis of the virginal conception.[62] He spent considerable time reviewing the evidence for the historicity from the point of view of church authority, concluding that it was, in fact, part of the infallible teaching of the church reflected in the early creeds and apostolic teaching. He also reviewed how this belief "interlocks" with other church doctrines such as the sanctity of Mary, and the sinlessness and divine sonship of Jesus—all of which seem to harmonize with the doctrine of the virginal conception. Other doctrines such as the preexistence of Jesus as Son of God (which pushes his origin and identity back before his conception) and the authentic humanity of Jesus seem perhaps less aligned with the doctrine of the virginal conception but not absolutely contradictory. He also noted that this doctrine, while not affirmed by all post–New Testament early Christian sources, had "reasonably wide affirmation."[63]

At this point Brown turned to a review of the biblical evidence. He noted he would be relatively brief, saving a full consideration for a later publication—what was to become his major 1977 study, *The Birth of the Messiah*.[64] The explicit biblical evidence for the virginal conception is found only in the infancy narratives of Matthew and Luke. Possible echoes in such texts as Paul's statement that Jesus was "born of a woman" (Gal 4:4) or Mark's enigmatic reference to Jesus as "son of Mary" (Mark 6:3) or in John's declaration that Jesus was "born, not of blood or the will of the flesh or of the will of man, but of God" (John 1:13) are judged as too ambiguous to be considered firm proof that these other New Testament writers were aware of the tradition of the virginal conception. Brown agreed that, although some modern interpreters might see the assertion of the virginal conception by Matthew and Luke as an intentional *theologoumenon*, it is most likely that the evangelists themselves accepted this as historical. The affirmation of the virginal conception was not created by either evangelist (whose accounts are independent of each other) and must have been received by them as a firm conviction of the Christian community prior to their composition of their Gospels.

Brown then considers the evidence that might be mustered either against or for historicity. He notes that, in general, the infancy narratives seem to contain material that is of a dubious historical nature such as dreams, angels, a guiding star, the Magi and their gifts, the slaughter of the innocents, and so forth. These seem to be elements included in the narrative either from "folklore" or from reflection on Old Testament events and motifs. Also problematic, as noted earlier, is the silence of the rest of the New Testament concerning the virginal conception. On the other hand, arguing in favor of historicity, how does one explain the origin of the idea of virginal conception. Suggested parallels of marvelous births of heroes found in Greco-Roman or other ancient literature are not convincing, since in most instances they involve a super-human hero impregnating a woman—very different from the assertion of the virginal conception. Likewise, there are no real antecedents in the Old Testament or other Jewish traditions. "And so, no search for parallels has given us a truly satisfactory explanation of how early Christians happened upon the idea of a virginal conception—unless, of course, that is what really took place."[65]

Finally, there is the strange charge of "illegitimacy" concerning Mary's pregnancy, a charge raised in Matthew's infancy narrative (Matt 1:18–19) and echoed in Mark 6:3 (i.e., identifying Jesus as the "son of Mary" instead of the son of Joseph) and John 8:41 (where Jesus's opponents say, "We are not illegitimate children"). Later Jewish traditions also consistently raised this accusation against Jesus. This persistent tradition concerning the irregularity of Jesus's conception may reflect a historical reality that can be explained only by the virginal conception or, as Brown notes, by "accepting a very unpleasant alternative."[66]

This assessment of the biblical materials led Brown to his final conclusion: "My judgment, in conclusion, is that the totality of the *scientifically controllable* evidence leaves an unresolved problem—a conclusion that should not disappoint since I used the word "problem" in my title [that is, of the chapter, not the book itself]—and that is why I want to induce an honest, ecumenical discussion of it."[67] In other words, Brown believed that his application of the historical-critical method does not rule out the historicity of the virginal conception, even though other exegetes dealing with the same evidence and attempting to be equally objective might conclude that it does not appear to support historicity. Brown forthrightly confessed that his fidelity to Catholic doctrine guides his conclusion but did not force it. As he mentions in an important footnote, "I am not afraid that an honest discussion of the virginal conception will lead to a traumatic choice between fidelity to modern exegesis and fidelity to a teaching Church, provided that both the Bible and tradition are subjected to intelligent historical criticism to find out exactly what was meant and the degree to which it was affirmed. Inevitably, however, openness to discussion will be misrepresented as denial of tradition."[68]

Conclusions about the Meaning of the Virginal Conception

Brown concluded his study of the virginal conception somewhat abruptly. His real goal in this instance was not to delve deeply into the meaning of this doctrine within the theologies of Matthew and Luke, nor to trace its development in the history of the church's teaching, nor its implication for Christology or Marian devotion within the church today. His main objective was to demonstrate the positive contribution of historical-critical biblical methods in support of traditional church teaching. His hope was that future discussion of the virginal conception and of the role of Mary herself within Christian tradition would be reinvigorated and become ecumenically engaged because of a review of the biblical and theological tradition surrounding this teaching. To this end, he urged that this discussion "be pursued in an atmosphere of pastoral responsibility."[69] A cavalier approach to the question might jeopardize the profound truth embedded in a doctrine such as that of the virginal conception. It was, he noted, a doctrine that had served the church well through the centuries, emphasizing both "the reality of Jesus' humanity and his uniqueness as God's Son."[70]

This doctrine has also given attention to the essential role of women within Christianity, a realization, Brown noted, even more urgently needed in modern times:

> Leaving aside Protestant minimalism and Catholic exaggeration in Mariology, can any of us fail to see that, in all those centuries when no woman could stand publicly in the sanctuaries of churches, it was symbolically significant that a statue of the Virgin stood there. If by Church law a woman could not preside at the ceremonies that brought about Jesus' eucharistic presence, no one could deny that by God's law it was a woman and not a man who brought about Jesus' historical presence. It must be with an awareness of what the virginal conception has meant to Christianity that we theologians and church historians and exegetes begin our ecumenical discussion of it.[71]

The Problem of the Bodily Resurrection of Jesus

As with the "problem" of the virginal conception, Brown's foray into the question of the bodily resurrection of Jesus was triggered by the ongoing debate in the church about the role of biblical scholarship in relation to a fundamental doctrinal teaching of the church. Some modern theologians who were believing Christians, Brown noted, nevertheless were calling into question the notion of the "bodily" resurrection of Jesus and even whether "resurrection" terminology itself was appropriate in a modern era for affirming the triumph of Christ over death. As he put it,

> Once again, as we saw in proposing to discuss the virginal conception of Jesus, the thought of questioning an ancient formulation produces strong reactions. Liberals, for whom fidelity to the NT is not a major issue, will instinctively feel

sympathetic toward the possibility of divesting Christianity of something so antiquated as the imagery of a dead body coming to life. And fundamentalists, who are incapable of distinguishing between a truth and its formulation, will immediately conclude that a questioning of resurrection language represents a loss of faith in Jesus' triumph over death.[72]

Brown noted that some theologians objected to "resurrection" language and the notion of bodily resurrection for several reasons. Speaking of bodily resurrection, for example, might downplay the notion of transformation essential to the meaning of *resurrection* and confuse it with *resuscitation*. Also, some New Testament traditions themselves seem to move beyond resurrection language, for example, the imagery of Hebrews about Christ as High Priest entering the heavenly sanctuary, or the exaltation language used in the hymn of Philippians 2:9–11 and in Ephesians 4:10, or the formula that "He [Christ]...lives by the power of God" in 2 Corinthians 13:4 and "Christ died and lived again" in Romans 14:9. Others note that the only way the ancient Jewish mind could formulate the victory of Christ over death was to use the concrete language of resurrection. Some would also say that resurrection language is inherently inadequate and therefore misleading in trying to explain a reality that totally defies human description and experience.

To respond to this debate and consider alternate formulations of traditional doctrine, Brown insisted, meant first examining closely, through judicious use of the historical-critical method, the "real intent" of the New Testament language that affirmed the bodily resurrection of Jesus. To do so, Brown laid out what he considered the chronological stages of the proclamation of resurrection in the various New Testament accounts, beginning with the creedal formula and resurrection appearances noted by Paul in 1 Corinthians 15:3–8, then the formulas found in the Acts of the Apostles, then the resurrection appearances narrated in the Gospels, and, finally, the tradition of the empty tomb.

Weighing the evidence in Paul's important text in 1 Corinthians 15 with the other New Testament evidence led Brown to conclude, "There never was one unanimously accepted tradition with a complete geographical or chronological sequence of appearances."[73] A review of the various gospel appearance stories also suggests that these accounts cannot be harmonized either by location or sequence of events. However, the various accounts agree in affirming that the risen Jesus did appear to the Twelve, "an appearance that is all important for the Church since through it the Twelve are commissioned for their future task."[74] Also important is that the gospel accounts unanimously, although in various ways, affirm "the radically changed status of the one who appears, reflecting the eschatological dimension of the Risen Christ. The post-resurrectional confession is not simply 'We have seen Jesus' but 'We have seen *the Lord.*'"[75] Thus the resurrection appearances involve not only an encounter with the risen Lord but a revelation of a reality that goes beyond ordinary experience.

Finally, Brown turned to the tradition of the discovery of an empty tomb. He emphasized that, in itself, an "empty" tomb is ambiguous; the gospel accounts themselves refer to alternate possible explanations such as the disciples "stole" the body of Jesus (Matt 27:64) or that the gardener had taken the body away (John 20:15). It is only in the light of the early community's conviction of Jesus's resurrection that the empty tomb becomes part of the Easter proclamation.[76] Only at that stage was the discovery of the empty tomb woven into both the passion narratives with the story of the burial of Jesus and the women coming to anoint the body of Jesus after the close of the Sabbath, and into the resurrection appearance traditions with the angelic messenger at the tomb explaining to the women witnesses its meaning, and the subsequent traditions of Mary Magdalene and Peter and the Beloved Disciple coming to the tomb and pondering its meaning.

Brown then summarized what he believed a historical-critical examination of the New Testament materials confirms about the resurrection: "The resurrection of Jesus, along with his exaltation and his giving of the Spirit, constituted an eschatological event—the beginning of the end-time. The categories of space and time, the categories of ordinary human experience such as 'seeing" and 'speaking' supply us with a language that is only analogous and approximate when we use it to describe the eschatological."[77] The silence of the New Testament in not describing the actual moment of the resurrection is testimony to the eschatological nature of the event.

At the same time, the tomb of Jesus was not itself part of the eschatological event but was fixed in time and place. If the location of the tomb were known to the Jerusalem Christians and if in fact the remains of Jesus were still there, it is hard to imagine that the disciples could have claimed that God raised Jesus from the dead. The tradition that the tomb was known and was empty, Brown affirmed, "is considerably older than the Gospel narratives that have been built around the discovery of the empty tomb."[78] The disciples would come to understand why the tomb was empty in the light of resurrection faith. "The tomb supplied an important element in the continuity between the career of the earthly Jesus and that of the risen Jesus, so that there was a tendency to take the language appropriate to one career and apply it to the other career, e.g., body, see, touch."[79]

It is precisely at this point that Brown rejoined the question about the church's doctrine of "bodily" resurrection. "And so from a critical study of the biblical evidence I would judge that Christians can and indeed should continue to speak of a *bodily* resurrection of Jesus. Our earliest ancestors in the faith proclaimed a bodily resurrection in the sense that they did not think that Jesus' body had corrupted in the tomb. However, and this is equally important, Jesus' risen body was no longer a body as we know bodies, bound by the dimension of space and time."[80] This makes room for the essential truth that resurrection involves transformation and mystery. Yet, Brown noted, the Christian doctrine of *bodily* resurrection effectively affirms what God has done, not only for all of humanity, but also for Jesus himself. "It was not an evolution in human consciousness, nor was it the disciples' brilliant insight into the meaning of the crucifixion—it was the sovereign action of God glorifying Jesus of Nazareth. Only because God has done this for His Son are new possibilities opened for His many children who have come to believe in what He has done."[81] Additionally, Brown observed that bodily resurrection also has implications for the future destiny of creation itself. "The problem of the bodily resurrection is not just an example of Christian curiosity; it is related to a major theme in theology: God's ultimate purpose in creating."[82] Remarkably, Brown edged up to a question that would later engulf theology, namely, the relation of Christian doctrine to ecology.

As in the question of the virginal conception, Brown's ultimate purpose was not to provide a full study of the New Testament teaching on resurrection, nor the meaning of bodily resurrection for Christian teaching and practice. What he wanted to demonstrate was that a thorough historical-critical examination of the New Testament can both ultimately support and give new insight into the meaning of traditional church doctrine.

CONCLUSION

A review of these popular works of Raymond Brown opens the window into his overriding pastoral purpose, his Catholic sensitivity, and his sense of vocation. He was intent on showing that use of modern biblical scholarship, exercised in a responsible way, was not reductionist or dismissive of traditional Catholic teaching. He dared to test this conviction on some of the most burning issues being debated among Catholics in the wake of the Second Vatican Council—the nature of the biblical writings themselves and their historical grounding; the origin and evolution of church order; the origin and authority of the hierarchy; the proper roles and authority of priests, bishops, and pope; the role of women, including the issue of ordination to priesthood; the historicity of the virginal conception of Jesus; and the meaning of bodily resurrection. Along the way, he also delved into the question of the diverse ecclesiologies of the New Testament,[83] the evolution of Christology,[84] the development of dogma, and the challenge that virtually all these questions posed for Catholic engagement in ecumenical dialogue.

While Brown would not style himself a "theologian" as such, his philosophical training and his theological acumen and sound knowledge of Catholic tradition were evident throughout his writings. He was not just a literary or historical technician interested only in analyzing in an objective way the biblical texts and their historical contexts. He had constantly in mind the theological and pastoral consequences of biblical inquiry. As Kevin Duffy described Brown's methodology, the "philosophy of the practitioner of the method"—a phrase that Brown himself also used—was always in play. For Brown, this meant something of a "hermeneutic of grace" when it came to finding a valid biblical basis for traditional Catholic doctrine.[85] He believed—and intended to demonstrate in his lecturing and writing—that a thoughtful and responsible dialectic between theology and exegesis, or between the Bible and church dogma, would be fruitful not destructive. Fending off the attacks of what he termed "fundamentalist vigilantes" in the church was a byproduct of this conviction, a painful dimension of Brown's life that we will consider later.[86] While Brown's major academic works endure as resources for serious biblical inquiry, his engagement with the hotly debated theological and pastoral issues of the church during his lifetime, some of which may have faded in subsequent years in intensity and interest, give a clearer view of the man, his character, and his Christian commitment.

CHAPTER 5

SIGNATURE EXEGETICAL WORKS

EXPLORING THE JOHANNINE LITERATURE

Through his multitude of lectures, articles, and books on the burning pastoral and doctrinal issues of the postconciliar church, Raymond Brown gained a reputation as one of the most influential and well-known Catholic scholars of his day, acclaimed by *Time* as "probably the premier Catholic Scripture scholar in the United States."[1] However, it is his major academic works that are likely to carry his name into the future; these are encyclopedic in scope and depth and will remain for some time as essential reference points for biblical scholarship. In fact, the reputation Brown earned through these substantial academic achievements gave a depth of authority to his more popular writings. No one could accuse Raymond Brown of being superficial or frivolous in his grappling with biblical interpretation; his in-depth studies of the gospel literature such as his acclaimed two-volume massive commentary on the Gospel of John inoculated him from this type of accusation, even from those who would be severely opposed to his biblical interpretation and its impact on the church.

All during the time he was composing these major works, Brown was also producing the steady stream of briefer and more popular works considered in the previous chapter, while also teaching graduate courses, directing doctoral students, and keeping up a heavy load of lectures and workshops in North America, Europe, and Asia—a reflection of his prodigious work habits and sheer stamina. Our goal here and in the next chapter is not to attempt a summary of the several thousand pages of these academic blockbusters but to chart the context that led Brown to these particular topics, to explore his approach, and to weigh some of his major conclusions and their contribution to ongoing biblical scholarship.

Among Brown's major works, his exploration of the Johannine literature remains his signature achievement, especially his Anchor Bible multivolume commentaries on the Gospel of John and the Epistles of John and his exploration of the evolution of the Johannine community in *The Community of the Beloved Disciple*.[2] His fascination with the Johannine writings spanned his professional career, with the first volume of the Gospel of John commentary published in 1966 while he taught at St. Mary's Seminary and University in Baltimore and the second volume in 1970 on the brink of his move to Union Theological Seminary. The commentary on the Johannine Letters (1982) would appear during his tenure at Union. As we will note later, he had begun but never completed work on a major revision of his commentary on the Gospel of John at St. Patrick's in Menlo Park, California, shortly before his death.

Before turning to his individual works, we can mark some of the characteristics that cut across Brown's academic volumes. First, they are encyclopedic in size and scope.[3] As virtually all his reviewers noted, Brown, in each instance, seems to have read and assessed a vast number of articles, comprising almost all the available secondary literature, with one of his major goals to bring this body of scholarship to his audience. His revisions of *The Birth of the Messiah* and his posthumously published materials for a planned revision of his commentary on the Gospel of John bristle with updated bibliographical references. Even when he published the second volume of his commentary on the Gospel of John four years after the first volume, he began the second volume with an assessment of the articles and books that had been published in the meantime on matters covered in the previous volume. While Brown was not shy in evaluating the viewpoints of these sources, his disagreements were expressed with courtesy and respect (except in the case of some of his far–right-wing critics). The readers of Brown's works who persevered through his footnotes and appendices came away with a full review of current scholarship on the issue under discussion. As more than one reviewer noted, his references were also scrupulously accurate.[4] This thoroughness did not always lead to exciting reading, but it earned Brown a reputation for meticulous and reliable scholarship.[5]

Second, Brown was consistent in his use of the historical-critical method, which he applied not only to the specific biblical book or, in the case of his work on the infancy narratives and the passion accounts, to particular biblical passages, but also to the sources and composition history of these texts. Brown treated the Pauline writings in his *Introduction to the New Testament,* but the main focus of his academic work remained the Gospels. He was interested not only in capturing as thoroughly as possible the "intended" meaning of the biblical author in the final form of the Gospel text but also the prehistory of the Gospel materials and the possible interrelationship of these various traditions and sources. As we will note, Brown held tenaciously to the proposed developmental framework for the composition of the Gospels that had been enshrined in *Dei Verbum* itself (no. 19), namely, a threefold stage: (1) rooted in the historical setting of Jesus and his contemporaries, (2) developed in the pastoral setting of the early community, and (3) finding full literary expression in the Gospels through the composition of the evangelists. Even as he proposed a more complex articulation of the tradition history of the Johannine materials, this basic developmental format remained intact. This same framework enabled Brown to affirm the ultimate historical grounding of the Gospel materials while also making room for theological development of these materials in the ongoing life of the early Christian community.[6]

Brown's confidence in the historical-critical approach also gave his work an ecumenical spirit. More than once, Brown expressed his conviction that a fair-minded and rigorous application of this method leveled the sectarian field for biblical studies.[7] No matter what the nature of an exegete's religious commitment, he believed that the application of the historical-critical method—distinct from the theological and pastoral interpretation of the Bible's meaning—should lead to a similar range of conclusions about the origin, context, and intended auctorial meaning of a passage under consideration. Thus, he had no restraint in incorporating a full range of Protestant, Orthodox, and Jewish scholarship in his academic writings. The reader of Brown's scholarly writings would have no doubt about his Catholic commitment, which he always stated forthrightly. But, at the same time, he did not use his Catholic theological or pastoral perspective to rule out of bounds tackling issues and viewpoints that would not be in sympathy with Catholic tradition. This "non-sectarian" quality of Brown's work won the respect of non-Catholic scholars, and his work would be used widely in the Protestant world. It would also lead to his having a leadership role in the professional academic societies that previously seemed to be the exclusive reserve of Protestant scholars, and earned him an impressive list of honorary doctorates and other public recognitions from Protestant and secular universities.[8]

Engaging in the highest quality biblical scholarship and rigorously applying the historical-critical method, while at the same time remaining faithful to his Catholic identity, was one of Brown's fundamental principles. Devoting his energy to major academic works gave him the opportunity to demonstrate the truth of this principle for all to see.

THE GOSPEL OF JOHN

No work established Raymond Brown as a highly respected biblical scholar more than his commentaries on the Johannine literature. His fascination with the Johannine writings began early in his scholarly career, particularly with his formative experience at Johns Hopkins University under the direction of William Foxwell Albright.[9] In the preface to the first volume of his Anchor Bible Commentary on the Fourth Gospel, Brown acknowledges the decisive influence of Albright: "By chance this volume has a publication date which falls very close to the seventy-fifth birthday of Professor William F. Albright, born May 24, 1891. The writer remembers that his first article on John was the product of one of the Professor's seminars at the Johns Hopkins University. And so he would like to take this occasion to acknowledge frankly his debt to the scholarship, example, and generosity of this great biblical scholar. *Ad multos annos.*"[10]

Exploring John's Gospel in depth brought together for Brown several threads of his biblical interests. Guided by Albright who, as the then dean of biblical archaeology, defended the fundamental historical grounding of the Bible, Brown would deal head-on with the debate about the historical roots of the Fourth Gospel that dominated much of Johannine scholarship at the time. Likewise—once again because of his fellowship in Jerusalem made possible by his time at Johns Hopkins and Albright's sponsorship—Brown utilized his immersion in the Dead

Sea Scrolls and their connection to Palestinian Judaism to break fresh ground in exploring the Jewish roots of John's Gospel. Tackling John's Gospel in this format would enable Brown to fully deploy his historical methodology on a biblical text of great complexity and depth.

The thought of writing a major commentary on the Fourth Gospel came early to Brown. In an April 1959 letter to his provincial, Fr. Lloyd McDonald, he spoke enthusiastically of an invitation to contribute a brief commentary on John in the newly established series, "New Testament Reading Guides," published by Liturgical Press under the direction of its general manager, William Heidt, OSB.[11] In asking his provincial's permission to accept this invitation, Brown noted that the series, although directed to a wide audience, was a serious effort, meant to utilize the best of current biblical scholarship. He added that this would be a good opportunity because he already had in mind "a full-scale commentary on John's Gospel. There is nothing in English by a Catholic that would even approach the Protestant commentaries that have been floating about."[12] His brief commentary in the Collegeville series, which was published in 1960, would become very popular and broke the ground for his major academic commentary that would appear six years later.

Brown's association with Albright also paved the way for his opportunity to be part of the newly established Anchor Bible series. The seed that planted the idea of the Anchor Bible was a proposal made to Albright by Jason Epstein, the founder of Anchor Books, a publishing house established in 1953.[13] He proposed a new edition of the King James version of the Bible that would reflect modern biblical scholarship. Albright sent one of his students, David Noel Freedman, a convert from Judaism and later an ordained Presbyterian minister and budding Old Testament scholar, to discuss the proposal with Epstein. Instead of simply annotating the venerable King James translation, Freedman proposed—and Albright accepted—that an entirely new translation be made. Together, Albright and Freedman proposed a twenty-eight-volume, "pocket-sized" paperback series, geared for a popular audience, that would consist of a fresh translation along with brief annotations. Translations of longer biblical books would be in a single volume, with briefer books bundled together in single volumes. As their plans developed, the original idea morphed into a hardback format and a projected series of thirty-eight volumes. An important feature would be the ecumenical nature of the project, with Protestant, Catholic, and Jewish scholars collaborating on this new American version of the Bible. This, too, reflected the influence of Albright, who had gathered an ecumenical and interreligious group of graduate students at Johns Hopkins. Many of Albright's students, in fact, would become contributors to the series.

A fateful turn for the series occurred in 1963 when Albright selected Brown to be on its editorial board, along with himself and Freedman, and to do the commentary on the Gospel of John and the Johannine Letters.[14] Brown was both excited by this prospect of being part of such an ecumenical project but also somewhat nervous. This was still at a time when ecumenical relations were both novel and somewhat fragile. Accordingly, Brown wrote to Cardinal Richard Cushing, archbishop of Boston, in April 1963 to get his clearance—the original idea for an ecumenical commentary series had been hatched at a conference that took place at Harvard, located within the boundaries of the Archdiocese of Boston. "Since this [project] is an outgrowth of the Harvard Colloquium [of which Cushing was one of the sponsors], may I turn to your Eminence for advice. Is this type of project a legitimate outgrowth of the intentions you had in sponsoring such a scholarly colloquium? Would you give your blessing to my editorial participation in this project? [signed] "Yours obediently in Christ." Cushing replied affirmatively: "In the light of the present ecumenism and especially the recent Harvard Colloquium, I beg you to serve as one of the editors.... Delighted to bless your participation to this scholarly publication."[15] Brown also wrote in a similar vein to no less than Cardinal Bea, whom Brown had met in Rome and who was the champion of ecumenism at the Council. After describing the project, Brown stated, "Therefore I turn to you for guidance on this question, in order to be sure that my acceptance would be truly serving the Church and be conformable to the desires of the Church's authorities. May I ask your Eminence, would you give your blessing to my editorial participation in this project?"[16] Both these letters reflect not only Brown's ecclesial loyalty and sensibilities, but also his shrewd strategy of keeping church authorities informed of his work and appealing for their support. As we will discuss later, the typical support that Brown received from ecclesiastical authorities was a consternation to his ultraconservative opponents who considered Brown heretical.[17]

Not content with the idea of writing simply an annotated translation of the Gospel, Brown pressed from the outset to do a full-fledged scholarly commentary, a change in format that would raise the bar for the entire series. As he noted in the preface to his commentary, given the amount of scholarship on the Fourth Gospel and the numerous questions being raised about the Gospel, "a translation with brief notes would serve no purpose here."[18] Albright and Freedman eventually agreed. Albright had recognized from the beginning that Brown was an exceptional scholar and brought to the project a Catholic who did not shy from employing the historical-critical method with rigorous objectivity. Freedman, too, recognized Brown's abilities and would remain a lifelong friend and respected editor of Brown's Anchor Bible work, including his three volumes on the Johannine literature, his 1994 two-volume work, *The Death of the Messiah*, and his 1996 *An Introduction to the New Testament*, which appeared in the Anchor Bible Reference Library series, a later offshoot of the commentary series. Freeman, who died in 2008, agreed that "Brown's Saint John's Gospel revolutionized the Anchor Bible, and a lot of New Testament scholarship."[19] Brown's was the first New Testament commentary in the series. Later, following Brown's mold, other contributors would provide multivolume commentaries on some Old and New Testament books.[20]

The Anchor Bible Commentary:
The Gospel according to John

Brown began his work on his commentary at a time when Johannine studies were undergoing a seismic shift. Earlier critical scholarship had placed John's Gospel late in the first or even into the early part of the second century and believed it was strongly influenced by Hellenistic culture and religious perspectives, reflecting even a kind of early Christian Gnosticism. Thus, the value of the Fourth Gospel for revealing any of the historical circumstances of Jesus of Nazareth was minimal at best. The highly influential commentary on the Gospel of John published by the German scholar Rudolf Bultmann in 1941 was a landmark study proposing this view.[21] However, the discovery of the Dead Sea Scrolls in 1948 and their eventual publication triggered a reassessment of this position. Now some of the thought patterns and rhetorical style of John's Gospel, previously judged to be reflective of later Hellenistic culture, were found in sectarian Jewish documents rooted in the intertestamental period of Palestinian Judaism. Brown himself was one of the first scholars to have direct access to these materials through the work on the concordance he was assigned during his fellowship year in Jerusalem.[22]

In taking up his own commentary, Brown was fully aware of the many commentaries, each with distinctive viewpoints, that had preceded him. He was convinced "that the time had come to gather the fruit of the brilliant but isolated contributions of his predecessors and to make a synthesis of what is of value in their very divergent approaches to the Gospel."[23] While he would exhaustively catalogue the views of his predecessors, Brown's own commentary turned out to be much more than a "synthesis" of previous views. Some guiding principles would shape his work: (1) He wanted to develop a "moderately critical theory about the composition of the gospel." Intrigued by features of John's Gospel that suggested it had been edited at various stages, Johannine scholarship had developed numerous hypotheses about the sources behind the Gospel and the process of its composition. One of the major contributions of Brown's commentary would be a cogent proposal about the identity and history of the Christian community that stood behind the Gospel. (2) Brown's commentary would also demonstrate his conviction "that the gospel is rooted in historical tradition about Jesus of Nazareth." Here, too, Brown's viewpoint would run counter to that of Bultmann and other Johannine scholars who doubted the historical value of the Fourth Gospel. (3) Finally, he wanted his historical-critical analysis of the Gospel to be as objective and credible as possible and not dictated by his own confessional stance. As he put it, "As we have come to realize, sincere confessional commitment to a theological position is perfectly consonant with a stubborn refusal to make a biblical text to say more than its author meant to say."[24]

These goals, including that of providing a synthesis of previous scholarship, would be achieved by Brown. The architecture of the commentary would reflect the original intention of the Anchor Bible series but go far beyond it. Each section of the commentary would begin with a fresh translation of the Gospel text that Brown described not as "prose of formal literary beauty" but rather a "rendering into the ordinary American English of today."[25] Following the translation was a series of notes that explained the translation and, in some cases, moved toward interpretation. In his volume on *The Epistles of John*, the notes section would be greatly expanded, made possible by the luxury of being able to devote 812 printed pages to biblical texts that were less than 6 pages long! After the notes came the "Comment"—the meat of Brown's commentary. This section was usually divided into "Comment: general," which gave an overview of the meaning of the passage, and "Comment: detailed," which dove deeper into the structure and content of the biblical text being considered. Each segment concluded with specific bibliography. A series of appendices at the end of the volume took up important and often controverted topics, and the volumes were armed with a series of indices.

In his extensive introduction (146 pages), Brown laid out his views on the composition history of the Gospel, what would turn out to be one of the most influential aspects of his commentary. Previous interpreters had explained the seams and some duplications in the present form of the Gospel as due either to accident (the leaves of an ancient manuscript had been mistakenly shuffled—an unlikely explanation), or to a combination of various sources, or reflective of various editions of the text. Bultmann, for example, had proposed that the Gospel was a combination of a "signs (or miracle) source," a collection of revelatory discourses, and a form of the passion and resurrection narratives. Others had attempted to trace in detail various editions of the Gospel that led to its present form. Brown was not content with any of these single alternatives and came up with his own proposal, one that over time would be refined and elaborated in his subsequent work, *The Community of the Beloved Disciple.*[26]

Brown proposed that the Gospel in its present form was the result of a five-stage development experienced by an early Christian community, one rooted in the history of Jesus of Nazareth, then extensively influenced by the postresurrection life of the community, and finally shaped by a "Redactor" into the canonical Gospel of John.

1. In the first stage, a body of material concerning the words and works of Jesus developed that was similar to but independent of the materials that would lead to the Synoptic traditions. Brown would attribute the unique flavor of this Johannine material to its origin in "heterodox" Judaism (in John's account, Jesus's first disciples are recruited from those of the Baptist) and possibly early Samaritan influence (reflected in the story of the Samaritan woman and the Samaritan community accepting Jesus in John 4 and the paucity of Davidic, that is, Jerusalem-based, motifs in John).

2. A second stage took place within the context of the post-Easter early Christian community and would lead to the

shaping of these traditions about Jesus into characteristic Johannine patterns. This stage was particularly formative. Various key members of the Johannine community in their ministry of preaching and teaching shaped the Gospel materials further into the Johannine pattern, adding drama to the miracles stories, weaving sayings of Jesus into long discourses, using the category of Wisdom to understand Jesus's identity, and so on. However, in this Johannine "school of thought and expression," the "principal preacher was the one responsible for the main body of Gospel material" (p. xxxv).

3. At this stage, the material shaped during stage two was organized into a consecutive gospel. "This would be the first edition of the Fourth Gospel as a distinct work" (p. xxxv). Brown believed that the "principal preacher" who directed the developments in stage two would also be responsible for this first edition of the Gospel and was the one Brown would refer to as the "evangelist" in his commentary.

4. Stage four represents a secondary edition of the Gospel. Although it is possible, as some suggest, that the Gospel underwent several editions, Brown believed that most of the features of John can be explained through one edition. At this stage, some material such as the story of the man born blind in chapter 9 would be adapted to the experience of tension between the synagogue and the early Christian community in the late '80s and '90s. It is probable also that the Johannine community moved from its location in Palestine to a place in the Gentile Mediterranean world, possibly Ephesus.

5. Brown attributes the final stage of the Gospel's composition to the "Redactor" who not only retained the material from stage four but worked in additional material, some of it stemming from previous stages in the life of the community and some of it causing a duplication of materials. He points to the extensive discourse material in chapters 13—17 of the Gospel and perhaps the material in chapters 11—12 preparing for the passion story (whose introduction may have led to the move of the account

of the cleansing of the temple from the end of Jesus's ministry to its beginning in chapter 2). The addition of the postresurrection Galilean appearances in chapter 21 may also have been added at this time. Brown also believed the redactor added further material about the sacraments, intensifying a sacramental perspective already present in the Gospel, and may have affixed the Prologue (John 1:1–18) to the beginning of the Gospel as well.

Brown realized that much of his proposal for the development of the community leading to the final form of the Gospel was speculative, particularly regarding details. On the other hand, the basic outline he proposed fits into the basic developmental stages in the formation of all the gospel literature. "A distinctive figure in the primitive Church preached and taught about Jesus, using the raw material of a tradition of Jesus' works and words, but shaping this material to a particular theological cast and expression. Eventually he gathered the substance of his preaching and teaching into a Gospel, following the traditional pattern of the baptism, the ministry, and the passion, death, and resurrection of Jesus" (p. xxxviii).[27]

Brown's views about other key aspects of the Fourth Gospel stemmed from his conviction about the development of the Johannine tradition, a tradition rooted in first-century Palestinian history. He notes, for example, that John's Gospel, while appearing as more abstract than the Synoptic Gospels, reflects accurately some of the historical, social, and geographical details consonant with Jesus's own day. The Gospel refers, for example, to specific details of Jerusalem that would have been obliterated in the destruction of 70 AD: the sheep's gate (5:2), the pools of Bethesda (5:2–3), and the pool of Siloam (9:7, 11). The evangelist is also familiar with the significance of various Jewish festivals: Tabernacles or Booths (7:2), the Feast of the Dedication (10:22), and Passover (12:1; 18:28, 39; 19:14, 31, 42). The Gospel is also aware of the Samaritans, their religious history, and their relationship with Judean Jews (chapter 4). Much of the religious language of the Gospel found in the discourses fits into similar rhetorical and dualistic patterns in the Dead Sea Scrolls.

Brown wavers on the issue of whether John's Gospel was totally independent of any literary contact with the Synoptic Gospels, particularly in the case of parallel stories such as the multiplication of the loaves, the walking on the water, and the passion narratives. Contrary to the assertions of direct contact proposed by Frans Neirynck and many of his colleagues at the University of Louvain, he concluded that "the evangelist drew the material for his stories from an independent tradition, similar to but not the same as the traditions represented in the Synoptic Gospels"[28] He did concede, however, that in the long period of time in which the Johannine Gospel was gestating, there may have been some "minor cross-overs" between the two streams of tradition (p. xlvi).[29]

What, Brown asks, does all this imply about the historical reliability of John's Gospel when it comes to its portrayal of Jesus? Each of the four Gospels, he notes, compose a portrayal of Jesus that is theologically charged, while rooted in history. The theological portrayal is particularly strong in the case of John. Brown judiciously concludes,

> From all these remarks it should be clear why we must be very cautious about the use of John in scientifically reconstructing in detail the ministry of Jesus of Nazareth, even as we must be careful in so using the other Gospels. We do believe that John is based on a solid tradition of the works and words of Jesus, a tradition which at times is very primitive. We believe that often John gives us correct historical information about Jesus that no other Gospel has preserved, for example, that, like John the Baptist, Jesus had a baptizing ministry for a period before he began his ministry of teaching; that his public ministry lasted more than a year; that he went several times to Jerusalem; that the opposition of the Jewish authorities at Jerusalem was not confined to the last days of his life; and many details about Jesus' passion and death. Yet, in evaluating the Johannine picture of Jesus, we cannot neglect the inevitable modifications made in the various stages of Johannine composition. (pp. l–li)

Curiously, in the section of his introduction to his commentary "Crucial Questions in Johannine Theology," Brown included summations of John's ecclesiology, sacramentalism, eschatology, and Wisdom motifs, but not Christology. Although he touches on the subject in the segment on "Wisdom motifs," Brown does not deal directly with an overall consideration of John's portrayal of Jesus.[30] He seemed to recognize this lacuna in his proposed revision of Johannine commentary whose introduction does include a section on "Christology." There, Brown concentrated on the Johannine portrayal of Jesus as the "Son of Man" and as personified "Wisdom."[31]

Brown's conclusions about other aspects of the Gospel reflect the "moderately critical" approach" he intended to employ in his commentary. In weighing the religious influences that may have shaped the unique theological perspective of John's Gospel, Brown was not convinced of the prevailing view that John's perspective was mostly influenced by later Hellenistic religious influences. He gave most weight to the Gospel's Palestinian Jewish background, including the Old Testament itself and, in particular, Jewish Wisdom traditions.

> In sum…we suggest that into Johannine theological thought patterns has gone the influence of a peculiar combination of various ways of thinking that were current in Palestine during Jesus' own lifetime and after his death. The Christian preachers interpreted Jesus the Christ against the background of the OT [Old Testament], and the preaching behind the Fourth Gospel was no exception. However, the Fourth Gospel has done this not so much by explicit citation as by showing how OT themes were implicitly woven into Jesus' actions and words. In particular, this Gospel has gone much further than the Synoptics in interpreting Jesus in terms of the OT figure of personified Wisdom. Some of the background of Jesus' thought is to be found in the presuppositions of the Pharisaic theology of his time, as these are known to us from the later rabbinic writings. It is no accident that Jesus is called a rabbi more frequently in John than in any other Gospel. Moreover, in John the thought of Jesus is expressed in a peculiar theological vocabulary that we now know to have been used by an important sectarian Jewish group in Palestine.[32]

Brown gave considerable space in his introduction to the standard questions of the date, location, authorship, and purpose of the Gospel. He concluded that the final stage of the Gospel was written toward the end of the first century, and probably in Ephesus, as many ancient traditions about the place of its origin had identified. Brown gave more detailed discussion to the question of the authorship of the Gospel. After weighing the evidence, he would not rule out the ancient tradition that John, the son of Zebedee, may have been the original eyewitness source of the Gospel.[33] However, the development of the Johannine tradition in its subsequent stages was probably the work of a close disciple of John, one who perhaps was in turn to be identified with the "Beloved Disciple" mentioned in the Gospel, and who would become the "principal disciple" whose "transmission of the historical material received from John was marked with dramatic genius and profound theological insight, and it is the preaching and teaching of this disciple which gave shape to the stories and discourses now found in the Fourth Gospel" (p. ci). In the final stage, the redactor would draw on this previous stage to compose the Gospel as we now have it.

Brown believed that the purpose of the Gospel was not primarily polemical, as some had suggested. While Docetism, which denied the authentic humanity of Jesus, was a yawning problem for early Christianity, Brown was not convinced that its refutation was a primary purpose of John. A more proximate concern for the Gospel were those Jewish Christians who had not yet broken free of their allegiance to the synagogue. The final stages of the Gospel were not written in Palestine, in Brown's view, but in the Diaspora, where Jewish Christians may still have been ambivalent about full immersion in the Christian community. Beyond this specific group, the Gospel intended to be a source of encouragement for all believing Christians, both Gentile and Jewish. Its purpose was not "missionary" in the sense of reaching out beyond the Christian community but "internal," meant to bolster the faith of community itself. "Perhaps, however, we may best say that much of the Gospel is addressed to the Christian believer without distinction of whether his derivation is Jewish or Gentile. This is a Gospel designed to root the believer deeper in his faith" (p. lxxviii).

One final issue taken up by Brown deserves consideration, namely, the Fourth Gospel's portrayal of the "Jews."[34] Far more than the other Gospels, John uses the term *Jews* rather than specific designations such as "scribes," "Pharisees," "priests," and so on, as in the Synoptic Gospels.[35] This usage, Brown suggests, reflects the post-70 context of the Gospel's composition. The term *Jews* becomes "almost a technical title for the religious authorities, particularly those in Jerusalem, who are hostile to Jesus" (p. lxxi). Brown asserts that the term *Jews* in John "has nothing to do with ethnic, geographical, or religious differentiation." People who are ethnically, religiously, and even geographically Jews (even in the narrow sense of belonging to Judea) are distinguished from "the Jews." He points to such examples as John 9:22, where, in speaking to the parents of the man born blind, the Gospel notes they feared "the Jews." Likewise, the paralyzed man in John 5:15, himself a Jew, is portrayed as informing "the Jews." John accentuates the tension between Jesus and the Jewish authorities because one of the Gospel's purposes is to justify Christian claims over against Jewish unbelief (examples would be John 8:44–47, 54–55). This polemic is also connected to the Gospel's desire to win over those Jewish Christians, just mentioned, who had not yet broken with the synagogue and become fully immersed in the Christian community.

Thus, Brown concludes, "John is not anti-Semitic; the evangelist is condemning not race or people but opposition to Jesus" (p. lxxii). Unfortunately, at this point in his career Brown did not address the influence of John's characterization of the Jews on subsequent Christian anti-Semitism or anti-Judaism. Noting the narrow and abstract meaning of the term *Jews* in John's Gospel and attributing its hostility to the post-70 circumstances, where tension was mounting between early Christianity and the Jewish authorities, were important steps in giving some historical context to this issue. In later publications, Brown himself would be more aware of the implications of John's characterization of the Jews, particularly when he became a close friend with other Jewish scholars, especially during his New York sojourn. He would also have an important influence on a key church document on this issue in his role as a member of the Pontifical Biblical Commission, namely, the 2002 document *The Jewish People and Their Sacred Scriptures in the Christian Bible*.[36]

A Singular Achievement

Before turning to Brown's commentary on the Epistles, it is important to note the singular achievement of his Gospel commentary. Brown completed the first volume of his commentary when he was thirty-seven years old, the second volume would appear four years later. He was still young and had been doing graduate teaching at St. Mary's for less than seven years. Yet he produced a commentary of over 1,200 pages that would command the attention of biblical scholarship worldwide and substantially influence scholarship and popular views about the origin and content of John's Gospel down to the present time. J. Louis Martyn, who would become a close colleague and friend at Union Theologi-cal Seminary, mentions in his final tribute to Brown his experience in first reading this new commentary. In a telephone conversation with Brown about another matter, Martyn took the occasion to tell him "that I wished heartily to congratulate him on the superb first volume of his commentary on the Fourth Gospel. My colleague John Knox had handed me a few days earlier a set of the page proofs, and, fascinated, I had put other things aside to dip into what was obviously a major work. Ray's immediate response to my word of congratulation was a rather dramatic silence, the precise implications of which escaped me at the moment, but which, with time, I learned to interpret as the reflection of a strain of genuine modesty."[37]

Brown was by no means done with his academic publications on the Johannine literature with the completion of his two-volume com-mentary. Later would come his further elaboration of the Gospel's ori-gin and composition in *The Community of the Beloved Disciple* (1979) and his major commentary on the Epistles of John (1982). As already noted, he was about to start the cycle all over again in the late 1990s with a complete revision of his commentary when death intervened. He had signed his contract for the book in May of 1996, with a projected publication date of November 1, 2000. He had completed a first draft of the introduction to his revision and some partial notes about specific passages. This is the work titled *An Introduction to the Gospel of John*, edited and commented on by Francis J. Moloney.[38] Perhaps, Maloney speculates, the most significant change Brown may have put into his planned revision, was, under the influence of narrative criticism, to pay more attention to the literary form of the Gospel as it now stands and less focus on the composition history of John's Gospel. Yet the original two-volume Anchor Bible commentary on the Fourth Gospel would remain Brown's most significant academic achievement and would be the warrant for his academic credentials for the rest of his life.

THE EPISTLES OF JOHN

Brown's 1982 commentary, *The Epistles of John*, completed his trio of major Anchor Bible commentaries on the Johannine literature.[39] As noted earlier, Brown considered the twelve-year gap between the second volume of the Gospel commentary and this work to be salutary since it gave him time to think through the full destiny of the Johannine tradition, from its origin and development presented in his Gospel commentary and refined in *The Community of the Beloved Disciple* (1979) to its final outcome that would be taken up in the commentary on the letters. Given Brown's intricate analysis of the ecclesial situation reflected in the Johannine Epistles, it seems fitting that he dedicated the volume to Archbishop Jean Jadot, who had recently completed his service as Apostolic Delegate to the United States (1973–80). Jadot's enlightened tenure as Apostolic Delegate and the quality of the episcopal appointments promoted by him had been prized by the proponents of the reforms of the Council, but he would be moved more into the shadows as the papacy of John Paul II took hold.

The format of the commentary on the epistles followed the general pattern Brown had set in his Gospel volumes, including a substantial introduction that ran for 146 pages, out of an overall volume of 812 pages, making Brown's commentary on these epistles among the largest ever produced. The brevity of the epistles and their complexity prompted Brown to greatly expand the notes that analyzed the texts in great detail. Most of the introduction to the commentary would be devoted to his elaborate hypothesis about the relationship of the epistles to the Gospel of John and the Johannine tradition and to the ultimate outcome of the intrachurch struggles that seemed to be the major concern of all three letters. As is obvious to any reader of these New Testament letters, 1 John is much longer and more theological in content, whereas 2 and 3 John are very brief and deal with specific situations in the communities addressed by their author.

The Struggle behind the Epistles

Brown's interest in detective work was given full rein as he attempted to trace in considerable detail what were the underlying problems reflected in these texts.[40] From his analysis he concluded that probably the same author wrote all three letters, with 1 and 2 John written at roughly the same time, around AD 100, and 3 John a bit later, perhaps around AD 110, putting them a decade or more later than the final redaction of the Gospel. The letters were addressed to small local communities who were scattered around the region—most likely around Ephesus, the place where Brown believed the final version of the

Gospel of John had also originated. The fact that the Book of Revelation addressed a series of such communities in the western coastal region near Ephesus offered somewhat of a confirmation of this scenario.

Central to Brown's elaboration of the circumstances addressed in the epistles was his conviction that the problem facing the communities was not due to some outside influence, such as Gnostic-oriented persons who were leading the communities astray. Rather, Brown believed that the dispute between what he termed the "adherents" who were aligned with the author of the letters and the "secessionists" he was opposing, stemmed from different interpretations of the Johannine tradition, a tradition fixed in the Gospel of John. Each side of the debate represented different viewpoints that led the Johannine communities to "become increasingly divided over the implications and applications of Johannine thought" (p. 69). Even prior to the writing of 1 John this division had developed into a full scale "schism," with the secessionists separating themselves from the communities loyal to the viewpoint of the author.

Brown attempted to trace what exactly were these differing viewpoints. He believed that the high Christology of John's Gospel, with its emphasis on the preexistence of Jesus and his divine status and, at the same time, the reality of his becoming "flesh" and thus being truly human, was the fundamental source of the divide. The author of 1 John insists on fidelity to "what was from the beginning, what we have heard, what we have seen with our eyes, what we have looked at and touched with our hands, concerning the word of life" (1 John 1:1). The author believes that his interpretation of the Johannine tradition is the true one, the message the recipients of the letter have heard "from the beginning" (1 John 2:7, 24; 3:11; 2 John 5, 6). The secessionists, on the other hand, have departed from the truth; "they are so progressive that they have lost their roots in the teaching of Christ (2 John 9). They do not understand the 'gospel' as it was 'from the beginning' while the author does" (p. 97). They have diminished the significance of Jesus's earthly life— finding his identity as the preexistent Word of God, with his "glory" revealed at the moment of his baptism by John, as eclipsing the importance of his earthly ministry. The emphasis in 1 John 5:6 that Jesus is "the one who came by water and blood, Jesus Christ, not with the water only but with the water and the blood" was intended to refute this viewpoint of the secessionists. It was not a matter of Jesus's divine status being revealed only at his baptism but his "glory" was also revealed in his earthly ministry of teaching and healing and, above all, in his death out of love, that is, "in blood" as well as in water. The interpretation of the tradition promoted by the secessionists could lead to a denial of the fully authentic humanity of Jesus, something affirmed in the Gospel concerning the "Word made flesh" (John 1:14). This diminishment of the salvific importance of the earthly and exemplary life of Jesus could also downplay the importance of moral behavior—the ethic condensed in Johannine tradition with the love command. Likewise, the slogan of the secessionists that Brown detected in 1 John 1:8, 10, claims they "have no sin." While the author would agree that those who believed in Jesus were children of God, he is also convinced that Christians can and do sin and need forgiveness (see 1 John 2:1–2), something that the slogan of the opponents seemed to overlook.

Brown asks if there is not a contradiction in the author repeatedly referring to the love command and the failure of the secessionists to adhere to this essential teaching of Jesus, while, at the same time, the author himself seems to ignore this command regarding his opponents whom he condemns bitterly. Here, Brown mobilizes his own interpretation of the love command that is a mainstay of Jesus's teaching in the Gospel. Brown is convinced that by focusing the command to love "one another" or "brothers," the Johannine love command does not extend to all human beings or to one's enemies—"only true believers in Jesus are the children of God and, therefore, brothers" (p. 85).[41] When applied to the situation behind the epistles, "this means that for the author 'brothers' were those members of the Johannine Community who were in communion (*koinōnia*) with him and his fellow witnesses to the tradition, and who accepted his interpretation of the Johannine Gospel (*angelia*; see 1 John 1:4–5)" (p. 85). Thus, rejecting the secessionists did not involve a violation of the love command; they themselves had violated the command in separating from the brethren Jesus had commanded them to love.

The Aftermath

Brown completes his treatment of the Johannine literature by speculating about the fate of the Johannine communities represented in the epistles. He notes that beyond these three epistles no further literary evidence of the Johannine community exists. It is possible, he concedes, that such communities survived but left no trace in history, "but it is far more likely that most of the author's adherents were swallowed up by the 'Great Church,' while the secessionists drifted off into various 'heretical' movements…movements that finally were rejected by the Great Church."[42]

In both instances, adjustments would be required. Over time, the secessionists would feed the development of deviations from orthodoxy such as Gnosticism, Montanism, and Docetism. For the author's adherents, the more charismatic and fluid structure of the Johannine ecclesial communities would have to adapt to the developing hierarchical order of mainline Christianity. Brown sees evidence of this already happening in 3 John. Here, the conflict is not so much about the supposed doctrinal errors of the secessionists as in 1 and 2 John, but a conflict about authority in a local church. The author, the "Presbyter" or Elder, takes exception to the assertion of authority on the part of Diotrephes, whom Brown believes was a local church leader attempting to control who was welcomed as a teacher in the community—a move perhaps prompted by the danger posed by the secessionists. The author, on the other hand, supposes that his role as "the Elder" (3 John 1), and therefore the privileged interpreter of the Johannine tradition, should override local authority. As Brown observes,

> The hostility of the Presbyter toward Diotrephes may have been based on the true judgment that such a step [i.e., resisting the emissaries of a "provincial Johannine church"] represented a radical departure from the Johannine tradition where the paraclete was the teacher and there was an equality among disciples. But if the Presbyter was a Johannine purist, figures like Diotrephes may have been more perceptive about the only practical way in which the substance of the Johannine tradition could be preserved against secessionist inroads. If such a theory is correct, it was not the Presbyter-author of the Epistles but an emerging Johannine church leader like Diotrephes who was responsible for leading the Johannine remnant into the Great Church.[43]

One final, related question was whether the epistles had any influence on the final redaction of the Gospel itself. The most likely candidate would be the so-called appendix to the Gospel found in John 21, which probably was added later in the composition history of the Gospel. Here, too, there seems to be a juxtaposition of the "Great Church" represented by Peter, and the Johannine tradition represented by the Beloved Disciple. This account of a Galilean resurrection appearance shows respect for both streams of tradition, yet Peter is given pastoral authority by the risen Christ ("feed my sheep") while the Beloved Disciple is not. At the conclusion of the scene, Jesus appears to predict Peter's martyrdom (John 21:19), but also implies that the Beloved Disciple will continue to live beyond Peter (John 21:22–23, "he will remain until I come"). Brown surmises, "Since no similar pastoral role is given to the Beloved Disciple, we may be hearing a symbolic description of the structural difference between two different types of churches. The churches with shepherd-bishops are being told that they must recognize the legitimacy of the churches of the Beloved Disciple, which had no human shepherds, while the latter churches are told that the shepherding roles of the bishops are not contrary to the will of Christ."[44]

Even though the implications of chapter 21 of John's Gospel might reflect similar circumstances as that posed by the secessionists in 1 and 2 John, Brown does not think the author of 3 John would accept the idea of shepherd-bishops being on a par with the authority of the Elder. Thus, it is unlikely that the Johannine Epistles had any direct literary influence on the final redaction of the Gospel.

Even though the end of the Johannine communities leads either into the world of heterodox Christianity or into absorption by the Great Church, Brown considers the original Johannine communities to have left an enduring legacy. "The ultimate victory for the original Johannine Community was to have its preexistence Christology accepted by the Great Church and become Christian orthodoxy. And so it may not be too romantic to think that, while some of the adherents of the author of the Epistles were accommodating themselves to the ecclesiology and structure of the Great Church (perhaps to the author's displeasure), that Church was accommodating itself to the Christology of the Johannine Christians."[45] The ultimate acceptance of the Johannine Epistles into the New Testament canon toward the end of the second century proved that Johannine Christology was fully compatible with orthodoxy and was not the preserve of the Gnostics. "The secessionists, perhaps the larger branch emerging from the schism, may have seemed to triumph by taking GJohn [the Gospel of John] with them down their paths to even more *outré* christologies that would be rejected as heresies....But eventually the comment patterned upon GJohn that the epistolary author left behind (known to us as I John) accomplished the purpose for which it was written—it saved the Johannine Gospel, no longer for the elect of the Johannine Community but for the Great Church and for the main body of Christians ever since."[46]

With this commentary Brown completed his published views about the origin, development, and content of the Johannine community. Putting this portrayal together drew on all of Brown's scholarship and, at times, his daring imagination. His articulation of the development and fate of Johannine Christianity would be refined as he went along and even was subject to some adjustment and simplification in the revision of his commentary on the Gospel he had begun but was never able to complete.[47] He remained modest about his hypotheses, hoping that they would be cogent enough and sufficiently grounded in the evidence provided by the biblical texts to spark discussion and further development on the part of the scholarly community. In his preface to *The Community of the Beloved Disciple*, he confessed, "I warn the reader that my reconstruction [of the Johannine tradition] claims at most probability; and if sixty percent of my detective work is accepted, I shall be happy indeed....With all those cautions let me confess that I find the material I present in this book exciting, and I wholeheartedly invite the reader to share my excitement in seeing familiar material come together in a new way."[48] These words bear testimony to the fact that despite his immersion in details, Brown, acting as the exegete-detective, never lost his enthusiasm for his lifelong scholarly vocation.

CHAPTER 6

SIGNATURE EXEGETICAL WORKS

THE BIRTH AND *DEATH OF THE MESSIAH* AND *AN INTRODUCTION TO THE NEW TESTAMENT*

Along with his exploration of the Johannine literature, three other major publications contributed to Brown's lasting academic legacy: his massive commentaries on the infancy narratives and the passion accounts and his comprehensive introduction to the New Testament. In his *An Introduction to the New Testament,* Brown also tackled the issue of the modern quest for the historical Jesus. All these works bear the encyclopedic qualities of depth and scope we discovered in his commentaries on the Gospel and Letters of John.

THE INFANCY NARRATIVES

In between the completion of his two-volume commentary on the Gospel of John and his commentary on the Johannine Epistles, Brown worked on his massive study of the infancy narratives of Matthew and Luke. The first edition appeared in 1977 while he was well situated in his tenure at Union Theological Seminary in New York. A second revised and expanded edition was published in 1993 after he had moved to St. Patrick's Seminary in Menlo Park. This would be the only major work for which Brown produced a significant "updated" version, as he labeled it.[1]

Brown explains in the preface to his original edition his reason for turning to this part of the New Testament. A historical-critical study of the infancy narratives was, he believed, the "last frontier to be crossed in the relentless advance of the scientific (critical) approach to the Gospels."[2] Some conservative Christians may not be aware that "the infancy material has an origin and a historical quality quite different from that of the rest of the Gospels."[3] They would accept without question that events such as the visit of the Magi following a guiding star or the appearance of the angels to the shepherds have the same historical value as the stories of Jesus's ministry. Some more liberal Christians, on the other hand, consider the infancy narratives as "folklore devoid of real theology...fit only for romantics or the naïve."[4] In both cases, such estimations of the infancy narratives have led to their relative neglect in modern biblical scholarship, even though the wondrous stories of the infancy narratives—along with the vivid accounts of the passion narratives—are the parts of the Gospels that have had a great influence on Christian theology, art, and poetic imagination, not to mention the challenge they pose for preachers at Christmas.[5]

The neglect of the infancy narratives on the part of modern biblical scholarship was a void that Brown wanted to fill with a major commentary. He was willing to address the many historical questions raised by these narratives, but his primary objective was to explore "the role these infancy narratives had in the early Christian understanding of Jesus."[6] As was the case for all his work, Brown believed that the proper application of the historical-critical method to these texts would enhance, not destroy, the impact of these revered accounts on Christian faith. For this reason, his commentary was intended to be "both scholarly and intelligible...and to reach a variety of audiences: fellow scholars, students of theology and of the Bible, and interested Christians."[7] He also recognized Roman Catholic interest in the infancy narratives because of Marian devotion. "As a Roman Catholic myself, I share their faith and their devotion; but it is my firm contention that one should not attempt to read later Marian sensibilities and issues back into the New Testament. (I do not mean that there is no need to relate the NT to later theology, but one must respect historical development.) I see no reason why a Catholic's understanding of what Matthew and Luke meant in their infancy narratives should be different from a Protestant's."[8]

The format for his work would follow the model of his Anchor Bible Commentary on the Gospel of John, with a fresh translation, followed by notes, and concluding with commentary and bibliography. However, the nature of the infancy narratives called for some adaptation of the formula. After a relatively brief (forty pages) introduction to the infancy narratives as a whole, he would treat Matthew's and Luke's infancy narratives separately (labeled "Book One" and "Book Two"), including an introduction to each. He hoped that this separate treatment would demonstrate how the infancy narrative fits into the overall theology of each Gospel and thus "offer some reasons for differences between the infancy narratives."[9] Even more important for the specific character of this volume compared to his work on the Johannine literature, Brown was not focused primarily on determining the composition history of either Matthew or Luke but rather the relationship of their infancy narratives to their Gospels as a whole.

Brown began his study by charting the evolution of critical biblical scholarship concerning the infancy narratives, a history encompassing three stages:

1. The first stage was the realization that the infancy narratives were different from the body of the Gospels and were probably formed last in the development of the gospel tradition. The Gospels, in effect, developed "backwards." The focus of the earliest Christian preaching was the death and resurrection of Jesus, as seen in the creedal formulas found in Paul (1 Cor 15:3–4) and in Acts (2:23, 32; 3:14–15; 4:10; 10:39–40). In the developing gospel traditions, this would lead to the formation of the passion narratives. Christian preachers turned their attention subsequently to the accounts of Jesus's ministry of teaching and healing. The development of Christology and curiosity about the origin of the human Jesus would lead ultimately to the formation of the infancy narratives of Matthew and Luke. Mark's Gospel, beginning with an Old Testament quotation and the ministry of John the Baptist, and the Gospel of John through its Prologue affirming the preexistence of the Word, would also be

concerned about the origin of Jesus's mission but in ways very different from Matthew and Luke.

2. The second stage was to consider the historical value of the infancy narratives. Here, several difficulties arise. Unlike the accounts of Jesus's public ministry, it is difficult to identify who might have been the "corroborating witnesses" for the events of Jesus's conception and birth. Although traditional explanations suggested Mary and Joseph as possible sources, this is very uncertain. Joseph seems to be off the scene during the public ministry of Jesus, and Mary is never cited in the body of the Gospels as a source for information about Jesus's origin. In the case of Matthew's infancy narrative, it is Joseph, not Mary, who is the center of attention. There is also the problem of "conflicting details." There is accord about the affirmation of the virginal conception of Jesus, about the identity of his parents as Mary and Joseph, about his birth in Bethlehem, and his later residence in Nazareth (the latter information could have been deduced from witnesses to the public ministry of Jesus), and about his birth during the reign of Herod the Great. On a myriad of other details, however, it is virtually impossible to harmonize the differences between Matthew's and Luke's accounts. It is likely that both Matthew and Luke drew on such sources as reflection on the Scriptures and some "folkloric" traditions available to their communities to shape their infancy narratives, as well as motifs to be found in Jesus's public ministry and now reflected back into the events of his origin.

3. The final "stage" explores the infancy narratives as illustrative of each evangelist's particular theology. Brown notes that the focus of scholarship "has shifted away from the pre-Gospel history of narratives and sayings about Jesus [i.e., in the infancy narratives] to the role of those narratives and sayings in the finished Gospels. What message is the evangelist trying to convey to the Church through them? This shift of focus can be dangerous if it leads to a neglect of questions of source, historicity, and literary genre; but is healthy in its reaffirmation that the primary task of exegesis is to make sense of the existing text."[10]

This quest for tracing how the specific infancy narratives of Matthew and Luke both prepare for and reflect the portrayal of Jesus and his message found in the body of their Gospels is the driving force of his massive study. As promised, Brown does directly engage some of the historical issues raised by the infancy narratives, for example, the virginal conception of Jesus, the location of Jesus's birth in Bethlehem, the Davidic descent of Jesus, and the census of Quirinius, among others. But his main interest is in the evangelists' theological portrayal of Jesus and his identity, and the function of the infancy narratives as overtures to Matthew's and Luke's Gospels as a whole. In this Brown was in line with the method of "redaction criticism" that was becoming increasingly popular in biblical scholarship on the Gospels. The focus here was on the specific perspective brought to the gospel materials by each evangelist's perspective, a perspective influenced by the community and context in which the Gospel was composed. The accumulation of "redactions" or "edits" traced to the evangelist enabled one to track the particular theological perspective of the Gospel. In the case of the study of the infancy narratives of Matthew and Luke, that theological quest is summarized in masterful conclusions or what Brown terms "epilogues" to each of the "Books" of his commentary.

Matthew

Matthew, Brown notes, uses the infancy narrative (Matt 1—2) as a "remarkable preface to his Gospel."[11] While John the Baptist is the immediate lead-in to the Gospel with his proclamation of God (as in Mark's Gospel), Matthew portrays the whole of God's activity in Israel as the ultimate preparation for the advent of Jesus as the Messiah. This is achieved through the genealogy that traces Israel's history from its origin in Abraham to its culmination in Jesus. Some of the events that Jesus and his family experience embody elements of Israel's own history such as the infancy of Moses, the threat of Pharaoh (e.g., Herod and Archelaus), taking refuge in Egypt (Joseph), and being called out of Egypt to the promised land. Matthew's account is laced with scriptural quotations and allusions, as will be the case with the body of his Gospel, demonstrating that Jesus "fulfills" the Scriptures (see Matt 5:17). Jesus also experiences, even in his infancy, the hostility of the authorities, but Joseph, the just man, provides continuity with Israel through his fidelity to the law and his protection of Jesus, ultimately bringing him and Mary to the safety of Galilee, which Matthew describes as the "Galilee of the Gentiles"—anticipating the ultimate mission to the Gentiles that will form the climax to Matthew's narrative. Above all, Matthew affirms the identity of Jesus as the Messiah, the Son of David and Abraham, but also as the "savior" and the unique "son of God," as evident in Matthew's explanation of the significance of the name "Jesus" and especially that of "Emmanuel," "God with us," which affirms Jesus's "divine sonship" alongside his identity as the Davidic Messiah.[12]

Brown also underscores the effectiveness of Matthew's infancy narrative, whose elements are "known by many who know little else of the Gospel" and has been the "subject of countless plays, poems, hymns, and pictures."[13] His final summation is worth quoting:

> There are preachers who are uneasy about the popularity of this story, feeling that it serves as a palliative for true Gospel. But this is to neglect the fact that the infancy narrative contains both the cross and the God-given triumph. Herod stalks the trail of the magi, a menacing reminder that, while the star of the newborn King has shone forth in purity and simplicity, there are those who seek to blot out that light. If the infancy story is an attractive drama that catches the imagination, it is also a substantial proclamation of the coming of the kingdom and its possible rejection. The dramatis personae may be exotically costumed as Eastern potentates and as a Jewish king and priests, and for that reason they are not easily forgotten. But beneath the robes one can recognize the believers of Matthew's time and their opponents. And, indeed, a perceptive reader may even recognize some of the drama of the Christian proclamation and its fate in all times.[14]

For Brown, no matter how technical his exegesis might become, the pastoral significance of the biblical text was never out of sight.

Luke

Brown's analysis of the Lukan infancy narrative demonstrated its similar functions to that of Matthew—creating a strong link to the Old Testament and serving as a prelude to the Gospel as a whole. Yet the dramatically different structure of Luke's first two chapters and the characteristic tonalities of his theology fashion an infancy narrative very different from that of Matthew's Gospel. Important, too, is that the probable audience of Luke's Gospel is a "church of the Gentile mission in the 70s or 80s,"[15] whereas the probable context of Matthew's narrative was "written in Syria by an unknown Greek-speaking Jewish Christian, living in the 80s in a mixed community with converts of both Jewish and Gentile descent."[16]

Brown believes it is likely that Luke joined the infancy narrative of chapters 1 and 2 to the body of his Gospel as a last step in the formation of his overall narrative. Matthew seems to have begun his composition moving organically from the opening verse in Matthew 1:1 and through the infancy narrative into the events of Jesus's public ministry. But, in the case of Luke, it is more difficult to trace a seamless literary thread from the opening scenes into the rather formal and dramatic beginning of Jesus's public ministry in Luke 3:1–2 ("In the fifteenth year of the reign of Emperor Tiberius, when Pontius Pilate was governor of Judea, and Herod was ruler of Galilee, and his brother Philip ruler of the region of Ituraea and Trachonitis..."). The presence of the genealogy in chapter 3 of Luke, after the account of Jesus's baptism, also makes more sense if the original beginning of Luke's Gospel had not included an infancy narrative.

Brown spends considerable time discussing the possible source or sources the evangelist used in composing his infancy narrative.[17] He doubts that there was an intact pre-Lukan infancy narrative that was simply fused to the beginning of the Gospel by the evangelist. It is more likely that Luke drew on several sources and knitted them together:

It was Luke himself who combined and fleshed out these traditions, incorporating a Christian creedal formula about Jesus as son of David and Son of God, and portraits of JBap [John the Baptist] and Mary gleaned from the Gospel account of the public ministry. With a sense of parallelism, he constructed an annunciation of JBap's conception to match the annunciation of Jesus' conception, exhibiting theological care to keep JBap on a lower level. The characters of JBap's parents he constructed on the pattern of Abraham and Sarah from the OT, as part of his plan to make the infancy narrative a bridge between Israel and Jesus.[18]

True to his word, Brown was particularly interested in the theological intent of Luke's infancy narrative. Like Matthew's account, Luke is interested in providing the connection of Jesus's origin with Israel, but he is less obvious. Where Matthew constructs Jesus's genealogy to trace his Davidic descent and lead into his conception, Luke's genealogy is related to Jesus's baptism and is traced back to Adam. Where Matthew chooses to highlight Joseph's role, Luke puts the spotlight on John the Baptist and Mary. Another significant difference is the role played by the Jewish authorities. In Matthew, there is overt hostility and threat on the part of Herod and even the Jerusalem establishment, reflective of the post-70 context of the Gospel of Matthew as a whole. Luke omits mention of any threat against Jesus by the Jewish authorities in his infancy narrative.

> In fact, Luke…shows a consistently favorable picture of Jews who almost instinctively recognize the infant Jesus as the fulfillment of the Law, the prophets, and the cult. As the Spirit is poured out on their representatives (Mary, Zechariah, Simeon), they burst into poetic praise of what God has done for His people, and thus the days of the infancy anticipate the outpouring of the Spirit of prophecy at Pentecost. Luke is more interested in establishing the continuity of the Christian movement with Israel than in anti-synagogue apologetics. His heroine Mary will embody that continuity—she responds obediently to God's word from the first as a representative of the Anawim of Israel (1:38); she appears in the ministry as a representative of the ideals of true discipleship (8:19–21); and she endures till Pentecost to become a Christian and member of the Church (Acts 1:14).[19]

At the end of his detailed analysis of Luke's account, Brown brings together the rich harvest of his overall conclusions about both infancy narratives. Although he had demonstrated in the body of his study that Matthew and Luke provide very different accounts of Jesus's origin, "there is a common understanding of the birth of the Messiah."[20] Both accounts "stress the intrinsic connection of that birth with what has preceded in Israel" and both "develop the Christological significance of the birth and thus its incipient continuity with what will follow in the

Gospel. For both evangelists the infancy narrative is the place where the OT and the Gospel most directly meet."[21]

The 1993 Update

One of Brown's hopes in producing his massive study of the infancy narratives was that it would inspire modern biblical scholarship to give more attention to these important yet complex parts of the gospel literature. The success of *The Birth of the Messiah* accomplished that goal. As he notes in the preface to his supplement, nearly five hundred books and articles had appeared since his 1976 publication, many of them in direct dialogue with Brown's work. This impressive response prompted Brown to compose an "update" to his original work, *The Birth of the Messiah: A Commentary on the Infancy Narratives in the Gospels of Matthew and Luke: New Updated Edition*.[22] The designation "updated" rather than "revised" accurately captures the unusual format and purpose of this work that appeared fifteen years after his original study. Brown's views developed in his original volume had not changed in any substantial way. Rather, his primary purpose was to interact with a substantial number of the studies that had appeared in the interim, particularly those that directly engaged his own views. In the new volume, the original text and pagination of the 1976 edition remained untouched with the new material added as a supplement at the end of the original material, with notes in the supplement referring to pertinent sections in the original text. Additionally, Brown fully updated the bibliography. The general sequence of the supplement followed the outline of the original, with comments first on the general introduction to the infancy narratives, then a separate consideration of Matthew's (Book One) and Luke's (Book Two) narratives. Among the appendices found in the original edition, only "Appendix IV" dealing with "The Virginal Conception of Jesus" received an "updated" treatment.

Most of the supplement is taken up with Brown's detailed interaction with the numerous books and articles dealing either with the infancy narratives in general or with specific passages and issues raised by these texts. As Brown had anticipated, a lot of attention was paid to the question of the historicity of the infancy narratives and, in particular, the implications for the objectivity of the historical-critical method and its alignment with church doctrine. Naturally, much of the debate about historicity focused on the evangelists' assertion of the virginal conception of Jesus. Brown would take this up not only in the supplement proper but in the revised "Appendix IV." On this question, Brown's study had provoked criticism from both the left and the right. Brown had not wavered from his original position that the proper application of the historical-critical method would neither unequivocally confirm or rule out of bounds the historical truth of the virginal conception.[23] As he had expressed it, "I came to the conclusion that the *scientifically controllable* biblical evidence leaves the question of the historicity of the virginal conception unresolved; yet there was better evidence for historicity than against."[24] Critics on the left questioned whether Brown pulled his punches about historicity to avoid contradiction with church dogma. Particularly annoying for Brown were the views of the Episcopalian Bishop John Spong who accused Brown as a Roman Catholic of being forced to "constantly discipline his scholarship in the service of the official teaching and dogma of his tradition. That makes it difficult for him to follow his scholarship if it leads to ecclesiastically unacceptable conclusions."[25]

Even more acute were the reactions of some conservative Roman Catholic scholars who asserted that Brown's measured conclusion about historicity put him at odds with Catholic teaching. Brown saw this as a failure on their part to appreciate the careful distinctions present in his views. He continued to affirm, based solely on a historical-critical analysis of the biblical texts, that the historicity of the virginal conception cannot be definitively proven by the biblical evidence nor can it be ruled out. In fact, Brown himself believed that the evidence favored historicity even if not definitively so. But in articulating his own viewpoint on the meaning of the virginal conception and guided by the teaching authority of the Roman Catholic Church, Brown was comfortable in affirming the historical reality of the virginal conception.

To clarify his position further, he listed four possible views concerning the historicity of the virginal conception:[26]

1. *Exegetical evidence establishes the historicity of the virginal conception.* Based on his analysis of the evidence, Brown did not agree, affirming that the evidence leaves the question of historicity unresolved.
2. *Church teaching does not require belief in the virginal conception.* While conceding he was not a theological

expert on this issue, he believed that the virginal conception was "infallibly taught."

3. *Theological arguments cannot guide exegesis in the issue of the virginal conception.* Here, Brown contended mainly with more liberal critics who believed he was allowing his theological convictions to taint his objectivity about the biblical text. Brown disagreed vigorously, asserting that critics who ruled out theological perspectives altogether were, in fact, also coming to the text with their own brand of secular theology. He noted that the early church's beliefs did not derive from their study of the New Testament; rather, the New Testament expressed the faith of the community.

4. Finally, *exegetical evidence disproves the virginal conception.* Here, Brown appealed to his meticulous analysis of the infancy narratives that confirms that both Matthew and Luke—independently of each other—clearly affirm the virginal conception.

One final issue to which Brown gave considerable attention was the thesis of his former student, Jane Schaberg.[27] In both the body of his supplement and in "Appendix IV," Brown systematically rebutted her thesis, which asserted that the motif of the virginal conception was used to mask the illegitimacy of Jesus's birth (as Joseph first concludes in Matt 1:18–19) and, furthermore, that Mary's pregnancy was probably the result of being raped. God's protection of Mary (through Joseph in Matthew's account) and the favor bestowed on her in Luke's account of the annunciation were the theological affirmations of the evangelists, proclaiming the traditional biblical doctrine of God's favor for the poor and downtrodden.[28] Luke's account of Mary's visitation to Elizabeth implied her need to avoid the shame of her pregnancy. Brown conceded that charges of Jesus's illegitimacy were not only echoed in Matthew's account but also became something of a staple in some later Jewish anti-Christian polemics. However, the assertion that the conception of Jesus was due to rape has no evidence in the biblical text and was never raised in antiquity. Additionally, he believed it "destroys the theological identity of Jesus intended by Matt in 1:18–25. Jesus is not the son of an unknown. He is truly *Son of God* through creative generation in the womb of Mary from the Holy Spirit of God; Jesus is truly *Son of*

David through acceptance by the Davidic Joseph, who named as his son the child thus conceived in Mary's womb."[29] As Brown concluded, "One should not decry solitary scholarship [such as Schaberg's isolated thesis], but it does leave one open to the suspicion that the proposed insight is in the interpreter's eye rather than in the author's intent."[30]

The sensational nature of Schaberg's thesis and its amplification in the press and its endorsement by Spong's popular book *Born of a Woman* resulted in severe criticism of Schaberg and even personal threats against her. This was painful, not only for Schaberg, but for Brown, too. Along with his strong refutation of her work, Brown added some words of support: "Schaberg's thesis has aroused anger as it has been sensationalized...; and so it should be emphasized that she has sought to argue as a scholar, is generally fair to other views, and shows no intentional tone of irreverence in her depiction of Mary as a rape victim. The reason her thesis will remain utterly implausible to most other scholars need have nothing to do with an establishment position or fear of church reaction."[31]

Conclusion

Brown's study of the infancy narratives remains a classic resource. No other study has matched it in scope and depth.[32] The "updated" edition provided the opportunity for Brown to interact with the scholarly literature that had appeared since the original edition of his study, but it did not substantially alter or advance his views about the infancy narratives. Brown's description of the origin, purpose, structure, and theology of the infancy narratives of Matthew and Luke will continue to be a point of reference for biblical scholarship for many years to come. But this academic achievement—like most of Brown's work—was prompted by pastoral concerns, namely, the hold that the infancy narratives had on Christian faith and imagination, and the depth of their proclamation about the identity of Jesus.

THE DEATH OF THE MESSIAH

Brown signed his contract with Doubleday to produce a study of the passion narratives on March 11, 1981, with a due date set for September 30, 1990, a date that was later moved to October 1992. But

Brown had been working on this massive study for over ten years and, as he wrote to his provincial, Gerald Brown (no relation), in 1989, "I have made an oath that I write nothing else until I do [finish it]."[33] It would be titled *The Death of the Messiah: From Gethsemane to the Grave: A Commentary on the Passion Narratives in the Four Gospels* and would appear in two volumes.[34] In many ways, this undertaking would be the most challenging of his major exegetical works. The literature on the passion narratives was vast, and in analyzing and comparing the texts of all four Gospels, the scope of this study was more extensive than he had attempted before. His work on this project began while he was at Union and would not be completed until he had moved to Menlo Park. His preparation included making various aspects of the passion narratives the subjects of his many public lectures as well as teaching courses on this topic at Union. He also devoted his last sabbatical during his Union years (1988–89) to feverish work on this text. Half of that sabbatical year he spent in Rome, and he noted in his letter to his provincial that he had written five hundred pages, spending most of his time in the library of the Pontifical Biblical Institute. He planned to do another five hundred pages when he moved to California, but, he confessed, "It gets harder and harder every day."

Why the passion narratives? No doubt his work on the infancy narratives and the successful impact of *The Birth of the Messiah* led him to turn next to the passion accounts. In both instances, Brown's pastoral instincts were at work. While somewhat neglected by biblical scholarship, popular piety as well as art and music feasted on the Christmas stories. The same was true for the accounts of Jesus's suffering and crucifixion. As he noted in the preface, "Aesthetically, more than any other section of the Gospels, indeed even more than the infancy narrative, it [the passion narrative] has captured the attention and imagination of dramatists (passion plays), artists, and musicians. Literarily, passion vignettes have left their mark on language and imagery: thirty pieces of silver, Judas' kiss, cockcrow, washing one's hands of blood."[35] Likewise, the death of Jesus was "the most public moment of his life as figures known from Jewish or secular history (Caiaphas, Annas, Pilate) crossed his path."[36] Even more important is the place the death of Jesus on the cross holds in Christian theology as "the key element in God's plan for the justification, redemption, and salvation of all," and spiritually, "the Jesus of the passion has been the focus of Christian meditation for countless would-be disciples who take seriously the demand of the

Master to take up the cross and follow him," a focus that would also be reflected in the fact that the passion accounts are the "center piece of Lent and Holy Week, the most sacred time in the liturgical calendar."[37] Thus, Brown concludes, "In sum, from every point of view the passion is the central narrative in the Christian story."[38]

The Format and Method

Brown wrestled with the design of his study. In general, he would follow the format of his other commentaries on the Johannine litera- ture and the infancy narratives, that is, a fresh literal translation of the text, followed by extensive notes and broader commentary, accompa- nied by a voluminous bibliography and a series of appendices on spe- cific issues. However, for this work he changed the order of the notes and commentary, leading with the commentary section to make the content of the passion accounts more accessible to the reader. But the fourfold passion accounts raised a challenge he had not faced before; should he pursue a "vertical approach" that would consider each of the four passion accounts in turn, similar to his approach in dealing with the infancy narratives of Matthew and Luke? Or was it prefera- ble to proceed "horizontally," immediately comparing the four parallel accounts of each scene in the passion story?[39] Brown decided that the "horizontal" approach was preferable in a part of the gospel literature where all four evangelists were tantalizingly close. At the same time, he assured his readers he was not trying to "harmonize" the four accounts and would pay attention to "the 'vertical' chain of thought peculiar to each Gospel read consecutively."[40]

At the outset Brown reminded his readers of his general suppo- sitions about the Gospels and their formation, a subject that he had addressed in most of his commentary writings, and the particular pur- pose of this commentary. His stated goal was "to explain in detail what the evangelists intended and conveyed to their audiences by their nar- ratives of the passion and death of Jesus."[41] He parsed each word of this goal. The evangelists were not eyewitnesses but were composing their Gospels at the culmination of a developmental process that was rooted in the history of Jesus and his disciples but also proclaimed in the preaching and ministry of the early church. This stream of mainly oral tradition would be absorbed variously by each of the evangelists. Brown accepted the working hypothesis of the so-called two-source theory that asserted that Mark was the first Gospel written and was used as a primary source by Matthew and Luke, combined with other sources used independently of each other to form their distinctive Gospels. John's Gospel drew on its own stream of tradition, independent of the Synoptic Gospels but in some instances reflecting similarities with the oral tradition that fed the Synoptic Gospels. Each evangelist imposed his own unique theological perspective on his Gospel account.

While recognizing that one cannot be completely confident about retrieving the intention of an ancient writer, Brown believed that careful analysis could yield a reasonable sense of what the author intended. Further complication was the fact that any author's intent may be different from what was actually "conveyed" by the language used. Yet here, too, Brown believed that in most instances what the author conveyed through a written text represented what the author intended to say.

Equally important was the "audiences" of the gospel writers. He recognized that the circumstances of the audiences addressed by the evangelists may each be distinct and that this could leave an impact on the text. For example, the fact that Mark would spell out the meaning of Jewish customs, such as the washing of hands before meals (Mark 7:34), suggested that his audience was not Jewish. In the references to the tearing of the Temple veil in the Synoptic passion accounts, would the audience of the Gospels know which veil was being referred to? Educated guesses might also need to be made about the extent of acquaintance an audience had with the Jewish Scriptures. As Brown concluded, "Combing the Gospel to detect the likely mentality of its audience is not an easy task."[42]

Brown emphasized the fact that the passion accounts were "dramatic narratives" [his term], in fact, the most extensive narrative segments of the gospel literature. The interpreter needed to consider the dynamics and literary structure of a narrative. This is reflected in part by Brown's choice to divide his analysis of the passion account into "acts" and "scenes." The four acts were (1) the prayer/arrest of Jesus, (2) the Jewish trial, (3) the Roman trial, and (4) the crucifixion. Within each "act" Brown also detected one or more "scenes." While attention to the contours and dynamics of a narrative was important, Brown remained skeptical about the overly complex literary and structural methodologies employed by some modern exegetes. In making his point, Brown cited a particularly obscure quotation from G. Bucher, who took a structuralist approach to an analysis of Matthew's passion narrative. At the end of the quotation, Brown comments wryly, "Despite my deep

145

concern for narrative and its structure, I have no idea whether I meet what is envisaged in those words."[43]

The Historicity of the Passion Accounts

Brown devoted considerable attention to the question of the historicity of the passion narratives. Here again, his instinctive moderation and good sense enabled him to weave through some difficult and controversial material. His fundamental perspective about the Gospels as a whole was expressed in this way: "In this commentary I shall work with the understanding that the Gospels are distillations of earlier Christian preaching and teaching about Jesus. The individual evangelists organized what they took over from such a background to communicate to their audiences an interpretation of Jesus that would nourish faith and life (as John 20:31 states explicitly)."[44] This formulation was counter to the views both of those who assumed that everything narrated in the Gospels is historical and those who dismissed out of hand any historical value for the Gospels.

Brown applied this general framework about the evolution of the Gospels to the specific question of the historical value of the passion accounts. The fundamental message of the passion account reflects the core message of early Christian preaching, a tradition reflected in the Pauline formula of 1 Corinthians 15:3–5, namely, that Jesus's death was "in accordance with the Scriptures" and that he was buried, and that he was raised again on the third day, "according to the Scriptures." The creedal formula cited by Paul here and its elaboration in the overall message of Paul and the other New Testament writers is that the death and resurrection of Jesus form the source of Christian salvation. To further explore this meaning, the early Christians turned, understandably, to their Scriptures, the Old Testament, finding in the prophecies of Isaiah, the Psalms, and other texts the backdrop for the sufferings and triumph of Christ. The passion narratives themselves are filled with such allusions to Scripture such as the division of Jesus's garments, the offering of vinegary wine, the formulation of the final words of Jesus, and so on.

However, Brown insists, this does not mean that the passion accounts are devoid of history or are simply *theologumena*, that is, purely theological affirmations put in narrative form. While the evangelists themselves were not eyewitnesses to the events of the passion and surely the "eyewitness memories of Jesus came down to the evangelists [with] considerable reshaping and development,"[45] this does not preclude that some historical information has left its mark on the narratives such as the circumstances of Jesus's arrest, the kind of charges brought against him at his trial, and the reality of his crucifixion and burial. "Thus from the earliest days available historical raw material could have been developed into a PN [passion narrative] in the course of evangelistic use and it might have been embellished and added to by Christian imagination."[46] In other words, the theological intent of the passion narratives does not thereby preclude their containing some fundamental historical information. Brown takes exception to the view of scholars such as Helmut Koester and, in particular, John Dominic Crossan, who contended that the early Christians had no interest in the historical details of what happened regarding the death of Jesus. Brown quotes the assertion of Crossan: "It seems to me most likely that those closest to Jesus knew almost nothing about the details of the event. They knew only that Jesus had been crucified, outside Jerusalem, at the time of Passover, and probably through some conjunction of imperial and sacerdotal authority."[47] As Brown retorts, "[Crossan] does not explain why he thinks this 'most likely,' granted the well-founded tradition that those closest to Jesus had followed him for a long period of time, day and night. Did they suddenly lose all interest, not even taking the trouble to inquire about what must have been a most traumatic moment of their lives?"[48] Likewise, the creedal formula cited by Paul in 1 Corinthians 15:3–5 and Paul's reference to the Last Supper on the eve of Jesus's death (1 Cor 11:23–26) belie the fact that the early Christians were not interested in the historical details of Jesus's death; the reference to "burial" in 1 Corinthians 15:4 was not drawn from Scripture but from the memory of the community, as was the fact that Jesus celebrated a final Passover with his disciples. Crossan himself would speculate, without any evidence to support his hypothesis, that Jesus was not buried but his body left exposed and eventually eaten by dogs.

Affirming that the passion accounts were not devoid of historical information did not mean that it was easy to detect such historical information. Here, Brown would refer to the sort of criteria used by explorers of the historical Jesus such as "multiple attestation," that is, materials found in a variety of sources; "coherence" of some incidents with other passages that had multiple attestation; "embarrassment," that is, this material ascribed to Jesus that would most likely not have been invented by the early church; and "discontinuity" or "dissimilarity," that is, material that is unique compared to the ordinary social context of the times. The application of these criteria is not conclusive, however, and Brown conceded that there is much we do not know about the circumstances of Palestine in the time of Jesus, such as the details of Jewish and Roman law concerning capital punishment.

In view of this, Brown laid out five principles that would guide his historical and theological inquiry in his commentary on the passion narratives:

1. The need to be aware of the difference between history and tradition. The assertion that some aspect of the text is derived from "tradition" does not mean that it necessarily goes back to the time of Jesus himself but may date from early Christian traditions that developed some time after the death of Jesus but prior to the formulation of the passion narratives.

2. Likewise, judgments about the historicity of details may be only "probable" and would rarely have absolute certitude. As Brown notes, "When we are dealing with accounts written over nineteen hundred years ago by non-eyewitnesses about a death that had occurred some thirty to seventy years before, certitude about the historicity of details is understandably infrequent."[49]

3. Although he would take up these issues, the primary concern of a commentary is not the reconstruction of pregospel traditions or in detecting history, but "making sense of what the biblical writers have given us."[50]

4. Brown's approach would not attempt to "harmonize" the four passion narratives. Attempting to harmonize the four accounts presumes that each one is reporting history, but, in fact, along with some historical remembrance, the evangelists are portraying the events to proclaim the meaning of Jesus's death in accord with the perspective of each of their Gospels.

5. The purpose of the commentary is not to explore history but what the evangelists conveyed through their accounts. As Brown puts it, "While I have a deep respect for historical investigation, I regard an obsession with the historical to be as great an obstruction to understand the Gospel PNs

as the cavalier assumption that Christians knew nothing about what happened. It is not tautological to insist that the Gospels are primarily evangelistic; to make them dominantly reportorial is a distortion."[51]

The Theology of the Passion Narratives

After cutting through the brush of the historicity question, Brown turned to the theological dimension of the passion narratives that would be the primary guiding interest of his commentary. He used the term "theology" deliberately, rather than the "Christology" of the passion narratives, for "what happens to Jesus in the passion and the way he responds to it are revelatory of the God whose rule or presence he proclaimed."[52] More precisely, the "theology" the commentary will focus on is "how *the evangelists* understood the death of Jesus, not how Jesus understood his own death or how his death was understood in the broad range of early Christianity."[53] To illustrate the specific theology of each evangelist, Brown conceded that he had to work around his chosen "horizontal" approach to the passion accounts. While comparing similar scenes across all four accounts, he wanted also to be alert to the consistent theological outlook of each evangelist.

The work of determining the theology of each passion account, as well as comparing and contrasting the evangelists' way of presenting the various scenes of their overall narrative, consumed the attention of his massive commentary. Before setting out on that task, Brown presented what he called a "short preview" of those outlooks. The passion narratives of Mark and Matthew had the most similarities to each other, presenting a Jesus who is abandoned by his followers and must face his hour alone, thus enduring the cross in a particularly agonizing way. Especially in Mark, the disciples abandon their master at his time of greatest need. Jesus dies alone, crying out in anguish in the opening words of Psalm 22 (quoted by both Mark and Matthew) but is vindicated by God, just as the disciples who fail will ultimately be reconciled with the risen Jesus. To the stark account of Mark, Matthew adds some motifs peculiar to his Gospel, primarily his tendency to attribute responsibility for the death of Jesus to the Jewish authorities, while at the same time presenting Gentiles more favorably (e.g., Pilate's wife, who intervenes on Jesus's behalf, and Pilate himself, who washes his hands to assert his innocence).

While still a passion story, Luke's account has a more positive tone. Jesus dies as he lived, as a prophet and martyr. The exemplary character of Jesus is apparent in the passion account—praying for his disciples and Peter, forgiving his executioners, consoling the Jerusalem crowd, and promising paradise to the criminal who is crucified alongside him. This exemplary character of Jesus's death will also be reflected in Acts such as the witness of Stephen at his moment of death. Instead of the lament Psalm 22 on his dying lips, the Lukan Jesus cites Psalm 31, entrusting his spirit to his Father. Luke also has access to traditions unique to his account, such as the encounter with Herod Antipas during his trial before Pilate. Contrary to those who question whether Luke's passion story portrays the salvific dimension of Jesus's death, Brown cites Luke 22:20, where at the Last Supper Jesus refers to "my blood which is poured out for you," and Paul's words in Acts 20:28, which speak of the church saved "with the blood of His own Son."

As is the case throughout his Gospel, John's account deviates in a more pronounced way from the Synoptic versions. Hostility to Jesus on the part of the Jewish authorities is emphasized throughout the body of John's Gospel and points to his death, as does the final "sign" performed by Jesus in the raising of Lazarus (John 11). In the passion narrative itself, Jesus appears to be in command and the account has an overall triumphant tone. As foreseen in the Gospel, Jesus, the Son of Man is "lifted up" in return to the Father. The moment of Jesus's death is the culmination of his mission from the Father to reveal God's love for the world and so Jesus's final words are "it is completed." Jesus is buried in the manner of a king, as it was proclaimed on his cross, with his identity as "King of the Jews" written in four languages.

Brown adds some final comments on the distinctiveness of the Johannine account. "It has been said," he notes, "that until the moment he dies, the Marcan Jesus is a victor only in the eyes of God; the Lucan Jesus is a victor in the eyes of his believing followers, but the Johannine Jesus is a victor for all to see."[54] Some readers might find it difficult to identify with the triumphant Jesus of John's account, which seems "scarcely a human way to die." Yet, Brown concludes eloquently, "This is the narrative that has made Good Friday good. It is a narrative for all those who in the course of history have been persecuted by the powerful, but whose sense that God is with them has made them realize how little power any worldly authority really has. Those who believe in Jesus have eternal life, and like him they can say, 'No one takes it from me.'

It is a passion seen so totally with the eyes of faith that the victim has become the conqueror."[55]

The Pre-Marcan Passion Narrative

Brown takes up one other major issue in his introduction, namely, a closer look at the prehistory of the passion tradition, specifically the question of whether there was a "pre-Marcan" passion account that served as the source for the version that appears in Mark's Gospel.[56] Put in its most direct terms, did the evangelist Mark have access to an older and already formulated version of the passion narrative that he incorporated into his Gospel, or was the composition of the passion narrative primarily the work of Mark himself? Since Brown, in accord with most scholars, believed that Mark's Gospel served as the primary source for the accounts of Matthew and Luke, this question also touches on the issue of the historical reliability of the passion accounts.

After surveying various opinions on the topic and sifting through the textual evidence himself, Brown concluded that there was probably no developed passion account, whether written or oral, prior to the composition of Mark's Gospel. This did not mean that Mark created his narrative out of whole cloth, or that it was simply theology expressed in a narrative format. Rather Mark's account was a "preeminent distillation of the way Jesus was proclaimed in apostolic or, at least traditional preaching. Paul (1 Cor 15:11) offers us evidence that there was a common apostolic preaching about Jesus: Having given a traditional sequence about Jesus (died, buried, raised, appeared) and having mentioned Cephas (Peter), the Twelve, James (the brother of the Lord) and all the apostles, Paul says, 'Whether then I or they, so do we preach [*keryssein*] and so do you believe.'"[57] Thus the passion account composed by Mark "embodied a traditional or widely accepted pattern, i.e., that *Mark constituted a good summary of the main lines of the Jesus tradition familiar to major Christian communities from earlier preaching*."[58]

Both Matthew and Luke would incorporate Mark's passion narrative into their respective Gospels, adding special material of their own— some of which were drawn from traditional sources available to them and other embellishments that may have been primarily the work of the evangelist himself.[59] It is worth quoting Brown's summary of his position at the conclusion of his long introduction to his commentary:

151

To summarize, the thesis which I shall work in this commentary is that on the preGospel level (before tradition had been channeled into lines of development leading to any one of the four Gospels) there existed at least a sequence of the principal stages in the death of Jesus, along with some stories about episodes or figures in that death. There may have been one or more preGospel *narratives* of the passion composed from this material, but neither the fact nor the wording of the contents of such a narrative can be established persuasively....Mark wrote his PN without use of any of the other canonical PNs. The Matthean PN drew heavily on Mark's PN; yet Matt has incorporated into the material taken from Mark a body of popular and imaginative tradition....The Lucan PN also drew heavily but more freely on Mark's PN. No other PN was used by Luke; but there were oral traditions...that he combined in orderly fashion with the material drawn from Mark. Some of those preLucan traditions (perhaps in a preGospel form) were also known to John. John did not use any of the Synoptic PNs in writing his own account, even though some of the preGospel tradition on which he drew resembled material on which Mark and Luke drew. Whether or not a preJohannine PN had already been shaped is not possible to determine.[60]

Conclusion

As was the case for his previous major works, Brown's study of the passion narratives was well received and, for a work of this type, a "bestseller."[61] While studies of the passion accounts continue to appear, Brown's major study remains an enduring point of reference. Its strength lies not only in making a painstaking case for the particular theology of each evangelist's passion account but also in its meticulous and forthright assessment of the historicity of the passion narratives and the path of their formation in early Christianity. The composition of his commentaries on the infancy narratives in *The Birth of the Messiah* and on the passion narratives in *The Death of the Messiah* had consumed a major portion of more than seventeen years of his academic life, even more if one counts his revision of *The Birth of the Messiah* that appeared in 1993, simultaneously with his work on the passion narratives. As we

Brown attended the Sulpician seminary college,
St. Charles, Catonsville, Maryland, 1945–46.

At work on the Dead Sea Scrolls at the famed
"scrollery" in Jerusalem. The priest in the Roman collar
is Patrick Skehan, a scholar Brown greatly admired.

At his desk in the early years of his teaching at St. Mary's
Seminary and University (1959–71). The photo of his parents
that he kept on his desk throughout his life is visible.

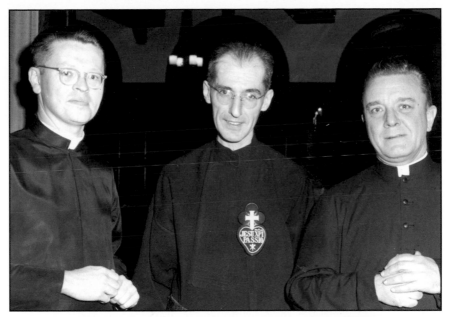

With fellow biblical scholars Barnabas Mary Ahern, CP,
and John J. Castelot, SS, Baltimore, February 1962.

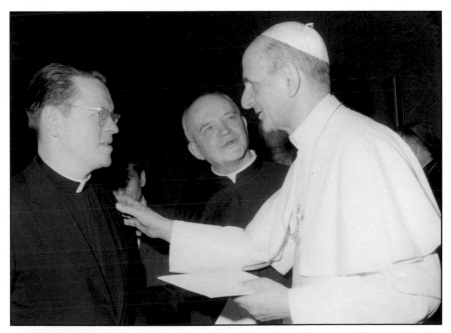

With Pope Paul VI, probably at the time of Brown's first
appointment to the Pontifical Biblical Commission (1972–78).

Wearing his honorary doctoral robes from the
University of Uppsala, 1974, one of thirty-one
honorary doctorates awarded Brown.

With his Mormon friend Truman Madsen, a leader in
the Church of Jesus Christ of Latter-Day Saints.

Meeting with Pope John Paul II and with Brown's close friend
Archbishop John Quinn of San Francisco.

With Phyllis Trible at the retirement party for
Eileen Tobin (Brown's secretary) in 1990.

With Sandra Schneiders, IHM, Granada,
July 1992, before the international
Society for New Testament Studies
meeting in Spain.

A social evening with friends in Phyllis Trible's apartment at
Union Seminary, mid-1990s: left to right, Raymond Brown
(laughing at a description of him in a detective story), Seth Casten
(the Union librarian), Sarah Ryan, PBVM (a friend and former student),
Agneta Enermalm (a New Testament colleague, lower right, back
view), and Phyllis Trible reading from the detective story.

With Pope John Paul II and Cardinal Joseph Ratzinger
at the time of Brown's second appointment to the
Pontifical Biblical Commission in 1997.

Brown visiting the Sulpician cemetery at St. Charles Villa, Catonsville, Maryland, in 1985 (his final resting place).

noted earlier, besides these blockbuster commentaries on the infancy and the passion narratives, Brown published numerous other, briefer, and more popular studies on these materials, including his essays on the virginal conception.[62] He himself noted this concentration on these particular portions of the gospel literature: "But whatever the judgment of others, I thank God's providence that has permitted me to spend so many years of my life in commenting on the biblical accounts of Jesus' birth and death. Not only have I learned more of the one for whom 'Messiah' (*Christos*) became a second name, but I have come to respect deeply the skill of the evangelists without whose contribution that name would not be known in all its profundity. In a small way may my work make their work better known."[63]

AN INTRODUCTION TO THE NEW TESTAMENT

Raymond Brown's final major work was published in 1997, only a year before his death.[64] Unlike his other major works we have reviewed, this was not a commentary but intended, as its title states, to be an introduction to the entire New Testament. In many ways, it represents Brown's most comprehensive and mature assessment of the New Testament writings.

As we have seen often, a hallmark of all of Brown's publications was his desire not to overlook the pastoral impact of his books and articles, even the most academic ones. In this case, he was determined that his *Introduction* would be at the service of the nontechnical reader, presumably someone starting out on a serious exploration of the New Testament. He spells out his intended audience in his first paragraph: "...both readers who have become interested in the NT on their own and readers who take NT beginning courses on different levels (e.g., Bible study groups, religious education, college surveys, and initial seminary classes)."[65] In view of that audience, he would avoid any Greek citations and provide a bibliography of English titles only, including many more popular level works than his other commentaries would. Because his goal was to acquaint his audience with the New Testament itself, his treatment of each New Testament book would begin with a summation of its contents, before tackling some of the critical issues involved. Despite Brown's best intentions, the heft of his *Introduction*, its voluminous bibliography, and some of the exhaustive analysis of issues surrounding the New Testament books would make this a formidable textbook for much of the audience Brown wanted to reach. Based on his sterling reputation, the book sold well, but one suspects it remained on the shelves of many who purchased it, except for graduate students or as a resource for teachers.[66]

The Format

The basic content of Brown's *Introduction* followed a standard pattern, beginning with a nearly one-hundred-page survey of the nature of the Bible and of the New Testament itself, its varied historical background, the issues involved in interpreting the New Testament texts, and then in the body of his work, a book-by-book study, emphasizing the content of each New Testament book and the particular issues it raised for interpretation. The order in which he treated the New Testament books was a combination of the canonical order (he begins with the Gospels and the Acts of the Apostles, and then the Pauline materials and the remaining books of the New Testament) but overlaid with his surmise about the chronological sequence in which the books were composed; thus in the opening section on the Gospels, Mark is treated first, followed by Matthew, Luke (and Acts), and then the Johannine literature (including the Johannine Epistles). The Pauline letters are sorted out between the ones surely composed by Paul, lined up in a probable chronological order, and then the "Deutero-Pauline" letters. A final major section treated the remainder of the New Testament books, concluding with Revelation. In keeping with his pastoral concerns, he would close his analysis of each New Testament book with a section titled "Issues and Problems for Reflection" that would explore some of the specific challenges of the individual book (e.g., the question of the role of Peter raised by Matt 16:16–19). There are only two appendices, one dealing with the quest for the historical Jesus and the other treating Jewish and noncanonical Christian writings pertinent to the New Testament.[67]

Select Issues

The nature of Brown's *Introduction*, spanning as it does all the New Testament books, prohibits an attempt to summarize its contents. He had elaborated his views about the circumstances and content of

each of the Gospels in his previous major works on the Johannine literature in his Anchor Bible Commentaries, on Matthew and Luke in *The
Birth of the Messiah*, and on all four Gospels in *The Death of the Messiah*.
However, in this final major work there are some questions that Brown
addressed in detail either for the first time (e.g., his views on Paul) or in
a more developed way (e.g., his articulation about the nature of a "text,"
his view of biblical revelation and inspiration, and his frontal critique
of the Jesus Seminar and other modern attempts at constructing the
"historical Jesus"). We will examine each of these in turn.

Interpreting the Biblical Text

As discussed in chapter 3, Brown's most fully developed views
on biblical interpretation can be found in his *Introduction*.[68] He spent
considerable time spelling out the various methodologies for interpreting the New Testament that had developed in the modern age, such as
textual criticism, historical criticism, source and form criticism, redaction criticism (which he preferred to call "author criticism"), canonical
criticism, structuralism, narrative criticism, rhetorical criticism, social
criticism, and advocacy criticism. After surveying this dizzying array
of methodologies, he noted that no single approach is adequate but,
depending on the exegete's purpose, some combination of these methodologies was called for.

He elaborates on his own approach by returning to the fundamental distinction that he had addressed several times before, namely,
the distinction between the "literal" meaning of the biblical text and
its "wider" meaning, along with a consideration—a newer one for
Brown—of the nature of a text and its meaning beyond the intention
of the author.[69]

Inspiration and Revelation

To this important discussion Brown added a section on the notion
of biblical "inspiration" and "revelation," theological issues rarely taken up
in an introductory text, or, for that matter, in exegesis in general. Brown
in his typical forthright manner believed it was important to deal directly
with these issues and that it did not detract from an "objective" or "scientific" approach but could help student readers be aware of their pre-
suppositions about such questions.[70] Brown found unacceptable both

the views of those who held that inspiration was a theological fiction to be ignored and those who believed that God had virtually dictated the words of Scripture without any significant human agency. Brown's own intermediate viewpoint was fully in accord with Roman Catholic teaching that had been articulated at the Second Vatican Council in its Decree on Divine Revelation, *Dei Verbum*. God is the ultimate source of Scripture (or "author" in this special sense), but this does not override full human agency in the composition of the Scriptures.[71]

One's perspective on biblical inspiration corresponded with the related question of "inerrancy." Here, too, Brown adopted the perspective found in Vatican II, namely, a kind of "qualitative" view of inerrancy "whereby all Scripture is inerrant to the extent that it serves the purpose for which God intended it."[72] That "intention" was identified by *Dei Verbum* as "that truth which God wanted put into the sacred writings for the sake of our salvation."[73] Regarding the notion of revelation itself, Brown also steered a middle ground, based on his Roman Catholic tradition, between those who dismissed the notion of divine revelation or found it irrelevant, and those who consider every word of Scripture as the product of revelation. Some Protestant Christians would not identify the totality of Scripture with revelation but contend that Scripture contains revelation and, therefore, would negate any subsequent theological positions or practices "that are not to some degree explicit in Scripture."[74] The Roman Catholic position, to which Brown adhered, was "that revelation involves both God's *action* for human salvation and the *interpretation* of that action by those whom God has raised up and guided for that purpose."[75] The Scriptures both describe God's actions (in Israel and in Christ) and interpret them. Thus, Scripture remains a normative source of revelation yet there is also the need for ongoing interpretation that is also guided by the Spirit and represents, in Catholic teaching, authentic tradition. Thus, "tradition" in Roman Catholic understanding, "embodies the post-scriptural interpretation of the salvific action of God described in Scripture."[76] This perspective would allow such dogmas as the immaculate conception of Mary and the assumption to be viewed as authentic, biblically rooted teaching, even though not explicitly affirmed in Scripture.

When all was said and done, Brown conceded, there remained the need for the church to develop a more refined theology of revelation and inspiration and its relationship to the Scriptures, especially in the wake of modern biblical studies. Traditional notions of "inspiration" presumed a single biblical author whereas modern biblical exegesis detected many authors and complex weaves of traditions and sources for many biblical books. Deeper philosophical theological probes into exactly what is meant by "inspiration" and "revelation" in Catholic tradition were required. These same types of questions would be posed later by the 2008 General Synod of Bishops on the question of the "Scriptures in the Life and Mission of the Church." Latin American bishops in particular expressed concern about the inroads of Pentecostal groups among their people, based in part on the attraction of a simplistic notion of inspiration as divine "dictation" to the biblical authors, with the accompanying view that the Bible was without error in all matters, including scientific ones. In his post-synodol response, *Verbum Domini* (2010), Pope Benedict XVI agreed about the need for further development of a Catholic theology of biblical inspiration and asked the Pontifical Biblical Commission to take up the question.[77] In response, in 2014 the Biblical Commission issued an extensive study of the issue, *The Inspiration and Truth of Sacred Scripture.*[78]

The Pauline Literature

The great majority of Brown's writings focused on the Gospel literature, with only tangential glances at Paul's writings. The necessary scope of his *Introduction* gave him the opportunity to elaborate his views on Paul, and he would devote 274 pages—a third of his overall *Introduction*—to this subject.[79] If this were less familiar territory for Brown's scholarship, it is not evident in his confident, clear, and richly documented treatment. He took up the standard questions regarding Paul: his background (born in Tarsus as described in Acts; probably a Roman citizen), his education (rooted both in Greco-Roman rhetoric and Jewish traditions), and his history as a Christian (from his conversion through his missionary career and his ultimate martyrdom in Rome). He also described the form and function of ancient letter writing and its relationship to the Pauline corpus, as well as the relationship of the Paul portrayed in Acts with the Paul known from his letters (a historical link through Luke is probable but the evangelist has his own theological perspective in describing Paul's missionary contribution).

Before turning to individual epistles, Brown considered the essential features of Paul's theology. Paul's theology was not systematic but has to be culled from his various pastoral writings, hence there is some inconsistency. Of central importance is understanding Paul's attitude toward Judaism.[80] Brown does not directly address what has been an ongoing debate among Pauline scholars, namely, the traditional view of Paul's relationship to Judaism that believed that after his encounter with the risen Christ, Paul severed his ties to his Jewish heritage—versus the so-called "New Perspective" that emphasized Paul's continuity with Judaism, even as he reconsidered his Jewish heritage in the light of Christ.[81] The "New Perspective" was prompted in a particular way by a reassessment of Palestinian Judaism from which Paul emerged. Instead of being characterized as a legalistic tradition that Paul eventually found burdensome in the light of Christ, authors such as E. P. Sanders viewed Palestinian Judaism as a form of "covenantal nomism," in which fidelity to the law was a response to the foundational grace of the covenant. Paul was not anti-Jewish nor was Judaism lacking a sense of salvation as response to God's grace; Paul's problem with Judaism was simply that it was not Christianity.[82] In other words, the key difference for Paul was faith in Christ as God's promised Messiah. Later proponents of the "New Perspective," while accepting the basic premise that Paul did not completely break with his Jewish heritage, will point to other factors that came to distinguish Paul from most Palestinian Jews.[83]

It is somewhat surprising that Brown did not explicitly refer to this dominant debate in Pauline scholarship, a debate in full swing at the time Brown was composing his *Introduction*. He includes Sanders's key work, *Paul and Palestinian Judaism*, in his bibliography but does not directly engage his work. Perhaps he felt it was too subtle a debate for the kind of readers of the *Introduction* he had in mind. Nevertheless, there is reason to believe Brown was sympathetic to the general views of the "New Perspective." One author he does cite in this regard was the influential essay of Krister Stendahl, "The Apostle Paul and the Introspective Conscience of the West."[84] Stendahl had warned modern interpreters not to view Paul through the lens of Martin Luther's own internal struggles. Luther's sense of personal guilt, and his reaction to what he deemed the legalism and formalism of medieval Catholicism, was not the kind of prism with which Paul viewed his own Jewish heritage. As Brown noted, "Luther's struggle with guilt and sin cannot be used to interpret Paul's outlook on his preChristian past."[85] In his discussion of Romans 9—11, Brown would also emphasize Paul's extraordinary love for Israel and his Jewish heritage.[86] It is amazing that Paul says he is willing to be cut off from Christ and be damned for the sake of his Jewish kinsmen. As Brown notes, "Giving the lie to all who say that he denigrates Judaism, he lists with pride the marvelous Israelite privileges (Romans 9:4–5)."[87]

Brown also vigorously refuted those who attempted to portray Paul as the true "founder" of Christianity. Some would claim that the historical Jesus had been, in fact, "a Jewish peasant of a reformist bent, criticizing hypocrisy and some of the entrenched religious attitudes and institutions of his times." It was Paul who transformed the memory of this historical Jesus, "Hellenizing" him, making Jesus the Son of God.[88] As Brown pointed out, few scholars today would put this quite so crudely, but making Paul the exclusive architect of a high Christology, as some modern interpreters do, moves in the same direction. Although Paul was a creative proclaimer of the gospel, he also stood in a stream of tradition and such titles as "Son of God" or "Lord" already had their roots in Palestinian Christianity prior to Paul, as reflected, for example, in the early Christian hymn that Paul quotes in Philippians 2:6–11, which portrays Christ in exalted terms.

While downplaying the notion of Paul as the "founder" of Christianity, Brown does not underestimate the enormous contribution of Paul to our understanding of the gospel. His own pastoral letters, along with the "Deutero-Pauline" letters written by his later disciples, form an incredible theological and pastoral heritage and make up a major portion of the New Testament Scriptures. "The ultimate gift of Paul," Brown concludes, "is to have preached a gospel that had enormous power in itself and therefore could not be chained or silenced even when its proponents were. Readers who keep in mind *the apostle whose preaching unchained the gospel* will not allow the Pauline message to be buried beneath details," while doing the work necessary to analyze his various letters.[89]

The Quest for the Historical Jesus

Brown's intention in his *Introduction* was to focus on the existing New Testament texts and not to spend time considering the prehistory of the New Testament traditions (an exception would be his recap of the evolution of the Johannine tradition). Thus, the subject of the quest for the historical Jesus was relegated to an appendix.[90]

Brown begins with a quick survey of the quest that had developed over the last two hundred years. The optimism of nineteenth-century scholarship about identifying the features of the historical Jesus was punctured by the work of Albert Schweitzer, who concluded that the historical Jesus detected by many scholars was simply the mirror image of their own perspectives. Schweitzer himself believed that Jesus understood himself as an apocalyptic Messiah whose death would bring about the end of the world and, therefore, was a "noble failure." As the quest moved into the twentieth century, the viewpoint of Rudolf Bultmann was influential. Because the New Testament writings were so theologically charged, Bultmann thought that the search for the historical Jesus was impossible and that there was little, if any, connection between the circumstances of the historical Jesus and the gospel portrayals of him. Yet Bultmann believed that the gospel portrayal of Jesus had religious significance, posing an existential challenge to modernity.

Despite the pessimism of Bultmann and others about the validity of the quest for the historical Jesus, later twentieth-century scholars renewed their efforts to detect, as Brown put it, "historical features beneath the Gospel presentation," such as the works of the highly respected German scholars Ernst Käsemann and Günther Bornkamm.[91] They shared Brown's own perspective that the historical grounding of Christian faith legitimized the search for the historical moorings of the gospel traditions.

From this rapid survey, Brown concentrated on several "current" attempts in the quest for the historical Jesus, dating from approximately 1980 to Brown's own time. He notes two basic tendencies, one a more conservative approach that would detect a basic "Christology" already in the lifetime of Jesus, in that Jesus would have been conscious of his "unique relationship to God and reflected that outlook in his speech and attitudes."[92] Brown himself was sympathetic to this tendency: "The scholarly practice of assigning the introduction of certain Christological titles to specific postJesus stages in the geographical and temporal spread of Christianity is now seen to be too simple. Therefore, a continuity between Jesus' lifetime and the Gospels portraits may be more inclusive than hitherto thought."[93]

On the far opposite pole were the views of the "Jesus Seminar," led at the time of Brown's writing by Robert Funk (1926–2005) and John Dominic Crossan. Funk, the seminar's founder, had been raised in a strict Pentecostal environment, and by his own admission, the work of the seminar was in reaction to the strictures he had experienced as a young man. The Jesus Seminar began in 1985 and ceased to exist sometime around

2006, with the death of Funk and the winding down of attention to the seminar's work. In its heyday during the 1980s and '90s it claimed a lot of public attention through shrewd public relations efforts and numerous published reports and spin-off books; its sensational claims about the historical Jesus were amplified in the popular press. The active members of the seminar numbered around seventy-five and, as Brown pointed out, were, except for someone like Crossan, relatively unknown. In a footnote, Brown observed (no doubt, with some satisfaction) that in 1995 no member of the distinguished theological faculties of Harvard, Yale, Union, Princeton, Duke, Emory, Vanderbilt, the University of Chicago, or any major European university were members.[94] One of the methods of the seminar, ridiculed by its critics, was its voting method, using color-coded beads in deciding which sayings or actions of Jesus in the Gospels had any historical grounding.[95]

In many ways, the Jesus Seminar represented the exact opposite of Brown's methods and assumptions in exploring the historical traditions behind the Gospels. First, the seminar began with a priori principles that excluded any supernatural reality, ruling out such New Testament assertions as bodily resurrection, Jesus's exorcisms, his foreknowledge of his death, and the eschatological character of Jesus's ministry. This led to an exceptionally skeptical stance regarding the historicity of most of the gospel material. For example, only one saying of Jesus in Mark and none in John were voted as authentic. Brown also found offensive the sensational nature of the publicity created by the seminar. The members of the seminar gave the impression they were "liberating" Jesus "from the tyranny of the 'religious establishment,' represented in church or doctrinal tradition and Christian worship."[96] Given Brown's own respectful dealing with church tradition and practice, the cavalier attitude of the seminar on this point was particularly galling. He also lamented that the widespread publicity given the claims of the seminar could give the impression that these were standard views of most biblical scholars, whereas, in fact, numerous highly respected scholars severely critiqued the work of the seminar.[97]

Brown particularly targeted the work of John Dominic Crossan, perhaps the most well-known participant in the seminar.[98] Several features of his approach Brown found objectionable. For example, Crossan asserted that sources as the reconstructed Q and apocryphal Gospels such as the Gospel of Thomas, the Secret Gospel of Mark, and a reconstructed form of the Gospel of Peter dated from before AD 60 and were more historically reliable than the canonical Gospels—a highly speculative position rejected by most scholars.[99] Crossan also describes the kind of social unrest that might have been present in some of the larger cities of Palestine during the lifetime of Jesus as also present in the small farming village of Nazareth—a scenario also questioned by many scholars. Crossan views Jesus as "a combination of an itinerant Cynic preacher and illiterate Galilean peasant, who was strongly egalitarian," thereby falling under the same criticism raised by Albert Schweitzer a century before. The Jesus portrayed by Crossan turns out to be someone with a modern face. Finally, Brown views Crossan's perspective as epitomizing the antisupernatural bias of the seminar as a whole: no demons and thus no exorcism; no supernatural miracles (although some charismatic healings of those with schizophrenia-like symptoms); the passion narratives created mainly by reflection on the Old Testament; no Jewish trial (the Romans were solely responsible for Jesus's execution); Jesus's body was abandoned and probably eaten by dogs, therefore no empty tomb. As Brown concluded, "Inevitably Crossan has been accused of flights of imagination that compromise his claims to a historical approach."[100]

Brown judged that, unlike the work of the Jesus Seminar, other attempts to describe the historical Jesus were more convincing, such as the work of E. P. Sanders, who portrays the historical Jesus against the Jewish backdrop of an "eschatological prophet," or scholars who give careful attention to the probable social circumstances in Palestine at the time of Jesus such as the German scholar Gerd Theissen and the American Richard Horsley. Others such as Elizabeth Schüssler Fiorenza, working from a feminist perspective, contended that very early traditions portrayed Jesus as the embodiment of Divine Wisdom. Brown reserves particular praise for his colleague and mentee John P. Meier, whose first two (of a projected six) massive volumes on the historical Jesus had already appeared. Titled *A Marginal Jew: Rethinking the Historical Jesus*, Meier's work applied the classical methods of historical criticism with exceptional rigor and comprehensiveness.[101] As the title indicates, Meier places the historical Jesus within a thoroughly Jewish context, albeit a Jew with unique views and identity. As Brown approvingly notes, "From Meier's massive work a more traditional Jesus emerges—one having considerable in common with the Jesus Christ described in Paul and the Gospels."[102]

Brown concludes his survey of the quest with his characteristic balance. The difficulty of finding scholarly consensus about a portrayal of the "historical Jesus" is a caution against one's faith in the ability of scholarship to arrive at certainty. No matter how objective and thorough scholars might be in their search, the results are always going to be limited. Therefore, it would be foolish to make the "historical Jesus" portrayed by scholars as the norm of Christian faith. Some of the results, such as asserting a Jesus who was simply a wise Cynic preacher and teacher, or a deluded apocalyptic prophet could hardly be the object of Christian faith.

At the same time, Brown did not advocate abandoning the quest for the historical roots of the Gospels or Christian faith:

> Following the principle of *fides querens intellectum* (faith seeking intellectually respectable expression), Christian belief has nothing to fear from solid, careful scholarly research. Such a position requires openness on both sides. On the part of church authorities, there should be a recognition that past phrasings of faith are time-conditioned and are susceptible to being rephrased. Through critical biblical study, what was once assumed to be a necessary aspect of belief (e.g., creation in six days with rest on the seventh) may prove to be only a dramatic way of phrasing what remains essential (namely, that no matter how things came into existence, it was through God's planning and power). For their part scholars would do well to avoid a rhetoric whereby their discoveries are presented as certain, making the discoverers the infallible arbiters of Christian faith. Biblical books are documents written by those who believed in the God of Abraham and the Father of Jesus Christ; good sense suggests that communities sharing that faith have an authority in dealing with those books.[103]

Few quotations better sum up the spirit and purpose of Brown's own scholarly work.

It would not do Brown justice to confine a summary of his views about Jesus to his interaction with the Jesus Seminar or the quest for the historical Jesus. Brown also used his theological acumen to write eloquently about the Christ who was the object of Christian faith. As he observed so often in his writings, the use of the historical-critical method to analyze the biblical materials did not have to result in compromising the fullness of orthodox Christian faith in the identity of the Jesus of the Gospels. One of his most explicit efforts in this regard was his work, *An Introduction to New Testament Christology*, published in 1994, at the same time he was working on *An Introduction to the New Testament*.[104] He intended this study of Christology for a broad audience. He would draw on several essays and lectures he had previously given on the subject but completely reworked them into a coherent and seamless whole with their inclusion in this book.

Brown covered the various images of Jesus portrayed in the New Testament and addressed numerous recurring questions about Jesus he had wrestled with over the years, such as Jesus's self-knowledge and the question about the nature of the resurrection. Most impressive was Brown's ability to link the New Testament Christologies to the later classic christological formulations of the church. One particularly eloquent example is his concluding reflection on the creedal formulas of Nicaea and Chalcedon about the humanity and divinity of Jesus. A student had asked Brown why these questions debated at Nicaea about the full divinity of Jesus were relevant, if Jesus was our God-given Savior. Brown offered the following eloquent reply, a reply worth quoting at length:

> If Jesus is not "true God of true God," then we do not know God in human terms. Even if Jesus were the most perfect creature far above all others, he could tell us only at second hand about a God who really remains almost as distant as the Unmoved Mover of Aristotle. Only if Jesus is truly of God do we know what God is like, for in Jesus we see God translated into terms that we can understand. A God who sent a marvelous creature as our Savior could be described as loving, but that love would have cost God nothing in a personal way. Only if Jesus is truly of God do we know that God's love was so real that it reached the point of personal self-giving. This is why the proclamation of Nicaea was and is so important—not only because it tells us about Jesus, but because it tells us about God. Indeed were it otherwise, the Nicene proclamation would scarcely be faithful to a Jesus who preached the kingship of God.
>
> So also do I think that the proclamation of Chalcedon about Jesus as true man (as well as true God) has enduring value, even for those who cannot pronounce Monophysitism.

Again, unless we understand that Jesus was truly human with no exception but sin, and limited, as indicated prima facie in the biblical evidence [he refers to chapters 3 and 4 of his book, where he takes up the issue of Jesus's human consciousness], then one understands that God loved us to the point of self-subjection to our most agonizing infirmities. A Jesus who walked through the world with unlimited knowledge, knowing exactly what the morrow would bring, knowing with certainty that three days after his death his Father would raise him up, would be a Jesus who could arouse our admiration, but a Jesus still far from us. He would be a Jesus far from a humankind that can only hope in the future and believe in God's goodness, far from a humankind that must face the supreme uncertainty of death with faith but without knowledge of what is beyond. On the other hand, a Jesus for whom the detailed future had elements of mystery, dread, and hope as it has for us and yet, at the same time, a Jesus who would say, "Not my will but yours"—this would be a Jesus who could effectively teach us how to live, for this Jesus would have gone through life's real trials. Then his saying, "No one can have greater love than this: to lay down his life for those he loves" (John 15:13), life with all the agony with which we lay ours down. We would know that for him the loss of life was, as it is for us, the loss of a great possession, a possession that is outranked only by love.

In the 4th and 5th centuries the question of Jesus as God and man was not an abstract question debated in the scholars' chambers; it was a question of what God and Christianity were all about. I submit that, if we take the trouble to understand, it remains all of that even in our century.[105]

CONCLUSION

It proved fitting that his *An Introduction to the New Testament* should be the final major publication of Raymond Brown. Here, more than anywhere else in his vast body of work, he had the chance to provide his views about the whole of the New Testament. The depth and clarity of his exposition revealed his amazing erudition, his scholarly integrity, his courageous application of critical methodology to the biblical writings, and his abiding respect for the religious dimensions of the Scriptures. Most reviews of his *Introduction* were strongly positive. Bruce Metzger (1914–2007), professor emeritus at Princeton Theological Seminary and a legendary scholar in his own right, described it as "a monumental piece of scholarship." Daniel Harrington, SJ (1940–2014), then professor of New Testament at the Jesuit Weston School of Theology, declared it to be "the best Introduction to the New Testament available." Some, such as biblical scholar Anthony Saldarini in a *New York Times* review, judged that while Brown's work represented the best of classical Western scholarship, other emerging methodologies, including those drawing on other cultural experiences, will need more attention in the future.[106] Brown himself would not be offended by such a criticism. In what turned out to be his last major publication, he had forthrightly stated, "*Different approaches to the text must be combined so that no 'criticism' becomes the exclusive manner of interpretation.* Interpreters who employ the various forms of criticism in a complementary way will arrive at a much fuller meaning of the biblical texts."[107]

CHAPTER 7

ECUMENISM AND INTERFAITH RELATIONS

Ecumenism was one of the most enduring interests of Raymond Brown. Along with his championship of the historical-critical method, his concern for Christian unity appears in virtually all his writings, including several essays and at least one book totally dedicated to that subject.

Like so many aspects of his life, Brown's strong ecumenical spirit was first kindled by his experience at Johns Hopkins University. There, he met his greatest mentor, William Foxwell Albright, whom Brown would later call simply, "my Teacher" or "the Professor."[1] Albright himself was a man of great integrity and deep Christian piety, born in Chile of Methodist missionary parents who were serving there. It is likely that this was the first Protestant whom Brown got to know and respect on such a deep level, not just for his exceptional scholarship and erudition, but also for his sense of integrity and reverence for the Scriptures. Also important was Brown's acquaintance with several Protestant peers who were his fellow students in the Semitics department of Johns Hopkins and in his year-long fellowship in Jerusalem, where he stayed at the facilities of the American Society for Oriental Research (later named The Albright Institute in honor of its first and most distinguished director) and worked alongside other Protestant scholars.[2]

His ecumenical involvement would intensify when he accompanied his bishop, Joseph Patrick Hurley of the Diocese of St. Augustine, to the first session of the Vatican Council in the fall of 1962.[3] While there, Brown was unexpectedly invited to lunch by Msgr. Jan Wille-brands, who had been appointed by Pope John XXIII in 1960 to be the secretary for the newly established Secretariat for Promoting Christian Unity, upon the recommendation of the highly influential ecumenist, Cardinal Augustin Bea, SJ.[4] Willebrands had been involved in ecumeni-cal work since the early 1950s in his native Netherlands, where he served as rector of the regional seminary at Warmond near Leiden. Aided by fluency in six languages, Willebrands was involved in building bridges, particularly with the Anglican and Russian Orthodox churches. He was instrumental in persuading representatives of the Orthodox churches to attend the sessions of the Second Vatican Council as observers from 1962 to 1965. At the time he met with Brown, Willebrands served at the Council, preparing the documents relating to Scripture and tradition, ecumenism, religious freedom, and relations with non-Christian reli-gions. Later, Willebrands would be made a bishop and then a cardinal, and appointed in 1969 by Pope Paul VI as president of the Secretariat for Promoting Christian Unity, succeeding Cardinal Bea after his death. Even after his resignation as archbishop of Utrecht, Willebrands contin-ued his work as president of the Secretariat and played a leading role in the Vatican, particularly in ecumenical affairs. He passed away at the age of ninety-six in 2006.

The purpose of the lunch hosted by Willebrands was to have Brown meet Lukas Vischer of the World Council of Churches, who at that time was its official observer to the Vatican Council.[5] Vischer had asked Willebrand's assistance in finding a Roman Catholic scholar for an upcoming plenary conference of the Faith and Order Commission.[6] In Brown's own words:

> Faith and Order had some biblical input into its documents, but it was being torn apart by criticism from the German scholars, that it was pietistic, ignorant, not critical. They had decided to bite the bullet and invite Ernst Käsemann to give a talk at the Montreal Plenary meeting in 1963.... Hitherto Roman Catholics had very little to do with [the] World Council; in fact there was a meeting at Evanston, near Chicago, and local Catholics were forbidden to participate. But now because the Council was showing itself open to ecu-menical work, the Faith and Order Commission wanted a Catholic to speak opposite Käsemann. Somebody, perhaps a

Protestant scholar, whom I knew through Hopkins, had suggested my name to them and they told Willebrands that I would be the one whom they would be willing to have. So I wound up getting into ecumenism that way. The Roman ecumenical office asked me to give one of the two major talks on Biblical Criticism at the Montreal Conference in 1963. And through that I got involved with the World Council, Faith and Order Commission, and stayed involved for over a quarter of a century with them. I've been very lucky in being in the right place at the right time.[7]

Ernst Käsemann (1906–98) was one of the world's preeminent Lutheran biblical scholars, noted among other things for his research on the historical Jesus.[8] He had been a doctoral student of Rudolf Bultmann, but in his later years moved far beyond the views of his master in laying out various working principles that could help detect historical materials within the gospel tradition. A classic and somewhat forbidding German scholar, he would also do work on the social implications of the Christian message, taking a more radical turn after his daughter was kidnapped and killed in 1977 during the troubles in Argentina. For a young, relatively unknown scholar such as Brown to be paired with Käsemann at a plenary meeting of the Faith and Order Commission, and the first Catholic to be so invited, was a singular honor. Brown's paper was on "Unity and Diversity in New Testament Ecclesiology," which was later published in the official journal of the SNTS.[9] That topic would reemerge in Brown's later work, *The Churches the Apostles Left Behind*.[10]

An amusing encounter with Käsemann would take place a couple of years later in 1967. Käsemann was in the Washington, DC, area for a conference, and Brown took the opportunity to invite the great scholar to speak to the faculty and seminarians of St. Mary's. Brown was proud that Käsemann accepted but also anxious that things would go well. To make sure, Brown, in his characteristically meticulous way, went around to all the classes at the seminary beforehand and told the students not to ask Käsemann any questions: "Listen, this is a very, very serious German biblical scholar. You guys do not know enough to ask him a question so please, please listen respectfully and applaud, but no questions." When the time came for the lecture, Käsemann delivered a dense lecture on the theology of Paul. Trouble began to brew when near the end of the talk, Käsemann announced that he had left the last page of his lecture in his room and would have to go and retrieve it. After a few minutes, he returned and completed his lecture. When the applause died down, Brown rose to close the session, but, contrary to Brown's instructions, a seminarian in the far back of the room raised his hand for a question— someone, by the way, that witnesses say was the least academically endowed of the entire student body! He challenged the great German professor about his quotation of Rudolf Bultmann, whom the student observed was "not a believing Christian." This critique of his mentor angered Käsemann, who replied, "I have known Professor Bultmann. He is a great Christian gentleman. I despise people who are spreading these awful rumors about him." With that, Brown hastily shut down the session—his carefully prepared defense against any embarrassment having failed miserably.[11]

Despite this setback, Brown's ecumenical enthusiasm would not dim. In his early days of teaching at St. Mary's, he began to organize "Ecumenical Invitation Days" at the seminary. Several times a year, Protestant pastors from the surrounding area would be invited, along with representatives of their congregations, to a daylong program, involving lectures, discussion, and prayer together. Later, this ecumenical activity inaugurated by Brown would lead to the establishment in 1968 of the highly successful Ecumenical Institute at St. Mary's, which offers degrees and certificates in ecumenical theology, one of the first such institutes to be established.[12] Of major importance, of course, was his move to Union Theological Seminary in 1971—a move, as we have seen, that was prompted in part by his desire to learn what life was like in the world of a leading Protestant seminary.[13] Here he would teach Protestant graduate students, serve as director of doctoral dissertations for several Protestant students and future ministers and teachers, live on the campus of a Protestant institution, and have prominent Protestant faculty colleagues. Several of the people at Union would become close friends and collaborators, such as fellow faculty members Phyllis Trible, J. Louis Martyn, and George Landes.[14] Brown would also maintain close friendships with several of his graduate students as they moved on to careers of their own.[15]

His positive experience at Union and the deep friendships with Protestants he treasured did not, however, prevent Brown from offering, in a frank ecumenical spirit, some pointed critiques of Protestantism. This was especially the case with a chapter in *The Critical Meaning of the Bible* titled "Moving All the Churches to Reform."[16] It had originated as a lecture Brown gave at Princeton Theological Seminary in 1979 at an ecumenical service commemorating the fifteenth anniversary of the Second Vatican Council's decree on ecumenism. After tracing the amazing ecumenical gains among both Catholics and Protestants since Vatican II, Brown offered some challenges to Protestant church life, most of them based on his experience at Union Theological Seminary, which, he bluntly stated, had given him "concern for the future of Protestantism."[17] First, he feared that an overemphasis on social concerns was substituting for theological rigor. "I grow fearful that some Protestants have forgotten a basic concern of the Reformation, namely, the Gospel rightly preached."[18] Second, while some criticize Roman Catholicism as "hung up on sex," with its frequent admonitions about marriage, sex, birth control, and abortion, Brown wondered if mainline Protestant churches had "gone to the opposite extreme."[19] After all, the New Testament did address repeatedly the need for sexual moral values. He concluded, "I have no sympathy for a Church that 'butts into' everything, but no sympathy either for a Church that is afraid to say anything about sex."[20] Likewise, he wondered if the leadership of mainline Protestantism had forfeited their responsibility to correct theological aberrations such as deviant christological understandings or inadequate understanding of and respect for sacramental life. He also wondered about the importance of the unity of the "church" for mainline Protestants. While Catholics struggle with authority and other issues, there is a reluctance to splinter off and an aversion to church division. "The freedom to form a splinter Church should not be praised as the freedom of the Gospel. Dividing the Church is an offense to the Gospel, and the purpose of true reform is to heal our divisions in loyalty to the Gospel."[21] Finally, he questioned the "indifference of the authorities of the liberal Protestant Churches to what their theologians say....I would rather live in a Church whose authorities can get excited and worried over what theologians are saying, even to the point of chastising them, than in a Church that ignores them."[22] Brown concluded this series of blunt challenges by stating that his desire was "to serve as a friend." At the same time, he recognized that he was an "outsider" and understood true reform would come "from those who know the strength of their Protestant Churches and can work with love and sympathy to make them even more what they should be."[23]

THE LUTHERAN–ROMAN CATHOLIC DIALOGUE AND COLLABORATIVE STUDIES OF PETER AND MARY

Another important ecumenical experience for Brown was his involvement in the Lutheran–Roman Catholic National Dialogue begun in 1964, jointly sponsored by the U.S. Bishops' Committee for Ecumenical and Interreligious Affairs and the USA National Committee of the Lutheran World Federation.[24] Brown was a leading member of this dialogue, serving from 1965 to 1974. From these discussions he would develop strong lifelong friendships with a number of Protestant biblical scholars such as Paul Achtemeier (1927–2013) of Union Theological Seminary in Richmond, Virginia, Karl P. Donfried of Smith College, and John Reumann (1927–2008) of the Lutheran Theological Seminary in Philadelphia and a leading ecumenist in the Lutheran community.[25] Out of this dialogue would come two influential collaborative publications in which Brown had a leading role, *Peter in the New Testament* and *Mary in the New Testament*.[26]

In 1973, the topic chosen for the dialogue was the issue of "Papal Primacy and the Universal Church." The members of the dialogue realized that to throw new light on this contentious issue they would need to do a thorough study of the role of Peter in the New Testament, as now viewed by modern biblical scholarship. Brown and Reumann were assigned to head a task force of biblical scholars who were members of the dialogue to do a collaborative study.[27] The task force developed a formidable work schedule, meeting for three hours or more in fifteen sessions between October 1971 and 1974 at Auburn Seminary on the campus of Union. One or more sessions were devoted to a study of the role of Peter reflected in Paul's letters, the Gospels, the Acts of the Apostles, and the Petrine Letters. Various members would be assigned to guide individual sessions by preparing a list of leading questions for the task force to address. The resulting discussions were recorded in minutes that Brown himself would work up into a mature draft; the accumulations of these drafts, ultimately edited by Brown and Donfried, led to the contents of the book. Later the members would, without exception, express their great satisfaction with this method.

Brown himself had already taken up in his earlier writings the question of the role of Peter in the New Testament and the relationship of this material to the eventual development of the papal office.[28] Anyone familiar with his views could see his fingerprints all over the content of this collaborative work. The book dealt successively with the historical role of Peter as a leader among the disciples and his role in the emergence of the early church. It then turned to the various images and symbolic roles Peter seemed to take in subsequent New Testament traditions. The authors used the term "trajectory" to describe these symbolic roles for Peter that extend beyond his historical role. These symbolic roles identified Peter as the "great Christian fisherman" or missionary (Luke 5); as the "Shepherd of Sheep" or pastor (John 21; Matt 16:19; 1 Pet 5); as "Christian Martyr" (John 21:18–19; 1 Pet 5:1); as a "receiver of special revelation (Mark 9:2 and parallels, i.e., the transfiguration; Acts 5:1; 10:9–16; 12:7–9); as "Confessor of the True Christian Faith" (Matt 16:16–17) and guarantor of the faith against false teachers (2 Pet 1:20–21; 3:15–16); and Peter as "weak and sinful man" (Gal 2:11–14; and the gospel portrayals of Peter, especially in the passion narratives).

The authors noted that there is a plurality of images associated with Peter and some of these developed in the trajectory "from earlier to later images."[29] The same might be said of Paul, whose image also develops in the later Deutero-Pauline letters such as Colossians, Ephesians, and the Pastoral Letters, which portray the Apostle in his apostolic sufferings and witness or as a pastor guiding his successors. However, the authors concurred that the Petrine trajectory "eventually outdistanced the other apostolic trajectories" such as those of Paul or the other Twelve Apostles.[30] The ecumenical implications of this study of Peter, the authors note, are modest but still significant: "The ecumenical discussion [of Peter] must involve not only the historical figure but also the continuing trajectory of [Peter's] image in the New Testament and beyond…whatever way we answer these questions [i.e., what factors prompted the trajectory of symbolic images and "how does God's providence and His will for His church enter into the trajectory"]. Thus, they concluded, "Shifting the focus to the developing symbolic roles for Peter raises the question of how the New Testament portrayal of Peter can relate to diverse ecclesiologies of today."[31]

This groundbreaking ecumenical study of Peter was an instant success and would be translated into six languages and widely used in other ecumenical circles.[32] That success and the fact that the Lutheran–Roman Catholic National Dialogue was turning to the topic of papal infallibility and teaching authority prompted the authors to propose another such collaborative study—this time on the portrayal of Mary in the New Testament. Although the Dialogue was dealing with papal authority, the issue of Mary was germane because of the recent papal definitions of the dogmas of the immaculate conception and the assumption of Mary. Brown himself in 1974 had asked to be excused from further participation in the national dialogue because of the press of other commitments; however, he was happy to again provide the leadership for this ecumenical study. This proposed study of Mary was approved by the Dialogue authorities but was considered an independent work since their official focus was specifically on papal infallibility and therefore the proposed study of Mary in the New Testament was not officially sponsored as part of the Dialogue's documentation in the way the study of Peter was. The task force for this project would be expanded to include two Episcopalian scholars and two from the Reformed tradition.[33] Joseph Fitzmyer, SJ, a longtime friend and collaborator of Brown, would also join the editorial team, along with Brown, Donfried, and Reumann. The task force adopted a similarly rigorous work schedule, meeting in ten sessions between September 1975 and December 1976, with Brown continuing to play his leading role in the ultimate drafting of the reports of the task force's work that would form the final content of the book. It is safe to say that no other member of the task force was as familiar with the scholarship on this subject as was Brown. He was on the brink of publishing his massive commentary on the infancy narratives, *The Birth of the Messiah* (1977), and had also worked extensively on the issue of the virginal conception of Jesus, with his book on that subject appearing in 1973.[34] As was the case with the Task Force's study of Peter, Brown's viewpoint was evident throughout this book on the New Testament portrayal of Mary.

While the overall format would be the same as with the study of Peter, the nature and limited scope of the New Testament texts on Mary called for a different approach. Mary is mentioned in the four Gospels and in Acts in varying ways; only once and somewhat obliquely in Paul's reference to Christ as "born of a woman," which is primarily a christological statement (Gal 4:4), and less possibly in Revelation chapter 12, where the symbolism of the Woman probably refers to Israel and the church and only in post–New Testament traditions is connected with Mary. Given their importance in the gospel portrayals, the authors also considered several Old Testament motifs that may have influenced the evangelists. The authors laid out their suppositions about the nature and sources of the Gospels and, in particular, the infancy narratives—viewing them as Brown had in his *The Birth of the Messiah*, namely, that the infancy narratives drew on minimal historical traditions, Old Testament motifs, and portrayals of Jesus and Mary found in the body of the Gospels.[35] They agreed that the minimal portrayal of Mary in the Gospel of Mark suggests that "she did not follow Jesus about as a disciple during the ministry" (p. 284) but was nevertheless "from the first a member of the post-Easter community" as testified in Acts 1:14. There is significant attention given to Mary in the infancy narratives; Matthew portrays her particularly in connection with the virginal conception but Luke has a rich array of reflections on Mary. Luke not only affirms the virginal conception but portrays Mary as a "faithful hearer of the word" (p. 235).

Mary has a limited role during the public ministry of Jesus. Mark's portrayal tends to the negative, with Mary and Jesus's family not understanding him (Mark 3:2–35). Both Matthew and Luke move to adjust Mark's version, removing the negative hues and, especially in Luke's account, including her among the "eschatological family of Jesus," that is, among those who hear the word of God and keep it" (see Luke 8:21; 11:28). John's Gospel begins by presenting Mary in a somewhat ambiguous light in the Cana story (John 2:1–12) as someone who is not fully aware of Jesus's mission, but she reappears in an important scene in the passion narrative (John 19:25–27), where she is portrayed as part of the "new family" of Jesus signified by the Beloved Disciple. She becomes the mother of the disciple "par excellence" (p. 289). While this motif might not be explicit in John's account, this scene opened the way for future Marian symbolism connecting Mary with the church, as would develop in the patristic period.

The authors also considered the significance of the virginal conception in Matthew's and Luke's accounts. As Brown himself had concluded in his own previous studies, "The task force agreed that the historicity of the virginal conception could not be settled by historical-critical exegesis, and that one's attitude towards church tradition on the matter would probably be the decisive force in determining one's view whether the virginal conception is a theologoumenon or a literal fact."[36] The authors agreed, however, that the virginal conception had in any case important theological significance, with Matthew's account emphasizing that Jesus is the Son of God through the power of the Spirit, and Son of David, as the adopted son of Joseph. Luke's portrayal coincides with that of Romans 1:3–4, that Jesus was constituted Son of God at his conception.

The overall conclusion of the task force's study was, as in the case of Peter, relatively modest but paves the way for future and diverse developments within the unfolding traditions of the church:

> We were able to trace some lines of development [within the New Testament] which were increasingly positive in portraying Mary as a disciple par excellence and as the virgin. In later centuries these positive lines dominated and were greatly enhanced. If the churches today are not in agreement as to how they evaluate Mary, it is not only because they have reached different conclusions about the post-NT developments, but also because they give different emphases to the varied elements in the NT itself.[37]

In both these collaborative studies, in which Brown had a leading role, the goal was to "remove confusion about the biblical evidence, so that discussions among the churches may be facilitated."[38]

LINKING NEW TESTAMENT DEVELOPMENTS WITH CHURCH TRADITIONS

Finding a credible link between evolving New Testament motifs and later church traditions was an essential ecumenical task for Brown and appears in many of his lectures and writings. Perhaps his most explicit statement of this was his book *The Churches the Apostles Left Behind*, published in 1984.[39] Brown himself was particularly proud of this book, and it represents one of his most creative discussions of New Testament ecclesiology and its ecumenical implications. As Brown noted on its dedication page, this book is essentially "ecumenical." It originated as the Sprunt Lectures, which Brown gave at Union Theological Seminary in Richmond, Virginia, in 1980, the first Catholic to do so at this venerable Protestant institution.[40] Translating his notes for those lectures into a written and documented text took several years, for which Brown was grateful, since presenting the lectures in various formats in the intervening years had deepened his perception of the issues.[41]

He saw this work as similar to what had commanded his attention in his commentaries on the Johannine literature and his work with John Meier, *Antioch and Rome*, namely, tracing the evolution of New Testament motifs and their significance for later post–New Testament traditions. His specific purpose in this ecumenical book was to pose an intriguing question to various New Testament books: "…from the viewpoint of their diverse understanding of what was important for survival and growth after the death of the apostles."[42] He reaffirmed at the outset his tenacious conviction that by using the historical-critical method in an appropriate way, both Protestant and Catholic exegetes should arrive at the same conclusion about what the New Testament texts *meant*, but not necessarily about what they *mean*. This was evidently true concerning ecclesiology, as the widely diverse structures of the Christian churches manifested. Brown's purpose in this book was to identify some key trends in some of the varying ecclesiologies of the New Testament and what link could credibly be made to later post–New Testament developments.

To accomplish this, he developed a key distinction in the unfolding phases of the early New Testament communities. He estimated that by the late 60s of the first century, the leading apostles and first-generation followers of Jesus had passed from the scene. Traditional Catholic theology had asserted that biblical revelation in the strict sense closed "with the death of the last apostle." In fact, this is more of a theological than a strictly historical affirmation. There continued to be a formative period in the development of the New Testament writings that extended beyond the physical death of the apostles but was shaped by apostolic traditions. This was the period in the latter third of the first century in which, except for Paul's authentic letters, most of the New Testament writings took their final form. Brown dubbed this the "sub-apostolic" period—to be distinguished from the "post-apostolic" period that emerged at the end of the first century. This key distinction set the agenda for Brown's book: "I shall examine a number of different church situations reflected in the sub-apostolic works of the New Testament… concentrating on the most important element that enabled each church to survive after the apostolic hero or guide had departed the scene."[43]

Before examining individual New Testament books, Brown affirmed that in fact various strands of tradition emerged in the subapostolic period. Here he was influenced by the work of Kirsopp Lake, the noted Anglican scholar and Harvard professor, whose work *Landmarks in the History of Early Christianity* had detected different lines of tradition developing in the great urban centers of Rome and Ephesus where early Christianity thrived.[44] Different from Lake, however, Brown would see several currents emerging in the subapostolic period, not all of them identified by their location. This would include at least three different post-Pauline traditions exemplified respectively in the different theologies of Ephesians and Colossians, the Pastoral Letters, and Luke's Acts of the Apostles. In his earlier works, Brown had also tracked two fundamental and conflicting currents in the Johannine community from this period.[45] Other currents would be exemplified in the Synoptic Gospels, Hebrews, 1 Peter, and the Book of Revelation. As Brown concluded, "We have found a remarkable sub-apostolic variety of thought."[46]

From this groundwork Brown would devote the rest of his book to brief descriptions of how various subapostolic communities responded to his leading question about what were the most important elements that enabled these communities to survive once their founding apostle or apostolic guide was off the scene. In each case he would identify what he saw as a key sustaining principle or theological ideal but also some liabilities or potential weaknesses that were yoked to these strengths. For example, the Pastoral Letters would emphasize the importance of sustaining structures and sound teaching, but this could involve the liability of some rigidness; Colossians and Ephesians emphasized the church as the "Body of Christ" and an emphasis on personal holiness, but this could lead to an overidealization of the church and impede reform; Luke-Acts emphasized the charismatic role of the Spirit but this could also lead to a lack of discipline; 1 Peter has a beautiful emphasis on the church as a witness to the world, but this perspective could also lead to a sense of exclusivism; and the Johannine ecclesiology emphasizes the disciple's bond of love with Christ, but this could encourage individualism. Matthew's Gospel is commended for its incorporation of Jewish tradition, and Brown declared that the community discourse of Matthew 18, with its emphasis on humility, pastoral care, and forgiveness, was "the most profound practical treatment of church in the NT and exemplifies Matthew's nuance in anticipating the dangers that the church faces from the very fact that it is structured and has authority."[47]

ECUMENICAL IMPLICATIONS: STRENGTHS AND CHALLENGES

These diverse New Testament ecclesiologies, Brown insisted, were not being proposed as ecclesial "models" but only as the answer to the specific question about key principles or qualities needed for survival found in each tradition. The question posed by such a review for the Christian churches today is how to deal with this diversity, especially in view of the fragmented nature of contemporary Christianity. One could reject or ignore the diversity and claim a divine imperative that all Christian communities must be uniform. Or one could use the diversity of the New Testament traditions as an excuse to justify the current disunity and conflict among Christian communities. But, as Brown forcefully notes, "Most of the NT was written before the major breaks in *koinōnia* [i.e., "communion"] detectable in the second century and so NT diversity cannot be used to justify Christian division today. We modern Christian have broken *koinōnia* with each other; for, explicitly or implicitly, we have excommunicated each other and/or stated that other churches are disloyal to the will of Christ in major issues. Such a divided situation does not have NT approbation."[48]

Instead, he proposed, the diversity of the New Testament ecclesiologies can be both a strength and a challenge for modern Christianity. Each of us, he says, cherishes the particular Christian community that has nourished our faith. "A study of the diverse emphases in NT churches may illustrate for us the strengths that we admire in our own church and increase our appreciation for how that church has remained faithful to the biblical heritage."[49] But this same diversity can also be a challenge:

A recognition of the range of NT ecclesiological diversity makes the claim of any church to be absolutely faithful to the Scriptures much more complex. We are faithful but in our own specific way; and both ecumenics and biblical studies should make us aware that there are other ways of being faithful to which we do not do justice....In short, a frank study of NT ecclesiologies should convince every Christian community that it is neglecting part of the NT witness....I contend that in a divided Christianity, instead of reading the Bible to assure ourselves that we are right, we would do better to read it to

discover where we have not been listening. As we Christians
of different churches try to give hearing to the previously
muffled voices, our views of the church will grow larger;
and we will come closer to sharing common views. Then
the Bible would be doing for us what Jesus did in his time,
namely, convincing those who have ears to hear that all is
not right, for God is asking of them more than they thought.
That could be the *metanoia* [repentance] that would prepare
the church for the kingdom.[50]

It would be hard to express the ecumenical significance of the New
Testament more succinctly or more eloquently than this.

SUMMING UP: BROWN'S LECTURE AT THE RATZINGER CONFERENCE

In January of 1988, Brown would make an important address on
"The Contribution of Historical Biblical Criticism to Ecumenical Church
Discussion." The occasion was the Emmaus Conference, sponsored yearly
by *First Things*, a conservative theological journal. The conference in 1988
was held in New York and organized by the prominent Lutheran churchman and later a Roman Catholic, Richard John Neuhaus.[51] The topic
concerned biblical interpretation. The headliner for the conference
was none other than Cardinal Joseph Ratzinger, then the prefect of the
Vatican Congregation for the Doctrine of the Faith. Ratzinger gave a
now famous address on the philosophical roots of the historical-critical
method. As we have already noted in chapter 3, Brown was invited by
Neuhaus to consider the ecumenical implications of historical-critical
methodology. Later, having heard Ratzinger's address, Brown would
add an important "addenda" to his published talk, laying out his own
views of the historical-critical method and how it could be employed
in a proper way in the context of a community of faith.[52] The surge of
criticism from ultraconservative groups that were dismayed by discovering Brown's name on the agenda, and both Neuhaus's and Ratzinger's
support of Brown, will be considered in the next chapter.[53]

Important for our topic here is what Brown had to say regarding historical-critical investigation of the Bible and its meaning for

ecumenism. It is clear that the approach Brown laid out in his two collaborative books on Peter and Mary in the New Testament and especially in *The Churches the Apostles Left Behind* was in full play here. In his Emmaus Conference address, Brown made several key affirmations about ecumenism and the appropriate role of the historical-critical method. First, he affirmed the essential ecclesial context of ecumenical dialogue. Such dialogues were not secular academic discussions but carried out on the part of believing communities for whom such factors as revelation and biblical inspiration, the content of the canon, and reverence for the Scriptures as the Word of God in contexts of liturgy and devotion were in play, even though such theological convictions may be understood differently among the participants. The "moderate and adopted" use of the historical method of biblical interpretation could not afford to have the kind of antisupernatural bias that the method may have accrued in other settings.[54] This comment was, in fact, in anticipation of the sharp critique of the European brand of historical criticism that Cardinal Ratzinger would address at the same conference.[55] Brown also recognized the limits of the historical-critical method when used appropriately in an ecumenical context, rejecting an "imperialistic claim that the meaning [of a biblical passage] detected by the historical critical methodology exhausts the meaning of the sacred text."[56] This perspective was already apparent in his earliest writings on the *sensus plenior*. Subsequent Jewish and Christian readings of the Scriptures would find meanings in the sacred texts appropriate to new contexts; this was the case, for example, with Marian devotion within Roman Catholic tradition.[57] He also was wary of giving too much weight to the idiosyncratic views of individual scholars; drawing on a wide array of scholarly opinion was an important corrective to misleading sensational or trendy views proposed by a few.

Brown also conceded that the kind of ecumenical dialogue in which the historical-critical approach to the Bible would be used involved a small number of contemporary Christians. The Orthodox churches of the East were, by and large, not yet comfortable with ecumenical dialogue or modern biblical scholarship. The same was true of many Evangelical branches of Christianity for whom ecumenical dialogue with other Christian denominations was seen as compromise, and participants in such dialogues were sometimes disciplined for such activity. Still others considered the Scriptures themselves to be without much relevance and viewed ecumenical activity as meaningless.

Nevertheless, Brown was convinced that for those contemporary Christians who were committed to ecumenical dialogue—among whom was certainly the Roman Catholic Church in the wake of Vatican II—modern biblical criticism could play a very constructive role. He listed several, all of them having echoes in his other writings, particularly in *The Churches the Apostles Left Behind*:

1. Historical-critical study of the Scriptures can give the churches a more realistic view of developments within their own structures and theology, beyond the explicit affirmations of the New Testament. "No church," he noted, "that has faced up to the results of serious biblical criticism can deny that in its theology, structure, and liturgy it has gone considerably beyond the New Testament churches with their inchoative diversities. That recognition leads to a consideration of how development in the course of past history shaped stances that are now regarded as definitive—stances that were once explained as clearly inculcated in the New Testament."[58] While contemporary churches may take comfort in tracing such developments to their biblical roots, the fact that there are diverse lines of development in the New Testament should raise the question for a church to ask why it has chosen one line of development over another. It may also prompt a particular · church to recognize "that another church has followed a different biblical line of development and thus preserved another biblical value."[59] This self-reflection, Brown contended, "is not an affirmation of relativism but an encouragement to the churches to face ecumenism as an essential enrichment rather than a grudging concession. Evaluating the strength and directness of the line of development may also help a church to distinguish in [i.e., among] the importance of traditional positions and thus to appreciate a 'hierarchy of doctrine.'"[60] This might lead to a healing of divisions not just horizontally across denominational lines but a healing "vertically," between the past and the present.

2. Brown also believed that examining carefully how various churches over time absorbed in different ways

the diverse lines of developments in the New Testament would help churches today "to deal more astutely with the ongoing church-shaping developments of our time." Thus, contemporary Christian communities today could be prompted "to recover genuine elements of the biblical heritage that may have been lost or minimalized in the tradition."[61] Examples might be how to absorb the consciousness of the enlightenment and the advances of science, or adaptations of church structures and ministries in response to modern needs.

3. Last of all, Brown turned from a focus on ecumenical scholarship and the use of modern biblical scholarship to the effect of biblical criticism on "ordinary people," using as an example the recent experience of Roman Catholicism. He observed that in the past forty years, since Pius XII's groundbreaking encyclical on Scripture, *Divino Afflante Spiritu*, the transformation within the Catholic Church has been astounding.[62] The revival of Catholic biblical scholarship, confirmed by Vatican II, led to a dramatic change in which clergy and laity who had previously shown little interest in the Bible— quite different from the Protestant experience—were now excited by the rediscovery of the Scriptures and their impact on religious education, liturgy, preaching, theology, and religious discussion. This change, in turn, "opened lines of communication between religiously interested Catholics and Protestants, even to the point of shared Bible classes and readings."[63] He observed that "in other Christian churches critical scholars have alienated Bible readers; in Catholicism critical scholars have had a role in creating Bible readers and the relationship between the two has remained good."[64]

CATHOLIC-JEWISH RELATIONS

Parallel with Brown's lasting commitment to ecumenism was his involvement with Judaism. The latter journey, however, had a different path and pace than his long-term ecumenical interest. Brown's commitment to ecumenism was forged in the very beginning years of his own vocation as a biblical scholar and teacher and never wavered. The same is true in many ways concerning his interest in Judaism, but here his own views and writings developed significantly, as had the perspective of Roman Catholicism itself.

Vatican II's Declaration on the Relation of the Church to Non-Christian Religions, popularly known by its opening Latin words, *Nostra Aetate* ("In this age of ours..."), was among the Council's most revolutionary statements. This was particularly true of the document's statements about the church's relationship with Judaism. It noted the special bond between Christianity and Judaism: "Since Christians and Jews have such a common spiritual heritage, this sacred Council wishes to encourage and further mutual understanding and appreciation. This can be obtained, especially, by way of biblical and theological enquiry and through friendly discussions."[65] The Council dealt explicitly with one of the most painful causes of Christian anti-Semitism, the chronic accusation that Jews collectively were responsible for the death of Jesus. "Even though the Jewish authorities and those who followed their lead pressed for the death of Christ (cf. John 19:6), neither all Jews indiscriminately at that time, nor Jews today, can be charged with crimes committed during his passion." It went on to add,

> The Jews should not be spoken of as rejected or accursed as if this followed from holy Scripture....Indeed, the Church reproves every form of persecution against whomsoever it may be directed. Remembering, then, her common heritage with the Jews and moved not by any political consideration, but solely by the religious motivation of Christian charity, she deplores all hatreds, persecutions, displays of antisemitism leveled at any time or from any source against the Jews.

This bold statement overturned centuries of prejudice on the part of the church and Christians.[66] It was against the backdrop of this amazing transformation that Brown would begin his professional work as a biblical scholar and professor.

Nostra Aetate was officially approved on October 28, 1965, a few years after Brown had begun his teaching career at St. Mary's, but the ferment for change leading up to the declaration would have been in play before the beginning of the Council and was spearheaded, in part, by Cardinal Bea, whom Brown came to know in Rome.[67] Pope John XXIII's famous greeting, "I am Joseph, your brother," in welcoming a Jewish delegation to the Vatican, reflected the tone of his papacy regarding Judaism. At the first Good Friday service where he presided as pope in 1959, he instructed that the traditional petition that referred to the Jews as "perfidious" be repeated without the offending word. In Baltimore, too, relations between Catholics and Jews had become cordial and mutually respectful, ultimately leading to the establishment at St. Mary's of the Ecumenical Institute that would include Catholic–Jewish dialogue as part of its mission.[68] Hanging over the whole question of Christian–Jewish relations and urging its redress was the raw gaping wound of the Holocaust.

However, Brown's first close contact with Judaism was not by way of the Catholic–Jewish dialogue but through his immersion in graduate biblical studies. Here again, his experience at Johns Hopkins was pivotal. His mentor, Albright, was a leading biblical archaeologist and was the scholar most responsible for determining the date and significance of the Dead Sea Scrolls discovered in 1948.[69] As noted earlier, one of Brown's first graduate experiences was participating in a seminar on the Dead Sea Scrolls conducted by Albright. Later, as part of his Hopkins program, Brown would spend a year's fellowship in Jerusalem working daily in the "scrollery" along with Joseph Fitzmyer, putting together a concordance for the Dead Sea texts.[70] While in Jerusalem, Brown also had the opportunity, either with ASOR members or faculty and students of the École Biblique, to visit several biblical archaeological sites. Early on, as we have noted, Brown's biblical interests focused on the Johannine literature and its emergence from Palestinian Judaism.[71] Brown was a leading proponent of those who believed that the taproot of the Johannine tradition was not to be found in the wider Greco-Roman world—what had been a consensus of much prior Continental scholarship—but within the dynamic diversity of first-century Palestinian Judaism.[72]

Thus, Brown's first close relationship with Judaism was not with contemporary Judaism and its relationship with the church but with the emergence of Christianity from its matrix in first century Judaism. His focus was historical and biblical, not contemporary or ecumenical. As it turned out, however, Brown would concentrate much of his work on two sets of New Testament materials that have been most problematic for Christian–Jewish relations: namely, the Gospel of John with its characteristic and strongly polemical references to the "Jews," and the four passion narratives that assign major responsibility for the death of Jesus to the Jewish authorities. As we have already noted in discussing Brown's Johannine commentary, he recognized the manner in which John's Gospel, different from the Synoptics, used the collective term "the Jews" throughout his Gospel, mainly as a way of characterizing Jesus's opponents, particularly the Jewish religious authorities.[73] Brown attributed the hostility that John's Gospel exhibits toward the "Jews" as resulting at least in part from the context in which the Gospel was formed, as the Johannine community experienced deep tension with the majority Jewish community and, consequently, moved over time further away from its own Palestinian Jewish roots. He therefore concluded that "John is not anti-Semitic; the evangelist is condemning not race or people but opposition to Jesus."[74] Missing from Brown's earlier discussions of this feature of John was any mention of the later impact of such anti-Jewish polemic in fomenting Christian anti-Semitism. He seemed to believe that understanding the original social and religious context of such statements was sufficient to neutralize their toxic potential.

Brown's later discussion of these anti-Jewish texts would take a very different tone. He would remain faithful to the task of fitting such materials into their original historical context but now he would deal with the consequences not only of what such texts *meant* but what they came to *mean* in subsequent Christian history. An important influence on Brown's awareness was the strong friendships he developed, particularly during his time at Union Theological Seminary. One important influence was his collaboration with J. Louis Martyn. As already noted, these two colleagues forged a warm personal friendship, doing joint teaching and with Brown frequently enjoying the hospitality of Martyn and his wife. Martyn was particularly sensitive to the anti-Jewish impact of the Johannine materials and hit it head on in his writings and in his classroom presentations.[75]

Perhaps even more significant for his familiarity with contemporary Judaism was Brown's friendship with Burton Visotzky, an outstanding rabbinic scholar who, after his ordination in 1977, joined the faculty of the Jewish Theological Seminary, located across the street from Union.[76] The two seminaries, particularly during the fresh ecumenical period of the 1970s and '80s, when Brown was at Union, had built close relationships between their two faculties, sharing classes, lectures, and fellowship over kosher meals. Even before Visotzky's ordination, he and

Brown had forged a close friendship that had a mutual impact on both their scholarship and teaching. Brown referred to Visotzky as "my rabbi" and Visotzky delighted in using the same term of affection and respect for Brown, considering him also "my rabbi." As it turned out, Brown would also be an advisor for the doctoral dissertation of Claudia Setzer, Visotzky's wife at the time. Brown would enjoy their hospitality and was both a mentor and supporter of Setzer during her doctoral work. Brown's long-term interest in first-century Jewish literature found further guidance in Visotzky's expertise, just as Visotzky took guidance from Brown about early Christianity and the New Testament, partaking in some of Brown's courses at Union. Visotzky noted that after his arrival at Union, Brown would first vet with Visotzky or another Jewish scholar any of his writings dealing with Judaism before submitting them for publication. Brown also lamented the fact that Christian students at Union did not have enough familiarity with Jewish religious literature; he arranged for Visotzky to give a seminar on rabbinic texts, the first to be held at Union.[77]

There is no doubt that through these interactions with Jewish scholars at Jewish Theological Seminary and in many other venues, Brown's awareness of the negative impact of some New Testament texts increased exponentially and would become apparent in his writings. A prime example is his treatment of the issue regarding the passion narratives, an issue that involved all four Gospels and their portrayal of Jewish involvement in the death of Jesus. His two-volume *The Death of the Messiah*, was published in 1993 after Brown had moved to Menlo Park, California, but the bulk of the work was done during his later years at Union, where he was most intensely involved in relationships with the Jewish community.[78] In any case, it is in this work that Brown most directly and extensively dealt with the issue of the anti-Jewish aspects of the gospel texts and their subsequent influence on Christian anti-Semitism, particularly the question of Jewish responsibility for the death of Jesus.

Following his chosen format for dealing with the four passion narratives seriatim, Brown would examine each of the four Gospels' manner of assigning responsibility for the death of Jesus to both the Jewish authorities and the Romans. But before considering the trial of Jesus in each of the Gospels, Brown devoted nearly seventy pages to the question of the role and responsibility of the Jewish authorities in the condemnation of Jesus.[79] With his characteristic attention to detail, Brown

addressed such questions as the role of Roman governance in Palestine at the time of Jesus's death, the respective role of the Sanhedrin
and Jewish religious authorities in capital cases, and the possibility they
could themselves carry out the death sentence. He not only combed
evidence within the Gospels but also in Josephus and other Jewish and
Roman sources. His fundamental conclusion was that probably there
was involvement of some Jewish religious authorities in handing Jesus
over to the Romans, who alone in such cases could carry out capital
punishment.

At this point, however, Brown was acutely aware of how this assertion of the passion narratives, which Brown considered to have a historical basis, would fuel Christian condemnation of Jews throughout
the centuries. He therefore directly dealt with this issue. He candidly
noted "some have advised me against devoting even these few pages to
the issue [i.e., Jewish responsibility and/or guilt for the death of Jesus].
They have warned me that whatever I write will be dismissed as Christian self-justification or as inadequate. I would do better, they tell me,
to treat the antiJewish issue as I treated the implications of the passion
for Christian spirituality and for the systematic theology of the redemption, namely, as very important subjects that lie outside the scope of
a book dedicated to commenting on what the Gospels report." Brown
answered his own question:

> NonChristians need more tangible evidence that a Christian
> commentator is aware of and concerned about the harm-
> ful way in which the PN's have been misused against Jews;
> and Christian readers need to be forcefully reminded of the
> hostile elements in their own reading of the PN's. As for
> Christian self-justification, these remarks are aimed only
> at intelligibility. I would not dare to justify or condemn the
> attitudes either of 1st-cent. Christians or of their opponents,
> about whose motives and consciences we are ill informed.
> However, if we can more clearly perceive and understand
> those 1st-cent. attitudes, we may be able to judge our own
> attitudes and self-justifications.[80]

Brown went on to survey the question in each of the four evangelists, concluding with some key observations that put first-century Jewish involvement in the death of Jesus into perspective.[81] First, "One must

understand that religious people could have disliked Jesus and still be good and sincere people." Some of the stances Jesus took could be perceived as offensive—his association with sinners and those who did not observe the law, his sharp criticism of the religious leaders, and so on. Second, "in Jesus' time religious opposition often led to violence." (At the time of his writing this, Brown contrasted the virulence of ancient religious strife to the more peaceful conditions of today—a contrast he might temper in view of the violence undertaken by some religious groups today.) Third, he noted that we are trying to determine "responsibility" rather than "guilt;" that is, we are not in a position to judge the personal integrity of those involved in the condemnation of Jesus. We can only assign "responsibility" based on what appears to have been the role taken by various individuals and groups in the matter.

Finally, "the religious dispute with Jesus was an inner Jewish dispute." For Brown, this was a key factor leading to the subsequent irresponsible interpretation of the biblical texts in fomenting anti-Semitism. As a contrasting example, Brown pointed to the fate of Jeremiah the prophet who was condemned by his own people and in an apocryphal tradition was even executed. Even though the notion of "blood guilt" borne by the people is part of the story of Jeremiah, "no one," Brown noted, "suggests that the blood of Jeremiah needs to be avenged."[82] Both Jews and Christians can read the story of Jeremiah as Scripture, "as an outstanding example of the innocent just one made to suffer by the leaders of God's own people." The story as such is similar to the story of Jesus's own condemnation and innocent death, but "the case is emotionally different because those who thought that Jesus was right ultimately became another religion…Christians spoke to Jews of *your* leaders doing this to our savior, while for Jews (in centuries past) it was our leaders doing this to *their* (false) prophet. Perhaps the 'our,' 'your,' and 'their' outlook cannot be overcome, but it will help readers of this commentary if they can remember that it was not thus when the crucifixion was taking place and even when the story was first taking shape."[83]

Brown returned to this point with even greater clarity in his later book, *An Introduction to the New Testament*:

In the Christian picture of what was done to Jesus, at first there was nothing anti-Jewish in depicting the role of the Jewish authorities in his death; for Jesus and his disciples on one side and the Jerusalem Sanhedrin authorities on the other were all Jews. The depiction of those Jews opposed to Jesus as plotting evil was not different from the OT depiction of the wicked plotting against the innocent [as before, Brown appealed to the example of Jeremiah]....Nevertheless, the account of Jesus' passion was eventually "heard" in an antiJewish way. A major factor was the conversion of Gentiles to the following of Jesus. Sometimes the early Christian communities encountered the hostility of local synagogue leaders, and they saw a parallel between this hostility and the treatment of Jesus by the authorities of his time. Now, however, the issue was no longer on an intraJewish level: That other group, the Jews, were doing these things to us Gentile Christians and were responsible for the death of Jesus.[84]

Brown was correct in predicting that his efforts to explain and defuse the anti-Semitic interpretation of the passion narratives would be deemed both inadequate and as an attempt at Christian self-justification. John Dominic Crossan in his own book on the issue would level both accusations at Brown's work.[85] Right at the outset of his work, Crossan took sharp issue with Brown's commentary on the passion narratives. This was not the first time the views of both scholars were in conflict. Brown had earlier critiqued Crossan's assessment that such extracanonical material as the Gospel of Peter was earlier than the canonical Gospels, whereas Brown believed that such texts were later and derivative from the canonical materials.[86] As discussed earlier, Crossan, a longtime professor at DePaul University in Chicago, had also been a leading figure in the Jesus Seminar, a group that Brown judged as "trendy" and "sensationalist" in its views without much academic credibility. An even more fundamental divergence between the two was their assessment of the historical grounding of the Gospels. In a review of Brown's book in the *New York Times*, Peter Steinfels recounts a quotation of Crossan where he offered a dissenting opinion to Brown's *The Death of the Messiah*. "'Basically the issue is whether the passion accounts are prophecy historicized or history remembered,' said John Dominic Crossan, a professor of religious studies at DePaul University in Chicago. 'Ray Brown is 80 percent in the direction of history remembered. I'm 80 percent in the opposite direction.'"[87] At the same time, Crossan wanted to make clear that he was not accusing Brown himself of anti-Semitism: "[Brown's] book *The Death of the Messiah* is acutely aware of the problem of antiJudaism, and he has a special section entitled 'Responsibility and/or Guilt for the Death of Jesus' (383–97). No one could read that chapter and accuse Brown of either anti-Judaism or anti-Semitism....I do not find any unfair, illegitimate, or invalid criticism of Judaism's religious tenets anywhere in Brown's book, and I emphasize that most strongly to offset any misunderstanding."[88]

Foremost among several criticisms of Brown's work that Crossan raises is his fundamental disagreement with Brown's view that there is some historical basis to the Gospels' accusation that some Jewish religious authorities were involved in the condemnation of Jesus. He finds particularly offensive Brown's cautious conclusions that often assert "probability" or "not impossible" or "not implausible" in making judgements about the details of possible Jewish involvement. This is especially true regarding the passion accounts that Crossan himself sees as originating as "defensive fiction" on the part of the originally small and fragile Jewish Christian sect over against the threats of the majority Jewish community. Blaming the Jews rather than the Romans deflected negative attention directed at the early Jewish Christian community. "It is quite possible," Crossan observed, "to understand and sympathize with a small and powerless Jewish sect writing fiction to defend itself. But once that Jewish sect became the Christian Roman Empire, a defensive strategy would become the longest lie. The passion narratives challenge both the honesty of Christian history and the integrity of Christian conscience."[89] For Crossan, there is no historical basis to the passion narratives; they are, in effect, prophecy drawn from the Old Testament turned into narrative. From this vantage point, Crossan finds Brown's work wholly inadequate and ultimately intellectually dishonest. Given the fact that Crossan sees the passion accounts and their assertion of complicity in the death of Jesus as "fiction," he believes that the responsibility of the Christian exegete is to say so, and to denounce the passion accounts and their tragic consequences in later history, culminating in the Holocaust itself. He notes, "There may well be some stories in the New Testament that one can leave as 'maybe historical' and avoid asserting one's best historical judgment or reconstruction about them. But the passion-resurrection stories are different because they have been the seedbed for Christian anti-Judaism. And without that Christian anti-Judaism, lethal and genocidal European anti-Semitism would have been either impossible or at least not widely successful. What was at stake in those passion stories, in the long haul of history, was the Jewish Holocaust."[90]

Apparently in Crossan's view, the subtleties of historical exploration in the case of potentially dangerous texts such as the passion narratives should give way to a consideration of their negative impact in later Christian interpretation. Crossan's view coincides with Brown in judging that the original arena for these narratives was an intra-Jewish conflict but that the stakes changed when Christianity and Judaism became separated. In contrast to Crossan, however, Brown still believed that the potential historical dimensions of the passion accounts, like the Gospels, deserve to be considered as carefully and objectively as possible. One could not, in effect, cut the Gordian knot and declare the passion narratives to be without historical merit, even in view of their later role in Christian interpretation.

It is interesting that over time Brown's conclusion that some Jewish religious authorities played a role in the condemnation of Jesus became accepted by some prominent Jewish scholars.[91] Surely in play for Brown was his lifelong attempt to constructively relate the historical context of the New Testament (i.e., part of what the text "meant") to later Christian interpretation.[92] For him, it would be just as impossible to completely denounce the passion narratives as "defensive fiction" and without any historical or theological merit, as it would be for him to overlook their potential for later Christian anti-Semitism.

Brown's commitment to building a stronger relationship with the Jewish community would also include his significant contribution as a member of the Pontifical Biblical Commission (PBC). As noted earlier, in 1996 Brown was invited for the second time to be a member of the Pontifical Biblical Commission by Pope John Paul II, with the recommendation of then Cardinal Joseph Ratzinger, the prefect of the Vatican Congregation for the Doctrine of the Faith under whose jurisdiction the PBC operated.[93] At the prompting of Pope John Paul himself, the PBC was beginning its work on a document addressing the relationship of the Old and New Testaments and its implications for contemporary relationships between Christianity and Judaism. The pope had noted that several postconciliar texts dealing with the bond between Christianity and Judaism had appeared, dealing with implications for the liturgy and religious education, but as yet there was no official study that directly addressed the implications of the Scriptures for Jewish–Christian relations. In his extended preface to the Commission's final work, which would be published in 2002,[94] Ratzinger himself, who, as prefect of the Congregation for the Doctrine of the Faith, served as official presider over the sessions of the PBC, forthrightly stated two serious questions facing the church in relationship to Judaism "under the shock of the Shoah": First, "can Christians, after all that has happened, still claim in good conscience to be the legitimate heirs of Israel's Bible?" Second, "In its presentation of the Jews and the Jewish people, has not the New Testament itself contributed to creating a hostility towards the Jewish people that provided a support for the ideology of those who wished to destroy Israel?"[95]

It was regarding the second question that Brown would make a significant contribution to the PBC's final document, even though Brown himself would not live to see the publication of the final version of the Commission's text. The working procedure for the PBC typically involved individual members of the Commission being asked to compose papers on various aspects of the issue under consideration. These individual papers would be discussed by the Commission in plenary sessions, then recast considering the discussion, and overtime worked into a final consensus text by a team of redactors. The procedure, in fact, was not unlike the process that Brown and his colleagues had used in composing the collaborative works *Peter in the New Testament* and *Mary in the New Testament.*[96] Not surprisingly, Brown was asked by Albert Vanhoye, SJ, then secretary for the PBC (a role that was akin to being the facilitator and leader of the Commission's discussions) to address the potentially anti-Jewish and anti-Semitic aspects of the Johannine literature. In an earlier letter to Vanhoye, Brown had already urged that the PBC not limit its attention to the historical context of the New Testament materials but consider the contemporary impact of these texts and their significance for the Catholic–Jewish dialogue.[97] In his reply, Vanhoye thanked Brown for his suggestion and agreed this was a direction the PBC document should take.[98]

To that end, Brown prepared a document that he submitted to the PBC, dealing with the meaning of the "Jews" in the Gospel of John and its implications for today. Given the nature of the Commission's work, this was not a paper meant for publication but as a contribution to the Commission's ongoing work on the topic.[99] Comparing Brown's essay with the final text of the PBC clearly shows that much of what Brown wrote was incorporated into the document.[100] His consistent views on John's Gospel developed over the years of his work on the Johannine literature is apparent. Some key perspectives of Brown's on the context of John's Gospel included the following: the fundamental Jewish roots of John's Gospel; John's use of the term "the Jews" in the majority of cases to refer to the opponents of Jesus, mainly the religious authorities; the social and religious context of the Johannine community with its growing tension with the majority of Jews; and its gradual separation and development over time into an entity with a differing sense of identity over against the Jewish community. Brown was also convinced that the problems created by later interpretation of John should not be addressed by editing offensive words or passages out of the New Testament or by referring to "Judeans" instead of "Jews" in John's text, but, rather, by informed teaching and preaching about the Johannine text and by condemnation of Christian anti-Semitism.

Although he did not have a direct hand in its formulation, Brown would certainly have agreed with the powerful conclusion of the PBC's document:

> The example of Paul in Rm 9–11 shows that, on the contrary, an attitude of respect, esteem and love for the Jewish people is the only truly Christian attitude in a situation which is mysteriously part of the beneficent and positive plan of God. Dialogue is possible, since Jews and Christians share a rich common patrimony that unites them. It is greatly to be desired that prejudice and misunderstanding be gradually eliminated on both sides, in favour of a better understanding of the patrimony they share and to strengthen the links that bind them.[101]

Raymond Brown, through his writings, particularly on the Gospel of John and the passion narratives, and through his personal friendships with Jews, embodied this spirit. Sonya Cronin's final assessment of Brown and Judaism, after evaluating a broad spectrum of New Testament scholars on this topic, offers this summation:

> Of the scholars we evaluated that wrote comprehensive works on John, Brown began dealing with anti-Judaism the earliest (as early as 1970). His sensitivity towards anti-Judaism in John grew consistently since the beginning of his career (1960). It involves both his biblical interpretation,

which has sought historical answers for the Johannine hostility towards "the Jews" and his direct addresses to the reader that combat potential anti-Judaism among his readers without actually judging the first-century community. Because of Brown's utilization of Catholic statements, and his identity first as a Catholic and secondly a biblical scholar, Brown has been able to represent the Catholic Church as a leader in the fight against anti-Judaism, both in biblical interpretation, and in general attitudes. As he grew more prominent in his scholarship, he became a significant voice in leadership, contributing to the formation of official Church statements. In his own careful yet truly committed way, he not only deeply influenced a generation of Catholic scholars, but has provided the resources for people of all perspectives to address the problem of anti-Judaism in the New Testament.[102]

CONCLUSION: AN ECUMENICAL SPIRIT

Raymond Brown's commitment to ecumenism and the Christian–Jewish dialogue had deep roots in his experience as a biblical scholar. The employment of the historical-critical method, he believed, was itself common ground for both Catholic and Protestant scholarship. Perhaps somewhat optimistically, he was convinced that an objective use of the historical-critical method on the biblical text would yield common results about what the text "meant" across denominational boundaries. In a similar vein, he devoted a lot of his scholarship to tracing the diverse developments of early Christianity's "sub-apostolic" texts and their impact on the later diversity among Christian ecclesiologies. Here, too, was a way that the various Christian denominations might not only learn mutual respect for each other's differences but also find a challenge regarding their fidelity to the biblical roots of the church.

His appreciation of the Jewish roots of the New Testament and his concentration on the Johannine literature and the passion narratives also led him over time to realize the impact of these texts on later hostility between Jews and Christians, due mainly to Christian anti-Judaism and anti-Semitism. As was the case with his ecumenical instincts, Brown's relationship with Judaism was not simply academic but found its passion in warm and enduring friendships. There is no evidence of Brown's attitude to Islam. No doubt if he had lived a few more years, the explosion of world events may have led him to an engagement with Islam and its writings.

Yet there was more to Brown's innate ecumenical spirit than his academic commitment and experience. He was also endowed with a natural curiosity that led him to explorations beyond the familiar, a curiosity and interest that was coupled with respect for the religious convictions of others, even as he maintained his own unwavering fidelity to his Catholic identity. One example of this was Brown's great interest in the Mormons. In 1974, he was invited to give the Welch Lecture at Brigham Young University in Provo, Utah. Many of his Sulpician colleagues testify that Brown delighted in knowing a lot about the Mormons and their customs and beliefs. As was the case with his interest in Protestants and Jews, however, that interest was not purely intellectual. A lovely letter Brown wrote in 1996 to a Mormon friend for inclusion in his seventieth birthday tribute book could be a final word on his generous and open ecumenical spirit:[103]

Dear Truman,

When many of your LDS friends read this book, they may raise their eyebrows at the sight of a letter from a Catholic priest who considers you and your wife and family as dear friends. Many of my Catholic friends raise their eyebrows when they hear that I am very fond of Mormons who have shown me warm kindness. Both of us can rejoice that God does not raise His eyebrows when His children love one another. (We could probably have a theological debate on whether God has eyebrows!)

I was asked to recall favorite memories [a request for the birthday tribute book]. I have two. When we went up from St. Louis to Nauvoo, you shepherded me through what once had been an impressive city. Then we visited the site where Joseph Smith was martyred. Ann choked up, and I saw your own reverence. How much abstract debate fades into the background when one sees true belief. The other memory was when we visited a yet unconsecrated temple. As we went about, the news that Truman Madsen was on the scene circulated, producing among the staff awe close to adoration. It was like being shown through

St. Peter's by the Pope! Yet for my religious background the Pope is number 1, and to keep you humble I have to tell you that even in your context I cannot consider you number 1. But you had the outstanding wisdom to marry a wonderful Lady who for you (and for me) is number 1.

Many more years. Ray

As is often the case, an inclination to ecumenism and interreligious dialogue transcends intellectual curiosity—which, no doubt, Raymond Brown had—and is prompted by a genuine interest in and respect for people who may be very different from one's own experiences and circumstances. Raymond Brown, who was involved in ecumenism all his professional life, was one of those people.

CHAPTER 8

OPPOSITION AND CONFLICT

The impact of the Second Vatican Council on the Catholic Church and the concurrent turmoil and social changes taking place in the world at the time of the Council created an atmosphere that proved challenging to many traditional institutions, including the church itself. Some theologians and bishops, who championed reform and renewal at the time of the Council, turned cautious over time as some of the implications of this change became apparent.[1] This dynamic and turbulent post–Vatican II environment generated some heated opposition to biblical scholars who were viewed as one of the pistons driving the reforms of the Council. Raymond Brown, because of his reputation as a scholar and, even more, because of the impact of his lecturing and popular publications, was considered the leader of the pack. The goal in this chapter is not to rebut Brown's opponents or to restate in detail his views on the various contested issues such as the virginal conception or the establishment of the New Testament priesthood— positions we have previously explained. Instead the purpose is both to document this aspect of Brown's professional career and to try to understand the reasons why such opposition was directed at him.

SETTING THE STAGE: CATHOLIC BIBLICAL SCHOLARSHIP IN THE UNITED STATES

In June 1976, Brown accepted an honorary doctorate from the University of Louvain. It was among the first of thirty-one such honorary degrees he would receive over the course of his remarkable career.

He had been relieved to learn that Louvain was willing to pay his travel expenses for the occasion, lamenting to his community treasurer that in some instances he had to pay his own expenses to receive such honors. The address he would deliver on this occasion would be published in the Fall 1976 edition of *Louvain Studies* and was titled "Difficulties in Using the New Testament in American Catholic Discussions."[2] Perhaps it was the formal setting for his address in the venerable aula of the University and before an audience composed of the prestigious and progressive faculty and honored guests of this medieval Catholic university (founded in 1425), or it may have been that the mounting criticism he was receiving back in the United States had put him in a more somber mood—in any case, the tone of this address is part lament, part critique of the state of American Catholic biblical scholarship, an unusual topic for Brown.[3] What Brown commented on in this article sets a framework for the opposition he would endure, particularly from some more traditional Catholic sources, an opposition that would dog him all his professional life.

The occasion of receiving his honorary doctorate, Brown noted, coincided with the American bicentennial of 1976, and Louvain itself had made a significant contribution over the years to Catholic biblical scholarship (he cited as an example, the distinguished Belgian and Louvain scholar, Msgr. Lucien Cerfaux, who even had a national postage stamp issued in his honor!), therefore he chose to focus on the state of Catholic biblical scholarship on the American scene.

His observations centered around two critical points. First, Brown contended that "because of its origin and history, Catholic NT scholarship in the U.S.A. has for the most part been mild and somewhat slow to come to grips with sensitive areas that crucially affect Christology and ecclesiology." To a certain extent, this was because there was a "lack of a first-class American Catholic graduate biblical school." This situation was further impeded by the Vatican demand that "all teachers of the Bible in seminaries and universities must have Roman degrees"—a condition, he noted, that would make the development of a high-quality American Catholic biblical school even more difficult. Second, biblical scholarship in America before and during the Council was strongly influenced by French Catholic scholarship, which, in Brown's view, was "mild and very concerned to reconcile the new developments with scholastic theology and patristic authority. For that reason, it made biblical criticism palatable in a conservative Catholic intellectual world"

(p. 146). Some, he noted, "romanticize" the Second Vatican Council as the "high-water mark of Catholic biblical criticism." In fact, "it was through the Council that biblical criticism won elementary acceptance in Catholic circles."

It was similar with the work of the Pontifical Biblical Commission during and after the Council. Its 1964 "Statement on the Historical Truth of the Gospels" became the backbone of the Council's Dogmatic Constitution on Divine Revelation, *Dei Verbum*, and, importantly, "won for the Church the acceptance of a developmental approach to the Gospels, recognizing that the final Gospels go considerably beyond the ministry of Jesus and that later Christology had been retrojected into the accounts of the ministry" (p. 147). Yet this crucial perspective—one that Brown himself repeatedly appealed to in his writings—"was very moderate and avoided really thorny issues," such as the question of the "limited human knowledge of Jesus."[4] Thus, contrary to popular opinion, in the wake of the Council "Catholic NT scholarship was just growing up" (p.148). Brown conceded that the scene was changing, however, with the influx of younger scholars in the field, many of whom had been influenced by more progressive German Catholic scholarship and at schools such as "Johns Hopkins, Harvard, and Yale."[5]

This undeveloped state of Catholic biblical scholarship in the United States led, in Brown's estimation, to somewhat "antiquated" views about key issues, such as the authorship and dating of the New Testament books, for example, presuming that the Apostle John was the author of the Gospel of John or assuming that Luke was the companion of Paul or the attributing of Pauline authorship to the Deutero-Pauline works, such as Colossians, Ephesians, and the Pastoral Letters. Even more significant was the hesitation of many American Catholic biblical scholars to address forthrightly the implications of modern biblical scholarship for such sensitive doctrinal issues as the virginal conception of Jesus[6] or the postresurrectional nature of Jesus's promises to Peter in Matthew 16:18, and the realization "that it [Mt 16:18] cannot be used to determine the intentions of Jesus during his ministry in regard to the Church" (p. 151). The commission of the risen Christ to his disciples in the final scene of Matthew's Gospel may be "a distillation from the Christian experience of the first century." "Such a conclusion," he notes, "would be a sharp challenge to what I call blueprint ecclesiology where it is imagined that Jesus told the apostles precisely what to do and they followed out specific commands. This blueprint ecclesiology leaves subsequent generations no real possibility of changing Church structure. Until there is a firm modern investigation of such questions as the post-resurrectional sayings of Jesus, NT criticism will not have made its real contribution to theological discussions" (p. 151).[7]

Even more crucial for the impact of modern biblical scholarship, Brown believed, is a proper understanding of the relationship of biblical criticism to church doctrine. Here, Brown was certainly touching the nerve center from which much of the opposition to him arose. He cited three aspects of the failure to understand the relationship between biblical scholarship and church doctrine.[8] First, some may "attempt to solve modern critical problems on the basis of dogmatic statements phrased in a pre-critical era" (p. 152). That was the case, for example, with such assertions as "Christ founded the Church" or "Christ instituted the sacraments." These assertions were a kind of ecclesiastical shorthand, "statements…phrased before the insight now accepted by the Church that the Gospels give a picture of Christ that goes considerably beyond the historical ministry of Jesus of Nazareth" (p. 152). Here once again, Brown appealed to the 1964 statement of the Pontifical Biblical Commission on the threefold evolution of the gospel tradition. These traditional church formulations are, in fact, "a distillation from the whole NT picture and from the whole of first-century Christian history" (p. 152). With a notion that so many of his critics would oppose, Brown believed it was the Spirit sent by the risen Christ that guided the foundation of the post-Easter church and the evolving formulation of its structures. Such a perspective allowed one to bridge the gap between these traditional formulations and the results of modern biblical scholarship: "Since we hold through faith that the Holy Spirit was at work in that growth [of the early church] and since there was real continuity from the first stage to the last, there is no real difficulty with the affirmation that Christ founded the Church. But, as we have seen, such a doctrinal affirmation does not solve the problem of Jesus' intentions during his ministry" (p.153).

A second casualty of not appreciating the proper link between biblical scholarship and church doctrine was "the forced interpretation of the silence of the NT in the light of later dogmatic interests." This fallacy, Brown speculates, might be related to the traditional doctrine that "revelation ceased with the death of the last apostles." However, this is to confuse revelation itself (i.e., embodied in Jesus Christ and his apostles) with the *formulation* of revelation, a process that continues to develop beyond the New Testament period. Brown used the example of ordination to illustrate his point. The New Testament is silent on the question of who presided at the Eucharist, but many Catholics would nevertheless affirm that it was the apostles and their successors, that is, the bishops and priests, who must have presided in the New Testament period since this is the affirmation of later church teaching. Brown, on the other hand, believed that the formal designation of who was authorized to preside at the Eucharist was a later—and valid—church decision. "Later Church practice of confining the celebration of the Eucharist to the ritually ordained is a valid limitation no matter who celebrated the Eucharist in NT times" (p. 154). Brown concluded, "Thus, I contend that it is a misuse of the argument from silence to assume that the first-century custom had to be the same as the later custom—there is no doctrinal need to do so and most of our information points in the opposite direction. Those who want to base the legitimacy of the Catholic priesthood on such dubious assumptions from silence expose us to the justified distrust of our fellow Christians" (p.155).

Finally, another deviation, like the argument from silence, "is the tendency to neglect or underplay texts that do not accord with later dogmatic positions." The church's belief in the inerrancy of Scripture, as stated in the formulation of *Dei Verbum,* refers to "that truth which God wanted put into the Sacred Writings for the sake of our salvation"; it does not thereby "guarantee a biblical author's general theology which is betrayed incidentally in his writing" (p. 156). Thus the author of Job may deny that there is an afterlife, but that is not a major teaching of his book. For a pertinent New Testament example, Brown turned to Marian devotion. Catholics who draw only on Matthew and Luke for their biblical portrayal of Mary also should consider the fact that Mark's Gospel does not share this type of portrayal. Mark depicts Mary and his blood family as not followers of Jesus, in contrast to his discipleship family who were. Rather than force Mark's portrayal into conformity with Catholic tradition on Mary, Catholic tradition must recognize that there were other patterns, even though, Brown believed, "the Lucan direction is the correct direction for the future of the Christian community" (p. 157).

Brown concluded his article with a plea that the church seriously engage the findings of sound biblical scholarship, even if it might challenge some traditional doctrinal formulations. It was not the role of biblical scholars to make such reformulations—that is the proper role of legitimate church authority. Hopefully, however, Catholic biblical scholarship might play a "consultative" role in the process. "There are those in the Church who charge that biblical criticism is barren and that we need a more spiritual reading of the Bible. Criticism may be barren in the hands of certain practitioners, but some who make the charge would dearly like to distract Catholics from a frank and honest discussion of the origins of Christianity and in the Church of today" (p. 157).

OPPOSITION IN DIFFERENT SHADES

In his 1976 address at Louvain, Brown clearly stated the issues that made him a lightning rod for those who considered modern biblical scholarship a threat to the life of the church. The views that his opponents considered toxic were in many cases the very ones to which Brown was most committed as a scholar, a historian, and a Catholic. In our review of these writings, both popular and scholarly, we have encountered his characteristic perspective over and over. Brown firmly believed that the result of critical biblical scholarship, exercised in the context of Christian faith and in fidelity to the church's tradition, led to certain key outcomes. They might be summarized as follows:

1. The Gospels were the result of an evolutionary development in the early church, with their roots in the life of Jesus and his mission but their content and tone influenced by the preaching of the early community and ultimately set in writing through the composition of the evangelists in the context of their communities. Brown repeatedly appealed to the endorsement of this perspective stated in the 1964 statement of the Pontifical Biblical Commission on the "Historical Truth of the Gospels" and the absorption of this perspective in Vatican II's *Dei Verbum*.
2. A concurrent conviction was that the development of the church and the formulation of the New Testament were under the guidance of the Holy Spirit. The portrayal of Jesus's teaching on such matters as the founding of the church, the institution of the church's vital structures and it ecclesiastical order, and its fundamental convictions about the identity of Jesus were prompted by the Spirit

and attributed to the authority of the risen Christ within the post-Easter community.

3. Continuity between the New Testament and the post–New Testament church was to be rooted in the diverse lines of development that emerged, particularly in the "sub-apostolic" writings of the New Testament such as the four Gospels, the Acts of the Apostles, and the Deutero-Pauline and other New Testament literature. It was in alignment with these Spirit-driven developments that one could find the biblical foundations for such later traditional doctrinal formulations such as "revelation ceased with the death of the last apostle," or "Jesus instituted the sacraments," or "Jesus founded the church."

4. While the formulation of doctrine and accountability to authentic church teaching were the responsibility of legitimate church authority (i.e., the pope and the bishops and the Ecumenical Councils), biblical scholarship exercised responsibly could play a "consulting" role in pointing to the implications of the findings of sound biblical scholarship for the life and renewal of the contemporary church.

Some of the criticism leveled at Brown was particularly vicious and mean-spirited—branding him a heretic and a renegade priest, questioning his motives, and distorting his positions. In his article offering a tribute to Brown at the time of his death, his longtime friend and fellow scholar, Joseph Fitzmyer, SJ, spent considerable time exposing this type of criticism. As he noted,

> Since the death of Brown, many have recalled the great things that he had achieved in his lifetime, and many have been the deserved eulogies of this renowned Scripture scholar. Because the "venomous" criticism of him had died down somewhat in the last decade before he died, it is all too easy to forget what an ordeal he went through in the seventies and eighties of this century. The criticism of those who attacked him stemmed from a pettiness that could not brook either the notoriety that Brown had begun to enjoy or the good effect of his teaching and writing about the written Word of

God on American Catholics, and indeed on Catholics and Protestants of the whole world.[9]

Particularly egregious examples were the attacks of the magazine *Triumph*. This journal was founded in 1966 by L. Brent Bozell Jr., the brother-in-law of the noted conservative writer William F. Buckley, founder and editor of *The National Review*. Bozell's views were something of an unusual mixture. He resigned as an editor of *The National Review* because of its opposition to some aspects of Catholic social teaching; he was opposed to the Vietnam War, and felt that Buckley was "too soft" on abortion. Yet Bozell and his magazine were ardently opposed to Brown and his brand of biblical scholarship. Fitzmyer quotes a mock "want-ad" purported to be placed by "R. E. Brown" seeking a faculty position, which appeared in an editorial of *Triumph* in 1973:

> *Personal.* Situation wanted: Are you a prestigious university, looking for an internationally known Scripture scholar with no dogmatic hang-ups? Then I'm the man for you. You'll never catch me affirming the virginal conception of Christ, the existence of Adam and Eve, the inerrancy of Jesus' knowledge, the Apostolic Succession. Do I make faith subservient to theology? Deny the validity of past formulations of doctrine? Deny literal truth to the Gospels? Yes, yes and yes again. We could make beautiful heresy together. Salary? Sufficient to support me in the style to which I have become accustomed. Reply to R. E. Brown, New York Review, Box 47.

> [reply] Mr. R. E. Brown, New York Review, Box 47. Dear Mr. Brown: We love you. Come home. (signed) The Catholic University of America.[10]

A later editorial mocked Brown again, asserting that his fellow Catholic biblical scholars "wouldn't renounce their faith in Brown if an archaeological find were to be dug up tomorrow saying 'Raymond Brown, who will go about during the twentieth century, is a fraud,' signed/Jesus of Nazareth, and attested to by a notary public."[11] Such crude attacks led to a resolution of the Catholic Biblical Association condemning *Triumph* for its attacks on Brown and other Catholic biblical scholars.[12] *Triumph* eventually ran out of steam and ceased publication in 1976.

Competing for these kind of crude attacks but lasting much longer and with much more intensity was a stream of editorials and articles in *The Wanderer* that appeared throughout the 1970s and '80s attacking Brown and his scholarship.[13] *The Wanderer*, published by a group of lay Catholics in St. Paul, Minnesota, and founded in 1867, claims to be the oldest Catholic newspaper in the country still in circulation, taking a decidedly conservative stance on both religion and politics. Fitzmyer cites a number of articles, bearing such sensational and provocative titles as "Some Modernist Errors," "The Deleterious Influence of Fr. R. Brown," "Heretics and Buffoons Meet in Washington," "Raymond Brown and the Charge of Modernism," "The Evil Fruit of Fr. Brown's 'Scholarship,'" "Fr. Brown Fathers Wild and Irresponsible Speculation," "Hans Kueng: The Doctrinal Image of Fr. Raymond Brown," "How Eccentric Can a 'Centrist' Theologian Be?" "The Continuing Mis-Adventures of Fr. Raymond Brown," "The Make-Believe World of Fr. Raymond Brown," "How Fr. Brown Stole Christmas," "Can Fr. Brown Steal the Center?" and "Fr. Brown Mispresents Bible, Catholic Church." *The Wanderer* even headlined the announcement of Brown's death, as "Fr. Raymond Brown, Modernist Scripture Scholar, Dead at 70," and the following week published a final attack on Brown, "Traditional Scholars Long Opposed to Fr. Brown's Theories."[14] Particularly galling for many of these writers was the fact that Brown was publicly respected by many cardinals and bishops and appointed by popes from Paul VI to John Paul II to a number of Vatican commissions, including twice being invited to be a member of the Pontifical Biblical Commission (the second time with the approbation of then Cardinal Joseph Ratzinger).

Other voices joined this chorus but in a more moderated tone. Perhaps the most extensive critique of Brown was the work of Msgr. George A. Kelly (1916–2004), *The New Biblical Theorists: Raymond E. Brown and Beyond*.[15] A priest of the Archdiocese of New York at the time he published this book in 1983, Kelly was a faculty member of St. John's University holding the John A. Flynn chair in "Contemporary Catholic Problems." As a former parish priest, he had been a champion of the labor movement and a strong advocate for social justice. During his priestly career, he would hold several important positions in the archdiocese, most notably serving as a director of the Family Life Bureau. He later would be the founder of the "Fellowship of Catholic Scholars" that continues to exist and has earned a reputation as a staunch defender of what it considers orthodox Catholic teaching. Cardinal O'Connor described Kelly as "a clerical James Cagney" and "foe formidable of theological and scriptural chicanery."[16] Lest it be supposed that by referring to "scriptural chicanery," O'Connor had Raymond Brown in mind, it should be noted that the cardinal also praised Brown as a faithful priest and servant of the church: "I never preach on Saint John without consulting your two volumes. You have been a brilliant scholar, a man of the Church and a true priest. We are all in your debt."[17]

Conceding that he was a prodigious scholar and the leading proponent of modern critical biblical studies in the Catholic Church, Kelly chose to focus his criticism on Brown as a prime exemplar of what was harmful about modern biblical scholarship. René Laurentin (1917–2017), who had sharply criticized Brown's study of the infancy narratives in *The Birth of the Messiah*, wrote a very brief preface that anticipates the tone of Kelly's work, noting, "The most modern theologians often say today is [sic] that theology is 'the expression of the people of God.' Such is said in theory, but theology often acts like an outside analysis, extraneous to that Faith, to the tradition which transmits it, and to the Holy Spirit who guarantees its dynamism, boldness, and its very existence."[18] Kelly offers a detailed analysis of Brown's works, focusing on the sensitive issues that were the usual subjects of such criticism: the historicity of the virginal conception, the foundation of the church, the priesthood and the episcopate, the human consciousness of Jesus, and the question of "pluralism" or the diversity of the New Testament concerning such questions as ecclesiology and Christology. As we have seen time and again, these issues that were the focus of much of Brown's writings continued to be neuralgic for more traditional Catholics.

In a concluding chapter, Kelly summed up his criticism of Brown under six headings:

1. He detected a change in Brown's viewpoint over the fifteen years since he first began publishing. He judges that Brown's 1967 book, *Jesus: God and Man*, was the work "of a Catholic scripturist trying to explore the mystery of Jesus' humanity," but his later writing on such topics "reads as if it were written by a nondenominational theologian activist reconstructing New Testament evidence to show that the Catholic Church in doctrine and practice has exaggerated the centrality of episcopal ministry in any Church supposedly established by Jesus."[19]

2. He accused Brown of unduly limiting "the data he will accept as persuasive." By this Kelly meant that Brown's "reconstructions" of the church and its practices in the New Testament can be persuasive only because Brown a priori excluded the writings of the early Apostolic Fathers such as Clement's First Letter to the Corinthians and the Letters of Ignatius of Antioch. "In an attempt to deny the existence of priesthood, monarchic episcopacy, apostolic succession in the first century, Brown explains away 1 Clement and the Ignatian letters as describing institutions not contemplated or commanded by Christ but new manifestations inspired 'by the Holy Spirit.'"[20]

3. Kelly asserted that Brown "has not been thoroughly evaluated by his peers." He speculates that church authorities remained silent when Catholic writers publicly "expound[ed] unusual religious theories," assuming that these "excesses and errors would be contained by peer criticism." But, in fact, this has not happened. Brown's books are reviewed by sympathetic "friends" who praise his scholarship while books promoting "traditional Catholic views have been treated severely."[21] Kelly's complaint is unfair to Brown's reputation; respect for Brown's work from his peers was earned through years of accomplished scholarship and was not some sort of entitlement or a gift of friendly reviewers. At the same time, Brown left little to chance, and when one of his books was published, he did not hesitate to try to get the book into the hands of reviewers who would understand what he was trying to accomplish.[22] Yet even when his books were reviewed by scholars appreciative of Brown, that would not guarantee completely favorable reviews.[23]

4. Kelly accuses Brown of writing and speaking "as if *Scriptura Sola* is [the] prevailing norm for Catholic exegesis."[24] Evidence of this is Brown's often repeated conviction that a Catholic's analysis of Scripture should be no different than that of a Protestant scholar. Here, Kelly overlooks Brown's careful distinctions that include the caveat of the historical-critical method "properly applied" and that the "philosophy of the practitioner of the method"—in

Brown's instance, his loyalty to Catholic tradition—must be taken into account.[25]

5. Kelly contends that Brown's "rhetoric in public controversy frequently obscures the issues in scholarly dispute." Here, Kelly seems to be accusing Brown of bad faith, asserting that in his public debates Brown downplays the weaknesses of the historical-critical methods and attacks his critics as "incompetent" or "old-fashioned." Brown's scholarly foes, "especially if they are older than age fifty-five, are passé as scholars, fearful captives of the right wing, or incompetent."[26] Brown, on the other hand, falsely "preempts the rhetorical center."[27]

6. Finally, in a lament raised by many of Brown's critics, Kelly asserts that Brown "is overprotected by American bishops." He cites defense of Brown by bishops such as Bishop James Rausch, then general secretary of the U.S. Catholic Conference, Archbishop John Whelan of Hartford, Connecticut, Cardinal Humberto Medeiros of Boston, and Cardinal Timothy Manning of Los Angeles. Archbishop John Quinn, who was a close friend of Brown, is cited as a particularly strong defender of Brown. Kelly remains perplexed by such support and ultimately blames such misguided support for Brown and others who hold similar views as "the failure of Vatican II Council Fathers to 'manage' the new Church directions they were beginning."[28]

One of Brown's own responses to these attacks from *The Wanderer* and from Kelly's book is worth noting. As noted earlier, Brown had shared the stage with then Cardinal Joseph Ratzinger at the Erasmus conference on biblical interpretation organized by Richard Neuhaus in 1988.[29] At that conference, Ratzinger had praised Brown ("I wish we had many scholars like Father Brown"), an endorsement that galled Brown's ultraconservative critics. Brown was mortified that his opponents in *The Wanderer* and other publications claimed he was using this statement of Cardinal Ratzinger "to give the impression that the Sacred Congregation for the Doctrine of the Faith has now approved all of his biblical theories." To counter this, Brown turned to what might seem an unlikely ally, Richard Neuhaus himself. Although Neuhaus was perceived by traditionalists as one of their own, he, in fact, admired Brown and had been the one to invite him to speak at the 1988 conference. In his letter of April 12, 1988, to Neuhaus, Brown asks the then still Lutheran pastor to intervene on his behalf with Cardinal Ratzinger (Neuhaus was well-known to Ratzinger): "I want to assure you (and if you have any contact with His Eminence I would appreciate it if you would pass on to Cardinal Ratzinger) that in public lecture or in printed articles I have never in any way used the Cardinal's January reference to me for self-promotion. It is another lie that I have even thought, never mind suggested, that the Cardinal and the Congregation had now approved my theories. To the contrary, I have observed extreme public caution about the January reference to my name. The only reference I have made to the January dialogue was to point out that His Eminence was opposed to radical criticism and to any return to fundamentalism or ultraliteralism."

Earlier in the letter, Brown lamented the constant stream of criticism he was experiencing from *The Wanderer* and from opponents like Kelly (to "whom they give continual honor"): "I regret that their incessant hatred for me has brought you [i.e., Neuhaus, who had been criticized for inviting Brown to speak at the conference] into its pages in such an antagonistic way. Despite 20 years of experience with the lies and divisiveness and paranoic hatred of that periodical I was still a bit startled by this particular article [an article by William Doino that appeared in the March 17, 1988, issue of *The Wanderer* attacking both Brown and Neuhaus]....The current article repeats all the usual lies, that I deny the virginal conception, the bodily resurrection, the foundation of the church by Christ, even though everything I have ever written clearly affirms these doctrines." As he concluded, "All of this reconfirms my very strong conviction that Catholic liberals like Thomas Sheehan [see further for Brown's critique of Thomas Sheehan] and Catholic fundamentalists like 'The Wanderer' are equally deleterious to an intelligent approach to Catholic doctrine, and the ongoing use of the Bible for nourishing Christian faith."

For his part, Neuhaus defended Brown publicly. In an article in the February 4, 1988, article of the *National Catholic Register* reporting on the "Ratzinger Conference" (as it came to be known), "The Catholic Moment," Neuhaus challenged conservative critics of Brown who claimed he was exaggerating Ratzinger's favorable opinion of him:

There is one more point on which some misunderstanding has already cropped up. It is no secret that some Roman Catholics view Father Raymond Brown as a most dangerous liberal. They were therefore surprised when the Cardinal declared at the Thursday morning news conference that he wished the Church had many more New Testament scholars such as Father Brown. I have read, and I have been told, that this must have been a slip of the tongue on the Cardinal's part, and that it is unfortunate that Father Brown will now be able to say that he works with the explicit blessing of the Congregation [of the Doctrine of the Faith]. Be assured, the Cardinal did not misspeak himself. I believe he was deeply and favorably impressed by Father Brown. To be sure, Brown's paper offered a much more positive reading of the current state of biblical scholarship than did the Cardinal's lecture. One reason for that is the difference between the American and European theological situations. But Father Brown readily recognized the legitimacy of the Cardinal's concern, and he was fully engaged in the conference's search for a scriptural scholarship that would better serve the community of faith.

Kelly's vigorous critique of Brown previously noted touches on all the controversial issues we have documented throughout our review of Brown's work. Very often, it should be noted, Brown's critics attacked what they saw as the errors and dangers of his conclusions about such issues as Christ's founding of the church, or the institution of the sacraments, or the human consciousness of Jesus, but in many cases, they did not lay out their own answers to explain the challenges that the biblical text itself posed for the more traditional formulations of such questions.

BROWN, THE APOSTOLIC DELEGATE, AND ARCHBISHOP LAWRENCE J. SHEHAN

Of all the opposition leveled at Brown, perhaps the most painful involved his interaction with Lawrence J. Shehan, the archbishop of

Baltimore, an experience of "opposition" to his work that occurred at the very beginning of his teaching and scholarly career and involving a church leader whom Brown greatly admired. Shehan (1898–1984) was a native of Baltimore and an alumnus of St. Mary's Seminary. As a parish priest in Baltimore, he was a leader in the pastoral life of the archdiocese, a pioneer in the movement for racial integration, the director of Catholic Charities, and active in ecumenical and interfaith outreach. In 1945, he was made an auxiliary bishop of the then combined Dioceses of Baltimore and Washington (they were made separate dioceses in 1947). He was later appointed as the first bishop of the newly established Diocese of Bridgeport, Connecticut, and, in 1961, he returned to Baltimore as the archbishop, where he would serve until his retirement in 1974. As archbishop, Shehan attended all the sessions of the Second Vatican Council and was a strong supporter of its reforms. In 1965, Pope Paul VI named Shehan as a cardinal.

In every way, Shehan was the kind of bishop that Brown admired, and he admitted that he considered Shehan something of a father figure for him. Shehan, too, had a warm relationship with Brown, becoming acquainted with him as a member of his seminary faculty at St. Mary's.[30] This would make the tension that developed between them even more painful to both men. The "first wave" of conflict came over two articles Brown had published in the *Catholic Biblical Quarterly* in the early 1960s; one was titled "Incidents that are United in the Synoptic Gospels but Dispersed in St. John," and the other, "The Problem of Historicity in John."[31] Both articles reflected Brown's characteristic view of the relative independence of the Gospel of John from the Synoptic tradition and the unique blend of evolving tradition and redaction on the part of the Johannine redactor. Brown surmised, for example, that the narrative of the Gethsemane prayer in the Synoptic Gospels was reflected in a very different format in John 12:27–28, and Jesus's words to Peter in John 21 reflected the kind of post-Easter setting that was also the probable original setting for Jesus's words to Peter in Matthew 16:16—the latter question much more likely to be red meat for Brown's critics.

The articles had come to the attention of the apostolic delegate, Archbishop Egidio Vagnozzi. Vagnozzi (1906–80) had been appointed as apostolic delegate to the United States in 1958 by the recently elected Pope John XXIII, having worked with the then Archbishop Giuseppe Roncalli when the future pope was the papal delegate to France after the Second World War. Even though appointed by Pope John XXIII,

Vagnozzi was known as a very conservative prelate, credited with the nomination of a generation of conservative bishops to the United States during his nearly ten-year span of office, returning to Rome in 1967. In his CBA oral history interview, Brown noted that Vagnozzi considered the four leading dangers facing the church before the Vatican Council were "the biblical movement, vernacular in the liturgy, lay participation, and the catechetical movement"—four of the central reforms that would in fact emerge from the Council. Vagnozzi, in alliance with the notorious Msgr. Joseph C. ("Butch") Fenton (1906–69) of the theology department at The Catholic University of America, had mounted attacks on several biblical scholars in the period leading up to the Council. He kept a sharp eye on the proceedings of the Catholic Biblical Association, whose headquarters were located at The Catholic University in Washington, DC.[32] No doubt the fact that Brown had published his articles in the *Catholic Biblical Quarterly*, the official journal of the Catholic Biblical Association, and was a seminary professor at St. Mary's in nearby Baltimore, brought him into the crosshairs of Vagnozzi's concerns.

Vagnozzi had prompted Shehan to warn Brown to cease publishing these kinds of articles, which the apostolic delegate thought questioned the historical truth of the Gospels. Shehan, who was on good terms both with Brown himself and with Fr. Lloyd McDonald, SS, Brown's provincial superior at the time, spoke personally and separately about the matter with each of the two Sulpicians. Brown followed up with a written explanation for Fr. McDonald of the views he had expressed in his articles, believing them to be in conformity with Catholic teaching and echoing views held by his peers at the Biblical Institute in Rome and at the École Biblique in Jerusalem. A couple of days later, on June 7, 1962, Shehan sent a formal letter to Fr. McDonald with his response to the matter:

> All things considered, I am convinced that it would be inadvisable at the present time for Father Brown to publish anything further along the lines of the two recent articles which appeared in the *Catholic Biblical Quarterly*. I realize that Father Brown has carefully analyzed the *Monitum* of the Holy Office and is following what he considers the correct interpretation of that document. One of Father Brown's articles, however, has caused concern to at least one person in high ecclesiastical authority in this country [i.e., Vagnozzi].

For him to go ahead with further writings along this line would probably be interpreted as a sort of rash daring, which at this point particularly he ought to avoid.

In his letter, Shehan went on to place the current "bitter dispute over the interpretation of the Holy Scriptures" in the context of the upcoming Second Vatican Council, which would begin in the fall of 1962, and he was confident that the Preparatory Commission of the Council would "ponder" the matter so it would be prudent to wait for their deliberations.

Shehan added his own estimation of Brown's frame of mind after his recent meeting with him. "After talking to Father Brown and carefully reading the explanation he has prepared, I have no doubt whatever that Father Brown accepts fully the historicity of the words and acts of Our Savior as presented in both the Synoptic Gospels and in that of St. John. I know, moreover, that Father Brown is prepared to accept any decision the Holy See makes. It is my considered opinion that he should wait to see what the Holy See says before publishing anything further along the lines of his two recent articles." As would become clear at a later phase of the controversy, Brown's view of the "historicity" of the words of Jesus in the Synoptics and John were quite different than those presumed by Shehan.

Brown's response in a letter to the archbishop on June 8, 1962, was totally compliant and even went beyond what Shehan has asked of Brown's provincial in his own letter.[33] "I hasten to assure you of my complete obedience and desire to cooperate. Any Catholic priest who undertakes to write on scholarly subjects must be ready, in a spirit of faith and Christian humility, to accept the fact that, although his opinions may be carefully presented, they will not always be considered prudent by all Church authorities. And so I accept your decision respectfully and without the slightest spirit of resistance." Brown pledged to "not publish further along the lines of some of my previous publications," and he had asked his provincial to provide the archbishop with a complete list of his writings that were in the process of being published, assuring him that if he had any hesitations about any of them, Brown would "withdraw any of these works which you indicate, no matter in what stage of publication it may be." He signed the letter, "Your obedient servant in Christ."

The utterly docile tone of Brown's letter to Shehan may indicate that this first serious brush with church authority had shaken the young scholar. Brown never lacked self-confidence, as his later works indicate, but at this early stage, he may have wondered if his future as a Catholic biblical scholar was in jeopardy. Yet Brown's letter the following day to his provincial has a somewhat different tone. He added a title to the list of his future publications he had prepared for Shehan's review, but then went on to express his dismay to Fr. McDonald:

> As I have had some time to think over what happened, I am more and more astonished at the severity of the action taken. The Delegate [Vagnozzi] told the Archbishop that he objected to a *suggestion* in one of my articles, but gave the Archbishop no direction to even talk to me about it. Yet on the strength of that I am partially silenced! All of the following have locked horns with the Delegate on the Scripture question, some face to face: R. Murphy, O. Carm; E. Siegman, C.PP.S, Barnabas Ahern, C.P.; Ignatius Hunt, O.S.B.; Neil McEleney (Paulist editor); John McKenzie, S.J.; Dave Stanley, S.J. and probably Vawter. He has spoken against some, written against others. Yet I am the only one that I know of who has had a direction against further writing. *Extraordinary.* (emphasis original)

He signed off, "I am sorry that you have to bear this as well as I. May God be good to us. In Christ, Ray Brown."[34]

Later, after Brown had replied to Archbishop Shehan and dutifully submitted his list of publications in process, he would learn the specific objection that Vagnozzi had concerning his views. In a long (four typed, single-space pages) letter to Fr. McDonald dated June 16, 1962, Brown reported that he had heard from Shehan that the apostolic delegate's problem was with his 1961 article in the *Catholic Biblical Quarterly*, "Incidents that are Units in the Synoptic Gospels but Dispersed in St. John," specifically with Brown's "*very carefully qualified statement*" (Brown's own emphasis) on page 159 proposing that "some" had suggested that the Petrine primacy text that Matthew's Gospel (16:16) locates as happening at Caesarea Philippi during the public ministry of Jesus may in fact have originated as a postresurrectional saying.[35] Apparently, Vagnozzi thought that such an opinion was contrary to a decree of the First Vatican Council that treated the Petrine primacy passage of Matthew as a "separate incident from the post-resurrectional scene in Jn 21."[36]

Brown spent the rest of his long letter spelling out for his provincial the reasons why many Catholic biblical scholars believe that the Petrine passage in Matthew 16 is "out of place" and is probably a postresurrection saying of the risen Christ, reasons that Brown would rehearse in his later writings on the subject.[37] He concludes with a reaffirmation of his loyalty to the Catholic tradition on the subject of the papal office: "Like all Catholic scholars I firmly believe that Jesus promised the primacy to Peter, that the words recorded in St. Matthew were spoken by him; that these words as interpreted by the Vatican Council grant the primacy also to his successors, the Bishops of Rome. Like many Catholic scholars I do not see that the above belief requires one to affirm that the words were spoken in the exact sequence given by Mt. I know of no statement of the Church that has ever decided this latter question." He assured his superior, "As I have said, I hope this will be the end of the problem because, out of respect, I certainly do not intend to pursue it."

A RENEWED AND PAINFUL CONTROVERSY

As it turned out, that would not be the end of the affair. The apostolic delegate's "silencing" of Brown would simply fade away as the deliberations and reforms of the Council engulfed the church, beginning in the fall of 1962. In one of its very first steps, the Council in effect rejected the Preparatory Commission's proposed declaration on Divine Revelation and the reform work of the Council would gain tremendous momentum.[38] As with many of the repressive actions taken by church officials against biblical scholars in the period leading up to the Council, there were no formal retractions, but the earlier edicts and disciplinary actions were simply ignored by all sides. Thus, Brown would continue publishing, taking up soon after this first brush with ecclesiastical censure such controversial issues as the human consciousness of Jesus and the historical basis of the virginal conception, as well as a string of publications on the evolutionary nature of the Johannine tradition and of the New Testament itself.

His relationship with now Cardinal Shehan continued to be friendly, despite the earlier incident. After Brown had delivered his inaugural lecture in 1971 at Union Theological Seminary on the virginal conception of Jesus, he had experienced a hail of criticism from some very conservative quarters. Brown had determined to publish his lecture in *Theological Studies*[39] and had sent a copy of the manuscript to Cardinal Shehan for his review, prompting the cardinal to write a remarkably positive response:

> It is unfortunate, and entirely beyond Father Brown's control, that many Catholics will judge what he said from sensational accounts. I hope that many bishops and priests will take the trouble to read the text when it appears in *Theological Studies* next March. Besides enriching their grasp of the New Testament, they will be exposed to a fine example of how to be, theologically and pastorally, both courageous and humble, critical and reverent. And they will be in a better position to deal with the inevitable distortions that are the fate of any notable effort to deal honestly with the truth of faith.... Ultimately it is reverence [before the mystery of Christ] that makes the work of a scholar like Raymond Brown a support, not a threat, to the faith of simple believers.[40]

When Brown was proposed for membership on the Pontifical Biblical Commission, Shehan generously supported his nomination. In a 1974 letter to William J. Lee, SS, at that time president of St. Mary's, Cardinal Shehan praised Brown, noting that he was Brown's "friend and supporter" and that along with his excellent scholarship, he had a "fine priestly character" and was loyal to the Holy See.[41]

Despite Shehan's words of praise in the wake of the Vagnozzi controversy, the issue of papal primacy and the institution of the priesthood would rekindle the tension between Brown and Archbishop Shehan. Brown's 1970 publication *Priest and Bishop: Biblical Reflections* would be the spark for an even more public dispute than the silencing by Vagnozzi.[42] Cardinal Shehan retired from his role as archbishop of Baltimore in 1974. He had expressed to some of the Sulpician faculty an interest in pursuing something of a scholarly career in his retirement and had raised the possibility of doing some teaching at the seminary, a request not received with much enthusiasm by the faculty. Shehan had earned a doctorate in theology from the Roman University of the Propaganda in 1923 but had not been involved in academic life throughout his distinguished career as a church leader. To prepare himself for a possible academic role, Shehan had done extensive reading in theology, including

Brown's recently published book *Priest and Bishop: Biblical Reflections.* Some of the views expressed in the book, particularly Brown's proposals concerning Christ's institution of the priesthood and the question of who presided at the Eucharist during the New Testament period, disturbed Shehan.[43]

In the June 14, 1974, issue of *The Catholic Review,* the official archdiocesan newspaper, Shehan had written a final pastoral letter prior to his retirement titled "Some Further Thoughts on the Priesthood." In this essay, Shehan referred to Brown's book and praised its description of the ideals of the priesthood but offered a mild critique of Brown's views that the term *priest* came into church use only after the New Testament period and that the notion of the Eucharist as a sacrifice was also developed after the New Testament.[44] In the meantime, the cardinal had continued to ruminate about the issue. Fr. Paul Purta, Brown's provincial, had alerted Brown about the report of a mutual priest friend, Fr. Frank Murphy, who noted "that the Cardinal, now that he spends much time alone in thought, reading, and reflection has developed some sensitivities and some crusades. One of his crusades is a defense of priesthood; one of his sensitivities is that not one Sulpician has written to acknowledge his writing on Priesthood."[45]

Brown wrote a gracious response in September of 1974, thanking the cardinal for referring to his book and for the "gentle" and respectful way he had expressed some differences of viewpoint. Brown went on to explain his viewpoints concerning the origin of the priesthood and underscored that, unlike some other more liberal viewpoints (he references Hans Küng), he believed "that the ministry of the eucharist (and therefore the priesthood) existed from the very beginning of the Church's existence." What he was attempting to do in his book is to show that the "terminology" for priesthood and sacrifice began to be employed by the church after the New Testament period. He concluded by thanking the cardinal for his support over the years: "The study of Scripture raises many difficult points, and the fact that I felt I had your confidence was always an assistance….Such gestures [of support] will always make it difficult for me to understand those who find Church hierarchy burdensome or a threat to scholarship."

At the same time, Shehan had been invited to give the annual Dunning Lecture on October 30, 1974, at the Ecumenical Institute of St. Mary's Seminary and University, an institute that Shehan himself had had a hand in inaugurating in 1968. With Brown's book still on his mind, he decided to make a critique of Brown's position the topic of his lecture, "The Priest in the New Testament: Another Point of View." Unfortunately, most people present—including Shehan himself—thought that the lecture did not come off well, with Shehan being on very unfamiliar terrain for such a complicated biblical topic. Brown, who was living in New York at this point, had not been present, but he had heard about the cardinal's remarks and, out of respect for Shehan, decided not to respond. Brown did, however, ask two of his Sulpician brethren, who were on the faculty of St. Mary's Seminary, to send to the cardinal a critique of his lecture. Their extended eight-page, single-spaced letter of November 18, 1974, provided a rather blunt point-by-point criticism of Shehan's views, branding them as "inaccurate." They prefaced their memo by stating they intended their comments, "as part of our service to you, our beloved pastor for many years, because we are priests of the Church, and because we share with Raymond Brown the responsibility of biblical and theological scholarship."[46] Despite the earnestness of the memo, the strategy may have backfired and only seemed to embolden Shehan in his determination to stand by his views. In the cardinal's August 1975 letter to Brown, he observed that "the talk drew an unusually sharp retort from Fathers Leavitt and Kselman."

The matter might have stopped there but Shehan was persuaded by others to publish his revised remarks. In the meantime, a mutual friend, the Sulpician Fr. Joseph Bonadio, told the cardinal that Brown, who had not been at the original lecture, was "somewhat concerned" about the cardinal's remarks and the prospect of them being published. In response, Shehan wrote to Brown a conciliatory letter, which included a copy of the manuscript he was submitting for publication.[47] He confessed that he began to realize he was in over his head prior to the lecture and tried to change the topic to something on ecumenism when he learned that the topic of the lecture had already been announced.[48] The cardinal was writing to Brown out of concern that his lecture might have offended Brown. He stated that he had given his revised manuscript of the talk for review by Fr. Jim Schaefer, a highly respected priest and pastor in the Archdiocese of Baltimore, "to make sure that the piece would not seem to be a reactionary diatribe and that it would contain nothing offensive to you. He assured me on both points and advised that it be published with the hope that a useful dialogue might be started on the points of difference." He concluded, "It is my hope that these differences in point of view will not mean a severance of what I have always treasured as a relationship of friendship. But I believe that a relationship which cannot stand the test of a difference of points of view is hardly worthwhile."

Shehan's article would be published as a two-part series in the November 1975 and January 1976 issues of *The Homiletic and Pastoral Review*.[49] The tension between Brown and Shehan that had first emerged under pressure from the apostolic delegate in 1962 would now break out again since the cardinal's criticisms were to be published in a national journal that had proven hostile to critical biblical scholarship. Brown wrote to Shehan a sharp letter on September 5, 1975, formally responding to Shehan's August letter and the manuscript to be published in the *Homiletic and Pastoral Review* that he had sent along with the letter. Brown's letter had a very different tone from his previous correspondence with the cardinal.[50] Brown confessed at the beginning of his letter that he was writing at "four in the morning of the day on which I rose," having just returned from Rome after giving a presentation on the priesthood to the "Second Consultation of American Bishops." He noted the irony: "Knowing that you have a sense of humor, I cannot resist telling you that my lectures to them contained the exact opposite of what you presented in your article."

In this long and angry letter, Brown declined to offer any public response to the cardinal's views but wanted, in the confines of a personal letter, to explain his own "concerns" and those of his Sulpician colleagues who had previously written their sharp rebuttal to Shehan's lecture. Brown took exception to the fact that Shehan's article would appear in *The Homiletic and Pastoral Review*, a journal he judged had "begun to slide off the purely scholarly spectrum into a journal of propaganda." He noted that earlier the *Review* had published Manuel Miguens's critiques of Brown's views on the infancy narratives but in that instance there was no concern on the part of anyone "other than the groans of some Scripture scholars at Miguens' incredible lack of historical method."[51] Brown went on to confront Shehan with the fact that "as you affirm clearly in your own article, you have no specialized expertise in this field…do I offend you (I know I am pressing you hard here) if I suggest that this article would not be accepted in an unaligned or neutral theological journal (which the H&P is not) if it came from the Rev. Lawrence Shehan and not from Lawrence Cardinal Shehan?" Furthermore, Brown lamented that on the last page of his article, Shehan had stated, "The thesis proposed by Father Brown, if accepted, would seem

to call into question the credibility of the Church's teaching authority as exercised at the highest level." No wonder, Brown explained, that
his provincial would be concerned when a cardinal had questioned the
orthodoxy of one of his priests, a priest who happens to be on "a commission of the Doctrinal Congregation (Holy Office) [Brown was referring to his recent appointment to the Pontifical Biblical Commission]
and has been bitterly attacked as a heretic by Catholic Fundamentalists."

Brown was obviously upset that, after he and Shehan had apparently decided not to pursue any public debate about the cardinal's Dunning lecture, he now discovered that Shehan's critical views of Brown
were going to be published in a hostile national journal. Brown went on
to challenge Shehan for deciding not to have his views vetted by other
biblical scholars, as Leavitt and Kselman had suggested in their memo
to Shehan (Brown mentions Vawter, Maly, Fitzmyer, Bourke, MacRae,
Skehan, "or any of the top Catholic biblical scholars in the country").
Would not their reactions and suggestions have strengthened your
exposition, he asks. "And if they had agreed with you, would you not
then have had a stronger case instead of having to have added that this is
the personal view of one long removed from specialized scripture studies?" Brown goes on at great length with this strong attack on Shehan,
his competence and his viewpoints, and ends with an even more personal lament. Brown recalls for Shehan that in Rome where Brown was
lecturing at the Pontifical Biblical Institute that the cardinal had assured
him, "Come back to Baltimore. You will always be welcome to teach in
my seminary!" Later, after Shehan had retired, Brown visited him and
discussed with him for an hour and a half about the content of Brown's
book on priesthood:

> I asked you…*whether you thought there was anything of doc-
> trinal concern in my book.* You took my hand and assured me
> that you had complete faith in my orthodoxy and had rec-
> ommended me to the Biblical Commission. I remembered
> that I gave the first half of my book on the priesthood as a
> clergy conference in your diocese, *with you present,* and that
> you had warmly thanked me for the service it rendered to the
> priesthood, which was one of the reasons I published it….
> Am I being oversensitive if I am hurt when I read in your
> Archdiocesan paper (three weeks after the conversation of
> October 1974 reported above) that you find in my book the

danger of viewing development of the Church as "a simply natural process"—*when I have insisted absolutely on the role of the Holy Spirit, the Third Person of the Trinity, in this development.* (emphasis original)

Brown concludes his long list of laments, reaffirming that he would still not respond publicly to the cardinal's criticisms, in part because of respect for a cardinal of the church "but more so and with all my heart because you have been a father to me and have been understanding in very difficult times back in 1962 and 1963 [a reference to Vagnozzi's silencing of Brown]. And while the child does not always understand the father, I know that your concern for me is still a fatherly concern. This was an awkward letter to write, but one that came from my heart in its openness. I think it would be even more awkward to respond to. Just keep me in your prayers, and that is sufficient response."

Brown expressed the extent of his frustration with the whole affair in a letter to his provincial, Paul Purta, just days after his impassioned letter of September 5 to Shehan: "I enclose a copy of the Cardinal's letter [August 18, 1975] to me (he sent his article) and my rather firm reply to him—I have had just about all his attempts at scholarship that I can stand."[52] In the meantime, Archbishop William D. Borders, who was Shehan's successor, had inquired of Paul Purta whether Brown would be open to serving on the Board of St. Mary's, despite the now public stress between Brown and Cardinal Shehan. In responding to Purta in this same letter, Brown stated that the dispute makes it "inconceivable that I could be named at the same time his [Shehan's] article appears to service on the board of a seminary in the Archdiocese for which he was responsible." Subsequently, Purta responded to Archbishop Borders with Brown's response, indicating two conditions under which he could even consider accepting the Board appointment: one, that Borders himself would inform the cardinal that this request came from the archbishop despite the "differences of opinion" between the two men and, second, that it would be made clear to the cardinal that Brown's appointment "does not represent Sulpician obstinacy and perversion; it is *not* insistence on 'inflicting' Father Brown on the Cardinal; it is *not* a response to the Cardinal's dissent from Father Brown's thinking" (emphasis original). At the end of his letter Purta diplomatically suggested to the archbishop that the Sulpicians would submit a name other than that of Fr. Brown to fill the open position on the Board.

On September 23, 1975, Shehan replied to Brown's impassioned letter of September 5. Its tone is cordial but somewhat restrained.[53] He did not refer to Brown's sharp criticism of him or the remarks that his manuscript submitted to *The Homiletic and Pastoral Review* was incompetent, nor to the pained personal nature of the letter. The cardinal lists the "threefold" purpose of his letter, the first of which was to inform Brown "that I have written to the Editor of the H. & P.R. to ask him to change the wording of my next to the last paragraph." This was the paragraph implying that Brown's views were not in accord with church doctrine—an accusation that was particularly painful for Brown. Shehan added a written postscript to the letter, noting "I have first talked to Fr. Baker [Kenneth Baker, SJ, the editor of *The Homiletic and Pastoral Review*] by telephone, have dictated to him personally the correction I wished made and have received from him assurance that the change will be made."[54] Second, Shehan reaffirmed that he did not accept Brown's "kind offer" not to respond to the two articles that were to appear. "If I am wrong I certainly shall not hesitate to acknowledge my mistake, I have repeatedly found that I lose nothing by admitting a mistake—quite the contrary. Naturally I am convinced that I am right or I would not have written." His third point seemed more conciliatory: Shehan wanted "to thank you for your book *Crises Facing the Church* and especially for the inscription which I find very touching, particularly under the circumstances. I marvel not only at your industry but especially at your productivity."[55]

A final paragraph responds to the concern that *The Wanderer* would use Shehan's published articles as the basis for an attack on Brown: "As for the danger of a headline in the *Wanderer*, I believe there is no probability of that happening. I have never been a subscriber, although someone rather frequently sends me a copy. I have never communicated with them in any way and, so far as I know, my name has never appeared in the paper. They apparently are not interested in anything I have to say and for that I consider myself fortunate." The cardinal concluded, "Again with gratitude for the book and with every best wish, I am Sincerely yours in Christ, Lawrence Cardinal Shehan, Former Archbishop of Baltimore."

That, it seems, was the end of the matter, although, as Brown had feared, the debate with Shehan would be cited by *The Wanderer* and other critics as proof of Brown's heretical leanings. Brown did his best to try to offset some of the damage to his reputation that he feared would result. On December 8, 1975, Brown wrote a letter to Archbishop Jean Jadot (1909–2009), at that time serving as the apostolic delegate to the United States from 1973 to 1980, briefing him on the background of the critical articles by Shehan that would appear in *The Homiletic and Pastoral Review*. One big difference from the first conflict between Brown and Cardinal Shehan in the early 1960s, was that Jean Jadot, rather than Egidio Vagnozzi, was serving as the apostolic delegate. Unlike his predecessor, Jadot had a doctorate in philosophy from the University of Louvain, was well versed in modern biblical criticism, and was supportive of Brown. Brown's particular concern was that a long digest of Shehan's article had been picked up by the National Catholic News Service, "omitting the few positive things he [Shehan] said about me, and giving the strong impression that I taught there was no priesthood, no eucharistic sacrifice, and no Church for the first seventy years of Christianity and that my views were substantially the same as those of Hans Kueng. Undoubtedly this calumny will be picked up by most of the Catholic newspapers of the country and create real fears about me in the minds of millions of ordinary Catholics." He did not ask Jadot to do anything specific but simply wanted to inform him about the matter. He ended the letter noting that Jadot's position "will forbid you to do more than to acknowledge it [i.e., the letter]. Please do not even bother doing that."

In fact, Jadot wrote in French a long and sympathetic reply to Brown. He had read Shehan's article and concurred with Brown's assessment of it. He also agreed with Brown's restraint in not openly opposing Shehan. At the same time, he wanted Brown to know of his personal support of him and his work: "I wish only to say to you that I have complete confidence in you and that your desire to remain within the limits of a healthy orthodoxy is well known to me....I know you pursue your research and your reflections in ways open to the Magisterium and that you are prudent in the manner in which you present the steps of your thought."[56]

Brown also wrote off the record to others, including Fr. Joseph Jensen, OSB, at that time the executive director of the Catholic Biblical Association (who in turn wrote a letter of support for Brown to Jadot[57]) and to Bishop James Rausch, then general secretary of the United States Conference of Bishops, briefing them on the debate with Shehan and sharing with them Jadot's supportive reply. He also alerted Archbishop Joseph Bernardin, at that time the archbishop of Cincinnati and one of the rising stars in the American hierarchy. Brown was concerned that

Shehan would attempt to have his article published in the *Osservatore Romano*, the Vatican newspaper, fearing that if that were to happen, "it would destroy whatever good will I have built up in Rome." Brown was not worried about his scholarly career (he noted that he had recently been elected president of the Society of Biblical Literature), but it would affect "my ability here and abroad to speak to priests and bishops and get them to understand what we are about in scholarly circles."[58] Bernardin replied that he would not be able to intervene directly to stop Shehan's article from appearing in the *Osservatore*, but "nevertheless, in a way that I would prefer not to disclose, I have made known to certain authorities in Rome your side of the story, basically as contained in your news release. Whether this will accomplish what we want I do not know, but at least I thought the background would be helpful to them." He signed off, "You know you have my confidence and support."[59]

While these steps undoubtedly protected Brown from further repercussions in Rome, for Brown and Shehan themselves, the whole controversy had been a painful and bruising personal exchange between two churchmen who had great affection and respect for each other but, sadly, got caught up in the dynamics of a volatile time in the life of the church.

CONCLUSION: *BIBLICAL EXEGESIS AND CHURCH DOCTRINE*

The most extensive response that Brown made to the avalanche of criticism he experienced was in his 1985 book, *Biblical Exegesis and Church Doctrine*.[60] In some ways, this publication was something of a patchwork quilt, compared to Brown's other more cohesive works. As he notes, it was stitched together from other previously published essays (nine of them are listed at the end of this study, some of which had been adapted for publication in book form). The tone is often polemical since his goal was to rebut some of the criticism he was facing from both the "ultraconservative" and "ultraliberal" fronts. As he notes in his preface, "Because of my optimism about the beneficial contributions of the biblical movement fostered by Vatican II, I am still stunned each time I encounter a distortion of these contributions by intelligent Catholic thinkers. I am not a foolish optimist; and so I anticipate the presence of ignorance and closed-minded bigotry even in the church—my problem is with those who should know better. Distortions are the peculiarity of the ultraconservative extreme of the Catholic spectrum; they are just as frequent on the liberal extreme. Even though neither extreme is necessarily bad-intentioned, their distortions must be refuted in order to assist Catholics who are seeking to understand modern biblical research."[61]

The opening section of the book repeats Brown's explanation and defense of the historical-critical method and its official acceptance by the postconciliar church.[62] The use of the method he is describing is by responsible Catholic scholars who employ it at the service of the church. Later in the book, he describes what he considers unfounded criticism from the left and the right. Exhibit number one on the left was a 1984 review of Hans Küng's book *Eternal Life?* by a Loyola professor of philosophy, Thomas Sheehan, that appeared in the *New York Review of Books*.[63] Sheehan, who was dubbed a "post-Christian agnostic," claimed that Küng's questioning of eternal life represented a consensus of liberal scholars who were casting doubt on such key traditional Catholic doctrines as the resurrection of the body, and Jesus's status as Son of God—a stance that Sheehan endorsed. Sheehan listed as representative members of this "liberal consensus" Catholic scholars such as Rudolf Schnackenburg, Roland Murphy, Pierre Benoit, John P. Meier, Joseph A. Fitzmyer, David Stanley, Rudolph Pesch, Walter Kasper, David Tracy, and, of course, Raymond E. Brown. Brown pointed out the total inaccuracy of such a listing, noting that four of the biblical scholars mentioned had been appointed by the pope to the Pontifical Biblical Commission (Brown, Benoit, Fitzmyer, and Stanley) and two (Schnackenburg and Kasper) to the Pontifical Theological Commission. Sheehan, from the liberal side of the spectrum, had completely misunderstood and misrepresented the views of the scholars named—all of whose biblical and theological views were faithful to Catholic doctrine.[64] In this instance, Brown was concerned with distortions of his views by *Catholic* sources. Other criticism, as we noted earlier, came from Protestant and secular observers who accused Brown of compromising his historical inquiry of the Bible in defense of Catholic doctrine.[65]

On the ultraconservative side, Brown chose as his target the French Catholic exegete René Laurentin.[66] Earlier in his career, Laurentin had done a careful study of the influence of Old Testament motifs on the infancy narrative of Luke's Gospel, but in more recent years had been strongly influenced by the Catholic charismatic movement and an interest in Marian apparitions.[67] Upon the publication of *The Birth of the Messiah*, Laurentin had launched a sharp criticism of Brown's use of the historical-critical method, asserting that it denied the evident historical basis of the narratives and represented the worst reductionist tendencies of the method.[68] Brown found Laurentin's criticisms unfair and unfounded, and provided an extensive list of his erroneous characterizations of his own work and that of Fitzmyer. In what may be a bit of overkill, Brown also listed in an appendix a number of errors and inaccuracies to be found in Laurentin's own work, apart from his criticism of Brown's exegesis.[69]

The most constructive part of the book is Brown's restatement of the relationship between exegesis and doctrine, the underlying source of the tension between Brown and most of his critics.[70] He begins by affirming the church's power to declare certain teachings infallible, but observing that there can be debate in the church whether and to what extent a particular doctrine has been declared infallible and also, an important aspect for Brown, that the church acknowledges there is a distinction between an infallibly taught doctrine and the language used to express that teaching. In noting its concerns about aspects of Hans Küng's questions about infallibility, the Office of the Doctrine of the Faith stated that the formulations of infallible teaching may be historically conditioned and subject to revision. A prime example is the movement from the formulations of faith in the New Testament traditions to their later reformulation in the doctrinal traditions of the post–New Testament church. The church's statement of its doctrine must be accountable to Scripture, but in its formulation of doctrine, the church will move beyond the biblical ways of expressing such teaching.

Brown cites three such examples in which the relationship between the content of the New Testament and later church doctrine proves to be "varied and complex." First, there are doctrines for which there is an abundant but incipient basis in Scripture. A prime example would be the central doctrine of the Trinity. While a clear conception or formulation of the Trinity was not yet present in the New Testament, there is abundant New Testament evidence about the distinct roles of Father, Son, and Holy Spirit to allow later church reflection, guided by the Spirit, to clearly enunciate this doctrine. Second, there are doctrines for which there is a slender basis in Scripture. Here, he refers, as an example, to the doctrine of the virginal conception of Jesus. A clear affirmation of the virginal conception of Jesus is found only in the Gospels of Matthew and Luke but apparently nowhere else in the New Testament literature. Yet the post–New Testament church would affirm this as a doctrine of faith. Similar examples might be the Petrine office; the leadership role of Peter within the church is affirmed in Matthew 16 and in John 21 but becomes more fully articulated as the Petrine office in the post–New Testament church. And, finally, Brown cites those doctrines "about which the Scriptures are Virtually Silent." One illustration of this would be the traditional doctrine of the continued virginity of Mary—a doctrine that was formulated in the churches of both the East and the West in the second to fourth centuries but about which there is no mention in the New Testament itself. Similar instances might be the doctrines of the assumption and the immaculate conception of Mary. Brown sees the development of such doctrines stemming from the church's reflection on the role of Mary in salvation history.[71]

In these and other examples of church doctrine that Brown cites, what is key is the recognition of the right of the Spirit-guided teaching authority of the church to develop and articulate anew Christian doctrine. Perhaps more than any other aspect of modern biblical scholarship and modern theology, this understanding of the legitimate development of doctrine, moving in harmony with but also moving beyond the express formulations of the New Testament, guided Brown's exegetical work and, at the same time, was a point of consternation for his critics. This notion of development was already evident within the New Testament itself, as, for example, the development of the earliest church's understanding of the person and mission of Jesus advanced from its foundation in the historical person and mission of Jesus of Nazareth, through to the post-Easter proclamation of the apostolic church, and into the formulations of the Gospels and what Brown called the "sub-apostolic" writings of the New Testament. Tracing these developments into the post–New Testament church provided the continuity between Catholic doctrine and its biblical foundations.

Raymond Brown was a tireless and visible defender of this viewpoint and, because of that, was also a prime target for those whose understanding of how church doctrine related to the Scriptures was very different. There is no doubt that this was the most painful part of his life as a biblical scholar and as a loyal Catholic. Assessing with great admiration Brown's capacity to bring the message of the Scriptures to a wider audience, his fellow Sulpician, Ronald Witherup, PSS, reflects that Brown may have allowed contention with his critics to "detract from the overall efficacy of his arguments. Unlike his critics, he never reduced his arguments to ad hominem diatribes; even when he replied vigorously to attacks against him, he always tried to keep the focus on the content. However, he did allow the criticism to affect him emotionally. He probably should have allowed this harsh criticism to roll off him as so much detritus of uninformed, frightened opinion. However, it was his pastoral sensitivity that goaded him to respond to these critics. The very people who could easily be swayed by the unbalanced arguments of a vocal few were the average persons in the pew—the audience that Brown thought deserved access to the best of biblical scholarship."[72]

CHAPTER 9

EPILOGUE

"THAT YOU MAY HAVE LIFE"

On Sunday, August 9, 1998, the Catholic Biblical Association of America (CBA) had gathered in the University of Scranton chapel for the opening Mass of its annual meeting. Bishop James Timlin, the bishop of Scranton, was to be the main celebrant and homilist. Right before the Mass was to begin, the bishop's master of ceremonies had created a tempest in the sacristy. As was the CBA's custom, several of the women members had been recruited to be lectors and ministers of communion at the Mass. However, as the master of ceremonies explained, in this diocese women were not to serve in such capacities when other ordained ministers were available to perform these roles. With no little consternation, the first "procession" to emerge from the sacristy were several grim-faced women, most of them seasoned scholars and even seminary professors, who had been summarily dismissed from their assigned roles. A ripple of tension moved through the congregation as people caught on to what had happened.

The regular procession of male ministers and concelebrant priests, along with the bishop, then emerged and the opening Mass got under-way. I was president of the CBA that year and wondered what the fallout from this incident might be as the meeting would continue over the next couple of days. During the distribution of communion, Fr. Ronald Witherup, PSS, then the U.S. provincial of the Sulpicians and himself a noted biblical scholar, came up to me and whispered with emotion in his voice the shocking news that he had just gotten word Raymond Brown had died suddenly.[1] He asked if I would make the announcement.

Stunned by the news, I went to the sanctuary where Bishop Timlin was seated, waiting for the distribution of communion to be completed. I told him I had just learned that Raymond Brown had died. He put his head down and told me, "Ray was my classmate at CU [The Catholic University of America]." I asked, "Bishop, would you like to make the announcement while all are gathered here?" He said, "No, please, you make the announcement."

As the distribution of communion was completed, I went to the pulpit and announced, "We just received very sad news. Ray Brown has died." There was an instant gasp that seemed to come from the entire congregation at once. Over the years, Raymond Brown had been an active member of the CBA, and was revered by his colleagues. He had taught several of them, saw himself as mentor to many more, and had, in fact, been a decisive factor in securing teaching positions for a remarkable number. But everyone there, whether they had known Raymond Brown personally or not, appreciated what he meant to the Catholic biblical renewal. The rest of the CBA meeting was shrouded in sadness at the passing of a great scholar and a formidable defender of Catholic biblical scholarship. The next morning, in one of the auditoriums of the University, there was a memorial Mass for Ray Brown, with virtually all CBA members present. I was asked to preside and Fr. Ronald Witherup, Brown's fellow Sulpician, gave a moving homily, the first of several tributes he would be called on to give over the next several days. Serving as lectors and communion ministers were the same women who had been dismissed from these roles the evening before. I suspect Ray Brown, a strong champion of women, would have appreciated that scene.

LIFE IN ABUNDANCE: THE FINAL YEARS

Brown's sudden death ended the final stage of his life, a very satisfying one for him. As noted earlier, Brown had decided to retire in 1990 from full-time teaching at Union Theological Seminary and move to St. Patrick's Seminary in Menlo Park, California, a seminary owned by the Archdiocese of San Francisco but founded and staffed by the Sulpicians.[2] His decision was not motivated by dissatisfaction with Union, as he had assured its president, Donald Shriver, in his resignation letter.[3] His years of teaching, directing doctoral students, and writing during his stay at Union had been the most productive and satisfying of his life. The flexible schedule he enjoyed there, with recurring brief sabbaticals and time for his usual amazing pace of lectures and workshops throughout the country, resulted in his widespread reputation as a premier Catholic scholar. But he realized that his biological clock was ticking. He was only sixty-two years old, yet he sensed that he had a limited number of years left and wanted to devote them to what he considered his most valuable and lasting contribution, research and writing.

By all accounts, he was able to achieve at St. Patrick's the style of life he was seeking. He was in the company of fellow Sulpicians, a relationship that had become even more important to him as retirement loomed closer on the horizon. The sustained attacks that had stalked him all through his years at St. Mary's and at Union seemed to have tapered off, probably due more to the spent energy of his critics than to any changes in Brown's core convictions. Being on the West Coast also brought him closer to his beloved friends, Sr. Kateri Sullivan and her extended family, who had become a second family to Brown. Kateri and some of her nephews came to visit him in Menlo Park regularly and continued to keep his tattered wardrobe operational.[4] Brown would dedicate what turned out to be his final publication "to the interrelated families Sullivan, Dodds, O'Connor and Grycz, with thanks for many personal kindnesses, and above all for what they have taught me by example about Christian love for one another."[5]

He had successfully fended off the overtures from Archbishop Quinn that he teach on the seminary faculty—or an even more frightening prospect for Brown—that he serve as a spiritual director for the seminarians. Brown had offered instead to speak in an occasional seminary class and would, in fact, offer some lectures now and then both in the seminary and in the Vatican II Institute, a residential sabbatical program for priests at that time located on St. Patrick's campus and run by the Sulpicians. Brown would also give some talks in local parishes. Then there was the mild weather of Palo Alto, where St. Patrick's was located, and the availability of a swimming pool on the campus that Brown took advantage of virtually every day. He had even hit pay dirt with his love for spicy food; the Mexican sisters who staffed the food service would take care of him on that score. He took turns with some other Sulpician faculty presiding at the sisters' daily Mass.

He also enjoyed the occasional vacation trip, as he had throughout his adult life. Together with John Kselman, PSS, Brown's trusted colleague who had edited and proofread virtually all his writings, he organized a trip to Greece in May 1995, promoted as a "Saints Paul and John Study Tour," with visits to several Greek cities and the islands of Samos and Patmos. Kselman noted that, in fact, most of the work of preparation for the trip would fall to him, but Brown was the maestro who had drawn a number of his lay and clerical friends to join the trip. Unfortunately, while on one of the islands, Brown had fallen off the back of a motorbike and seriously gashed his leg. He insisted on continuing the trip but had to keep his leg elevated for the remainder of the journey. Shortly before his death, he spent considerable time planning a visit to Sicily for April of 1999 that would include two of his dear friends, Kateri Sullivan and Phyllis Trible. They were to meet him in Rome—he had arranged for them to stay at the Lay Centre in Rome—and then travel together to Sicily. Sadly, the trip would never take place because of Brown's death.

He would continue to do lecturing and offer workshops for various groups, both across the country and abroad, but he was also making decisions to throttle back on, or even ceasing altogether, his extensive lecturing. In a June 7, 1991, letter to John Donahue, SJ, a friend and colleague who considered Brown a mentor, he wrote, "I have done well here [in Menlo Park] since my retirement in June 1990, and my writing is going at a satisfactory pace. That very success has caused me to think over carefully what I want to do in the future. I have turned 63, and there are some books I would very much like to complete. After 1993, I am not making any plans; for if finances permit in terms of covering room and board expenses, I might decide to stop lecturing."[6] He also decided to no longer give priests' retreats. In an August 31, 1995, letter responding to a request from Fr. William H. Flegge, a priest of the Diocese of Salt Lake City, Brown stated, "I have now decided that I should gradually withdraw from priests' retreats. I am at most a lecturer; and I do better service to the church by staying at my desk and writing—a task more urgent as I grow older."[7]

He also maintained his discomfort with cold weather, appreciated even more in the mild year-round climate of California. Responding to a request for a lecture from Fr. Jim Bacik, at that time chaplain at the University of Toledo Catholic Center, Brown had replied, "In general I do not accept obligations in the north during heavy snow periods of Jan, Feb, up to about March 20th."

Although he did cut back on the amount of his commitments in these latter years, Brown was still open to attractive opportunities and had made commitments for several lectures and workshops for the years ahead, including a presentation at the golden jubilee of his "home parish," St. Rose of Lima in Miami Shores, scheduled for October 10, 1998; another invitation to take part in the Los Angeles Religious Education Congress planned for February 1999; a lecture at the Emmaus Center in Minneapolis planned for May 1999; an address to a gathering of Dominican sisters and others religious of the Nordic countries also in May 1999; taking part in a special traveling seminar to the Holy Land in the spring of 2000 organized by Doris Donnelly of the Cardinal Suenens Center of John Carroll University; a retreat for the bishops of Region V in January 2001 ("Region V" includes the states of Alabama, Kentucky, Louisiana, Mississippi, and Tennessee, which would conform to Brown's rules about cold weather assignments); and a conference for his home diocese of St. Augustine planned for either late 1999 or early 2000. In responding to the bishop's request, Brown wrote, "Thus I am open to coming in 1999 or even January 2000 if you wanted to start the millennium—in fact that is a nice idea: God willing, my first lectures in another century (provided I last that long)."[8]

Another notable invitation that must have pleased Brown had come from none other than Cardinal Joseph Ratzinger, then prefect of the Congregation for the Doctrine of the Faith, inviting Brown to make a presentation at a planned Vatican conference for September 16–19, 1999, addressing the topic of "Interpretation of the Bible in the Church." In his letter of invitation, Ratzinger had urged Brown to accept because the conference could use his expertise on dealing with the issue of the relationship between biblical interpretation and Catholic doctrine.[9] This invitation once again demonstrated that the efforts of some of Brown's superorthodox critics to drive a wedge between Cardinal Ratzinger and Brown proved futile.

Despite the array of speaking commitments, Brown did focus on his research and writing that was his main objective in moving west. The ten years he was in California would be very productive as the list of his publications attests.[10] In 1993, he completed a revision of *The Birth of the Messiah*, dubbed a "New Updated Edition," which retained the content of the original 1977 edition but added extensive commentary on literature that had appeared in the intervening years. In 1994, he was able at last to bring to completion his major two-volume work, *The Death of the Messiah*, a study he had been laboring over for more than a decade. In the same year, he published one of his most theologically astute books, *An Introduction to New Testament Christology*, a tribute to Brown's acumen not only in biblical exegesis but in his sure grasp of Christology. In 1997, he published *An Introduction to the New Testament*, the last of his major studies and one he had begun in his later years at Union.

Scattered throughout this period were several more popular works aimed at helping preachers during the various liturgical seasons of the year: *A Risen Christ in Eastertime: Essays on the Gospel Narratives of the Resurrection* (Collegeville, MN: Liturgical Press, 1991); *A Once-and-Coming Spirit at Pentecost: Essays on the Liturgical Readings between Easter and Pentecost, Taken from the Acts of the Apostles and from the Gospel according to John* (Liturgical Press, 1995); *Reading the Gospels with the Church: From Christmas Through Easter* (Cincinnati: St. Anthony Messenger Press, 1996); and *Christ in the Gospels of the Ordinary Sundays: Essays on the Gospel Readings of the Ordinary Sundays in the Three-Year Liturgical Cycle* (Liturgical Press, 1998). He also continued to produce a stream of articles, book reviews, and audio tapes all during this period,[11] most of them on a more popular level, although in 1992 he did contribute the article on the "Infancy Narratives in the Gospels" for the newly published *Anchor Bible Dictionary*, edited by his longtime colleague and friend, David Noel Freedman.[12] He also contributed a chapter to the *Festschrift* for his close collaborator and friend at Union, J. Louis Martyn. Its title was "Further Reflections on the Origins of the Church of Rome."[13] Brown himself on more than one occasion had strongly discouraged plans to have a *Festschrift* of his own, feeling that the materials incorporated in such collections seldom saw the light of day, but he was more than happy to offer a tribute to his friend on the occasion of his retirement from Union, an event that many of Brown's associates believed had accelerated his own decision to leave Union.

His final publication was *A Retreat with John the Evangelist: That You May Have Life* (Cincinnati: St. Anthony Messenger Press, 1998). This was part of the series "A Retreat With…" published by the Franciscan press, with each volume offering a seven-part retreat imaginatively drawn from the writings of a spiritual master, such as St. Benedict or St. Francis de Sales. But Brown proposed a format somewhat different from the other volumes in the series. It was the "evangelist" himself who would present the seven conferences but aided by a "translator"—Brown himself—to help the "evangelist" speak to a modern audience. Brown was pleased with his idea and had sent a draft for review to Ronald

Witherup, PSS, to ask what he thought of it. Witherup liked what Brown had written but thought it was a bit stiff and he needed to add a bit of humor to make this format livelier—a suggestion that Brown followed, and the reader will discover some of this gentle humor throughout the work (e.g., suggesting that Nicodemus brought the abundant spices to anoint Jesus in a "wheelbarrow"). This lovely work, where Brown channels his vast knowledge of the Johannine literature into devout meditations, was an appropriate conclusion to his lifelong exploration of the Gospel. A poignant note: several friends to whom Brown sent inscribed copies (something he habitually did with both books and article offprints), received them by mail only a few days after they had learned of his death.[14]

THE FINAL DAYS

Brown's health had been generally good for most of his life. He had had his gall bladder removed when he was at St. Mary's. While he was at Union, he had a bout with varicose veins that required some surgery,[15] and the severe wound to his leg on the trip to Greece in 1995 had slowed him down a bit. More than once, Brown had mused with friends about how long he might expect to live. He was aware that both his parents had died relatively young and that both had suffered from cancer, something Brown feared for his own fate. He had also pondered what it would mean when he no longer had the energy to continue his work to which he had dedicated his entire adult life. After a 1985 visit to the Sulpician retirement center, St. Charles Villa, in Catonsville, Maryland, he wrote to his friend Joe Reynolds, the administrative assistant to the Sulpician provincial, "You were most gracious in taking me out to the retirement home; it had more effect on me than you probably realized. When we are busy in life we really do not see what is coming down the line and we put that in the back corner of our minds. In a way, it was a bit tragic to see some of those men whom I had known as vital and strong now vague and wandering; in another way it is a reminder of mortality that we all need. They will be more consistently in my prayers in the time to come."[16]

Nevertheless, his legendary energy and punishing work schedule continued. At the same time, he did not take good care of himself. He was notorious for eating junk food, savoring anchovy pizzas and canned pastas laced with hot sauce. He also resisted getting regular check-ups and would self-medicate, sometimes turning to doctor friends to provide him with medications. In early 1998, friends began to notice a decline in his health. Marion Soards, his former assistant at Union and now professor of New Testament at Louisville Presbyterian Seminary, was shocked at his appearance when he came on a visit in the spring; Brown looked pale and haggard. Robert Leavitt, PSS, a fellow Sulpician and former student of his at St. Mary's (and later president-rector of the school), had a similar reaction when he met Brown during his brief visit to the seminary around the same time. When Leavitt asked him if he was feeling all right, Brown replied that he was fighting some "allergies"—an explanation that Brown offered to several concerned friends.

In late May, Brown came to Chicago to receive an honorary doctorate from Catholic Theological Union (the last of the thirty-one he would receive). As was his custom during his visit, he stayed with some dear friends, John and Rosemary Croghan, who lived in Winnetka, a North Shore suburb of Chicago. They had known him for some years and were pleased to have him as a guest at their home. Previously, when giving lectures in the Summer Scripture Seminar sponsored by the Archdiocese of Chicago at Mundelein Seminary, Brown stayed with the Croghans, doing his work in their guest room. The only hitch was that Brown was not fond of dogs, and before coming down for breakfast, he would call out to have someone put their family dog outside before he would descend the stairs! Rosemary Croghan had been a nurse and one of their sons, John, was a physician. They, too, noticed with concern that Brown's health had declined. Once again, he explained it was the result of allergies, although the Croghans were skeptical. Even so, Brown seemed to be in good spirits and went through the ceremony at CTU without any problems. In his remarks that evening to the seminarians and lay graduates and their families and friends, he spoke, as usual, without notes. In retrospect, his words had a valedictorian spirit to them.[17] He remarked that he appreciated the invitation to receive the honorary degree from CTU "because I realize that you are honoring me for my Catholic faith and not just my scholarship." He was grateful for his vocation to the priesthood, which had sustained him all his life and had brought him into the lives of so many people around the world. He expressed gratitude to his parents and his early teachers, the Irish

Christian Brothers, for instilling in him a love of reading and an appreciation for the beauty of language. He had relished the novels of Charles Dickens and believed he had read all of them as a young boy. He also urged the graduates to be open to others and to engage with people of all types; the friendships and experiences he had with unfamiliar people and places had opened a new world for him, something he considered a great gift in his life. He advised a good dose of humility, realizing the limits of one's own views and the need to search lifelong and earnestly for God's wisdom. Above all, a love of Scripture had nourished him and guided him all his life—he wanted to leave that as his last word for the graduates, he said.

As the summer wore on, Rosemary Croghan continued to have concerns about Brown's health and over the next few weeks would call him occasionally to see how he was doing. On Saturday, August 8, she made one of these calls and Brown confided that at morning Mass with the sisters he had felt faint and had to sit down for a while. Mrs. Croghan was alarmed and urged him to see a doctor right away and not to treat this lightly. Brown had an aversion to doctors and was noncommittal in his response. Determined to change his mind, Rosemary had her physician son, John, who also knew Brown from his visits to their family, call Brown. He could detect Brown's labored breathing even over the phone and urged him to go to a doctor. Brown responded, "We'll see; we'll see." (In fact, some of Brown's reluctance was because he was preparing to leave that day for a lecture at Santa Fe, New Mexico—an assignment he was prompted to accept because his hosts had promised him a ticket for an evening outdoor opera performance, an offer too good for the opera-loving Brown to refuse.) Undeterred, Mrs. Croghan put a call through to Fr. Gerald D. Coleman, PSS, the rector of St. Patrick's Seminary and technically Brown's religious superior. It turned out he was on vacation, but Rosemary tracked him down and urged him to have someone at St. Patrick's coerce Brown into going to a doctor. He agreed and made the call.

Early that afternoon, two of Brown's Sulpician colleagues accompanied him to the Sequoia Heart and Vascular Clinic in Redwood City, only a short ride from Menlo Park.[18] The attending physician informed Brown that they would first need to run some tests to determine what might be the problem. Accordingly, Brown told his Sulpician brothers not to waste their time waiting but to return home to St. Patrick's and he would call them for a ride back when the tests were completed. The tests revealed that Brown's heart was enveloped in fluid, which was affecting his oxygen supply and the cause of his dizziness. When the doctor attempted to draw off some of the fluid to provide some relief, Brown went into immediate cardiac arrest and could not be revived. The time of his death was 3:15 p.m. on August 8. He was seventy years old. The Catholic chaplain, Fr. Anthony Chung, was summoned and Brown was anointed. What everyone, Brown himself included, expected to be an examination and some moderate treatment turned out to be a totally unexpected and shocking death.[19]

AFTERMATH

The news of Brown's death spread rapidly and messages of condolences and words of appreciation for his remarkable contributions came pouring into the Sulpician headquarters. Built over a lifetime, the worldwide network of Brown's friends and colleagues was remarkable. Reviewing his routine correspondence shows his easy familiarity with some of the most well-known and leading scholars in the world— Catholic, Protestant, and Jewish. They included people such as C. H. Dodd, the eminent British scholar and Johannine expert; Ernst Käsemann, the German Lutheran scholar; Pierre Benoit, OP, the renowned French Dominican and faculty member of the École Biblique, whom Brown had first met during his fellowship year in Jerusalem; Sean Freyne, the Irish scholar from Trinity College Dublin; Rudolf Schnackenburg, one of the best-known Catholic German scholars; Marius DeJonge, the Dutch scholar, Johannine expert, and longtime professor of New Testament at the University of Leiden; Oscar Cullmann, the eminent Swiss biblical scholar and theologian; and Martin Hengel of Tübingen, considered one of the world's leading historians of religion and an expert on first-century Judaism. Through respect for his scholarship and because of his leadership of professional biblical organizations both in America (the Society of Biblical Literature and the Catholic Biblical Association of America) and Europe (the *Studiorum Novi Testamenti Societas*), Brown was on a first-name basis with a vast network of biblical scholars. His sudden death registered with all of them and provoked an avalanche of words of sympathy and appreciation.[20]

A memorial Mass was held at St. Patrick's on Friday, August 14, filling the large seminary chapel. Archbishop William J. Levada of San

Francisco, who had succeeded Archbishop Quinn, was the celebrant. Also present was Cardinal Roger Mahony of Los Angeles, three archbishops, including John Quinn, Brown's friend in San Francisco, and five bishops, plus many Sulpicians, along with the seminarians of St. Patrick's and other friends. James Sanders, a professor of Old Testament at the Episcopal divinity school of Claremont, California, and a former colleague of Brown's at Union Theological Seminary, was asked by the interim president of Union, Richard Butler, to represent Union at the service. At the final benediction of the Mass, Mahony himself spontaneously and warmly praised Brown as a genuinely Catholic and "centrist" biblical scholar who had made a great contribution to the church. In his tribute to Brown at the Union memorial service that would take place later, Sanders described the moment and himself paid tribute to Brown's characteristic dual loyalty to critical biblical scholarship and to the church:

> Very significant in my mind, was the tribute offered by Cardinal Mahony that came just before the benediction and recessional led by the casket. Mahony spoke without notes, but it is clear upon reflection that the tribute was carefully conceived and delivered. In addition to expressing appreciation for Ray Brown's ministry of scholarship to the church at large, and especially to the Archdiocese of Los Angeles, the cardinal focused on Brown's centrist position in his New Testament scholarship and how he drew criticism from both the right and the left. Biblical scholars often criticized Ray for not carrying his application of the historical/critical method on to questions of the historicity of central Christian doctrines, especially the virgin birth and the resurrection. He seemed to hesitate at the crucial junctures and to stop short of where his method should take him. On the other hand, Ray's work was frequently under attack from conservative Catholics in the church for where his method did take him on other matters. While he was viewed by some on the left as critically less than candid, he was viewed by others on the right as heretical. Ray's centrist position in these respects was fully recognized in the order of service, in the homily, and in the two tributes.

I left the chapel with the distinct feeling that Cardinal Mahony's remarks, praising Ray's scholarly ministry, were a call to the whole church to regroup, right and left, at the point of understanding of Scripture and tradition to which Raymond Brown had led the way, and to view it as a milepost in the church's centuries-long pilgrimage of efforts to understand the mysteries of the faith with which it is charged. Ray was convinced that critical readings of Scripture enhanced the faith and did not challenge its essential core. He sacrificed the kudos he might have gleaned from the left, had he been more thoroughly critical in his views of the virgin birth and the resurrection, but he did so by the personal sacrifice, on the other hand, of being a lightning rod within the church for stinging criticism from conservatives of his use of critical methods. Ray's aim always was to bring Scripture to vibrant life for the church at this stage in its pilgrimage.[21]

Later, Sanders wrote to Mahony, thanking him for his remarks at the memorial service. In his reply, Mahony noted, "Ray was a wonderful and dear friend over many years, and I always appreciated his intelligence and his humility, and his New Testament scholarship will continue to influence all of us throughout the coming new century."[22]

The Mass of Christian burial took place on Monday, August 17, at Our Lady of the Angels Chapel, the parish of the Charlestown Retirement Community in Catonsville, Maryland. The chapel was located at what had been the College of St. Charles, the very place where Brown had entered the seminary and had his first encounter with the Sulpicians; it is still owned and operated by the Sulpicians. Cardinal William H. Keeler (1931–2017), archbishop of Baltimore (and Cardinal Shehan's successor) was the celebrant, and Bishop John J. Snyder of Brown's home diocese of St. Augustine was in attendance, along with Cardinal Bernard Law (1931–2017), at that point at the height of his influence in the American church, and several other prelates. Once again, Ronald Witherup, PSS, offered the homily. Brown's brother Robert, his sister-in-law Irene, and his nephew Robert Justin were also present. Marion Soards, Brown's assistant at Union and an ordained Presbyterian minister and professor of New Testament at Louisville Presbyterian Seminary, was invited to read the first reading. This time his dear friend Phyllis Trible was the official representative of Union Theological Seminary. He was buried in the Sulpician cemetery that is on the same property, and affixed over his grave would be the same steel cross and inscription that graced several rows of his Sulpician brothers who had preceded him in death.

Along with Phyllis Trible, three other dear women friends from Union had traveled together for the funeral, Sr. Kateri Sullivan, his long-time close friend from Los Angeles, and Eileen Tobin, who had been his trusted administrative assistant during his years at Union. She was a bright and intelligent woman who had not had any advanced educational opportunities but revered Brown and his work, and as she would remark in her eulogy at the memorial service to be held at Union, she appreciated the constant respect and affection he showed her.[23] Also present was Sr. Sarah Ryan, a mutual friend of Phyllis Trible and Brown. After the ceremony, the four women returned for a final sad farewell at the graveside before beginning the long drive back to New York. He was beloved by all of them, as he was by so many friends over his lifetime, and such friendship and love sustained him as well.

The memorial service at Union Theological Seminary took place on Friday, October 2, with moving personal tributes given by his former colleagues, James Sanders, J. Louis Martyn, Eileen Tobin, his assistant, and by Phyllis Trible, whose soaring tribute would later be published in *The Christian Century*.[24] After citing his exceptional academic accomplishments, Trible noted his personal warmth and kindness that was recognized by the outpouring of sadness and appreciation by so many students, faculty, and staff at Union at the time of his death:

> Although cardinals, archbishops, bishops, and countless priests attended the funeral services, neither their presence nor their words dwarf the outpouring of love for Raymond Brown that comes from all sorts and conditions of people throughout the world: the former student in Japan who became his translator; the Sisters from Mexico for whom he said Mass and who prepared the spicy food he enjoyed; the cloistered Carmelite Sisters in East Anglia, England, who received his lectures with gratitude; the parishioners at Corpus Christi Church in New York City whom he served for many years; and, just recently, certain teenagers in southern California who turned the tables by teaching him how to prepare for college these days. (Pack clothes, not books.)

These and countless more people bring to his death stories of his ministry to them. As the telling of stories continues in public and private, they give comfort in the midst of sorrow. They testify to this gracious and generous man whose happy demeanor and lambent humor were themselves a blessing. Through Ray the stories also witness to the One who came that we may have life.[25]

Weston School of Theology, where Brown's longtime colleague and collaborator John Kselman, PSS, was on the faculty, would also have a memorial service honoring Brown on September 23, 1998. Kselman gave the eulogy and included two memorable quotations of Brown about death. The first was his comment in the introduction to *The Death of the Messiah*: "A surprising number of people have asked if I plan a trilogy to conclude with *The Resurrection of the Messiah*. Responding with mock indignation that I have written two books on the resurrection (a response that conveniently ignores the fact that neither is truly a commentary), I tell them emphatically that I have no such plans. I would rather explore that area 'face to face.'"[26] The other was a quotation from his final publication, *A Retreat with John the Evangelist*, one of the most extensive reflections on the experience of death that Brown ever wrote. Putting words in the mouth of the "Evangelist," Brown observed,

No matter how often we renew our faith, there is the supreme testing by death. Whether the death of a loved one or one's own death, it is the moment where one realizes that all depends on God. We have been cautious during our life to shield ourselves with bank accounts, credit cards and investments, and to protect our future with health plans, life insurance, social security and retirement plans. Yet there comes a moment when neither cash nor "plastic" works. No human support goes with one to the grave; and human companionship stops at the tomb. One enters alone. If there is no God, there is nothing; if Christ has not conquered death, there is no future. The Lazarus story [chapter 11 of John's Gospel] speaks to such a moment. The "tos" and "fros" of the reactions show struggle even among the disciples and those who love Jesus as they face death. The Lenten/Easter mystery of crucifixion and resurrection victory is the appropriate moment to reflect on the promise: "I am the resurrection and the life. Those who believe in me, even if they die, will come to life. And everyone who is alive and believes in me shall never die at all" (11:25–26).[27]

A final memorial tribute was held during the Society of Biblical Literature (SBL)'s annual meeting in Orlando, Florida, on Sunday evening, November 22. Paul Achtemeier, the highly regarded professor of New Testament at Union Presbyterian Seminary in Richmond, who would serve as well as a president of the Catholic Biblical Association and the Society of Biblical Literature, was the presider at the ceremony. Five of Brown's associates were invited to comment on the different dimensions of his life: Professor Marion Soards on Brown as teacher; Dr. Phyllis Trible on his role as a colleague; Fr. Donald Senior, CP, on his role as a churchman; Fr. Daniel Harrington, SJ, on his scholarship; and Fr. Ronald Witherup, PSS, on his life as a Sulpician. In a postscript that Brown would have savored, a reporter from the *Wall Street Journal* wrote a column about the SBL meeting and included mention of the memorial service for Brown. He reported a comment one of the participants at the service shared with him on the occasion when Brown himself had addressed the SBL a few years back, after a hiatus of some years. "Brown had just given an address at the annual meeting, his first in perhaps a decade; the experience was therefore unfamiliar to the younger scholars. One of them was heard to offer this awed assessment: 'It was like a dinosaur. We hadn't seen one in a long time. And it was *really* big.'"[28]

When the immediate grief over Brown's death subsided and the public memorials were completed, it fell to Ronald Witherup, Brown's Sulpician colleague and then provincial superior, to serve as the executor of his estate. Brown had updated his last will and testament in December 1996 and, typically, included a detailed explanation of his assets and his meticulous directions about their disposition. He had in fact amassed a considerable estate.[29] Apart from buying his books and his extensive travels (with most of this reimbursed by the hosts of his lecturing and teaching), he lived very frugally—with a notoriously worn-out wardrobe, sparsely furnished living quarters, and virtually nothing spent on personal matters other than his beloved season opera tickets and some modest expenses for maintaining his stamp collection. As noted previously, over the years he had made a number of generous gifts to some of his students and graduates who were struggling financially. He also provided a steady stream of financial support to his Sulpician community. As a result, the stipends he received for his work and the royalties from his many publications enabled him to build up a sizeable amount of savings in a variety of accounts, most of which he had wisely invested under the direction of more than one investment counselor. The major share of his estate was to be given to his Sulpician community. However, he designated a generous bequest to his brother Robert and, in case he would be deceased before Brown's own death, less amounts were designated for his widow Irene and his nephew Robert Justin. A significant amount was provided for his dear friend Sr. Kateri Sullivan, explaining, "The Dodds family (husband, wife, 4 children, many grandchildren) and Kateri Sullivan, whom I have known since 1968, have constituted almost a second family to me since my parents died. I have spent holidays with them, and I had them visit with me in Jerusalem and Rome. I owe them much."[30] He explained that he was leaving the money to Kateri "because she is the least financially protected of the family. I want her to use it for herself freely in her lifetime, and whatever is in excess she might leave to help the least protected of the Dodds' grandchildren through college."[31]

Brown also laid down instructions for his beloved stamp collection (including its location and the combination for the safe where some of the stamps were stored), asking that it not be sold because he feared that the one who would sell it would not realize its worth, which Brown estimated might be as much as $75,000. He requested that it would be kept for at least another "25 years in the hope that within that span you find a Sulpician priest who would get interested in keeping it up, adding to it, and *ultimately returning it to the Society*" (emphasis original). Alas, as noted previously, mildew had damaged much of the collection in its transit from New York to California, and when the collection was professionally appraised, it was estimated to be worth $13,000. Providence spared Brown from finding that out during his lifetime, particularly since the damage was due to the way he himself had packed the stamps for the move.

In his explanatory letter accompanying his will, Brown also expressed a wish that his personal library be a gift to the library at St. Patrick's Seminary. Earlier, Brown himself had stated a desire that at least a portion of his personal collection would be lodged at St. Mary's in Baltimore. Ultimately, the Sulpicians determined that a good solution would be to bring the bulk of his collection (estimated at more than three thousand volumes), plus Brown's own personal papers and manuscripts and some of his personal effects to his alma mater at St. Mary's.

In 2002, the Sulpicians and Fr. Robert Leavitt, PSS, then president of the seminary, would dedicate a section of St. Mary's Knott Library as the "Raymond E. Brown Center and the Johannine Collection" as an addition to the library.[32] The following autumn, October 16–18, 2003, the seminary would celebrate the inauguration of the Center with a symposium in Raymond E. Brown's honor focusing on the Johannine writings, bringing together once more several of Brown's colleagues, friends, and graduate students.[33]

THE LEGACY OF RAYMOND E. BROWN

This review of Raymond Brown's life and work closes with a final, if incomplete, assessment.[34] What are the identifying characteristics of this extraordinary priest and scholar?

1. Clearly, Raymond Brown was the foremost champion and practitioner of the historical-critical approach to the Bible in modern Catholic Church history. He was convinced that the historical-critical approach could be employed in a way that had integrity as a historical methodology and, at the same time, was compatible with Christian faith and doctrine. By the historical-critical approach, Brown meant exploring, as objectively as possible and utilizing the sound and available methods of historical and literary research, the sources, the historical and social context, the nuances of the biblical languages and literary forms, the probable circumstances of the author or authors of the text and that of their probable audience.[35] He believed that the inquiry into this ensemble of factors in the formation of a text, applied as objectively as possible, would yield in a reasonable fashion "the meaning the ancient author intended to convey"—what Brown would describe as the "literal" sense of the biblical text. He realized that this so-called "literal sense" did not exhaust the meaning of a biblical text; there was a "more than literal" sense that accrued as the biblical text was read and interpreted by subsequent readers, including the practitioner of the method him or herself, and the community of faith. This

would lead to what he called "what the text means" or the "wider sense" of the text. Although Brown was not a theorist by inclination, he became more sophisticated in his ways of speaking of the nature of a text as his scholarship developed, especially as it would take on meaning extending beyond the original author's intentionality, a meaning created by the relationship between the text and its readers.

Equally important for Brown was the conviction that attention to the historical grounding of the biblical text was not only compatible with Christian faith but was a necessary byproduct of it. Christian faith was "incarnational," rooted in the belief that through Jesus Christ the sacred and the divine were fused with the human reality. This fusion, this "becoming flesh," was not limited to the incarnation of Jesus, the "Word made flesh," but, as the Second Vatican Council's Dogmatic Constitution on Divine Revelation, *Dei Verbum*, had affirmed, this incarnational reality was also characteristic of the Scriptures themselves. That is, the Bible was at once divinely inspired and humanly composed. Thus, orthodox Christian faith itself opened the path to a rigorous historical inquiry about the biblical text.

2. A corollary to Brown's confidence in the use of the historical-critical method was his conviction that the New Testament, in particular, reflected the ongoing development of the church's life, teaching, and structures beyond the lifetime and mission of Jesus of Nazareth. This, too, was a proposition enshrined in the Second Vatican Council's teaching through its incorporation of a three-stage development of the gospel tradition, rooted in the historical reality of Jesus of Nazareth but, guided by the Holy Spirit, undergoing development in the life of the earliest Christian community and fixed in writing by the evangelists and other New Testament authors in the last third of the first century. As noted previously, this developmental perspective, which Brown considered essential for understanding the connection between the New Testament and later, legitimate church

doctrinal teaching and ecclesial structures, was perhaps the major point of opposition for his conservative critics.[36] Brown fearlessly brought this developmental perspective to his consideration of the origins of the priesthood and episcopate, the papal office, the origin of the sacraments, the diversity and development of Christology, the diverse New Testament ecclesiologies and their connection to ecumenism, to specific and sensitive doctrinal issues such as the virginal conception and bodily resurrection of Jesus, and to the development of Marian devotion. As Kevin Duffy has observed, Brown's methodology should be described not only as "incarnational" but "ecclesial" as well.[37]

Brown was particularly equipped to make the connection between the biblical material and later church doctrine. He had training not only as a consummate biblical scholar but also had a strong background in philosophy and Catholic theology—and was able to draw on both when addressing sensitive issues such as the significance of the virginal conception of Jesus or the debate about the human consciousness of Jesus. Especially toward the end of his life, he expressed concern about some trends he saw developing that could threaten the bond between biblical scholarship and church doctrine. For example, he abhorred the kind of sensationalism associated with the Jesus Seminar that, in Brown's view, tried to make headlines by pitting the results of biblical scholarship against the traditional teachings of Christian faith. He also opposed the way some modern scholars exaggerated the value of the extracanonical writings, such as early gnostic texts, as if they were on a par with the canonical Gospels and writings. The devaluing of the New Testament canon, he believed, was without basis in history and dangerous for Christian faith. He also lamented that some younger Catholic scholars were expert in biblical methodology but had little or no theological training. Brown brought a deep and nuanced understanding of Catholic theology and doctrine to his exegetical work and was concerned about the future where such a combination would be more uncommon. The result he feared was that much biblical scholarship would be highly technical and specialized but unable to produce the kind of teaching and writing that would inspire Christian faith. If anyone was dedicated to the principle that biblical scholarship should be exercised in service to the community of faith—a principle insisted on by Pope Benedict XVI in his exhortation *Verbum Domini*, on the role of the Scriptures in the life and ministry of the church—it was Raymond E. Brown.[38]

3. Brown was also convinced that the employment of the historical-critical method and the resulting appreciation it created for both the development and diversity of early Christianity led to a life-giving Christian ecumenism, as well as a more profound respect for Judaism and an appreciation of the grounding of the New Testament in first-century Judaism.[39] All his professional life, beginning with his awakening in the ecumenical atmosphere of Johns Hopkins University, Brown was an active leader in ecumenism. This was reflected not only in his formal ecumenical roles such as membership on the Faith and Order Commission or participation in ecumenical dialogues, but in the respectful and open manner he always exhibited toward his Protestant and Jewish friends and colleagues. Throughout his life he maintained close friendships with people of very different faith traditions and styles of theology. This was not just the result of an amiable disposition and an outgoing personality—both of which Brown had—but was rooted as well in his faith conviction that being open to others and being humbly aware of one's own limited knowledge and perspective was life giving.

4. Above all, Brown's motivation for the tremendous energy and hard work he poured into his meticulous biblical research, his eloquent teaching and lecturing, and his prolific writing, was grounded in his vocation as a priest. His priesthood was the channel for expressing his Catholic faith and was the key to his profound pastoral mission. Being a Sulpician priest, dedicated to scholarship, teaching, and the formation of ministers of the church,

gave Brown the perfect context to express his faith and use his exceptional gifts of intellect and communication. The encyclopedic scope and depth of his major commentaries— the Johannine literature, the infancy narratives, and the passion narratives—can give the impression that Brown's interests were exclusively academic. His interest in these particular works seemed to be focused primarily on issues of sources, of historical context, of the minute nuances of the text. But when one steps back and reviews the wide range of Brown's publications and the topics of his lectures and workshops, it is clear that his primary interest was not confined to a detailed analysis of the biblical text but to the connection between the biblical text and contemporary Christian faith, not only the faith of the individual believer but the significance of the biblical message for the church, the community of faith. This is what drove him and what sustained him through the waves of opposition that he had endured. To characterize Brown as an academic who was interested only in historical and methodological concerns would be wide of the mark. His academic interests were at the service of his overwhelming pastoral interest. Brown himself reflected on this in an interview of Union faculty conducted by Malcolm Warford, who asked whether his scholarly pursuits were driven by "professional" concerns or out of contact with the church and ministry. "Strangely enough," Brown replied, "I've never really been interested in scholarship that doesn't have some significance for the Church....Pure scholarship, my mind responds to, but I really keep asking myself, what is this going to do?"[40]

Brown's identity as a Catholic priest was the motivation for his biblical scholarship, but it also suffused the manner of his personal life.[41] He was faithful to celebrating the daily Eucharist and praying the breviary. When his schedule permitted, he preferred throughout his life to be in a Catholic parish to celebrate Sunday Mass and to preach. The consistent wearing of his Roman collar when he taught and lectured was a visible sign of his commitment as a priest, but there were more important indicators than that. A Roman collar can be worn by someone whose personal manner of life does not reflect what that apparel is supposed to signify. Brown's friends who knew him well and on a daily basis all testify to his personal integrity. His notoriously simple lifestyle in clothing and food and personal effects was due in part to his intense concentration on his study and indifference to other lures. But people who knew him well were also aware that his simplicity of life was homage to the gospel and that he was impatient with priests or religious who lived an ostentatious life.

Above all, Brown had a keen pastoral sense in his dealings with others. In his first years as a teacher at St. Mary's, he seemed to adopt the severe professorial style that was the expected manner of that time and place. But later, evidently during his twenty years at Union, his manner as a professor had mellowed and his thoughtful pastoral style captivated both his students and his colleagues. Dr. Alexandra R. Brown, one of Brown's former students at Union and later professor of religion at Washington and Lee University, had composed an eloquent tribute to Brown for Union's memorial service at the time of his death. After noting his remarkable erudition and teaching skill, she added a beautiful tribute to Brown as a priest:

> While it goes without saying that he taught us well in the languages, tools and methods of biblical scholarship, he also taught by example something much rarer in our skeptical times—a way of integrating rigorous intellectual inquiry and faith without compromising either. Ray was, of course, as a Sulpician priest, explicitly committed to this integration; it has been frequently noted since his death that Ray always wore his Roman collar when teaching or lecturing. Indeed, we knew as we took notes in class and sat with Ray in conference and read his books that we were engaged with a mind and heart animated by love of the Church. And we learned in more personal ways too of his priestly calling. He somehow knew when we were more in need of a priest's than a scholar's counsel. I will never forget the morning during one crisis of my father's long critical illness when he stopped me quietly in the corridor at Union Seminary to tell me he had said mass for Dad that morning. Nor the time when he relieved my anxieties about academic performance by suggesting (with a wink) that I was guilty (and double so as a

Protestant!) of supererogation. In many quiet ways like this, and in ways we will never know, Ray was God's priest to us.[42]

When the Sulpician community and Paulist Press invited me to prepare this "intellectual biography" of Raymond Brown, they emphasized that they were not looking for a "hagiography" but an honest and fair portrayal. Indeed, Raymond Brown was not a plaster-of-Paris "saint" of the sort that hagiographers would relish. He was a genuine human being, with terrible eating habits and a boyish sense of humor, at times with a touch of overconfidence about his own opinions, a person who could be deeply hurt by hostile criticism, someone who enjoyed a Manhattan before dinner, and who loved the opera. (Some think the real reason he moved from Baltimore to New York was access to the Metropolitan Opera.) Yet he was also a mature man and a priest of great integrity. I had full access to his archives, all his personal correspondence and papers, his will, his death certificate, and his financial records. I have also interviewed numerous people who knew him as a fellow religious, as a professional colleague, as a teacher, as a friend. I also have read and reread almost everything he wrote. I can say without hesitation there is not a false note in all that I have seen.

As Brown himself reflected, he ended up in the biblical field by "accident" or luck: the outbreak of the Korean War and his bishop's decision to bring him home from Rome and the resulting conflict in the sequence of his courses at St. Mary's—all leading him to have to explore the Old Testament on his own and in so doing discovering "the most interesting thing I had ever done in my life." Brown's abiding love of Scripture was for him the ultimate expression of his Catholic faith and his love for the church. He knew it was a privilege to be able to spend his life studying and proclaiming the Scriptures as the Word of God—it was also the source of his deepest joy.

THE FINAL WORD

What might be the lasting impact of Raymond Brown's life and work? Brown was a classic example of what might be called an "ecclesial" scholar, steeped in a rigorous academic pursuit but with the totality of his work dedicated to the service of the church. His insistence on the use of the historical-critical method of inquiry in exploration of the Scriptures was salutary and timely, both for understanding the so-called literal meaning of the biblical text but also as a demonstration in the wake of the Second Vatican Council that the modern Catholic Church itself could absorb rigorous historical inquiry without compromising its convictions about the unique sacred character of the Bible. Like many other Christian scholars before and since, Brown's combination of genuine Christian faith, loyalty to the life of the church, and a fearless intellectual integrity ultimately won the respect of the church's leadership and rebutted the attacks and fears of his opponents. Future generations of Catholic scholars cannot afford to forget the witness that Raymond Brown and others like him have given to the church.

Because of their depth and rigor, Brown's major academic contributions, such as his commentaries on the Johannine literature, the infancy narratives, and the passion narratives, will remain valuable resources for biblical scholarship for some time to come. As we have argued throughout this volume, Brown did not confine his work to the use of the historical-critical method nor to discovering only the literal sense of the biblical text. His interests were also absorbed by the layers of meaning to be found in the Scriptures in the unfolding history of the church. There is no doubt that the current interests of biblical scholarship and its methods of interpretation have ranged more widely than Raymond Brown probably anticipated. Yet Brown's respect for the text in its original historical context, which he saw as an essential corollary of an incarnational faith, remains an important touchstone and point of reference for other creative approaches to biblical interpretation.

The original excitement of the Catholic biblical renewal stimulated by Vatican II has tempered, due in part to the routinization of the changes it had initiated. Much more Scripture washes over the life of the modern Catholic Church than at any time in its history, and even though much more needs to be done, this deeper exposure to the Word of God has left its impact on the church's liturgy, preaching, religious education, and theology. There is also little doubt that in the arena of ecumenism and interfaith dialogue, the Second Vatican Council brought revolutionary changes to the Roman Catholic Church, and the Catholic biblical renewal played no small part in that transformation. In a world fractured by divisions and violence, the effort to create bonds of understanding, respect, and friendship across religious lines is an urgent blessing. Raymond Brown was a courageous and tireless proponent of such ecumenical and interfaith commitment.

In short, Raymond E. Brown was an exceptional scholar and an exemplary member of the church whose example should not be forgotten. One could say that Brown, who died at seventy with many plans still unfolding, had his life cut short, but viewing his lifetime from beginning to end, a better summation would be that he had been gifted with "abundant life." One of his favorite texts from his beloved Gospel of John informed the subtitle of his last publication, "That You May Have Life," and describes the quality of the lifetime of experiences that was God's gift to him: "I came that they might have life, and have it abundantly" (John 10:10). Raymond E. Brown's life was blessed with a meaningful vocation to which he remained faithful, a superlative education in a field he loved, the opportunity to experience a vast expanse of the world, an exceptional talent for teaching and writing, the support of numerous friends who loved and cherished him all his life, a reputation for integrity that has remained unshaken (despite attempts of some of his critics), and a legacy of scholarship that inspired an untold number of readers and listeners. He truly was gifted with "abundant life."

When all is said and done, a good epitaph for this exceptional scholar and proclaimer of the Word might be the words of Pope Francis, himself a great lover of the Bible, found in his exhortation *The Joy of the Gospel*:

> The best incentive for sharing the Gospel comes from contemplating it with love, lingering over its pages and reading it with the heart. If we approach it in this way, its beauty will amaze and constantly excite us. But if this is to come about, we need to recover a contemplative spirit which can help us to realize ever anew that we have been entrusted with a treasure which makes us more human and helps us to lead a new life. There is nothing more precious which we can give to others. (no. 264)

May his memory be a blessing.

NOTES

FOREWORD

1. See, e.g., Raymond E. Brown, *Biblical Exegesis and Church Doctrine* (New York: Paulist Press, 1978), 54–85.

2. One example is the series of essays in Scott Carl, ed., *Verbum Domini and the Complementarity of Exegesis and Theology* (Grand Rapids, MI: Eerdmans, 2015), where Brown's scholarship is invoked numerous times on questions of method and interpretation.

INTRODUCTION

1. Historically, the Sulpicians used two sets of initials, *SS* in the U.S. province and *PSS* in the French and Canadian provinces. The system was not uniform and sometimes confusing. In 2014, by mandate of a General Assembly and approval of the Holy See, the Society of St. Sulpice adopted the uniform practice of using *PSS* and permanently suppressing the U.S. form *SS*. This decision, however, was not retroactive. So, Raymond E. Brown, whose Sulpician initials were always *SS*, will be referred to in this fashion. On the Sulpicians, see pp. 5–6.

2. See, e.g., *The Virginal Conception & Bodily Resurrection of Jesus* (New York: Paulist Press, 1973), 3–15. On the evolution of Catholic biblical scholarship during this period, see also Benedict Viviano, *A Short History of New Testament Studies* (Chicago: New Priory Press, 2016). On the Catholic biblical renewal in the United States during this period, see Donald Senior, "The Biblical Revolution of Vatican II and Its Impact on the Church in the United States," in *The Oxford Handbook of the Bible in America*, ed. Paul C. Gutjahr (New York: Oxford University Press, 2017), 520–30.

3. On this see the work of John W. O'Malley, *Trent: What Happened at the Council* (Cambridge, MA: Harvard University Press, 2013).

4. See Bernard Montagnes, *The Story of Father Marie-Joseph Lagrange: Founder of the Modern Catholic Bible Study* (New York: Paulist Press, 2006); also, Lagrange's own reflections in Henry Wansbrough, trans., *Père Lagrange Personal Reflections and Memoirs* (New York: Paulist Press, 2006).

5. Quoted in John Cornwell, *Hitler's Pope: The Secret History of Pius XII* (New York: Penguin, 2008), 37.

6. See pp. 53–58.

7. See Gerald P. Fogarty, *American Catholic Biblical Scholarship: A History from the Early Republic to Vatican II* (San Francisco: Harper & Row, 1989), 78–119. He charts the case of Henry Poels, a Dutch priest who was professor of Old Testament at the Catholic University of America, who was dismissed from his position because he was accused of being too liberal and holding a "Protestant view" of biblical interpretation, especially questioning the Mosaic authorship of the Pentateuch.

8. *Divino Afflante Spiritu*, no. 46.

9. Dated August 20, 1941, the Commission advised the bishops concerning "a small and denigrating anonymous work" that had been sent to the hierarchy in an attempt to defame Catholic biblical scholars by suggesting that the historical-critical method would pose "a most grave danger for the church and for souls."

10. See pp. 53–58.

11. On the origin, development, and significance of Vatican II's *Dei Verbum*, see the works of Ronald D. Witherup, *Scripture: Dei Verbum*, Rediscovering Vatican II (New York: Paulist, 2006), and *The Word of God at Vatican II: Exploring Dei Verbum* (Collegeville, MN: Liturgical Press, 2014).

12. "Instruction Concerning the Historical Truth of the Gospels," no. 4; see the English translation of the Pontifical Biblical Commission document by Joseph Fitzmyer, "Instruction Concerning the Historical Truth of the Gospels," *Theological Studies* 25 (1964): 402–8. Fitzmyer would mount a strong defense of the historical-critical method, including its reflection in the 1964 Biblical Commission statement, in *The Interpretation of Scripture: In Defense of the Historical-Critical Method* (New York: Paulist Press, 2008).

13. *Instruction Concerning the Historical Truth of the Gospels*, no. 10.

14. See chap. 3, pp. 59–75.

15. See John Donahue, "50 Years after *Divino Afflante Spiritu*," *America* (September 18, 1993): 5.

16. See *Dei Verbum*, no. 19n4.

17. It should also be noted that this basic Lectionary format was adapted by several mainline Protestant denominations.

18. E.g., a series of directives titled *The Program for Priestly Formation*, from the U.S. bishops, in collaboration with the Major Superiors of Men Religious, called for a substantial number of Scripture courses in seminary curricula. The U.S. bishops also produced extensive instruction for Sunday homilies to be biblically based; see, e.g., the 2013 USCCB document, *Preaching the Mystery of Faith: The Sunday Homily* (Washington, DC: United States Conference of Catholic Bishops, 2013).

19. Walter Kasper, *Jesus the Christ* (New York: Paulist Press, 1976); and Edward Schillebeeckx, *Jesus: An Experiment in Christology* (New York: Seabury, 1979).

20. Avery Dulles, *Models of Church* (New York: Image Books, 1974).

21. Some critics, however, questioned the extent to which the biblical materials cited at the beginning of these statements substantially influenced their major content and direction.

22. See *Dei Verbum*, no. 23, which encourages "sons" of the church to take up biblical studies.

23. The Pontifical Biblical Institute is a division of the Gregorian University and focuses entirely on graduate biblical studies. Some students pursue degrees in biblical theology at the Gregorian itself.

24. See chap. 9, pp. 231–32.

CHAPTER 1

1. See full bibliography of Brown's works by Michael Barré in John R. Donahue, ed., *Life in Abundance: Studies of John's Gospel in Tribute to Raymond Brown* (Collegeville, MN: Liturgical Press, 2005), 259–89.

2. One major exception is the oral history Brown agreed to provide at the request of the Catholic Biblical Association, which took place on December 3, 1996. John Endres, SJ, served as the interviewer. Henceforth, this document will be referred to as oral history interview with Raymond Brown.

3. Brown paid a brief tribute to the Irish Christian Brothers of his high school days in the preface to his 1994 book, *A Once-and-Coming Spirit at Pentecost: Essays on the Liturgical Readings between Easter and Pentecost, Taken from the Acts of the Apostles and from the Gospel according to John* (Collegeville, MN: Liturgical Press, 1994).

4. On Brown's friendship with Sullivan, see pp. 39–41.

5. Brown's father had worked as a young man on the renovation of the former McAlpin Hotel at 34th and Broadway in Manhattan; it was later converted into an apartment building and still exists as the Herald Towers. Reuben Brown bought some of the fixtures and marble benches from a renovation of the McAlpin to use in his home in Montvale, New Jersey.

6. St. Paul's is now a grade school only. The high school eventually was succeeded by St. Petersburg Catholic High School in 1973, formed by a merger of two Catholic secondary schools.

7. Letter of Raymond Brown to Fr. Van Antwerp from Miami Shores, May 26, 1963.

8. Letter of Raymond Brown to Fr. McDonald, June 21, 1963.

9. That "generosity" was also expressed in the fact that, as Brown gratefully noted in a later letter to his provincial, his father had paid his entire tuition through high school and college up until the time his son had joined the Sulpicians.

10. The College formally closed in 1969 when it was merged with St. Mary's College Seminary, also located in Catonsville. This college seminary, in turn, would close its doors in 1977.

11. On the origin of the Sulpicians and their history in the United States, see Christopher J. Kauffman, *Tradition and Transformation in Catholic Culture: The Priests of Saint Sulpice in the United States from 1791 to the Present* (New York: Macmillan, 1988).

12. Brown apparently excelled in academics from the outset of his schooling. In a letter of Brown's close friend Kateri Sullivan to Fr. Ronald Witherup on September 1, 1998, shortly after Brown's death, she mentions that Brown had given to her "a collection of medals of excellence he [Brown] received from grade one through his junior year of high school at All Hallows School in the Bronx."

13. Edward A. Cerny, SS (1890–1962), served as Dean and Registrar of St. Mary's Seminary and was himself a biblical scholar who had studied at The Catholic University of America and done further work

at the Pontifical Biblical Institute on both its Rome and Jerusalem campuses.

14. Oral history interview with Raymond Brown, 1.

15. This was probably Fr. Miles Andrew, SS (1900–1966), who taught Old Testament at St. Mary's from 1952 until his retirement in 1964.

16. Oral history interview with Raymond Brown, 1.

17. Being designated a "pontifical" seminary or university involves special approbation by the Vatican, with faculty holding degrees from Roman pontifical universities and approved by the Vatican. The baccalaureate and licentiate degrees are a standard European designation; a baccalaureate usually involves one year of graduate work beyond a college degree; the licentiate degree is roughly equivalent to a master's degree in the U.S. system, with perhaps an additional year of graduate work.

18. On this point, see chap. 3, pp. 66–68. A fuller treatment of *Sensus Plenior* would be the subject of Brown's doctoral dissertation for the STD from St. Mary's received in 1955; it would be published as *The* Sensus Plenior *of Sacred Scripture* (PhD Diss.; St. Mary's Seminary and University, 1955; later printed by photo-offset, Ann Arbor, MI: Edwards, 1960). Marion Soards, who would be Brown's assistant at Union Theological Seminary, noted that he had found by sheer luck a copy of Brown's dissertation on *Sensus Plenior* at a surplus book sale at the library of Southern Baptist Seminary in Louisville, Kentucky—the book was inscribed to "William Foxwell Albright."

19. Oral history interview with Raymond Brown, 2.

20. As his provincial superior at the time of Brown's death, Fr. Ronald Witherup had the sad task of sorting through his personal effects. In his closest he found several unopened new sweaters, shirts, and bathing suits given to Brown by friends, even though he continued to wear his infamously threadbare outfits.

21. See pp. 13–16, 112, 167.

22. Fr. Laubacher's vote tally seems a bit faulty; he accounts for 13 of the 14 votes, but we don't know what the remaining one vote was for.

23. The mansion had once belonged to a member of Napoleon's family and was donated to the Sulpicians with the understanding that it would be maintained. It continues to exist but now houses administrative offices of a girls' school adjacent to St. Mary's property.

24. Oral history interview with Raymond Brown, 2.

25. Letter of J. Linn, SS, March 10, 1956.

26. Letter from the house of solitude, March 10, 1956.

27. Oral history interview with Raymond Brown, 2.

28. At this point in its history, the École Biblique was not authorized by the Vatican to grant an STD in Scripture; graduates would have to take their doctoral exams before the Pontifical Biblical Commission in Rome.

29. Oral history interview with Raymond Brown, 2.

30. Oral history interview with Raymond Brown, 2.

31. The publication and analysis of the Dead Sea Scrolls had a long history in front of them before they would fully see the light of day; on this point, see John J. Collins, *The Dead Sea Scrolls: A Biography* (Princeton, NJ: Princeton University Press, 2013).

32. *CBQ* 19 (1957): 53–82.

33. "The Qumran Scrolls and the Johannine Gospels and Epistles," *CBQ* 17 (1955): 403–19, 451–55.

34. See "The Pre-Christian Semitic Concept of 'Mystery,'" *CBQ* 20 (1958): 417–43; "The Semitic Background of the New Testament *Mystērion*," *Biblica* 39 (1958): 426–48; 40 (1959): 70–87; and *The Semitic Background of the Term 'Mystery' in the New Testament* (Philadelphia: Fortress, 1968).

35. Letter of Raymond Brown to Fr. McDonald, October 3, 1948.

36. Fitzmyer, in his tribute to Brown at the time of his death, describes their work: "In those days we had no computers, and all the cards were written by hand. Such a concordance was badly needed by the seven-member editorial team appointed to piece together, study, and publish the close to 40,000 fragments from Qumran Cave 4. It was meant to help them in identifying tiny fragments, relating them to others, and translating them. There was also the plan that, once the fragmentary texts of Cave 4 were all published, we would be able to revise the tentative readings on the cards according to their final and definitive form and publish the concordance. Alas, in 1999 we are still awaiting the final publication of some of the fragmentary texts, and the concordance is now being produced with a computer systematically, as each volume in the series, Discoveries in the Judaean Desert, is published by the Clarendon Press of Oxford. The cards of that concordance, however, were eventually photographed in the late 1980s, printed in a restricted edition, and sent to those few editors to whom the fragments of Cave 4 had been originally entrusted for publication. Neither Brown nor I ever received a copy of that concordance, despite all the work we had put

into it." Joseph Fitzmyer, "Raymond E. Brown, SS: In Memoriam," *Union Seminary Quarterly Review* 52 (1998): 1–18, at 6–7.

37: See, e.g., the final chapter of Fitzmyer's *The Interpretation of Scripture: In Defense of the Historical-Critical Method* (New York: Paulist Press, 2008), where he praises Brown's work.

38. Allegro became something of a tragic figure. Although early on he was a valued member of the team of scholars analyzing the Dead Sea Scrolls, he later developed some bizarre and sensational theories about the origins of Christianity. His most famous work in this line was his 1970 book *The Sacred Mushroom and the Cross* (London: Hodder and Stoughton Ltd, 1970) that alleged that early Christianity originated as a clandestine cult centering around the use of hallucinogenic mushrooms and that the New Testament is written in code about these origins.

39. *The Jerome Biblical Commentary* for which Brown would be one of the principal editors; see pp. 80–82.

40. Oral history interview with Raymond Brown, 8.

41. *The Jerusalem Bible* was originally produced in French in 1956 by the faculty of the École Biblique in Jerusalem, translating from the original Hebrew and Greek. An English version appeared in 1966. Both the original French- and English-language versions were praised for their literary quality and used widely, especially in the Catholic world.

42. Letter of Raymond Brown to Fr. Van Antwerp, November 30, 1950. Despite his negative judgment about the Pontifical Biblical Institute at this point, Brown would later serve for a semester as a visiting professor there, with a course on the Gospel of John in 1973 and a course on the passion narratives in 1988.

43. See chap. 7, pp. 183–95.

44. See intro., pp. xix–xx.

45. See the letter of Raymond Brown to Fr. McDonald, November 14, 1958.

46. Even the modest Giovanni Battista, who would succeed John XXIII as Pope Paul VI, was quoted as remarking to a friend, Giulio Bevilacqua, that "this holy old boy doesn't realize what a hornet's nest he's stirring up." See Peter Hebblethwaite, *John XXIII: Pope of the Council*, rev. ed. (Glasgow: Harper, 1994), 502.

47. See intro., pp. xxi–xxvi.

CHAPTER 2

1. Interview with Fr. John Kselman, PSS, October 10, 2016. Robert Leavitt, PSS, also a student of Brown at this period, noted that it was usual that most of the faculty adopted a rather severe mien in their teaching roles so in this Brown was not exceptional; interview with Robert Leavitt, PSS, April 2, 2016.

2. See chap. 1, pp. 8–9.

3. *The Gospel and Epistles of John*, New Testament Reading Guide 13 (Collegeville, MN: Liturgical Press, 1960). This would prove to be the most popular commentary in the series, with new editions in 1965 and 1982. Brown would contribute the commentary on Deuteronomy (Old Testament Reading Guide 10) in the same series, published in 1965.

4. Later, as the number of Brown's written assignments and speaking engagements mushroomed, he and his provincial superiors agreed that it would be simpler and more efficient for Brown to send yearly reports of his many activities.

5. See chap. 5, pp. 109–30. He would publish the first volume of his Anchor Bible commentary on the Gospel of John in 1966 and the second volume in 1970, close to the end of his tenure at St. Mary's. Later publications included his work on the evolution of the Johannine community, *The Community of the Beloved Disciple* (1979) and the Anchor Bible commentary on the Epistles of John (1982).

6. See chap. 6, pp. 113–15.

7. On the details of this important project, see chap. 4, pp. 80–82.

8. See pp. 234–35.

9. Letter of Fr. McDonald to Bishop Joseph P. Hurley, September 10, 1962.

10. See chap. 7, pp. 167–83.

11. See oral history interview with Raymond Brown, 4.

12. He wrote to his provincial, Fr. McDonald, in a letter on October 21, 1966, "I love St. Mary's and the Sulpicians—there is no other Catholic seminary that would appeal to me at all. But I have real problems doing my research in the current atmosphere of seminary change. More important my continued distrust of the trend present in the Catholic seminary movement makes me feel like a fifth wheel rather than a contributing Sulpician." To soothe him, McDonald replied, "I hope you will not be too disturbed by the revolution through which we are passing in every element of life. What comes from God will remain and

what is purely human will necessarily fail." Letter of McDonald to Raymond Brown, January 13, 1967.

13. Brown looked back on his dissatisfaction with the situation at St. Mary's in a 1994 letter to Fr. William Lee, president of St. Mary's: "It was in this light that I discussed with you in March as to the general feasibility of the situation at St. Mary's without any date or definite plan. I found your remarks encouraging. At the same time, even in my brief few days at St. Mary's, I realized the difficulties. Being kept awake at two in the morning by deacons playing in the halls a kind of tag-game reminded me of my strong dislike for the lack of discipline that we have allowed to develop in our seminaries and that lack of discipline that inclined me to leave St. Mary's in the first place. And I began to wonder could I function again in a system that basically I think too unstructured. But the appointment of Fred Cwiekowski gave me hope that the incredibly poor administration of the recent rectorships might be coming to an end, and that better days were at hand. But I saw all too well the hard struggle he faces financially. And also, as I told both you and Paul [Purta, Brown's provincial], I was deeply worried by the "Pastoral rhetoric" that marked the January Sulpician documents. I remain afraid that we would drive out our young professors of academic standing by such rhetoric, and that we would be getting on a train that is going nowhere. I am thoroughly convinced that real intellectual intent is the most valuable and lasting thing we can give in a seminary."

14. See the full discussion of this episode in chap. 8, pp. 212–26.

15. Letter of Raymond Brown to Fr. McDonald, November 5, 1965.

16. See the letter of Raymond Brown to Fr. McDonald, February 19, 1967.

17. The Swiss biblical scholar Oscar Cullmann (1902–99) was a Lutheran known worldwide for his ecumenical involvement, especially establishing dialogue between Catholics and Lutherans in the wake of the Second Vatican Council.

18. An alternative Brown proposed was that he would teach an additional five hours of Scripture per week during the Fall 1967 semester at St. Mary's. He realized that "the students would complain about the amount of work, but let them scream."

19. On this, see Robert T. Handy, *A History of Union Theological Seminary in New York* (New York: Columbia University Press, 1987), esp. 263–65.

20. Woodstock was the first Jesuit seminary in the United States, founded in 1867. The move to New York City in 1969 was prompted in large part by the spirit of the times. The Second Vatican Council and the Jesuit Thirty-First General Congregation, which met in 1965 while the Council was in session, had encouraged a revitalization of seminary preparation. Other religious order seminaries at this same time also pulled up stakes and moved to an urban location, such as Washington Theological Union and Catholic Theological Union in Chicago, which were both founded in 1968. In May 1964, Cardinal Leo Joseph Suenens of Belgium was invited to speak on seminary education in the wake of the Council at Rockefeller Chapter at the University of Chicago. He suggested that future seminary education should be urban based, located near a great university, and ecumenical in spirit (see Paul Bechtold, *Catholic Theological Union at Chicago: The Founding Years, 1965–1975* [Chicago: Catholic Theological Union, 1993]). The offices and classrooms of the new Woodstock venture were located in Morningside Heights, directly across the street from Union, while faculty and students lived in apartments scattered in the surrounding area. The library was located on 125th Street. The Woodstock sojourn in New York was short-lived. The theologate was closed permanently in 1974, due to a desire to consolidate existing Jesuit seminaries in view of declining enrollment (at the time the Jesuits maintained six theologates in North America: Woodstock, Weston, Regis in Toronto, Chicago, St. Louis, and Berkeley) and some nervousness on the part of the Jesuit leadership about the lifestyle of the seminarians scattered in apartments in New York.

21. Brown listed Fordham, Notre Dame, University of San Francisco, Vanderbilt, McCormick Theological Seminary (Chicago), Weston College (Boston), Boston College, and Princeton Theological seminary. Brown would continue to be wooed by other universities as his career progressed, including Emory University, Duke University, as well as European schools such as the University of Louvain and the Pontifical Biblical Institute in Rome.

22. See the assessment of recent trends in Catholic seminary education and formation in Katarina Schuth, *Reason for the Hope: The Future of Roman Catholic Theologates* (Wilmington, DE: Michael Glazier, 1989); and her more recent follow-up study, *Seminary Formation: Recent History, Current Circumstances, New Directions* (Collegeville, MN: Liturgical Press, 2016).

23. E.g., located next to Columbia University, Union students were involved with the mushrooming Vietnam War and civil rights demonstrations that marked the period of the sixties and seventies. Brown, a fairly conservative man, was also dismayed at some of the sexual liberty sought by some students at the time. On the somewhat turbulent atmosphere at Union during this period, see Robert T. Handy, *A History of Union Theological Seminary in New York* (New York: Columbia University Press, 1987), esp. the chapter "Turmoil and Transition," 261–314.

24. In his remarks at the Union memorial service for Brown, October 2, 1998, his close friend and faculty colleague at Union, J. Louis Martyn, recalled Brown's love of opera and music: "As a number of his colleagues know, Ray was a true devotee of grand opera, one who could be seen on the subway to Lincoln Center carrying along the libretto in Italian. I think that devotion to the operatic scene was no accident. For, all of us who heard him do his own singing behind the lectern knew that we were hearing the Biblical arias sung with uncommon fidelity, with a contagious verve, and with the virtue of a simple clarity, behind which lay countless hours of meticulous research. In fact, Ray was himself a prima don in the good sense of the term, and he was that because he was theologically vocationed to play the role, and because he was able to remember where that vocation came from."

25. See *The Community of the Beloved Disciple: The Life, Loves, and Hates of an Individual Church in New Testament Times* (New York: Paulist Press, 1979), 7.

26. On such half-sabbaticals, Brown had given semester courses at the Pontifical Biblical Institute in 1973 and 1988, the Albright School of Archaeology in Jerusalem in 1978, and the North American College in 1983 and 1988.

27. Phyllis Trible mentioned in interview that she and Brown, along with some other faculty colleagues, would sit quietly on a set of couches along the walls of the board room where the faculty usually met. At other times, though, Brown became engaged with some heat in faculty discussions about faculty promotions and hirings, with Brown on the alert that academic standards would not be slackened. His friend and colleague George Landes had confided to a mutual friend about such moments when Brown became agitated: "I always feel uncomfortable when that happens."

28. In his remarks at a memorial for Brown at Union Theological Seminary shortly after Brown's death, Martyn offered this comment

about their friendship: "Among other scenes, I recall personally the first meeting of the Gospels Seminar in the Society of Biblical Literature in Toronto, 1969, a time when Ray was still at St. Mary's. As I found myself engaged in a heated debate with a colorful colleague from California—to whom neither Ray nor I bore any personal malice—I noted that Ray kept scribbling ammunition notes and slipping them across the table to me. That was a foretaste of things to come in seventeen years of genuine colleagueship. But the colleagueship was also attended by a genuine friendship, a development academics soon learn not to take for granted. Coming from rather different backgrounds and with quite different experiences in our own years as doctoral students, we soon found our complementarity to be more than collegial. It was enjoyable, ripening into a friendship that was marked precisely by the distinction between weak sentimentality and the kind of strong respect that includes mutual concern for the other's welfare. My favorite picture of Ray is one in which he is just on the verge of a smile. It is an intriguing picture because one senses that it itself has a future." October 2, 1998.

29. See chap. 5, pp. 109–30. Their reconstructions were not identical, however. Brown provided a summary and critique of Martyn's hypothesis in an appendix to *The Community of the Beloved Disciple*, 171–74.

30. According to John J. Collins, "Phyllis Trible, more than any other scholar, put feminist criticism on the agenda of biblical scholarship in the 1970s." John J. Collins, *The Bible after Babel: Historical Criticism in a Postmodern Age* (Grand Rapids, MI: Eerdmans, 2005), 78.

31. On her tribute to Brown, see chap. 9, p. 318n.23.

32. Letter of Kateri Sullivan to the Very Rev. Ronald Witherup, October 25, 1998.

33. "In Baltimore one of the many display cases contains his doctoral academic hoods. I was wondering if you ever considered taking his collar, a black jacket, blue windbreaker, a couple of pairs of pants, his beret and put them in a matching display case? As his doctoral hoods honor his monumental contributions to the church and his dedication to the 'gospel message,' the second case would witness to his unassuming and simple life style. It is the image of Ray that people who knew him carry in their memory."

34. The Lay Centre, now located in SS. John and Paul, the General Headquarters of the Passionist Congregation in Rome, is a highly respected independent Catholic institution that provides housing and

community living for lay students attending Pontifical universities in Rome.

35. See chap. 4, pp. 91–96, concerning Brown's engagement with the question of women's ordination in his *Biblical Reflections on Crises Facing the Church*; his article, "Roles of Women in the Fourth Gospel," *Theological Studies* 36 (1975): 688–99, was also widely quoted.

36. See Visotzky's tribute to Brown in John Donahue, ed., *Life in Abundance: Studies of John's Gospel in Tribute to Raymond E. Brown* (Collegeville, MN: Liturgical Press, 2005), 91–107.

37. Letter to William J. Lee, June 8, 1974.

38. The complex circumstances leading up to Mosley's resignation, most of them dealing with debates about the governing structures of Union, are described in Robert Handy, *A History of Union Theological Seminary in New York* (New York: Columbia Press, 1987), 291–306.

39. See p. 34.

40. No doubt among the projects Brown had in mind was the completion of his two-volume work on the passion narratives, *The Death of the Messiah* (to be published in 1994), that he had been working on for some time and longed to complete, as well as a major *Introduction to the New Testament* (to appear in 1997), and a complete revision of his commentary on the Gospel of John, which he would begin but not be able to complete. See chap. 6, pp. 131–66.

41. Letter to Donald Schriver, April 5, 1989.

42. See the letter to Gerald L. Brown, March 20, 1989.

43. Letter to Gerald L. Brown, August 2, 1988.

44. Written note to Edward Frazer, August 1977.

45. Letter of Raymond E. Brown to the Most Rev. John R. Quinn, July 5, 1988 (emphasis original).

46. Letter to Archbishop Quinn July 5, 1988. In accordance with Brown's wishes, a substantial portion of his library was donated to St. Patrick's Seminary; other remaining volumes, including Brown's collection of works on the Johannine literature, Qumran, and Judaica, would end up in a special section of the library at St. Mary's in Baltimore, dedicated to Brown's memory.

47. On this final stage of his life, see also chap. 9, pp. 232–37.

48. Witherup, who was provincial at the time of Brown's death and had the sad task of disposing of his personal effects, discovered new swimming trunks in Brown's closet that were never used; Brown preferred

retaining his old worn swim gear. Interview with Ronald Witherup, PSS, November 20, 2016.

49. See chap. 9, p. 234.

50. See chap. 9, pp. 234–35.

51. See chap. 7, pp. 167–83.

52. See chap. 8, pp. 199–230.

53. His good friend John Croghan, a trustee of the University, had nominated Brown to the Board of Trustees and was pleased that their response was immediate and positive. I am happy to note that the final honorary doctorate he would receive was from Catholic Theological Union in June 1998, only a few weeks before his death; on this, see chap. 9, pp. 238–39.

54. See chap. 7, pp. 167–69.

55. Brown won a host of annual national awards over his professional lifetime, including five National Catholic Book awards, five Catholic Press Association awards, three Biblical Archaeology Society awards, and two National Religious Book awards.

56. Oral history interview with Raymond Brown, 5.

57. *CBQ* 36 (1974): 466–85. This volume of the *CBQ* was dedicated to the honor of Patrick Skehan, whom Brown greatly admired; see chap. 1, pp. 18–19.

58. John L. McKenzie was a highly respected and erudite biblical scholar who began his career as a Jesuit but later, after a dispute with his community, joined the Diocese of Madison, Wisconsin, whose bishop at the time was Cletus O'Donnell, a friend of McKenzie. McKenzie was at home in both Old and New Testament scholarship and published singlehandedly in 1965 a *Dictionary of the Bible* that is still in print (New York: Touchstone Press). McKenzie was blunt and outspoken and was one of the remarkable group of Catholic biblical scholars who emerged during the Catholic biblical renewal at the time of the Council. Brown knew and respected McKenzie as a scholar, but their personal and professional styles were quite different. As Brown noted, "I guess I never shared much liking for John McKenzie, for I always found him a bit off-putting and arrogant" (oral history interview, p. 5). After he left the Jesuits, McKenzie moved from his position at Loyola University in Chicago, to brief stints in the University of Chicago Divinity School, the University of Notre Dame, and finally at Claremont in California. He passed away in 1991. The flavor of the man that Brown found off-putting is reflected in his blunt judgment about his fellow academics:

"I think my colleagues in theology and exegesis are open to the charge that they have become mandarins, who speak only to other mandarins about topics which are of interest only to mandarins in a style of discourse which is gibberish to any except mandarins, and one sometimes wonders about them too. Scholarship is and ought to be a form of public service and not an expensive enterprise dedicated to the production of a few more mandarins who can spend a leisurely life in the production of other mandarins."

59. See Brown's acknowledgment of this in *The Community of the Beloved Disciple*, p. 6. His original address was published in the *Journal of Biblical Literature* 97 (1978): 5–22.

60. The SNTS meets normally in European cities; however, it did hold international meetings in Claremont, California, in 1972; Durham, North Carolina, in 1976 (the bicentennial of the United States); and in Chicago in 1993.

61. His address was published as "*The Gospel of Peter* and Canonical Gospel Priority," *New Testament Studies* 33 (1987): 321–43.

62. See intro., pp. xviii–xix.

63. See chap. 8, pp. 199–230.

64. It is likely that this discussion was remote preparation for the PBC's publication of a major document on this topic in 1993, on the 50th anniversary of *Divino Afflante Spiritu*, Pius XII's monumental endorsement of modern Catholic biblical scholarship: *The Interpretation of the Bible in the Church*. On the importance of Pius XII's 1943 encyclical, see intro., pp. xix–xxi.

65. The full text of the report can be found in "Biblical Commission Report: Can Women Be Priests?" *Origins* 6, no. 6 (July 1, 1976): 92–96. For press reports, see *National Catholic Reporter* 12, no. 34 (July 2, 1976): 15. For an excellent summary of the salient points of the Commission's report—which was never formally published—and the document that was produced by the Congregation of the Doctrine of the Faith, see John R. Donahue, "A Tale of Two Documents," in *Women Priests*, ed. Arlene Swidler and Leonard Swidler (New York: Paulist Press 1977), 25–34.

66. These conclusions were expressed in the body of the Commission's text as follows: "It does not seem that the New Testament by itself alone will permit us to settle in a clear way and once and for all the problem of the possible accession of women to the presbyterate. However, some think that in the scriptures there are sufficient indications

to exclude this possibility, considering that the sacraments of eucharist and reconciliation have a special link with the person of Christ and therefore with the male hierarchy, as borne out by the New Testament. Others, on the contrary, wonder if the church hierarchy, entrusted with the sacramental economy, would be able to entrust the ministries of eucharist and reconciliation to women in light of circumstances, without going against Christ's original intentions."

67. The Congregation's document "Declaration *Inter Insigniores*: On the Question of Admission of Women to the Ministerial Priesthood," would appear in October 1976.

68. See chap. 4, pp. 91–96.

69. Rev. Msgr. Richard Malone is a retired priest of the Archdiocese of Philadelphia. He had served as an Adjutant for the Congregation of the Doctrine of the Faith from 1966 to 1977, and later was appointed executive director of the NCCB Committee for Pastoral Research and Practices.

70. See the letter of Richard Malone to Raymond Brown, August 10, 1976. Brown's report of his conversation with Muthig is in the form of an undated handwritten note.

71. Albert Deschamps, letter to Raymond Brown of November 28, 1978.

72. Brown received the letter of appointment from Cardinal Ratzinger on March 1 and responded on March 3: "Thank you for your letter of February 7th (3355/69) which I received March 1. I wish to express my sincere gratitude for the appointment as member of the Pontifical Biblical Commission for five years. I gladly accept and hope that my presence may be of service to the Church."

73. See the letter of Raymond Brown to Joe Reynolds, February 7, 1996. Brown included a suggested wording for the press release, emphasizing that he [Brown] was the only American appointed out of twenty scholars on the Commission.

74. Rome: Libreria Editrice Vaticana, 2002.

75. Later, Vanhoye would be honored by an appointment as a cardinal under Pope Benedict XVI.

76. Letter of Brown to A. Vanhoye, June 3, 1996. Brown also expressed his relief that he would be able to make the plenary session of the Commission planned for April 7–12, 1997, since he did not have any prior commitments during that time.

77. Letter of A. Vanhoye to Raymond Brown, July 11, 1996.

78. On a personal note, I was privileged to be appointed to the Biblical Commission in 2002, in effect, succeeding Brown as the American "representative" on the Commission. The statement "The Jewish People and Their Sacred Scriptures" was published during my first year on the Commission. Most of the members who had served with Brown during his truncated term were still serving on the Commission at the time I arrived and acknowledged his brief but substantive participation in its work.

79. See chap. 7, pp. 183–95.

CHAPTER 3

1. Brown served both as the director of a number of doctoral students and, for others, served on their doctoral advisory boards. Some of those whose dissertations he directed include Mary Boys, now Dean at Union Theological Seminary; Jane Schaberg (1938–2012), professor of religious studies and of women's studies at the University of Detroit Mercy; Sharon Ringe, professor of New Testament at Wesley Theological Seminary, Washington, DC; Martinus de Boer, professor of New Testament at the Vrije Universiteit in Amsterdam; Richard Sturm, who served for several years at the Northern Baptist Theological Seminary in conjunction with St. John's University; Marion Soards, professor of New Testament at Louisville Presbyterian Seminary; Craig Koester, professor of New Testament and Vice President for Academic Affairs at Luther Seminary, St. Paul, Minnesota; and Jennifer Glancy, professor of New Testament and Early Christianity at Le Moyne College, Syracuse, New York.

2. Michael Barré lists ten commercially produced tape series produced by Brown that are in addition to tapes made of his individual lectures and then circulated; see Donahue, *Life in Abundance*, 289.

3. See the complete list of Brown's publications provided by Michael Barré in Donahue, *Life in Abundance*, 259–89.

4. See *Responses to 101 Questions on the Bible* (New York: Paulist Press, 1990), 1–5. In fact, Brown gratefully dedicates this work "to so many people whose names, alas, I have never known or have escaped me, but whose faces and presence I recognize as they come back to lecture after lecture as I speak at different times and often in different places. This manifestation of their love of the Scriptures has been

a resurgent source of encouragement for me. This book is their book, for their interest and questions generated it." Brown was very proud of having thought of the format for this popular book and complained to Fr. Kevin Lynch, then head of Paulist Press, when Brown learned that his colleague and friend Joseph Fitzmyer, SJ, had apparently "stolen" his idea and was going to publish a book titled *Responses to 101 Questions on the Dead Sea Scrolls* (New York: Paulist Press, 1991). Lynch consoled him by wryly noting that probably not that many people had 101 questions about the Dead Sea Scrolls.

5. We will consider the contribution Brown made in his published works in chaps. 4—7, first by engagement with a number of publications that addressed "crises" facing the church and then turning to his major academic publications.

6. It should be noted that the fundamental importance of the literal meaning of the Scriptures, and the use of the historical-critical method to detect it, has been an important assertion of official Catholic teaching, reflected, for example, in the 1993 statement on *The Interpretation of the Bible in the Church* by the Pontifical Biblical Commission, and emphatically in Pope Benedict XVI's 2010 post-synodal exhortation *Verbum Domini*: "Before all else, we need to acknowledge the benefits that historical-critical exegesis and other recently developed methods of textual analysis have brought to the life of the Church. For the Catholic understanding of sacred Scripture, attention to such methods is indispensable, linked as it is to the realism of the Incarnation: 'This necessity is a consequence of the Christian principle formulated in the Gospel of John 1:14: *Verbum caro factum est*. The historical fact is a constitutive dimension of the Christian faith. The history of salvation is not mythology, but a true history, and it should thus be studied with the methods of serious historical research.' The study of the Bible requires a knowledge of these methods of enquiry and their suitable application. While it is true that scholarship has come to a much greater appreciation of their importance in the modern period, albeit not everywhere to the same degree, nonetheless the sound ecclesial tradition has always demonstrated a love for the study of the 'letter.' Here we need but recall the monastic culture which is the ultimate foundation of European culture; at its root lies a concern for the word. The desire for God includes love for the word in all its dimensions: 'because in the word of the Bible God comes to us and we to him, we must learn to penetrate the secret of language, to understand it in its structure and its mode of expression.

Thus, because of the search for God, the secular sciences which lead to a greater understanding of language became important'" (no. 32).

7. In *An Introduction to the New Testament* (Anchor Bible Reference Library; New York: Doubleday, 1997), Brown would refer to a number of such newer methodologies such as structuralism, narrative criticism, rhetorical criticism, advocacy criticism (under which he included liberationist, African American, feminist, and related studies). His comments on structuralism are particularly wry: "Often structuralists propose outlines of frightening complexity, causing nonstructuralists to wonder whether such intricacy is helpful and whether semiotic analysis produces results that could not have been obtained by commonsense exegesis" (p. 25). To prove his point, he cites in a footnote (n. 9) a particularly condemning judgment of the method by the French scholar L. Monloubou. Brown's reluctance to employ new methodology is also noted by Ronald Witherup in his assessment of Brown's legacy. Witherup, Brown's fellow Sulpician, reports a private conversation in which Brown confided that he "honestly felt too old for taking on new approaches to biblical studies." See R. Witherup, "The Incarnate Word Revealed: The Pastoral Writings of Raymond E. Brown," in *Life in Abundance: Studies of John's Gospel in Tribute to Raymond E. Brown*, ed. John R. Donahue (Collegeville, MN: Liturgical Press, 2005), 238–52, at 248.

8. Joseph Fitzmyer, "Historical Criticism: Its Role in Biblical Interpretation and Church Life," *Theological Studies* 50 (1989): 244–59, at 249. See also E. Krentz, *The Historical Critical Method* (Philadelphia: Fortress Press, 1975).

9. See intro., pp. xv–xix.

10. *An Introduction to the New Testament*, 35.

11. *An Introduction to the New Testament*, 35.

12. See pp. xix–xxvi.

13. See, e.g., the stout defense of the historical-critical approach and a review of its history by Joseph Fitzmyer, "Historical Criticism: Its Role in Biblical Interpretation and Church Life," *Theological Studies* 50 (1989): 244–59; and in his book, *The Interpretation of Scripture: In Defense of the Historical-Critical Method* (New York: Paulist Press, 2008). The latter is a compilation of several articles Fitzmyer wrote on this subject.

14. We will discuss this in more detail in chap. 8, pp. 199–230. Brown's most direct engagement with opposition from both left and

right can be found in his work *Biblical Exegesis & Church Doctrine* (New York: Paulist Press, 1985).

15. See Kevin Duffy, "The Ecclesial Hermeneutic of Raymond E. Brown," *Heythrop Journal* 39 (1998): 52. This is corroborated by the observation of Craig Koester, a former doctoral student of Brown and currently professor of New Testament at Luther Seminary in St. Paul, Minnesota, who spoke of Brown in most grateful terms. "The one challenge I found [in Brown's direction of his dissertation] was that I wished Ray had pushed me harder in terms of method. Ray's primary interest was in texts, and he could appreciate various ways of framing questions and doing inquiry. He did not want us to start with a thesis that would force us to bend the research to make it support what we thought we already know. That was very important. But we did not spend a lot of time working through the methodological questions that in turn shape interpretation." Interview with Craig Koester, November 20, 2016.

16. *The Critical Meaning of the Bible: How a Modern Reading of the Bible Challenges Christians, the Church, and the Churches* (New York: Paulist Press, 1981). Particularly important for his assumptions about method are chapters 1 and 2. As was the case with so many of his publications of this sort, the chapters originated as lectures given in various settings.

17. Raymond E. Brown, Joseph A. Fitzmyer, and Roland E. Murphy, *The New Jerome Biblical Commentary* (Englewood Cliffs, NJ: Prentice-Hall, 1990), 1146–75.

18. *An Introduction to the New Testament*, 20–47; we will discuss this major work of Brown in chap. 6.

19. See chap. 6, pp. 142–46.

20. *An Introduction to the New Testament*, 35.

21. As Brown would point out, different dimensions of the process that led ultimately to the written biblical text were the subject of a variety of biblical methodologies that all fell under the general umbrella of the "historical-critical method," such as form criticism, redaction criticism, literary criticism, etc.

22. See Brown's elaboration of this in *The Critical Meaning of the Bible*, 30.

23. *An Introduction to the New Testament*, 35.

24. See, e.g., his reflections in his article on hermeneutics in *The Jerome Biblical Commentary*, 1148–49, nos. 11 and 12. His reference here to the notion that the written text transcends the intention of the

author is brief and made somewhat reluctantly: "We may reject the systematic skepticism of literary critics about ever knowing the intention of a nonpresent author."

25. *An Introduction to the New Testament*, 39 (italics original).

26. *An Introduction to the New Testament*, 45. Brown cites here the work of Sandra Schneiders, *The Revelatory Text: Interpreting the New Testament as Sacred Scripture* (San Francisco: Harper, 1991). There is no doubt that Brown's reflections on the interaction of text and reader to produce meaning represented a development in his own understanding of hermeneutics. He credits Sandra Schneiders's work and ongoing conversations with her as having facilitated this development. Brown also found useful Schneiders's way of sorting out the intent of various approaches to the biblical text: speaking of the "world behind the text" (i.e., historical inquiry about context and sources, etc.), the "world of the text" (the literary and narrative dynamics of a biblical book), and the "world in front of the text" (i.e., the interaction between the text and its reader); see *An Introduction to the New Testament*, 28. At that time, Schneiders was on the faculty of the Jesuit School of Theology at Berkeley, and Brown, who was nearby in Menlo Park, appreciated his conversations with her. See also the helpful analysis of Robert Leavitt, "Raymond Brown and Paul Ricoeur on the Surplus of Meaning," in Donahue, *Life in Abundance*, 207–30, who situates Brown's method in relation to the reflections of Paul Ricoeur on textuality.

27. *An Introduction to the New Testament*, 37.

28. See pp. 100–103.

29. Raymond E. Brown, *The* Sensus Plenior *of Sacred Scripture* (STD Diss.; St. Mary's Seminary and University, 1955).

30. On this, see Hans Boersma, *Scripture as Real Presence: Sacramental Exegesis in the Early Church* (Grand Rapids, MI: Baker Academic, 2017).

31. *The New Jerome Biblical Commentary*, 1146–65.

32. *The New Jerome Biblical Commentary*, 1157.

33. See Raymond Brown, "The *Sensus Plenior* in the Last Ten Years," *CBQ* 25 (1963): 262–85.

34. *An Introduction to the New Testament*, 41. In *An Introduction*, Brown would also deal with the notions of biblical "inspiration" and "revelation"—both concepts necessary for the full picture of Catholic teaching on interpretation of the Bible; see chap. 6, pp. 155–57.

35. See *The Critical Meaning of the Bible*, 30–34.

36. See chap. 4, pp. 77–107.

37. *An Introduction to the New Testament*, 45 (italics original).

38. *The Heythrop Journal* 39 (1995): 37–56.

39. Duffy followed up on this by correctly stating Brown's view in his 1995 article, citing Brown's 1990 letter. See "The Ecclesial Hermeneutic of Raymond E. Brown," n. 53.

40. Brown elaborates on this subtle but important distinction in his essay "The Contribution of Historical Biblical Criticism to Ecumenical Church Discussion" in the collection of papers from the 1988 Erasmus Conference edited by Richard John Neuhaus and published as *Biblical Interpretation in Crisis: The Ratzinger Conference on Bible and Church* (Grand Rapids, MI: Eerdmans, 1989), 24–49, at 45. On this conference and Brown's contribution, see chap. 8, pp. 180–83. See also the discussion in Duffy, "The Ecclesial Method of Raymond E. Brown," 43.

41. See *The Critical Meaning of the Bible*, 41.

42. *The Critical Meaning of the Bible*, 41–43. As we will see later, the diversity of Scripture on such issues as the portrayal of Mary also opens the way to ecumenical harmony. See chap. 7, pp. 180–83.

43. Since Brown's contribution at this conference dealt primarily with ecumenism, we will take it up in chapter 7. See pp. 180–83.

44. See the 1988 Erasmus lecture by Cardinal Joseph Ratzinger, "Biblical Interpretation in Crisis: On the Question of the Foundations and Approaches of Exegesis Today," in Richard J. Neuhaus, ed., *Biblical Interpretation in Crisis: The Ratzinger Conference on Bible and Church* (Grand Rapids, MI: William B. Eerdmans, 1989), 1–23. Brown's contribution was titled "The Contribution of Historical Biblical Criticism to Ecumenical Discussion," in *Biblical Interpretation in Crisis*, 24–49. The "addenda" added later after Brown had heard the presentation of Cardinal Ratzinger is found on pp. 37–49.

45. "The Contribution of Historical Biblical Criticism," 38.

46. "The Contribution of Historical Biblical Criticism," 39.

47. "The Contribution of Historical Biblical Criticism," 40.

48. Reported by Peter Steinfels in the *New York Times*, February 1, 1988. Brown was grateful for this endorsement and quietly asked his provincial to spread the word about it to several news outlets. Archbishop John Quinn, Brown's good friend in San Francisco, wrote to Cardinal Ratzinger and thanked him for "your very positive remarks about Father Raymond Brown, the well-known American Scripture scholar. I have known Father Brown for some thirty-five years and have had

frequent contacts with him through the years. He has been consistently a very exemplary priest living a life of evangelical simplicity and of very deep Catholic faith. He is eminently respectful of the Magisterium of the Church and has been very effective in giving spiritual retreats for large groups of bishops all over the United States. Has been very unfairly and vocally attacked by those who do not understand his writings. I know this has been an immense source of suffering to Father Brown who is above all a man of the Church." Letter of Archbishop John R. Quinn to Cardinal Joseph Ratzinger, May 20, 1988. As noted further (see chap. 8, pp. 210–12), Brown's critics chafed at this brief endorsement by Cardinal Ratzinger, whose orthodox credentials were unassailable; several accused Brown of exaggerating Ratzinger's praise and using it to further his own ends.

49. "The Contribution of the Historical Critical Method," 40.

50. "The Contribution of the Historical Critical Method," 41. Brown noted, in response to a comment of Cardinal Ratzinger that few biblical commentaries are sold in Europe, that Neuhaus himself had stated "that my [i.e., Brown's] Anchor Bible *John* has had extraordinary diffusion in the English speaking world."

51. "The Contribution of Historical Biblical Criticism," 42.

52. "The Contribution of Historical Biblical Criticism," 42.

53. "The Contribution of Historical Biblical Criticism," 46.

54. "The Contribution of Historical Biblical Criticism," 47.

55. *Dei Verbum*, no. 13; see also the comments of Ronald D. Witherup, *Scripture: Dei Verbum*, 50–51 (see intro., n. 11), who notes that the "Incarnational" principle is cited both regarding the nature of Scripture and the Eucharist.

56. *The Critical Meaning of the Bible*, 21; see Brown's entire chapter, "The Human Word of Almighty God," 1–22.

57. *Responses to 101 Questions on the Bible*, 127.

58. Duffy, "The Ecclesial Hermeneutic of Raymond E. Brown," 52.

CHAPTER 4

1. See Benedict XVI, *Verbum Domini*, Post-Synodal Apostolic Exhortation, 2010, nos. 29–30.

2. The analogy between the incarnation and the historical grounding of the Scriptures had been cited in Vatican II and subsequent

official Catholic teaching; see, e.g., Pope Benedict XVI, *Verbum Domini*, esp. no. 15.

3. We will consider Brown's more purely academic contributions in chapters 5 and 6.

4. On Brown's methodology and his use of the phrase "philosophy of the practitioner of the method," see chap. 3, pp. 69–71.

5. See pp. 97–98; see also the contribution of Ronald Witherup, PSS, who underscores the pastoral contribution of Brown's writings in "The Incarnate Word Revealed: The Pastoral Writings of Raymond E. Brown," in Donahue, *Life in Abundance*, 238–52.

6. *The Gospel of John and the Johannine Epistles*, New Testament Reading Guide 13 (Collegeville, MN: Liturgical Press, 1960). Brown followed up with two revised editions of this work, one in 1965 and again in 1982.

7. Raymond E. Brown, Joseph A. Fitzmyer, Roland E. Murphy, eds., *The Jerome Biblical Commentary* (Englewood Cliffs, NJ: Prentice-Hall, 1968).

8. Bernard Orchard et al., *A Catholic Commentary on Holy Scripture* (London: Thomas Nelson, 1953). In his unvarnished manner, Fitzmyer characterized this earlier work as "mainly the product of retrograde British Catholic-biblical scholarship and horribly out of date even from the day of its completion." J. Fitzmyer, "Raymond E. Brown: In Memoriam," 5.

9. See the comment of John R. Donahue in, "Joseph A. Fitzmyer, SJ: Scholar and Teacher of the Word of God," *U.S. Catholic Historian* 31 (2013): 75n41, where Fitzmyer credits Brown with the original idea for *The Jerome Biblical Commentary*.

10. Letter of Raymond Brown to Fr. McDonald, February 12, 1961. One suspects that Brown's emphasis on the fact that the lion's share of the work would be done by others was intended to ease his superior's concern about overwork. In fact, most of the work would be done by the editors, especially Brown himself.

11. Letter of Raymond Brown to Fr. McDonald, September 2, 1961. McDonald's response on September 5 was brief and to the point: "You may have permission for the publication work listed in your letter of September 2nd. With kindest wishes…."

12. J. Fitzmyer, "Raymond E. Brown: In Memoriam," 6.

13. *The New Jerome Biblical Commentary* (Englewood Cliffs, NJ: Prentice Hall, 1990).

14. *The New Jerome Biblical Commentary*, xv.

15. See the online article of Francis T. Gignac, "The Revision of the New Testament of the New American Bible," Bible-Researcher.com, accessed February 6, 2018, http://www.bible-researcher.com/gignac1. html.

16. An infamous example of an overly casual translation was that of Matt 25:26, where the master calls the servant who buried his one talent, "You worthless, lazy lout!" A notorious error was found in Luke 1:17, which read "God himself will go before him" when the subject of the sentence is John the Baptist! The most recently revised New American Bible translation (NABRE) of 2011 is greatly improved in both the quality of the biblical translation and the annotations, combining the 1986 revision of the New Testament with the 2010 translation of the Old Testament. The New Testament portion of the 2010 translation is currently undergoing some additional revisions, particularly with an eye to the use of this translation in a liturgical context.

17. See, e.g., a number of articles related to the infancy narratives: "The Problem of the Virginal Conception of Jesus," *Theological Studies* 33 (1972): 3–34; "Jesus with Mary at Christmas," *NC News Service Supplement*, December 1972; "Luke's Description of the Virginal Conception," *Theological Studies* 35 (1974): 360–62; "The Meaning of the Magi, the Significance of the Star," *Worship* 49 (1975): 574–82; "The Meaning of the Manger, the Significance of the Shepherds," *Worship* 50 (1976): 528–38. Similarly, the appearance of *The Death of the Messiah* was preceded by a series of more popular studies and lectures. For example, "How to Read the Passion Narratives of Jesus," *Catholic Update*, April 1984; articles on each of the Synoptic passion narratives that appeared in *Worship* between March 1985 and 1986; and "The Burial of Jesus (Mark 15:42–47)," *The Catholic Biblical Quarterly* 50 (1988): 233–45. Brown continued to publish on these topics in a variety of popular journals even subsequent to the appearance of his major academic works.

18. Important exceptions would be the number of brief volumes that Brown composed as guides for preaching and for spiritual reading keyed to the various seasons of the liturgical year. See, e.g., *An Adult Christ at Christmas: Essays on the Three Biblical Christmas Stories—Matt 2 and Luke 2* (Collegeville, MN: Liturgical Press, 1978); *A Crucified Christ in Holy Week: Essays on the Four Gospel Passion Narratives* (Collegeville, MN: Liturgical Press, 1986); *Christ in the Gospels of the Ordinary Sundays: Essays on the Gospel Readings of the Ordinary Sundays in the*

Three-Year Liturgical Cycle (Collegeville, MN: Liturgical Press, 1998). As we will note later, his final publication was *A Retreat with John the Evangelist: That You May Have Life* (Cincinnati: St. Anthony Messenger, 1998).

19. Raymond E. Brown, *Priest and Bishop: Biblical Reflections* (New York: Paulist Press, 1970).

20. *Priest and Bishop*, 1.

21. *Priest and Bishop*, 3.

22. *Priest and Bishop*, 41.

23. *Priest and Bishop*, 41–42.

24. See chap. 8, pp. 199–212.

25. *Priest and Bishop*, 64.

26. *Priest and Bishop*, 73.

27. *Priest and Bishop*, 77.

28. We will consider the ecumenical perspectives of Brown on this and other issues later, see chap. 7.

29. See chap. 7, pp. 172–73, concerning Brown's major role in the composition of *Peter in the New Testament*.

30. Raymond E. Brown, *Responses to 101 Questions on the Bible* (New York: Paulist Press, 1990), 127.

31. *101 Questions*, 130.

32. *101 Questions*, 132.

33. Brown also took on the question of the evolution of authority structures in the church of Rome and came to the same conclusion in the work he coauthored with John P. Meier, *Antioch & Rome: New Testament Cradles of Catholic Christianity* (New York: Paulist Press, 1983), with Brown himself providing the material on Rome: "The connection between a Petrine function in the first century and a fully developed Roman papacy required several centuries of development, so that it is anachronistic to think of the early Roman church leaders functioning as later popes" (p. 163). In this same work, Brown affirmed that "single-bishop" structure did not exist in Rome until around 140–50 (p. 163).

34. *101 Questions*, 133.

35. *101 Questions*, 134; see also Brown's similar comments in *Biblical Reflections*, 77.

36. *Biblical Reflections*, 78.

37. "The Meaning of Modern New Testament Studies for the Possibility of Ordaining Women to the Priesthood," 45–62.

38. "The Apostolic Letter *Ordinatio Sacerdotalis* of John Paul II to the Bishops of the Catholic Church on Reserving Priestly Ordination to Men Alone," Rome, May 22, 1994.

39. It is noteworthy that in Brown's work *101 Questions*, written in 1990, some years before the pope's statement, he did not take up the issue of women's ordination, even though he addressed the topic of the biblical basis for Catholic priesthood. Brown was also sensitive to the false accusation that he was the one who had leaked the Pontifical Biblical Commission's stance on this issue. At the end of his essay on women's ordination, he notes that the Commission was going to take up this issue in 1975 (see chap. 2, pp. 53–57, on Brown's role on the Pontifical Biblical Commission and the issue of women's ordination). In that same year, the Women's Ordination Conference would be founded and continues to be a strong advocate for expanding women's roles within the church, including ordination to priesthood. The issue would burst into public view in 1979 during Pope John Paul II's first visit to the United States when Sr. Theresa Kane, RSM, then president of the Leadership Conference of Women Religious, asked the pope during a prayer service at the National Shrine of the Immaculate Conception to permit women to serve in all ministries of the church.

40. *Biblical Reflections*, 51.

41. *Biblical Reflections*, 49. Brown's humorous asides are innocent enough, particularly if delivered in concert with his audience in a lecture format. However, as the debate about women's ordination became more intense in Catholic circles, such remarks might be taken as indicating Brown did not view the issue with sufficient seriousness.

42. *Biblical Reflections*, 51. Brown would directly address the variety of New Testament ecclesiologies in his book *The Churches the Apostles Left Behind* (New York: Paulist Press, 1984). Since this work originated in an ecumenical context and was primarily directed to the ecumenical implications of diverse New Testament ecclesiologies, we will consider this book in the chapter on ecumenism; see chap. 7, pp. 176–78.

43. *Biblical Reflections*, 53.

44. For readers of a later generation, an "erector-set" was an elaborate and popular toy that included multiple small metal parts that could be assembled into various structures.

45. *Biblical Reflections*, 55–56.

46. *Biblical Reflections*, 56.

47. *Biblical Reflections*, 57.

48. *Biblical Reflections*, 58. Note that here and elsewhere in his writings Brown curiously refers to "sociology" as a factor in the development of the early church. By "sociology," I assume he means the social context of early Christianity not the science of sociology.

49. *Biblical Reflections*, 59.

50. *Biblical Reflections*, 59.

51. *Biblical Reflections*, 60 (italics original).

52. *Biblical Reflections*, 60n46. What Brown had in mind in referring to "theology schools for Catholic women" is not entirely clear. Did he foresee Catholic schools of theology that would be exclusively for women, or was he referring to Catholic schools of theology being more welcoming to women?

53. *Biblical Reflections*, 61.

54. Pope John XXIII, *Gaudet Mater Ecclesia*, October 11, 1962, no. 14. This was also emphasized in the Pontifical Theological Commission's 1989 statement on the "Development of Dogma": "This valorization of the pastoral character of the Magisterium underlines the distinction between the unchanging basis of faith, on the one hand, and the way this is expressed, on the other. The point is that the teaching of the Church, while always the same in meaning and content, should be passed on to mankind in a living way, and adapted to what the times demand (*GS* 62; cf. John XXIII, the Opening Discourse of Vatican II, 11 October 1962; *AAS* 54 [1962]: 792)."

55. See chap. 7, pp. 167–83.

56. *The Virginal Conception & Bodily Resurrection of Jesus* (New York: Paulist Press, 1973).

57. *The Virginal Conception*, 14.

58. *The Virginal Conception*, 14–15.

59. In this review, Brown had used the three-stage evolution of Catholic biblical studies from the end of the nineteenth century until the Council and beyond cited in our introduction (see intro., pp. xv–xxx); see further, *The Virginal Conception*, 1–20.

60. *The Virginal Conception*, 2.

61. See the letter of Raymond Brown to Fr. Paul Purta, December 18, 1971. In his book (p. 21), Brown notes that he had already given lectures on this subject earlier in 1971 at Lancaster Theological Seminary and at University College in Dublin. He would later publish a somewhat expanded version as "The Problem of the Virginal Conception of Jesus," in *Theological Studies* 33 (1972): 3–34. Although the overall title of his

book did not include the term *problem*, it is in the heading of the chapters dealing with these issues, a point Brown underscores. The "problem" was how to understand these two issues in the light of modern biblical and theological inquiry.

62. Brown noted that he was not addressing the tradition of the miraculous virginal birth of Jesus or that of the perpetual postpartum virginity of Mary.

63. *The Virginal Conception*, 32.

64. See chap. 6, pp. 131–42.

65. *The Virginal Conception*, 65.

66. A former doctoral student of Brown's, Jane Schaberg, would, in fact, assert that Jesus was illegitimate and that this was the origin of the tradition of the virginal conception in her work *The Illegitimacy of Jesus: A Feminist Theological Interpretation of the Infancy Narratives* (San Francisco: Harper & Row, 1987). She suggested that both Matthew and Luke were aware of the tradition of Jesus's illegitimacy and gave a theological interpretation in the form of the miraculous virginal conception. She went on to suggest that Mary may have become pregnant through rape. Brown vigorously disagreed with Schaberg's explanation and added a direct refutation of her view in the updated 1993 edition of *The Birth of the Messiah*. Their disagreement on this issue led to a painful strain in the relationship between Brown and his former student. On this, see Frank Reilly, "Jane Schaberg, Raymond E. Brown, and the Problem of the Illegitimacy of Jesus," *Journal of Feminist Studies in Religion* 21, no. 1 (2005): 57–80. Schaberg herself would be hounded by conservative critics for her view.

67. *The Virginal Conception*, 66–67 (italics original).

68. *The Virginal Conception*, 66–67n117.

69. *The Virginal Conception*, 67.

70. *The Virginal Conception*, 67.

71. *The Virginal Conception*, 67–68.

72. *The Virginal Conception*, 71.

73. *The Virginal Conception*, 96.

74. *The Virginal Conception*, 106.

75. *The Virginal Conception*, 112 (italics original).

76. *The Virginal Conception*, 121–22.

77. *The Virginal Conception*, 125.

78. *The Virginal Conception*, 126.

79. *The Virginal Conception*, 127.

80. *The Virginal Conception*, 127–28 (italics original).

81. *The Virginal Conception*, 128.

82. *The Virginal Conception*, 129.

83. See, e.g., *The Churches the Apostles Left Behind* (New York: Paulist Press, 1984), and the work coauthored with John P. Meier, *Antioch & Rome: New Testament Cradles of Catholic Christianity* (New York: Paulist Press, 1983).

84. See, e.g., *An Introduction to New Testament Christology* (New York: Paulist Press, 1994) and his earlier work, *Jesus: God and Man— Modern Biblical Reflections* (Milwaukee: Bruce, 1967). Of course, the topic of Christology was treated directly or indirectly in most of his writings, including his major academic works on the infancy narratives (*The Birth of the Messiah*) and the passion narratives (*The Death of the Messiah*), as well as in his commentaries on the Johannine literature. His *An Introduction to the New Testament*, one of his most comprehensive works, would also deal with Christology. We will consider these major academic contributions of Brown in chapter 6.

85. The term a "hermeneutic of grace" has been used in contrast to the method of a "hermeneutic of suspicion," the latter used often in feminist and other methodologies to detect the underlying biases in a text. By contrast, a "hermeneutic of grace" gives the benefit of the doubt, at least at the outset, regarding the intention or integrity of a text.

86. See chap. 8, pp. 199–230.

CHAPTER 5

1. *Time*, December 30, 1991.

2. We will consider Brown's other major works on the infancy narratives, the passion narratives, and his introduction to the New Testament in the following chapter.

3. In his annual report to the president and board of Union Theological Seminary, Brown confessed, "Every time I go through the process of spending an extra half year *after* submitting a typed manuscript, I make a resolve to write shorter books. Usually, it takes me about three years to forget that resolve." Annual report of May 15, 1982 (emphasis original).

4. This accuracy was also a tribute to Brown's collaborators. Brown acknowledged in particular the contribution of John Kselman,

PSS, himself a veteran biblical scholar, who served as Brown's personal editor for decades, and read through each of Brown's manuscripts to ensure accuracy. His assistant during his tenure at Union, Marion Soards, recalled being assigned by Brown to spend a summer checking and rechecking each of the multitude of references in Brown's manuscript for *An Introduction to the New Testament*.

5. As his more popular works demonstrated, Brown was capable of writing with passion and verve and some of the summaries of the meaning of biblical passages found in his commentaries are beautifully expressed.

6. On Brown's methodology, see chap. 3.

7. See chap. 7 on ecumenism.

8. See chap. 2, pp. 50–53, on Brown's role as a public scholar and the string of honorary doctorates he received from Protestant and secular universities.

9. See chap. 2, pp. 112–15.

10. *The Gospel according to John I–XII: Introduction, Translation, and Notes*, AB 29, p. vii. Brown refers to his article, "The Qumran Scrolls and the Johannine Gospel and Epistles," *CBQ* 17 (1955): 403–19, 559–74. Albright died in September of 1971, able to see the publication of Brown's second volume of his Johannine commentary published in 1970.

11. William Heidt, a member of the Benedictine community of St. John's in Collegeville, Minnesota, became director of Liturgical Press in 1950 and served in that capacity for 28 years. His energetic direction, fueled by the advent of the Second Vatican Council and the Catholic biblical renewal, would lead to the creation of the 46-volume, pamphlet-like biblical commentary series, the *Old Testament Reading Guides* and the 27-volume *New Testament Reading Guides*. This series, with many of the volumes revised and updated several times, had a very long shelf life. Brown's own contribution on the Gospel of John would go through three editions (1960, 1965, and 1982) and sell over a million copies. Heidt was also responsible for the establishment in 1962 of the bimonthly journal *The Bible Today*, now in its fifty-fifth volume. These efforts were part of the fascination with the Bible that swept through Catholicism at this period. Heidt himself had earned a PhD in the Semitics department of The Catholic University of America. His early enthusiasm for the Catholic biblical renewal waned in later years. He eventually moved to Holy Apostles Seminary in Cromwell, Connecticut, where he

taught Scripture from 1978 to 1996, before retiring to St. John's Abbey, where he died in 2000.

12. Letter of April 22, 1959, to Fr. McDonald.

13. See a helpful review of the history in a 1982 *New York Times Book Review* article by its then editor D. J. R. Bruckner (April 11, 1982) on the twenty-sixth anniversary of the highly successful series.

14. The original assignment was for Brown to cover both the Gospel and Epistles of John in two volumes. As his commentary on the Gospel mushroomed in size and was so well received, the editors and publisher agreed that the commentary on the Epistles would be a separate volume.

15. Letter of Cardinal Cushing to Raymond Brown, May 17, 1963.

16. Letter of Raymond Brown to Cardinal Bea, of the Vatican Secretariat for Promoting Christian Unity, May 8, 1963. There is no record of Bea's reply, but we can safely assume it was positive.

17. See chap. 8, p. 210.

18. *The Gospel according to John I–XII*, v.

19. *New York Times Book Review*, April 11, 1982.

20. Examples: Fitzmyer on the Gospel of Luke; Joel Marcus on the Gospel of Mark; Marcus Barth on the Letter to the Ephesians; some Old Testament commentaries such as those on the Psalms, Isaiah, and Jeremiah, would run to three volumes.

21. First published in German in 1941, Bultmann's commentary remains in print; see *The Gospel of John: A Commentary* (Louisville: Westminster John Knox Press, 1971).

22. See chap. 2, pp. 15–17.

23. *The Gospel according to John I–XII*, v–vi.

24. *The Gospel according to John I–XII*, vi.

25. He further commented that a biblical translation not be "too colloquial" or "border on slang" (p. vi). This is an echo, perhaps, of his negative experience regarding the fate of his translation of the Fourth Gospel at the hands of the final editor for the New American Bible translation.

26. *The Community of the Beloved Disciple: The Life, Loves, and Hates of an Individual Church in New Testament Times* (New York: Paulist Press, 1979). His full-blown theory about the Johannine community would appear in his commentary on the Epistles (1992), where he would attempt to trace the final stages of the Johannine trajectory. He notes in the preface that it was fortuitous that he had delayed the completion

of this volume due to the intervening publication of *The Birth of the Messiah* (1977). The stretch of time between his volumes on the Gospel and his commentary on the Epistles gave him the opportunity to reflect more fully on his hypothesis and, above all, to benefit from his interactions with his friend and colleague at Union, J. Louis Martyn (see preface, p. xiv.). As noted in his posthumous *An Introduction to the Gospel of John* (New York: Doubleday, 2003; New Haven: Yale University Press edition, 2010), edited and commented on by Francis J. Moloney, Brown would simplify somewhat the stages of development proposed in his earlier works but retain his basic hypothesis.

27. In the introduction to a proposed revision of his commentary on the Gospel that he was working on at the time of his death, Brown would further simplify this five-stage hypothesis but retained its basic character. See p. 124.

28. *The Gospel according to John I–XII*, xiv. Neirynck, a Belgian scholar of formidable erudition, was both a proponent of the two-source hypothesis as well as the hypothesis that the Gospel of John had some form of literary contact with one or perhaps all the Synoptic Gospels.

29. It should be noted that the possibility of "cross overs" between the Synoptic tradition and the Johannine tradition during the otherwise independent development of each stream of tradition has gained ground among Johannine scholars in recent years. See, e.g., the work of Paul N. Anderson, *The Riddles of the Fourth Gospel: An Introduction to John* (Minneapolis: Fortress Press, 2011).

30. See *The Gospel according to John I–XII*, cv–cxxxviii.

31. See *An Introduction to the Gospel of John*, 249–65.

32. *The Gospel according to John I–XII*, lxiv.

33. Later, however, Brown considered any attribution of the Johannine tradition to the Apostle John, the son of Zebedee, unlikely; see *An Introduction to the New Testament*, 368–69.

34. On Brown's engagement with Judaism, see chap. 7, pp. 183–95.

35. He notes that John uses the term "the Jews" some 70 times in his Gospel, compared to 5 or 6 times in other individual Gospels.

36. On both these points, see chap. 7 on the ecumenical and interreligious engagement of Brown. In the revised introduction to his commentary published after his death, Brown would give much more treatment to this issue; see *An Introduction to the Gospel of John*, 157–72.

37. J. Louis Martyn, "Raymond E. Brown in Memoriam: A Personal Word about a Friend and Yokefellow of Seventeen Years," September 1998.

38. *An Introduction to the Gospel of John*, ed. Francis J. Moloney (New Haven: Yale University Press, 2003). Moloney, a noted Johannine scholar in his own right, generously prepared the publication of Brown's text found on his computer after his death. The only intact revised text was the introduction Brown had worked on. The rest of the material were fragmentary comments on various sections of the Gospel. Thus, putting together Brown's materials was, as Moloney describes, a "daunting experience," having to touch up some of Brown's sentences and fill in the blanks. Moloney also used the opportunity in numerous "editor's notes" (clearly marked to distinguish his own views from that of Brown's) and in some alterations of Brown's text to compare and contrast Brown's views with his own, including calling into question Brown's hypothesis of multiple authors in the composition history of the Gospel as well as refuting other positions held by Brown. This led Allen Callahan in a review to wryly note that at times Moloney took on the role of the "Ecclesiastical Redactor" posited by Rudolf Bultmann, the redactor who stood in tension with the previous stage of John's Gospel, a position that Brown himself did not agree with, preferring to the see the final "Redactor" of John as complementing, not correcting, the work of the previous stages of the Gospel's composition; see Allen D. Callahan, "A Review of Raymond E. Brown's *An Introduction to the Gospel of John*," *Harvard Theological Review* 97 (2004): 229–34, esp. 231. On Moloney's work on Brown's planned revision, see also his "Raymond Brown's *New Introduction to the Gospel of John*: A Presentation—and Some Questions," *CBQ* 65 (2003): 1–21. This article originated as Moloney's presidential address at the sixty-fifth annual Catholic Biblical Association meeting at John Carroll University in Cleveland.

39. *The Epistles of John: Translated with Introduction, Notes, and Commentary*, AB 30 (New York: Doubleday, 1982).

40. On Brown's love of detective stories and his special passion for the *Mannix* TV series, see chap. 2, pp. 35–36.

41. This is a much-debated point; others would see John's love command having less of a sectarian viewpoint since John's Gospel affirms God's all-embracing love of the world as the purpose of Jesus's mission (see John 3:16). On this point, see D. Senior, "The Death of Jesus as Sign: A Fundamental Johannine Ethic," in *The Death of Jesus*

in the Fourth Gospel, ed. G. Van Belle (Leuven: University Press, 2007), 271–92; see also the emphasis on the "missionary nature" of the Johannine love command in Francis J. Moloney, *Love in the Gospel of John: An Exegetical, Theological, and Literary Study* (Grand Rapids: Baker Academic, 2013).

42. *The Epistles of John*, 103–4.

43. *The Epistles of John*, 107–8.

44. *The Epistles of John*, 111.

45. *The Epistles of John*, 112.

46. *The Epistles of John*, 115.

47. In his planned revision, Brown proposes three stages, but now incorporates his originally proposed stages 1 and 2 into a Stage 1 and also includes under stage 3 ("The Writing of the Gospel") the final evolution and separation of the Johannine community reflected in the conflicts apparent in the Epistles. See *An Introduction to the Gospel of John*, 62–86.

48. *Community of the Beloved Disciple*, 7.

CHAPTER 6

1. *The Birth of the Messiah: A Commentary on the Infancy Narratives in Matthew and Luke* (New York: Doubleday, 1977). The "updated" version, bearing the same title and published by Doubleday in 1993, was now included under the newly formed Anchor Bible Reference Series. As noted earlier, Francis Moloney edited the new introduction to Brown's projected revision of his commentary on the Gospel of John, but, strictly speaking, this was not Brown's publication since he had not had the chance to complete the final version even of the introduction to the commentary; as editor, Moloney used the opportunity to clarify and interact with Brown's own views. In a manner characteristic of both his frugality and consideration for his friends, Brown had a number of duplicated copies made of the new material from the updated version of *The Birth of the Messiah* so that his friends would not have to spend money on purchasing the entire volume. (I proudly have one of these copies inscribed "Best wishes, Ray.") His assistant Marion Soards notes that Brown was dismayed that he had purchased the full volume anyway!

2. *The Birth of the Messiah*, 7.

3. *The Birth of the Messiah*, 7.

4. *The Birth of the Messiah*, 7.

5. Brown's reference here to the influence of the passion narratives might have been a signal for his next major exegetical project, his two-volume study of the passion narratives; see pp. 142–53.

6. *The Birth of the Messiah*, 8.

7. *The Birth of the Messiah*, 8.

8. *The Birth of the Messiah*, 9. This optimistic conviction that the historical-critical method properly applied would lead to the same conclusions no matter what the confessional stance of the exegete was a hallmark of Brown's views. See chap. 3, pp. 69–70.

9. *The Birth of the Messiah*, 8.

10. *The Birth of the Messiah*, 38.

11. *The Birth of the Messiah*, 231–32.

12. *The Birth of the Messiah*, 153.

13. *The Birth of the Messiah*, 232.

14. *The Birth of the Messiah*, 232.

15. *The Birth of the Messiah*, 235.

16. *The Birth of the Messiah*, 46.

17. *The Birth of the Messiah*, 239–50.

18. *The Birth of the Messiah*, 247.

19. *The Birth of the Messiah*, 498–99.

20. *The Birth of the Messiah*, 497.

21. *The Birth of the Messiah*, 497.

22. The Anchor Bible Reference Library (New York: Doubleday, 1993).

23. See Brown's earlier treatment of the virginal conception discussed in chap. 4, pp. 131–42.

24. "Supplement," p. 698. Brown quotes here in part from his book on *The Virginal Conception & Bodily Resurrection of Jesus*, 66–67 (italics original).

25. See John Spong, *Born of a Woman* (San Francisco: Harper, 1992), 124.

26. See "Supplement," "Appendix IV," 698–708.

27. See pp. 141–42.

28. See Jane Schaberg, *The Illegitimacy of Jesus* (San Francisco: Harper & Row, 1987).

29. "Supplement," 601–2 (italics original).

30. "Supplement," 637.

31. "Supplement," 637. Jane Dewar Schaberg (1938–2015) had completed her doctoral studies under Brown's direction at Union in 1977 and went on to become professor of Religious Studies and of Women's Studies at the University of Detroit Mercy from 1977 through retiring as professor emerita in 2009. She passed away after a long illness at the age of seventy-seven in 2015.

32. Curiously, Pope Benedict did not cite Brown's work in his own study of the infancy narratives (Joseph Ratzinger, *Jesus of Nazareth: The Infancy Narratives* [New York: Image, 2012]). However, Brown is cited in Ratzinger's study of the passion accounts, noting that Brown did not rule out a historical basis for John's presentation of the trial of Jesus in John's account; see Joseph Ratzinger, *Jesus of Nazareth: Holy Week: From the Entrance into Jerusalem to the Resurrection* (San Francisco: Ignatius Press, 2011), 184.

33. Letter of Raymond Brown to Gerald Brown, March 16, 1989.

34. New York: Doubleday, 1994. Similar to *The Birth of the Messiah*, this would be part of the Anchor Bible Reference Library. Unlike Brown's commentary on the Gospel of John, the two volumes of this work appeared simultaneously.

35. *The Death of the Messiah*, vii.

36. *The Death of the Messiah*, vii.

37. *The Death of the Messiah*, vii.

38. *The Death of the Messiah*, vii.

39. On a personal note, I know that Brown wrestled with this issue. At the same time he was preparing his massive study, I had begun to publish a series of individual books on each of the four passion accounts, relating them to the theology of each evangelist (The Passion Series [Collegeville, MN: Liturgical Press, 1984–91]). On several occasions, Brown explained to me his own preference for the "horizontal" approach he was taking, giving me the impression that he was still not completely sure of his choice.

40. *The Death of the Messiah*, viii.

41. *The Death of the Messiah*, 4; on Brown's methodology, see chap. 3.

42. *The Death of the Messiah*, 11.

43. Commenting on the essay of G. Bucher, "Elements for an Analysis of the Gospel Text: The Death of Jesus," *Modern Language Notes* 86 (1971): 835–44; see *The Death of the Messiah*, 12n11. Brown seemed to find structuralist and semiotic methodology particularly obscure and

useless, a highly abstract approach that ran counter to his own more pragmatic inclinations; see also his comments in *An Introduction to the New Testament*, 24–25.

44. *The Death of the Messiah*, 13.

45. *The Death of the Messiah*, 14.

46. *The Death of the Messiah*, 14.

47. J. D. Crossan, *The Cross That Spoke: The Origins of the Passion Narrative* (San Francisco: Harper & Row, 1988), 405.

48. *The Death of the Messiah*, 15.

49. *The Death of the Messiah*, 22.

50. *The Death of the Messiah*, 22.

51. *The Death of the Messiah*, 24.

52. *The Death of the Messiah*, 25.

53. *The Death of the Messiah*, 25 (italics original).

54. *The Death of the Messiah*, 35.

55. *The Death of the Messiah*, 35.

56. *The Death of the Messiah*, 46–57. The question of a pre-Marcan passion account is also taken up in appendix ix (vol. 2, 1492–1524) written by Marion L. Soards, Brown's doctoral student and assistant while at Union Theological Seminary. Soards had written a paper on the issue of a pre-Marcan passion narrative for a seminar that Brown had conducted and had concluded such a pre-Marcan source did not exist. Soards would later compose his doctoral dissertation on Luke 22, under Brown's direction, and confirm his conclusions. From his interactions with Soards, Brown himself was persuaded to abandon the hypothesis of such a source for Mark's passion narrative. Soards, who was a cherished assistant for Brown, would eventually become professor of New Testament at Louisville Presbyterian Seminary.

57. *The Death of the Messiah*, 48. Brown believed, along with many other scholars, that the tradition attributed to Papias that Mark was the interpreter of Peter's proclamation may not be accurate but may be a shorthand way of asserting that Mark's Gospel reflected the content of early apostolic preaching.

58. *The Death of the Messiah*, 48 (italics original).

59. In the case of Matthew, Brown believed the evangelist drew on "folkloric" traditions available in his community but questioned to what extent Matthew himself composed this special material in his passion narrative. This led to a friendly debate with him on my part; see. D. Senior, "Revisiting Matthew's Special Material in the Passion Narrative:

A Dialogue with Raymond Brown," *Ephemerides Theologicae Lovanienses* 70 (1994): 417–24. In that same issue of the *Ephemerides*, Frans Neirynck, the formidable Belgian scholar who had great respect for Brown, offered a detailed review of *The Death of the Messiah* that was appreciative but also critical on some points; see pp. 406–16.

60. *The Death of the Messiah*, 92 (italics original).

61. Reviews at the time of Brown's publication were uniformly positive, including an extensive review by Peter Steinfels in the March 27, 1994, edition of *The New York Times*, who described Brown's study as "a work likely to profoundly influence the way Christians think about the Passion narratives." Some noted, however, that Brown's intent to trace the theology of each Gospel's passion narrative was hampered by his decision to compare each scene horizontally.

62. On Brown's more popular works, see chap. 4.

63. *The Death of the Messiah*, xi–xii.

64. *An Introduction to the New Testament* (Anchor Bible Reference Library; New York: Doubleday, 1997).

65. *Introduction*, vii.

66. To help remedy this, Brown's friend and former assistant, Marion Soards, published an abridged edition of Brown's *Introduction* that kept his basic analysis of the New Testament books, but severely trimmed his dealing with critical issues and substantially reduced the voluminous bibliography. See Raymond E. Brown, *An Introduction to the New Testament: The Abridged Edition*, ed. and abr. Marion L. Soards (New Haven: Yale University Press, 2016). Despite its formidable size and content, Brown's *Introduction* would sell over 100,000 copies in its first year of publication, an amazing amount for a religious publication of this size and a tribute to Brown's reputation.

67. We will consider Brown's views on the historical Jesus later, pp. 159–65.

68. See chap. 3, p. 63.

69. *Introduction*, 35–46.

70. *Introduction*, 34.

71. *Introduction*, 30–31. On the formulations of Vatican II's *Dei Verbum* on revelation and inspiration, see Ronald D. Witherup, *Scripture: Dei Verbum* and *The Word of God at Vatican II: Exploring Dei Verbum* (see intro., n. 11).

72. *Introduction*, 31.

73. *Introduction*, 31.

74. *Introduction*, 33.

75. *Introduction*, 34 (italics original).

76. *Introduction*, 34.

77. "Certainly theological reflection has always considered inspiration and truth as two key concepts for an ecclesial hermeneutic of the sacred Scriptures. Nevertheless, one must acknowledge the need today for a fuller and more adequate study of these realities, in order better to respond to the need to interpret the sacred texts in accordance with their nature. Here I would express my fervent hope that research in this field will progress and bear fruit both for biblical science and for the spiritual life of the faithful." *Verbum Domini*, no. 19.

78. Pontifical Biblical Commission, *The Inspiration and Truth of Sacred Scripture* (Collegeville, MN: Liturgical Press, 2014). The Commission focused on the Bible's own self-understanding of inspiration and inerrancy.

79. *Introduction*, 407–680.

80. *Introduction*, 438–39.

81. See James D. G. Dunn, *The New Perspective on Paul*, rev. ed. (Grand Rapids, MI: Eerdmans, 2008).

82. See E. P. Sanders, *Paul and Palestinian Judaism* (Philadelphia: Fortress Press, 1977).

83. See the discussion of recent trends in Michael J. Gorman, *Apostle of The Crucified Lord: A Theological Introduction to Paul & His Letters*, 2nd rev. ed. (Grand Rapids, MI: Eerdmans, 2017), 1–9.

84. See Krister Stendahl, "The Apostle Paul and the Introspective Conscience of the West," *Harvard Theological Review* 56 (1963): 199–215. See *Introduction*, 439n35.

85. *Introduction*, 439.

86. *Introduction*, 569–71.

87. *Introduction*, 571. On Brown's engagement with Judaism, see chap. 7, pp. 183–95.

88. *Introduction*, 571. However, this perspective on Paul, expressed even in the simplistic terms Brown derided, still exists. See, e.g., the recently best-selling work of Reza Aslan, *Zealot: The Life and Times of Jesus of Nazareth* (New York: Random House, 2013), who casually asserts that Paul consciously and deceptively redid the image of Jesus in a manner to make the Christian message more acceptable to a Roman audience. For a sharp critique of such a view, see Jerry L. Sumney, *Steward of God's Mysteries: Paul and Early Christian Tradition* (Grand Rapids: Eerdmans,

2017); and the article of Benjamin L. White, "The Traditional and Ecclesiastical Paul of I Corinthians," *CBQ* 79 (2017): 651–81, who exposes the late nineteenth and early twentieth century roots of this tendentious viewpoint.

89. *Introduction*, 455 (italics original).

90. See *Introduction*, "Appendix I," 817–30.

91. Bornkamm's work, *Jesus of Nazareth* (New York: Harper & Row, 1960), enjoyed great popularity. Brown, as we will note later in the chapter on ecumenism, was a great admirer of Käsemann. Brown had assessed the work of the so-called "post Bultmannians" in an earlier work coauthored with the Canadian Jesuit scholar P. J. Cahill, *Biblical Tendencies Today: An Introduction to the Post-Bultmannians* (Washington, DC: Corpus, 1969).

92. *Introduction*, 819–20. Brown cited the work of such scholars as Ben Witherington III, *The Jesus Quest: The Third Search for the Jew of Nazareth* (Downers Grove, IL: InterVarsity, 1995), who, in turn, refers to scholars holding this more conservative view such as J. D. G. Dunn, P. Stuhlmacher, and N. T. Wright.

93. *Introduction*, 820.

94. *Introduction*, 820n8.

95. Red beads—indicated the voter believed Jesus did say the passage quoted, or something very much like the passage (3 Points); pink beads—indicated the voter believed Jesus probably said something like the passage (2 Points); gray beads—indicated the voter believed Jesus did not say the passage, but it contains Jesus's ideas (1 Point); black beads—indicated the voter believed Jesus did not say the passage—it comes from later admirers or a different tradition (0 Points).

96. *Introduction*, 821.

97. Brown cited the names of such well-known scholars as Alan Culpepper, Richard B. Hays, Luke Timothy Johnson, Leander Keck, John P. Meier, and Charles Talbert; see *Introduction*, 821.

98. See, especially, Crossan's major work, *The Historical Jesus: The Life of a Mediterranean Jewish Peasant* (San Francisco: Harper, 1994). Brown also discusses the work of Marcus Borg, whose writings were also popular, but Brown found that Borg's attempt to find a meaningful spirituality in his study of the historical Jesus made his views "more attractive" to some who "would otherwise find the Seminar's claims offensive." *Introduction*, 823.

99. See Brown's strong critique of this view in "The Gospel of Peter and Canonical Gospel Priority," *New Testament Studies* 33 (1987): 321–43.

100. *Introduction*, 823.

101. John P. Meier, *A Marginal Jew: Rethinking the Historical Jesus*, Anchor Bible Reference Library (New York: Doubleday, 1991–). After volume three, the volumes of Meier's magisterial work would be published by Yale University Press.

102. *Introduction*, 827.

103. *Introduction*, 828.

104. *An Introduction to New Testament Christology* (New York: Paulist Press, 1994).

105. *An Introduction to New Testament Christology*, 150–52.

106. *New York Times*, December 21, 1997. See similarly, the comment of British scholar Marc Goodacre, "In a culture in which students are often eager to know about feminist hermeneutics, reader-response, liberation perspectives and deconstruction, the solid focus on historical-critical matters will inevitably be seen as a shortcoming. But this has an important and valuable pay-off: Brown's Introduction is useful but not exhaustive, and students will continue to need to take more than one book off the shelf." *Reviews in Religion and Theology* 3 (1998): 93–4.

107. *Introduction*, 28 (italics original).

CHAPTER 7

1. See, e.g., Brown's tribute to Albright "the Professor" in *The Gospel according to John I–XII*, vii.

2. See chap. 2, p. 27. Brown mentions this in his oral history: "I owe much to Hopkins, because half the people who studied there wound up teaching at Protestant Seminaries and Universities. David N. Freedman and Frank Cross [a highly respected professor of Scripture at the Harvard Divinity School] were there ahead of me, but they knew me through Hopkins. And thus I got into the Anchor Bible group." On this point, see chap. 5, pp. 113–14.

3. See chap. 2, pp. 26–27.

4. On Bea, see chap. 4, p. 81.

5. Vischer's (1926–2008) tenure with the World Council of Churches began in 1961 with his appointment as research secretary on

the council's Commission on Faith and Order. From 1962 to 1965, he was a WCC observer at the Second Vatican Council. He was director of the Faith and Order Commission from 1966 to 1979, then director of the Protestant Office for Ecumenism in Bern.

6. The "Faith and Order Commission" is a part of the World Council of Churches, whose purpose is to provide study and reflection on issues relating to ecumenism. It holds occasional plenary study sessions such as the one Brown was involved in in Montreal in 1963. The Commission consists of some 120 members, some of whom are not formal members of the World Council itself. This would include Roman Catholic representatives, a role that Brown himself fulfilled after appointment to the Commission by the Vatican.

7. Oral history interview with Raymond Brown.

8. His essay, "The Problem of the Historical Jesus," which was first published in 1954, was considered groundbreaking. The English translation of the article is found in E. Käsemann, *Essays on New Testament Themes*, Studies in Biblical Theology (London: SCM Press, 1964).

9. Raymond E. Brown, "The Unity and Diversity in New Testament Ecclesiology," *Novum Testamentum* 6 (1963): 298–308.

10. See pp. 176–78.

11. This incident was reported to me in an interview with Rev. Robert F. Leavitt, PSS, a former student and close colleague of Brown, who would later join the faculty at St. Mary's and become its president. His memory of the event was corroborated by other Sulpicians who were present. Leavitt was given the task by Brown of recording the lecture and noted that when Käsemann returned with the missing page to complete his lecture, he had only one more paragraph to read, raising the question why he would have to retrieve his written text to add one final paragraph!

12. The Institute still thrives, with over 750 graduates since its founding. Michael Gorman, the former dean of the Institute, now holds the Raymond Brown Chair at St. Mary's.

13. See chap. 2, pp. 30–32.

14. He dedicated his book *The Churches the Apostles Left Behind* to these three faculty colleagues among others with whom he had enjoyed long friendships; see further, pp. 176–78.

15. For a list of Brown's doctoral students, see chap. 3, p. 59n.1.

16. *The Critical Meaning of the Bible: How a Modern Reading of the Bible Challenges Christians, the Church, and the Churches* (New York: Paulist Press, 1982).

17. *Critical Meaning of the Bible*, 119.

18. *Critical Meaning of the Bible*, 119.

19. *Critical Meaning of the Bible*, 120.

20. *Critical Meaning of the Bible*, 120.

21. *Critical Meaning of the Bible*, 121.

22. *Critical Meaning of the Bible*, 122.

23. *Critical Meaning of the Bible*, 122.

24. Brown was also invited by the Vatican in 1982 to serve on the International Catholic–Methodist dialogue. While he was happy to serve on this important dialogue, his role was less prominent and did not lead to significant publications on his part as his involvement in the Catholic–Lutheran dialogue did.

25. Donfried and Reumann would serve as coeditors with Brown for the volume on *Peter in the New Testament*; Paul Achtemeier would be the first Protestant elected as president of the Catholic Biblical Association in 2000.

26. Raymond E. Brown, Karl P. Donfried, John Reumann, eds., *Peter in the New Testament: A Collaborative Assessment by Protestant and Roman Catholic Scholars* (Minneapolis: Augsburg, 1973). Raymond E. Brown, Karl P. Donfried, Joseph A. Fitzmyer, John Reumann, eds., *Mary in the New Testament: A Collaborative Assessment by Protestant and Roman Catholic Scholars* (New York: Paulist Press, 1978).

27. The list of names is something of a who's who among Catholic and Protestant scholars—the dialogue had included a few scholars other than Lutherans to broaden the discussion and to serve as a possible model for other such dialogues. On the list besides Brown and Reumann were the following: Paul J. Achtemeier, Myles Bourke, P. Schuyler Brown, Joseph A. Burgess, Joseph A. Fitzmyer, Karlfried Froehlich, Reginald Fuller, and Gerhard Krodel.

28. See chap. 4, pp. 89–91.

29. *Peter in the New Testament*, 166–67. Note that this and the subsequent book on Mary are collaborative texts, not the works of individual authors; thus, the quotations represent a common text achieved by consensus among the ecumenical team.

30. *Peter in the New Testament*, 167.

31. *Peter in the New Testament*, 168.

32. See the preface to *Mary in the New Testament*, v.

33. Reginal Fuller, Gerhard Krodel, J. Louis Martyn, and Elaine H. Pagels were added to the list of scholars who had worked on *Peter in the New Testament*.

34. *The Virginal Conception & Bodily Resurrection of Jesus*; see chap. 4, pp. 100–103.

35. See chap. 6, pp. 131–42.

36. *Mary in the New Testament*, 291–92; on Brown's viewpoint, see chap. 4, pp. 100–103.

37. *Mary in the New Testament*, 294.

38. *Mary in the New Testament*, 294.

39. New York: Paulist Press, 1984.

40. In 2009, the school changed its name to Union Presbyterian Seminary, partly to distinguish itself from Union Theological Seminary in New York as well as to affirm its sponsoring Presbyterian identity. The seminary was founded in 1812.

41. *The Churches the Apostles Left Behind*, 8.

42. *The Churches the Apostles Left Behind*, 9.

43. *The Churches the Apostles Left Behind*, 19.

44. Kirsopp Lake, *Landmarks in the History of Early Christianity* (London: Macmillan, 1920).

45. See chap. 5, pp. 125–30.

46. *The Churches the Apostles Left Behind*, 29.

47. *The Churches the Apostles Left Behind*, 38.

48. *The Churches the Apostles Left Behind*, 148.

49. *The Churches the Apostles Left Behind*, 148. At the time Brown had expressed this in his original Sprunt lecture, the Vatican had disciplined Hans Küng, and some in his audience expressed concern that the Roman Catholic Church was about to embark on a purge of dissenting Catholic scholars. Paradoxically, Brown, while not attacking Küng, expressed his appreciation for the Catholic Church's "serious concern for sound doctrine," which "is both a NT idea and a strength in the Christian picture, often best understood from within" (p. 149).

50. *The Churches the Apostles Left Behind*, 149–50.

51. Richard John Neuhaus, who died at seventy-two in 2009, was an ordained Lutheran minister, an erudite scholar, and an activist pastor. He was received into the Catholic Church in 1990 and ordained a Catholic priest by Cardinal John O'Connor, becoming a priest of the Archdiocese of New York. He was the founder and chief editor of the

journal *First Things*, which he continued to lead after his conversion to Catholicism. He was a strong advocate for the church's position on abortion and played an active national role in politics and religion.

52. "The Contribution of Historical Biblical Criticism to Ecumenical Church Discussion," *Biblical Interpretation in Crisis: The Ratzinger Conference on Bible and Church*, ed. Richard John Neuhaus, Encounter Series 9 (Grand Rapids: Eerdmans, 1989), 24–49. On the significance of Brown's "addenda" concerning historical biblical criticism, see chap. 3, pp. 71–74.

53. See chap. 8, pp. 210–12.

54. "The Contribution of Historical Biblical Criticism," 38.

55. See chap. 3, pp. 71–74.

56. See Cardinal Joseph Ratzinger, "Biblical Interpretation in Crisis: On the Question of the Foundation and Approaches of Exegesis Today," in *Biblical Interpretation in Crisis*, 1–23.

57. Here, Brown appealed to the collaborative text, *Mary in the New Testament*; see earlier, pp. 174–76.

58. "The Contribution of Historical Biblical Criticism," 34.

59. "The Contribution of Historical Biblical Criticism," 35.

60. "The Contribution of Historical Biblical Criticism," 35.

61. "The Contribution of Historical Biblical Criticism," 35.

62. This development is traced in the introduction, see pp. xix–xxx.

63. "The Contribution of Historical Biblical Criticism," 36.

64. "The Contribution of Historical Biblical Criticism," 37. Brown was writing this at a time when popular biblical study at the parish and diocesan level was at its zenith. In recent years there may have been some fall-off in enthusiasm as some of the novelty has worn off, but Brown's statement remains substantially true. See introduction, pp. xxviii–xxix.

65. All quotations in this section are from *Nostra Aetate*, no. 4.

66. Of course, like all the Conciliar statements, such a change in perspective did not appear miraculously but was the fruit of dialogue and collaboration on the part of some Christians and Jews much earlier than the Council, including the common involvement of Catholics and Jews in the U.S. labor movement in the 1930s and '40s. Similarly, there were ongoing dialogues seeking reconciliation of Christians and Jews in postwar Germany. Likewise, the Council's declaration would not automatically erase the scourge of anti-Semitism from the Christian

community. At the level of the Vatican, as well as in many dioceses, the groundbreaking work of *Nostra Aetate* has been followed by numerous statements attempting to advance the relationship between the church and Judaism, including the major 2002 statement of the Pontifical Biblical Commission, *The Jewish People and Their Sacred Scriptures in the Christian Bible*, in which Brown himself, as a member of the Commission, played a significant role in its formulation; see further, pp. 192–94.

67. See p. 167.

68. See p. 185.

69. A 2009 tribute to Albright by Thomas Levy and David Noel Freedman on behalf of the National Academic of science describes this moment: "In 1948 the scrolls were brought to the American School of Oriental Research in Jerusalem for evaluation, where they were photographed by John Trever. Trever airmailed two small Leica photographs of a column or two of the scrolls that had been brought to the school on February 18, 1948, by Metropolitan Athanasius Yeshue Samuel and Father Butros Sowmy of St. Mark's Monastery for the evaluation. David Noel Freedman recalls Albright saying that within an hour of first looking at the photographs he knew it was a genuinely ancient discovery and that the scrolls dated from the last two centuries BCE and the first century CE. As Mrs. Albright related the story, it may have taken Albright 20 minutes to form a judgment, and 19 of those minutes were spent trying to find his 1937 article on the Nash Papyrus, with photograph, somewhere on his stacked desk. This was an example of Albright's remarkable memory for form and detail. He recognized in the tiny Leica photographs four letters with distinguishing characteristics that were definitely older than those he had written about and dated in the Nash Papyrus over 10 years earlier. As editor of the *Bulletin of the American School of Oriental Research*, Albright published an article in the April 1948 volume announcing the discovery of the Dead Sea Scrolls. In the October 1949 volume Albright himself published one of the first scholarly articles on the scrolls' discovery, entitled 'On the Date of the Scrolls from Ain Feshkha and the Nash Papyrus,' that included a good infrared photograph of the Nash Papyrus for comparison. When news of Willard Libby's new method of dating ancient remains using carbon 14 (14C) reached Albright, he announced in an Associated Press article that he was eager to try out the new technique in Egypt and the Bible lands; Albright was always eager to apply new discoveries and new methods to archaeological and biblical research. Albright's early assessment of

the antiquity of the Dead Sea Scrolls played a critical role in determining the authenticity of this remarkable discovery, their importance for future scholarly research as well as their rapid purchase for museums in Israel and Jordan and their ultimate conservation for future generations." See Thomas Levy and David Noel Freedman, "William Foxwell Albright 1891–1971: A Biographical Memoir," National Academy of Sciences, Washington, DC, February 2009.

70. See chap. 1, pp. 13–16.

71. See chap. 5, p. 115.

72. See chap. 5, pp. 117–21.

73. See chap. 5, pp. 122–25. Note also the extended discussion in the work of Sonya Cronin, "Raymond Brown, 'The Jews,' and The Gospel of John" (Diss.; Florida State University, 2009), who traces the development of Brown's perspective on this issue. She describes the various nuances of meaning Brown detected in John's references to the "Jews" and also charts Brown's attention to the contemporary consequences of some polemical New Testament texts. Her dissertation is now published as a book, *Raymond Brown, "The Jews," and the Gospel of John: From Apologia to Apology*, Library of New Testament Studies 504 (New York: Bloomsbury, 2015).

74. *The Gospel of John I–XII*, lxxli.

75. See J. Louis Martyn, *History and Theology in the Fourth Gospel*, 3rd rev. and exp. ed. (Louisville: Westminster John Knox Press, 2003).

76. Visotzky also earned a reputation as a proponent of interreligious relations with both Christianity and Islam.

77. Visotzky confessed that he was very nervous at the beginning of this pioneering effort. Brown was there to introduce him at the first session, and when it became clear that Brown himself was going to stay for the duration of the presentation, Visotzky's nervousness increased. However, relief came when he observed that after a few minutes Brown characteristically fell asleep!

78. See chap. 6, p. 43.

79. See *The Death of the Messiah*, 328–97.

80. *The Death of the Messiah*, 386.

81. *The Death of the Messiah*, 391–97.

82. *The Death of the Messiah*, 396.

83. *The Death of the Messiah*, 396 (italics original).

84. *An Introduction to the New Testament*, 167. See also his similar comments in *A Retreat with John the Evangelist: That You May Have Life*

(Cincinnati: St. Anthony Messenger Press,1998). This was the very last published work of Brown; some copies sent to friends even arrived after his death. In the format of this lovely book, Brown has the "Evangelist" confess: "I am told that many have found references to 'the Jews' in my 'Gospel Message' offensive. When your Translator recounted for me the hatred for Jews that developed in subsequent centuries, I saw how passages I had written could be read in the light of that later experience and how meanings could emerge that I never dreamed of—a humbling discovery" (p. 69).

85. John Dominic Crossan, *Who Killed Jesus? Exposing the Roots of Anti-Semitism in the Gospel Story of the Death of Jesus* (San Francisco: Harper Collins, 1995).

86. See chap. 6, the discussion about the Jesus Seminar, pp. 160–62.

87. *New York Times*, March 27, 1994. National Section.

88. Crossan, *Who Killed Jesus*, 35.

89. Crossan, *Who Killed Jesus*, 36.

90. Crossan, *Who Killed Jesus*, 35.

91. See the article of John Pawlikowski, "Reflections on the Brown-Crossan Debate" (Memo of the American Interfaith Institute Staff, January 6, 2015), who notes the concurrence of such prominent Jewish scholars as Michael Cook, of Hebrew Union College, Cincinnati, and the late Ellis Rivkin in his 1997 work, *What Crucified Jesus? Messianism, Pharisaism, and the Development of Christianity* (Springfield, NJ: Berman House, 1997).

92. Crossan, a well-known and widely published scholar, is himself a Catholic, a former priest of the Servite Order, from which he later resigned and who is now professor emeritus of DePaul University. However, it would be fair to say that, unlike Brown, aligning the New Testament with later Catholic doctrine has not been a preoccupation of his scholarly work.

93. See chap. 2, pp. 57–58.

94. Pontifical Biblical Commission, *The Jewish People and Their Sacred Scriptures in the Christian Bible* (Rome: Libreria Editrice Vaticana, 2002).

95. *The Jewish People and Their Sacred Scriptures*, 11.

96. See chap. 7, pp. 172–76.

97. "I would like to see the topic [i.e., hostile passages about "the Jews"] enlarged to cover this second point as well because it is very important in relation to Jews today. At this very moment the American

Bible Society has published a "Contemporary English Version "of the NT which removes all hostile reference to the Jews, substituting other words. The Society wanted an imprimatur from the American Catholic Bishops but [I] was one of the scholars consulted who urged that such an imprimatur not be given (it will not)....There are Jewish groups who are pushing very hard to persuade Christians to emend the NT in this was [sic] we should not do this but it would be helpful if we commented on the meaning of hostile references to the 'Jews' and how they should be understood today in a way that is not offensive ecumenically. Just a suggestion." Letter of Raymond Brown to A. Vanhoye, June 3, 1996.

98. "Inspired by your letter, I have taken care to specify that our theme should extend to the relationship between Christians and Jews in the perspective of the relationship between the NT and the OT. As you have written, this theme is very current. We should study topics that are 'burning' [Fr. *brulant*]! I am all the more happy to be able to count on your competence and your experience" [author's translation from the French]. Letter of Albert Vanhoye to Raymond Brown, July 21, 1996.

99. A copy of Brown's document is in the Associated Archives of St. Mary's Seminary and University in Baltimore, titled in French (but with the content in English): "Points de vue divers sur les juifs dans Jean."

100. On this, see the dissertation of Sonya Cronin, "Raymond Brown, 'The Jews,' and The Gospel of John," esp. 183–90, now published as a book, *Raymond Brown, "The Jews," and the Gospel of John: From Apologia to Apology*. Her detailed comparison of Brown's paper and the final text of the PBC document shows that much, but not all, of Brown's viewpoints were incorporated into the final version of the PBC text. For example, Brown would concede that in the final versions of John's Gospel, as the rift with other Jews widened and as the Johannine community was more deeply immersed in the Gentile world, the term "the Jews" took on an anti-Jewish meaning in John's Gospel. But the PBC text asserts that there is "no question here of anti-Jewish sentiment since—as we have already noted—the Gospel recognizes that 'salvation comes from the Jews' (4:22). This manner of speaking only reflects the clear separation that existed between the Christian and Jewish communities" (*The Jewish People and Their Sacred Scriptures*, 175).

101. *The Jewish People and Their Sacred Scriptures*, 199.

102. Cronin, *Raymond Brown, "The Jews," and The Gospel of John*, 225–26. The culmination of Brown's view on the designation "the Jews"

in the Gospel of John and its potential for misinterpretation in the cause of anti-Semitism is found in the proposed revisions of his commentary on John published after his death in Moloney's work, *An Introduction to the Gospel of John*, 157–75. In dealing with the contemporary consequences of John's blanket and often polemical designation of Jesus's opponents as "the Jews," Brown notes, "Today, therefore, in proclaiming John preachers must be careful to caution hearers that John's passages cannot be used to justify any ongoing hostility to Jewish people, any more than one should appeal for justification in our times to the genocidal cleansings of Palestine described in the OT as God's instructions for Israel at the time of Joshua's conquest (Lev 27:28–29; Josh 6:21; 8:22; 10:38–39). Regarding the Bible as sacred does not mean that everything described therein is laudable" (p. 168).

103. Brown's friend, Truman Madsen, was a highly respected leader in the LDS and a professor of religion at Brigham Young University in Salt Lake City, Utah, and director of the university's Jerusalem Center for Near Eastern Studies. A contemporary of Brown, he passed away in 2009 at the age of eighty-two. It is not known how Brown first met Madsen.

CHAPTER 8

1. In his CBA oral interview, Brown himself observed that scholars such as Frank J. McCool, SJ (+2007), who taught at the Biblicum, and Barnabas Ahern, CP (+1995), who had played a significant role as a *peritus* at the Council, became "more conservative in the last days of [their] lives." Such prominent theologians as Joseph Ratzinger and Avery Dulles (1918–2008), originally strong proponents of the Council's reforms, have also been described as later growing more cautious in the wake of some of the directions that implementation of the Council would take.

2. See *Louvain Studies* 2 (1976): 144–58. This article of Brown's is not included in the otherwise comprehensive bibliography assembled by Michael Barré in Donahue, *Life in Abundance*, 253–89.

3. At the beginning of his article, Brown notes that earlier in his 1975 book, *Biblical Reflections on Crises Facing the Church* (pp. 3–19), he had "dealt with the frenzied discussion appearing in some American national Catholic newspapers and religious magazines which had

passed into the hands of right-wing extremists and which were being used as organs of attacks on theologians and biblical scholars" (p. 144). Brown had also just completed round two of a painful debate involving Cardinal Lawrence J. Shehan; see further, pp. 217–26.

4. The issue of Jesus's human consciousness would be one of the key issues seized upon by Brown's critics. Brown's contention that Jesus's human consciousness was limited and historically time bound was "translated" by some of his critics into asserting that Brown considered Jesus to have been "ignorant." Brown observed that the scholars present at the Council may not have realized some of the doctrinal implications of a developmental approach to the Gospels. "I was there," he noted, "and I certainly did not see all the implications I see now." He may have been stretching things a bit to impress his Louvain audience, since he was at the Council only for about a month; see earlier, chap. 2, pp. 26–27. In fact, several of the Louvain faculty he was speaking to had key advisory roles at the Council, such as Gustav Thils, Philip Delhaye, Louis Janssens, Gérard Phillips, and Frans Neirynck, all of whom served as *periti*, or official consultants serving their bishops at the Council.

5. I can only wonder what the Louvain faculty thought of this comment of Brown, which did not reference Louvain itself; from experience I know that German scholarship was appreciated by the Louvain faculty, but it considered its own work equal to or better than its German counterparts.

6. Here, Brown recalled his own treatment of these issues in his study *The Virginal Conception & the Bodily Resurrection of Jesus* (1973). Curiously, he does not refer to his studies on the Petrine texts in *Priest and Bishop* (1970) or *Peter in the New Testament* (1974).

7. Brown had developed this metaphor of a "blueprint" ecclesiology in his reflection on the issue of women's ordination in his work *Biblical Reflections on Crises Facing the Church*, 50–60; on this, see chap. 4, pp. 91–96.

8. Here, as in many other places in his writing, Brown appeals to the Vatican statement *Mysterium Ecclesiae*, issued by the Congregation for the Doctrine of the Faith in 1973. Brown underscored the significance of the fact that this document recognized the limits of doctrinal formulations, both in their time-bound language and the fact that some doctrinal statements are directed to specific historical circumstances that may no longer hold.

9. Fitzmyer, "Raymond E. Brown: In Memoriam," 12–13. The adjective *venomous* is a quotation from a comment of Cardinal Timothy Manning, former archbishop of Los Angeles, who defended Brown after he had been the object of public protests at the 1973 National Catholic Education Association annual meeting and at the Los Angeles Religious Education Congress. Manning, who himself was viewed as a very conservative prelate, nevertheless defended Brown in the archdiocesan newspaper: "He is a good and holy priest, and loyal to the Church. He is a Scripture scholar and limits his skill to his Scripture expertise. Fr. Brown, as a follower of Christ, is in good company when it comes to being criticized. Do not be led astray by the venomous critics of Fr. Brown." *Tidings*, April 4, 1980.

10. *Triumph* 8, no. 7 (July 1973): 8.

11. *Triumph* 8, no. 9 (November 1973): 8.

12. At its annual meetings, the Catholic Biblical Association routinely issues resolutions, such as thanks for its hosts and organizers of the meeting. However, in the years when members were being attacked, the Association frequently issued resolutions passed by the entire assembly defending the good name of biblical scholars under attack.

13. See Fitzmyer, "Raymond E. Brown: In Memoriam," 14–16. He also listed similar attacks by critics such as Rev. William G. Most and others that appeared occasionally in *The National Catholic Register*. Fitzmyer compared Brown's experience to that of the persecution experienced by Père Marie Joseph Lagrange at the end of the nineteenth century; see intro., pp. xvii–xviii.

14. See *The Wanderer* 131, no. 36 (September 3, 1998): 11; and no. 37 (September 10, 1998): 1, 11, an article written by a H. V. King. These latter steps prompted Fitzmyer to wonder if these Catholic editors and writers had ever heard of the Christian principle, *Nil nisi bonum de mortuis* ("Concerning the dead, [say] nothing but good"). Never one to mince words, Fitzmyer called the paper a *Käseblättchen* (literally, a "cheese leaflet"!).

15. George A. Kelly, *The New Biblical Theorists: Raymond E. Brown and Beyond* (Ann Arbor, MI: Servant Books, 1983). Another priest opponent of Brown was Fr. William G. Most (1914–99), who taught for forty years at Loras College in Dubuque, Iowa. Similar to Kelly's views, Most accused Brown of departing from orthodox Christian faith, especially in his views on the limited human knowledge of Jesus and Brown's interpretation of biblical inerrancy. See especially Most's work *Free from All*

Error: Authorship, Inerrancy, Historicity of Scripture, Church Teaching, and Modern Scripture Scholars (Libertyville, IL: Franciscan Maryville Press, 2008). On November 14, 1974, Most had written to Cardinal Šeper, at that time prefect of the Congregation of the Doctrine of the Faith, citing a list of Brown's alleged errors concerning the virginal conception, obedience to the magisterium, the origin of the priesthood and episcopate, the "ignorance" of Christ" (i.e., Brown's views about the human consciousness of Jesus), and Brown's alleged conviction that belief in demons was a "superstition." Most stated that he did not want to question Brown's "motives": "I have heard he [Brown] is quite sensitive about his orthodoxy, and believes he is orthodox....Yet the evidence I am about to submit indicates that probably he himself is confused, and, in virtue of that very confusion, has confused many others." Letter of Rev. William G. Most to Franjo Cardinal Šeper, prefect of the Sacred Congregation "for the Teaching of the Faith" [*sic*], November 14, 1974.

16. See Cardinal John J. O'Connor, quoted in the New York archdiocesan paper *Catholic New York*, July 15, 1999. Kelly passed away in 2004.

17. Letter of Cardinal John O'Connor to Raymond Brown, March 14, 1994.

18. *The New Biblical Theorists*, vii. Several reviewers sharply criticized Laurentin for his endorsement of Kelly's criticism of Brown and of modern Catholic biblical scholarship in general; see the reviews of J. Murphy-O'Connor, OP, in *The Bible Today* 22 (1984): 110, and Richard Sklba (later named auxiliary bishop of Milwaukee), *Catholic Biblical Quarterly* 46 (1984): 576–77. Sklba points to Kelly's use of sources as "hurried and superficial"; in fact, Kelly quotes a number of authors, giving page numbers but rarely indicating the book or actual source from which the quotation is taken. There is no bibliography included with his book.

19. *The New Biblical Theorists*, 116. The sarcastic tone of Kelly's comment here is found throughout his book.

20. *The New Biblical Theorists*, 121.

21. *The New Biblical Theorists*, 123.

22. John Meier reported that when Joseph Fitzmyer was editor of the *Catholic Biblical Quarterly*, he threatened to resign if Brown tried to control who would review his books in the journal.

23. See, e.g., the reviews of *An Introduction to the New Testament* by Anthony Saldarini and Marc Goodacre cited earlier, p. 166n.106.

24. *The New Biblical Theorists*, 127.

25. See chap. 3 on Brown's methodology.

26. *The New Biblical Theorists*, 131.

27. *The New Biblical Theorists*, 132.

28. *The New Biblical Theorists*, 143. Particularly galling for Kelly was the fact that Cardinal Terence Cook of New York had given a copy of Brown's book on the priesthood to each priest of the archdiocese, leaving Kelly to wonder, "Who was underwriting this largesse of Paulist Press?" See a later article of Kelly, "A Wayward Turn in Biblical Theory," *Catholic Dossier* (January/February 2000). In this final broadside at Brown (who had died nearly two years earlier), Kelly repeats a number of his accusations from his earlier book, including his assertion that the critique of Brown by Cardinal Shehan was "the first post-Vatican II critique by a bishop of a theologian."

29. See earlier, chap. 3.

30. On Brown's relationship with Shehan, see Ronald D. Witherup, "Raymond E. Brown, SS, and Catholic Exegesis in the Twentieth Century: A Retrospective," *U.S. Catholic Historian* 31 (2013): 1–26, esp. 17–21.

31. See *CBQ* 23 (1961): 143–60; and *CBQ* 24 (1962): 1–14.

32. As Brown noted in his CBA oral history interview, Vagnozzi at one point forbade the CBA to publish a resolution passed at its annual meeting at Mt. St. Mary's Seminary in Norwood, Ohio, August 28 to September 1, 1961, condemning the attacks on biblical scholars that were being mounted in the journal *The American Ecclesiastical Review* by Fenton and others. Incensed by these attacks, the CBA passed a resolution protesting these accusations of heresy that had appeared in this series of articles, "which do consistently charge Catholic scholars with gross ignorance of basic theological truths, if not of deliberately malicious perversions of these same truths, no evidence adduced of any particular error published by any scholar." The resolution went on to "repudiate any and all such attacks and affirms its desire and intention of promoting discussions which join honesty and candor with genuine friendship and mutual esteem." After some debate, the resolution was carried by an overwhelming majority. All such resolutions of the CBA were published in the *Catholic Biblical Quarterly*, the CBA's official organ. However, when its then editor, Roland Murphy, OCarm, prepared for the resolution's publication, he was summoned by Vagnozzi and forbidden to do so. Murphy insisted on the right of the Association

to publish its proceedings, but then Vagnozzi pressured Archbishop Patrick A. O'Boyle, archbishop of Washington, to intervene. Murphy reluctantly acquiesced but the anger of the CBA's members continued to smolder over what they saw as such unfounded and damaging attacks. On this entire episode, see Fogarty, *American Catholic Biblical Scholarship*, 298–310.

33. Letter of Raymond E. Brown to Archbishop Lawrence J. Shehan, June 8, 1962.

34. Letter of Raymond Brown to Fr. Lloyd P. McDonald, SS, June 10, 1962. It is interesting that in his CBA oral history interview, Brown references Vagnozzi's concerns about biblical scholarship during his tenure as apostolic delegate but does not mention his own personal and painful experience with the delegate.

35. *CBQ* 23 (1961): 143–60.

36. Both Vagnozzi and Brown were referring to a decree published in the compendium of church official teachings, *Enchiridion Symbolorum*, compiled by Henreich Denzinger and Clement Bannwart, SJ, no. 1822.

37. See, e.g., *Crises Facing the Church*, 63–83; also, his collaborative work, *Peter in the New Testament*, 83–100.

38. See intro., pp. xxii–xxvi. On the composition history of *Dei Verbum* at the Second Vatican Council, see also the work of Ronald D. Witherup, *Scripture: Dei Verbum*, Rediscovering Vatican II (New York: Paulist Press, 2006).

39. It would appear as "The Problem of the Virginal Conception of Jesus," *Theological Studies* 33 (1972): 3–34; on this topic, see chap. 4, pp. 100–103.

40. Quoted in an unpublished 1971 memo of Very Rev. Paul Purta, SS, Brown's provincial at the time. Purta had prepared the memo as a potential defense of Brown in view of the reactions to his article on the virginal conception. The remarks of Shehan were quoted by Fr. Thomas E. Clarke, writing in the Christmas issue of *America*.

41. Letter of Cardinal Lawrence J. Shehan to the Very Rev. William J. Lee, SS, November 15, 1974.

42. On this work of Brown, see chap. 4, pp. 83–89.

43. In the letter cited above to William Lee, Shehan stated that he had found "several things" in Brown's book "of concern to me." See further, R. Witherup, "Raymond E. Brown and Catholic Exegesis in the 20th Century," 18.

44. See the discussion of Brown's views in chap. 4, pp. 85–87.

45. Letter of Very Rev. Paul Purta to Raymond Brown, August 27, 1974.

46. See the letter of Rev. John S. Kselman, SS, professor of Biblical Studies and Rev. Robert F. Leavitt, SS, professor of Systematic Theology, to His Eminence, Lawrence Cardinal Shehan, November 18, 1974.

47. Letter of Cardinal Shehan to Raymond E. Brown, August 18, 1975.

48. "Finding I was 'in over my head,' as I began to write out a manuscript for the talk, I decided to change the subject for some innocuous topic dealing with ecumenism…only to find out that the topic I had proposed had been announced publicly."

49. Lawrence J. Shehan, "The Priest in the New Testament: Another Point of View," *Homiletic and Pastoral Review* 76 (November 1975): 10–23; and "Apostles and Bishops: Still Another Point of View," 76 (January 1976): 8–23.

50. Letter of Raymond E. Brown to His Eminence Lawrence Cardinal Shehan, September 5, 1975.

51. Manuel Miguens, OFM, was a Spanish Franciscan who taught for several years at The Catholic University of America. He took a very aggressive stance against the use of the historical-critical method and accused Catholic biblical scholars like Brown of being dangerous to the church. He himself had published studies both on the origin of the priesthood (*Church Ministries in New Testament Times* [Arlington, VA: Christian Culture Press, 1976]) and on the virginal conception—labeled by Miguens as the "Virgin Birth" (*The Virgin Birth: An Evaluation of Scripture Evidence* [Westminster, MD: Christian Classics, Inc., 1975]), neither of which, as Brown documents in *The Critical Meaning of the Bible*, 27–28, were well received. Brown pointed to Miguens as a prime example of misleading attacks on modern Catholic biblical scholarship. Miguens was denied tenure in 1983 after teaching six years at The Catholic University of America; he died in 2000.

52. Letter of Raymond Brown to the Very Rev. Paul P. Purta, SS, provincial, September 7, 1975.

53. Letter of Cardinal Shehan to Rev. Raymond E. Brown, SS, September 23, 1975.

54. Baker himself was a very vocal critic of Brown. In an editorial in the February 2004 issue of *The Homiletic and Pastoral Review*, Baker asserted that Brown was not a Catholic exegete.

55. Brown's book *Biblical Reflections on Crises Facing the Church* had just been published by Paulist Press in 1975. On this, see chap. 4, p. 89.

56. Letter of Archbishop Jean Jadot to Raymond Brown, December 24, 1975.

57. Letter of Fr. Joseph Jensen, OSB, to the Most Rev. Jean Jadot, December 23, 1975.

58. Letter of Raymond Brown to the Most Rev. Joseph L. Bernardin, December 22, 1975.

59. Letter of Most Rev. Joseph L. Bernardin to Raymond Brown, January 14, 1976.

60. New York: Paulist Press, 1985.

61. Raymond E. Brown, *Biblical Exegesis and Church Doctrine*, 8.

62. See chap. 3, pp. 60–63.

63. "A Revolution in the Church," *New York Review of Books*, June 14, 1984.

64. Sheehan responded to a similar criticism of his article that he had received from several theologians and that were referenced in a letter to the editor from Catholic theologian Stephen Englund (see *New York Review of Books*, November 22, 1984). In his response, Sheehan concluded, "I did raise the question about the basis on which any believer makes the claim that Jesus is the savior who offers and embodies God's salvation, that is, God himself. History cannot show this to be the case, not even the post-Bultmannian scholarship that Schillebeeckx uses and perfects. History can show only that Jesus apparently thought he was a special prophet in whose words and deeds God was present. Everything after that is a matter of faith; and since liberal Catholic theologians know that fact, I credited them with being (willingly or not) pious agnostics."

65. Typical would be the comment of the noted literary critic Frank Kermode, who in a review of Geza Vermes's study of the infancy narratives, erroneously makes Brown a "Jesuit scholar," mistakenly refers to the "Vatican Biblical Commission," and blithely questions Brown's integrity as a scholar: "Our indifference to the problems of Luke and Matthew does not affect professional scholars, whose exertions are unrelenting. Before the appearance of this little book by Geza Vermes I'd have advised anybody showing an interest in these matters to consult Raymond Brown's *The Birth of the Messiah*, a work of some six hundred pages which, like all Brown's numerous publications, is a monument to

his indefatigable though sometimes fatiguing scholarship. Brown's book must be eight or ten times as long as Vermes's, but unless you want every cranny of the topic examined in minute detail, Vermes will probably be enough. He of course uses Brown, and even allows himself a polite smile at his competitor, a Jesuit scholar, seemingly of skeptical temperament but always alive to the party line; willing to use the liberty, only recently acquired by Catholics, to take note of modern biblical scholarship, but careful not to cross that line. A statement by the Vatican Biblical Commission explains the rules: exegetes have full liberty to report their biblical researches so long as they do not question 'the truths of faith and morals.' The Church had long refused to allow its scholars participation in two centuries of modern Bible criticism, but it has slowly loosened the reins. The last book placed on the Index of Forbidden Books was added in 1959. It was about the Infancy Narratives. Brown lets you know when he is consciously sailing close to the wind; he enjoys a good measure of freedom but it is far from absolute." From Frank Kermode's review of *The Nativity: History and Legend* by Geza Vermes that appeared in the *London Review of Books* 29, no. 1 (January 2007): 40–41.

66. Brown also takes mild exception to some of the views of John McHugh in *The Mother of Jesus in the New Testament* (Garden City, NY: Doubleday, 1975), observing that "McHugh's exegesis was intelligent, mildly critical, and not fundamentalist; but I found that he bypassed the tough problems of modern exegesis." *Biblical Exegesis and Church Doctrine*, 69–70.

67. Laurentin's original study was *Structure et Théologie de Luc I–II* (Paris: Gabalda, 1957). Brown referred favorably to this book of Laurentin in *The Birth of the Messiah* (see, e.g., p. 266n9). Laurentin, who died September 10, 2017, at the age of ninety-nine, was a prolific author; most of his works were on Marian devotions and apparitions.

68. In a scathing review of Laurentin's work in the journal *Marianum* 47 (1985): 15–38, much of which is repeated in this work, Brown especially criticized Laurentin for his intemperate characterizations of the historical-critical method, including a description of this work as "the excrement of historical research"; Laurentin, *Les Évangiles de l'Enfance du Christ Vérité de Noël au delà des Mythes,* 2nd ed. (Paris: Desclée, 1983). It was translated into English as *The Truth of Christmas beyond the Myths* (Still River, MA: St. Bede's, 1985). The quote is from the English translation, p. 439. As Brown commented, "Such language is

not appropriate to scholarly discourse" (*Biblical Exegesis and Christian Doctrine*, 76).

69. See *Biblical Exegesis and Church Doctrine*, 157–61.

70. See chap. 2, "Critical Biblical Exegesis and The Development of Doctrine," in *Biblical Exegesis and Church Doctrine*, 26–53.

71. *Biblical Exegesis and Church Doctrine*, 44.

72. See Ronald Witherup, "The Incarnate Word Revealed: The Pastoral Writings of Raymond E. Brown," in Donahue, *Life in Abundance*, 238–52, at 246.

CHAPTER 9

1. Brown had in fact died on Saturday afternoon, August 8, but because Fr. Witherup was traveling to the Scranton meeting, his secretary was unable to reach him with the news until Sunday.

2. St. Patrick's Seminary and University was founded in 1896 and from the outset was staffed by the Sulpicians. However, in a dispute with Archbishop Salvatore J. Cordileone of San Francisco concerning the jurisdiction of the seminary, the Sulpicians reluctantly terminated their role as administrators and faculty in 2016.

3. See chap. 2, p. 46.

4. In an October 25, 1998, letter to Ronald Witherup, Kateri Sullivan commented, "For years I gave him [Brown] no peace about his pants. Several times I told him, 'This is the last time this jacket lining or pants pocket can be mended.' He told me I'd be sorry for my critical attitude because he was leaving his personal effects to me, and then I'd have to treat his pants with reverence and respect."

5. *A Retreat with John the Evangelist: That You May Have Life* (Cincinnati, OH: St. Anthony Messenger Press, 1998).

6. Letter of Raymond E. Brown to John Donahue, SJ, June 7, 1991. At that time, Donahue was the director of the Georgetown Bible Institute and had inquired about Brown's future availability to offer some lectures in the summer program.

7. Letter of Raymond Brown to Fr. William H. Flegge, August 31, 1995.

8. Letter of Raymond Brown to Bishop Snyder, May 1977.

9. "Given your expertise in the area, the Congregation [of the Doctrine of the Faith] would be most grateful if you would agree to

take part in the Symposium by presenting the twelfth topic of the program: Unity and diversity of concepts in the New Testament. The paper should approach the subject in a synchronic-theological manner as the preceding topic in the series (The witness of the New Testament books to a single kerygma) will be of a diachronic-historical nature." Letter of Joseph Cardinal Ratzinger to Rev. Raymond E. Brown, July 18, 1998. Brown replied quickly: "I accept with pleasure and the topic assigned is one in which I am interested." Letter of Raymond Brown to Cardinal Ratzinger, July 31, 1988.

10. The context and content of most of these publications have been reviewed in chaps. 4, 5, and 6.

11. See the listing in the bibliography prepared by M. Barré, in Donahue, *Life in Abundance*, 259–89.

12. David Noel Freedman, ed., *Anchor Bible Dictionary*, 6 vols. (New York: Doubleday, 1992), 3:410–15.

13. Robert T. Fortna and Beverly Roberts Gaventa, eds., *The Conversation Continues: Studies in Paul and John in Honor of J. Louis Martyn* (Nashville: Abingdon, 1990), 98–115. Another *Festschrift* for Martyn was edited by Joel Marcus and Marion Soards, *Apocalyptic and the New Testament: Essays in Honor of J. Louis Martyn*, Journal for the Study of the New Testament Supplement Series 24 (Sheffield: JSOT Press, 1989). For this volume, Brown wrote a moving personal tribute to his friend. Brown had confided to Soards that "Lou Martyn can do anything. He can write a monograph of the first order, and when my exercise bike broke, he came over and fixed it for me. He can do about anything." Brown, as noted earlier, was Martyn's peer in producing quality publications but not in the mechanical realm. Martyn earlier in his life had been a plumber and had a strong practical bent. See earlier, p. 3.

14. Both Phyllis Trible, his close friend and faculty colleague at Union Theological Seminary, and Eileen Tobin, Brown's former secretary while at Union, had the experience of receiving this book a few days after his death; see their comments in the Union Memorial Service booklet, October 2, 1998.

15. In his April 1987 annual report to the president and board of Union, Brown noted that his post-surgery condition was "not serious or painful but a nuisance that kept me pinned down for several months… having to lecture to a class while seated with one leg propped up on cushions."

16. Letter of Raymond E. Brown to Joseph M. Reynolds, October 22, 1985.

17. Characteristically, Brown did not have any notes or manuscript for his presentation at the commencement ceremony. I was president of CTU at the time and the next day wrote out detailed notes about the content of his address and later incorporated his advice to the graduates into an editorial for the school's newsletter, the *Logos*.

18. Later, some of Brown's Sulpician colleagues not on the scene wondered why Brown was not taken to a first-rate hospital such as the Stanford University Hospital not far away. In fact, the Sequoia Clinic, associated with the highly regarded Cleveland Clinic, was a top-rated center for heart disease and the best choice for Brown to get immediate care.

19. The official death certificate lists as the cause of death "Hemopericardium," the often catastrophic infusion of blood in the pericardium and "Fibrinous pericarditis," a more chronic condition resulting in a thickening of the membrane encasing the heart. At first the Sulpicians were going to order an autopsy for Brown but later decided against it, believing it would serve no purpose.

20. Not all the reactions were positive. True to form, on September 10, 1998, *The Wanderer* published an assessment of Brown by Henry V. King, branding Brown as "the late Modernist Scripture scholar." On the chronic opposition of *The Wanderer* to Brown, see earlier, p. 207.

21. From the memorial booklet for Raymond E. Brown, Union Theological Seminary, October 2, 1998.

22. Letter of Cardinal Mahony to Dr. James Sanders, August 24, 1998. In the letter, Mahony gently corrected Sanders for having inserted an "e" into his last name, noting that this was a result of British pressure, whereas the original Irish manner was to leave the "e" out. It is not known how Sanders, an Episcopalian of British descent, reacted to Mahony's observation.

23. In her poetic reflection at the Union Memorial service, Eileen Tobin recalled the visit of Brown's four women friends to this fresh grave, "We four women had played different roles in the life of Sulpician Father Raymond E. Brown, but we all knew Ray as friend. Ray viewed friendship as a sacred bond, a bond that entwined us all in the ultimate friendship, friendship with God. And if we were not aware of it in the beginning, we grew into that awareness as time went on. As we stood on either side of the unfinished grave, the words, "love," and "friendship,"

began to dance with each other somewhere inside of me until I saw them join, rooted in the same meaning. The dancing words embraced the four of us and the spirit of Ray in a unifying force that in no way lessened the pain, but plunged the sadness into a whole new experience. I began to see, visually, rather than feel, a new kind of energy. We were part of this death. Death and life are united, one inside the other, a continuing spiral toward oneness." Union Memorial Booklet, October 2, 1998.

24. *The Christian Century*, October 7, 1998.

25. Union Memorial booklet, October 2, 1998.

26. *The Death of the Messiah*, xii.

27. *A Retreat with John the Evangelist*, 53–54.

28. Cullen Murphy, "Old Stories, New Scholars," *The Wall Street Journal*, Friday, November 27, 1998, 9. As it turned out, the "participant" whose comments were quoted was David Garland, professor of Christian Scriptures at Baylor University's George W. Truett Theological Seminary. Brown gave a paper on the plausibility of Pilate's granting the body of the dead Jesus to Joseph of Arimathea. The room assigned was too small for someone of Brown's reputation and was jammed. Marion Soards was sitting next to Garland and after the lecture asked his colleague what he thought of Brown's presentation, prompting the response cited by Murphy; from a memo provided by Marion Soards.

29. Like other diocesan priests, the Sulpicians are not religious and do not take a vow of poverty; thus, they manage their own finances freely, such as owning property, making investments, paying taxes, and so on.

30. Raymond E. Brown, "Letter of Explanation to Accompany My Last Will and Testament," December 29, 1996, p. 4.

31. As noted earlier, Kateri Sullivan belonged to the group of Immaculate Heart of Mary Sisters who were coerced into breaking off from their original religious community under the tenure of Cardinal James F. McIntyre (1886–1979). No doubt Brown had this circumstance in mind in his concern for her financial vulnerability.

32. In a letter to Fr. Ronald Witherup, Kateri Sullivan, after admiring the idea of the proposed Center, had humorously suggested that in order to communicate the flavor of the man, one exhibit should put on display Brown's tattered coat, his worn-out sandals, and his favorite beret. Letter of Kateri Sullivan to R. Witherup, October 25, 1998.

33. The proceedings were published as John Donahue, ed., *Life in Abundance: Studies of John's Gospel in Tribute to Raymond E. Brown* (Collegeville, MN: Liturgical Press, 2005).

34. There have been a number of assessments of Brown's contributions to modern biblical scholarship. See, e.g., the essays of Ronald D. Witherup, "Raymond E. Brown, SS, and Catholic Exegesis in the Twentieth Century: A Retrospective," *U.S. Catholic Historian* 31 (2013): 1–26; and "The Incarnate Word Revealed: The Pastoral Writings of Raymond E. Brown," in Donahue, *Life in Abundance*, 238–52; Joseph A. Fitzmyer, "Raymond E. Brown, SS: In Memoriam," *Union Seminary Quarterly Review* 52 (1998): 1–18; Daniel Harrington, "A Teacher for Us All," *America*, August 29, 1988; and "John's Gospel Revisited," *America*, October 3, 1995; William Baird, *History of New Testament Research, Volume Three: From C. H. Dodd to Hans Dieter Betz* (Minneapolis: Fortress Press, 2013), 407–23.

35. On Brown's methodology, see chap. 3, pp. 59–75.

36. On this, see chap. 8, pp. 205–6.

37. See chap. 3, pp. 74–75.

38. "Here we can point to a fundamental criterion of biblical hermeneutics: *the primary setting for scriptural interpretation is the life of the Church*. This is not to uphold the ecclesial context as an extrinsic rule to which exegetes must submit, but rather is something demanded by the very nature of the Scriptures and the way they gradually came into being." Pope Benedict XVI, *Verbum Domini*, no. 29 (italics original). Further on, the pope reaffirmed this principle: "Their [i.e., 'Catholic exegetes'] common task is not finished when they have simply determined sources, defined forms or explained literary procedures. They arrive at the true goal of their work only when they have explained the meaning of the biblical text as God's word for today" (no. 33).

39. On this, see chap. 7, pp. 183–95.

40. Interview of Raymond E. Brown by Malcolm Warford, Union Theological Seminary, March 11, 1977.

41. In an interview about Brown, the Dominican biblical scholar Benedict Viviano, OP, expressed his conviction that Brown's example as a priest and scholar was a significant encouragement to American priests during the 1980s and '90s, when the priesthood was the subject of much criticism and its traditional authority questioned. It was during this period that substantial numbers of priests, both diocesan and religious, resigned. Brown, on the other hand, bore his priestly identity

openly, without apology or fanfare, and at the same time was recognized as a formidable scholar by his peers and even the general public. A veteran priest and longtime organizer of continuing education programs for priests in a midwestern diocese concurred with this assessment—noting that having Brown as a speaker at an event for priests would draw large numbers from the surrounding dioceses. Brown himself mentioned the appreciation he received from priests in the preface to his work *Priest and Bishop: Biblical Reflections*. In personal correspondence, he also mentioned that a bishop of a western diocese, where Brown had been invited by the director of continuing education to give a workshop, rudely snubbed him. Yet the priests of that diocese turned out in force and made it clear that they deeply appreciated Brown himself and what he had to say.

42. Tribute of Alexandra R. Brown, "Raymond E. Brown, SS: 1928–1998" from a fax to Dr. Phyllis Trible, dated October 1, 1988.

SUBJECT INDEX

Anchor Bible Series, 113–15
Antioch and Rome, 43, 177
Anti-Semitism, 57–58, 122–23, 183–95
Archelaus, 135
Aristotle, 164

Benedict, St., 236
Biblical Exegesis and Church Doctrine, 226–29
Birth of the Messiah, 131–42
  1993 update, 139–42
Bodily resurrection, 103–8
Brown, Raymond E.
  Assessment of contribution, 247–55
  Auburn Chair of Biblical Studies, 36
  Doctoral students of, 273n1
  "Ecclesial" hermeneutic, 74–75, 155–57
  Ecumenical interest, 167–71, 195–97
  Death of, 231–32, 237–40
    Impact of, 240–47
  Family background, 1–5
  Friendships, 38–43
    With women, 39–41

Honorary doctorates, 44, 238–39
Jerusalem, 16–20
"Incarnational" method of interpretation, 68–69
Major publications, characteristics of, 109–12
National awards, 270n55
Opera, love of, 35
Opposition to, 204–12
Pastoral focus, 77–80, 96–98, 236
Preaching, writings on, 281n18
Priesthood, 250–53
Public scholar, 50–53
Rome, 20–21
Response to criticism, 229–30
Saint Mary's Baltimore, 20–29
Saint Patrick's, Menlo Park, 43–50, 232–37
Seminary training, 5–13
Silencing of, 212–17
Stamp collection, 48–49
Structuralism, 275n7
Union Theological Seminary, 30–38

Catholic Biblical Association, 51–52, 311n32

323

INDEX OF MODERN NAMES